THE ARBITRATOR'S HANDBOOK

Revised Second Edition

THE ARBITRATOR'S HANDBOOK

Revised Second Edition

ð€

John W. Cooley

National Institute for Trial Advocacy

Reprint Permission
National Institute for Trial Advocacy
361 Centennial Parkway, Suite 220
Louisville, CO 80027
Phone: (800) 225-6482
Fax: (720) 890-7069
E-mail: permissions@nita.org

Cooley, John W., *The Arbitrator's Handbook*, Revised Second Edition (NITA 2009)

ISBN 978-1-60156-105-3
FBA 1105

Printed in the United States of America

Official co-publisher of NITA.
WKLegaledu.com/NITA

To John and Christina—
And in loving memory of Maria

Table of Contents

Chapter One—General Description of the Arbitration Process
1.1 Overview of the Arbitration Process 2
    1.1.1 Stages of the arbitration process 2
    1.1.2 Benefits and limitations of arbitration......................5
    1.1.3 Mandatory vs. voluntary arbitration 8
    1.1.4 Hybrid arbitration processes 9
    1.1.5 Application of arbitration to various types of disputes.............13
1.2 The Role and Authority of the Arbitrator 17
    1.2.1 The adversarial (common law) model 17
    1.2.2 The inquisitorial (civil law) model 19
    1.2.3 The international arbitrator 22
    1.2.4 Qualities of an effective arbitrator.......................24
    1.2.5 Maintaining neutrality and impartiality.................24
1.3 Arbitrator Ethics...26
    1.3.1 Canon I—Integrity and fairness of process 26
    1.3.2 Canon II—Disclosure of bias or conflicts of interest................28
    1.3.3 Canon III—No improper communications with parties..........29
    1.3.4 Canon IV—Fairness and diligence 32
    1.3.5 Canon V—Just, independent, and deliberate
            decision making 33
    1.3.6 Canon VI—Trust and confidentiality 33
    1.3.7 Canon VII—Integrity and Fairness in Arrangements for
            Compensation and Expense Reimbursement........................34
    1.3.8 Canon VIII—Truthful and accurate advertising 35
    1.3.9 Canon IX—Party-appointed arbitrators' duty to determine
            and to disclose their status 35
    1.3.10 Canon X – Exemptions for non-neutral party-appointed
            arbitrators...36

Chapter Two—The Arbitrator's Prehearing Functions and Duties
2.1 Initiation of Arbitration 37
    2.1.1 Reviewing the arbitration clause, the demand and response,
            and pertinent rules...37

2.1.2 Conflict check 48

2.1.3 Arbitrator's oath 49

2.1.4 Choosing the third arbitrator 50

2.1.5 Selecting chair of arbitration panel 51

2.1.6 Role of the chair of arbitration panel 52

2.1.7 The arbitrators' initial conference 53

2.1.8 Complying with court orders compelling or
staying arbitration 53

2.2 Conducting the Preliminary Hearing 54

2.2.1 Covering all pertinent topics 65

2.2.2 Considering procedural alternatives.........................65

2.2.3 Written order summarizing the results of the preliminary
hearing 68

2.3 Supervising Prehearing Discovery.....................................69

2.3.1 Deciding whether to permit discovery 69

2.3.2 Deciding what kind of discovery to allow 70

2.3.3 Deciding how much discovery to allow 70

2.3.4 Subpoenas 71

2.3.5 Ruling on discovery motions 72

2.4 Prehearing Provisional Court Remedies and Interim
Arbitration Awards..73

2.4.1 Prehearing provisional court remedies 73

2.4.2 Interim arbitration awards 73

2.5 Preparing for the Arbitration Hearing 74

2.5.1 Reading the pre-hearing briefs and materials 74

2.5.2 Anticipating procedural and evidentiary problems....76

2.5.3 Preparing lists of questions 76

2.6 Conducting a Site Visit 77

2.7 Withdrawal, Incapacity, or Death of an Arbitrator 78

Chapter Three—The Arbitrator's Hearing Functions and Duties

3.1 Arbitrators' Conference 79

3.2 Sequence of the Hearing–General 79

3.3 Arbitrator's Opening Statement..80

3.3.1 Personal introductions...81

3.3.2 Disclaimer of bias and partiality 81

3.3.3 Explanation of arbitration process and legal effect of award......82

3.3.4 Procedural ground rules...82

3.3.5 Arbitrator's instructions to testifying witnesses 82

3.3.6 Answering questions of parties or counsel.......................83

3.4. Handling Preliminary Matters...83

    3.4.1 Ruling on motions 83

    3.4.2 Confirming the witness schedule 84

    3.4.3 Swearing of witnesses..84

3.5 Parties' Opening Statements..84

    3.5.1 Basic differences between arbitration and trial opening
         statements 85

    3.5.2 Rule against argument..87

    3.5.3 Introduction and summary..88

    3.5.4 Presentation of facts..89

    3.5.5 Brief statement of law..89

    3.5.6 Comments on opposition's case 90

    3.5.7 Summary and request for relief..................................90

    3.5.8 Ruling on objections and responses 90

3.6 Understanding Basic Principles of Evidence 92

    3.6.1 General considerations 92

    3.6.2 Direct and circumstantial evidence............................93

    3.6.3 Relevance and materiality 94

    3.6.4 Hearsay and exhibits..94

    3.6.5 Affidavits..94

    3.6.6 Admissions of fact 95

    3.6.7 Stipulations of fact..95

    3.6.8 Judicial notice...95

3.7 Customary Procedure and Ethics of Direct Examination.................95

    3.7.1 Goals of direct examination.......................................95

    3.7.2 Basic rules governing direct examination 96

    3.7.3 Customary procedure governing adverse
         and hostile witnesses...97

    3.7.4 Customary procedure for redirect examination
         and rehabilitation 98

    3.7.5 Ethics of direct examination 100

3.8 Customary Procedure and Ethics of Cross-Examination.................101

    3.8.1 The role of cross-examination....................................101

    3.8.2 Basic rules governing cross-examination 101

    3.8.3 Customary questioning technique 103

3.8.4 Ethics of cross-examination 105

3.9 Permissible Impeachment...107

3.9.1 Role of impeachment 107

3.9.2 Prior inconsistent statements 109

3.9.3 Other prior inconsistencies...................................112

3.9.4 Character and "characteristic" impeachment 113

3.9.5 "Case data" impeachment....................................114

3.10 Expert Testimony 114

3.10.1 Standards for expert testimony 114

3.10.2 The expert's overview...115

3.10.3 Customary procedure for offering expert testimony..............116

3.10.4 Customary procedure for cross-examination of
expert witnesses 119

3.10.5 Ethics of expert examination 123

3.11 Foundations for Evidence...124

3.11.1 Evidentiary foundations—general 124

3.11.2 Customary foundations for testimonial evidence..................126

3.11.3 Customary foundations for documents 129

3.11.4 Customary foundations for real and demonstrative evidence 132

3.12 Hearing Exhibits 134

3.12.1 Ensuring introduction of all pertinent evidence..................134

3.12.2 Ensuring advocates' proper handling and use of exhibits 136

3.13 Ensuring Completeness and Accuracy of Transcripts 140

3.14 Ruling on Objections and Offers of Proof.............................141

3.14.1 Ruling on objections 141

3.14.2 Ruling on offers of proof 150

3.15 Arbitrator's Prerogative to Call Witnesses and Direct Introduction
of Other Evidence 150

3.16 Entertaining Final Arguments 151

3.16.1 Deciding whether to permit final argument.........................151

3.16.2 Role and function of the final argument............................151

3.16.3 Typical format, structure, content, and delivery of final
argument 154

3.16.4 Ethics of final argument 157

3.16.5 Ruling on objections during final argument 159

3.16.6 Arbitrator's questioning of advocates during final
argument 159

3.17 Concluding the Hearing 159

3.17.1 Determining when evidence will be "closed" 159

3.17.2 Determining whether the parties should file
post-hearing briefs 160

3.17.3 Setting post-hearing briefing or oral argument schedule 160

3.17.4 Arbitrator's final remarks 162

Chapter Four—The Arbitrator's Post-hearing Functions and Duties

4.1 Ruling on Post-hearing Motions 163

4.2 Reviewing Post-hearing Briefs and Proposed Findings and
Conclusions 164

4.3 Deciding the Merits of the Claims and Defenses 164

4.3.1 The decision-making process – general 164

4.3.2 The decision-making procedure 166

4.3.3 Customary standards for interpreting contract language 166

4.3.4 Customary application of the rules of substantive law 170

4.3.5 Application of basic contract, tort, and equity principles 170

4.3.6 Determining liability 174

4.3.7 Determining compensatory damages 177

4.3.8 Considering appropriateness of awarding punitive damages ... 177

4.3.9 Determining equitable and other remedies 178

4.3.10 Considering appropriateness of awarding
attorneys' fees, costs, and interest 178

4.4 Drafting the Award 179

4.4.1 Considering the nature and purpose of the award 179

4.4.2 Knowing the jurisdictional requisites of a binding award 180

4.4.3 Complying with time limits 181

4.5 Drafting the Opinion Supporting the Award–General 181

4.5.1 Reading the record of proceedings 181

4.5.2 The five parts of an opinion 184

4.6 The Opening 185

4.7 Summary of Claims and Defenses and Other Issues 186

4.8 Statement of Facts 186

4.8.1 Introduction 186

4.8.2 Mechanics of drafting a statement of facts 187

4.8.3 Writing with accuracy...196

4.8.4 Writing objectively 202

4.8.5 Writing to persuade 203

4.9 Discussing, Analyzing, and Applying Relevant Law or Equitable
Principles —General Considerations 204

4.9.1 Rules or contract provisions...204

4.9.2 Selecting and sequencing topics....................................204

4.9.3 Designing headings and subheadings............................205

4.9.4 Using charts, diagrams, and graphic illustrations
where appropriate..206

4.9.5 Using a simple and direct writing style. 206

4.10 Drafting the Ratio Decidendi..212

4.10.1 Introduction..212

4.10.2 Thinking like a judge 213

4.10.3 Using an effective analysis format 216

4.10.4 Knowing and applying the skills of legal analysis 217

4.10.5 Avoiding certain types of arguments 225

4.10.6 Using footnotes 226

4.10.7 Using quotations 227

4.10.8 Editing and proofreading 228

4.11 Drafting the Disposition 231

4.12 Drafting Findings of Fact and Conclusions of Law.................232

4.13 Signing and Issuing the Award 233

4.14 Retaining Jurisdiction to Enforce or Monitor Award 233

4.15 Enforcement, Challenge, and Appeal of Award 233

4.15.1 Enforcement of the award 234

4.15.2 Challenge of the award...234

4.15.3 Appealing the award 237

4.16 The Role of the Appellate Arbitrator 238

Chapter Five—Conducting the Cyberarbitration

5.1 Basic Definitions 242

5.1.1 Cyberspace 243

5.1.2 Electronic Dispute Resolution (EDR) 246

5.1.3 Videoconferencing..246

5.1.4 Telephonic Dispute Resolution (TDR) 246

5.1.5 EDR information acquisition and delivery technology 247

5.1.6 Online Dispute Resolution (ODR) 248

5.1.7 Cyberarbitration 249

5.1.8 Cybermediation 249

5.1.9 Cybernegotiation 249

5.1.10 Internet regulatory organizations and related terms 250

5.2 Comparison of Face to face, Telephone, and Written
Communication in Arbitration 251

5.2.1 Face to face communication in arbitration 251

5.2.2 Telephonic communication in arbitration 252

5.2.3 Written communication in arbitration 252

5.3 Benefits and Limitations of Cybearbitration 255

5.3.1 Benefits 255

5.3.2 Limitations 256

5.3.3 Confidentiality 258

5.3.4 Cost or financing of service 259

5.4 Ethics of Cyberarbitration 260

5.5 Comparison of Various Communication Modes in
Cyberarbitration 261

5.6 Cyberspace Netiquette 263

5.7 Gathering Relevant Internet Information 268

5.7.1 General 268

5.7.2 Search engines 269

5.7.3 Other Internet reference tools 271

5.7.4 Tips for using search engines 272

Epilogue

Truth Never Dies 275

Appendices

Contents of Appendices 277

A. Grounds for Various Arbitration Rulings 279

B. Arbitrator's Prehearing Functions and Duties Checklist 307

C. Arbitrator's Hearing Functions and Duties Checklist......................313

D. Arbitrator's Post-hearing Functions and Duties Checklist................327

E. Sample Arbitration Clauses for a Commercial Contract....................335

F. AAA Commercial Arbitration Rules 339

G. JAMS Comprehensive Arbitrations Rules and Procedures................361

H. AAA International Arbitration Rules..373

I. 1958 New York Convention on the Recognition and Enforcement
   of Foreign Arbitral Awards 387

J. AAA Supplementary Procedures for Online Arbitration....................393

K. The Code of Ethics for Arbitrators in Commercial
   Disputes—Revised 2004 399

L. Selected ABA Model Rules of Professional Conduct 415

M. American Bar Association Litigation Section's Civility Guidelines ...427

N. Uniform Arbitration Act 431

O. Federal Arbitration Act 455

P. Organizations Offering ADR Services 465

Preface

The model chosen for this work is the fair-minded judge—a truth-seeking judge who seeks balance and justice, law and equity, and who understands that the arbitrator's function has both artistic and scientific elements, requiring application of both intuitive and analytical skills. Guided by the fair-minded judge model, I have developed this book using what I call a "pracademic" approach—taking care to create, throughout, a judicious blend of practice and theory.

Organized into five chapters and an appendix of arbitration forms and rules, this second edition of *The Arbitrator's Handbook* provides a full range of features geared to assist the arbitrator in systematically performing his or her functions and duties competently and efficiently.

- Chapter one provides basic information regarding the nature of arbitration, including a description of its stages and types, as well as its benefits and limitations. It also defines the role, authority, and ethics requirements of the arbitrator.

- Chapter two describes the pre-hearing functions and duties of the arbitrator, focusing on the time of initiation of the arbitration as well as the preparation stage.

- Chapter three focuses on the arbitrator's hearing functions and duties. It covers such topics as the arbitrator's opening statement, handling of preliminary matters, and review of basic rules of evidence, and making rulings on motions and objections.

- Chapter four, regarding the arbitrator's post-hearing functions and duties, addresses such topics as ruling on post hearing motions, deciding the merits of the case, and drafting the award and the opinion supporting the award.

- Chapter five, a new chapter in this second edition, covers information useful to arbitrators when conducting a cyberarbitration.

- In addition, checklists are included in appendices A–D to ensure that the arbitrator does not forget to take key actions at critical stages of the arbitration process. The appendix also contains sample arbitration forms and rules.

One chapter of this second edition deserves special mention. Sections 3.6–3.11 and 3.16 of chapter three—concerning the arbitrator's duties and functions during the arbitration hearing—are partly a condensed adaptation of chapter five of *Arbitration Advocacy*, 2d, John W. Cooley with Steven Lubet (NITA 2003). Chapter three presents in an abbreviated, reader-friendly format, many of the evidentiary principles that are of direct concern to arbitrators and advocates alike. The comprehensive coverage of evidentiary topics there takes into account that some arbitrators who will use this handbook will not be lawyers and that some will be from countries whose arbitral evidentiary procedures are quite different from those used in the United States. In-depth explanations of these evidentiary matters and many helpful examples may be found in *Modern Trial Advocacy*, 3d ed., Steven Lubet, (NITA 2004).

I have undertaken to explain the arbitrator's role with several audiences in mind. First and foremost, I have written for arbitrators. I have deliberately crafted this handbook generically so that it will be useful to a wide variety individuals, lawyers and nonlawyers alike, serving in all types of arbitrator roles in a wide variety of private and public dispute settings—including those existing domestically, internationally, and in court-mandated arbitration programs. This is a book to use, not to simply read and place on the shelf. It is designed to be used by arbitrators during the preliminary stage of arbitrations and to be brought to the hearing sessions as a quick-reference tool or guide used during the course of the hearings. The book's organization, tailored to the sequential stages of the arbitration proceeding, contemplates continual reference by arbitrators as the hearing advances.

The second audience for whom I have written consists of the organizers of and participants in continuing legal education (CLE) programs in the United States and in other countries around the world. The step-by-step approach, the succinct presentations of useful information in chart form, and the analyses of critical process, procedural, and evidentiary issues make it an ideal teaching tool for arbitration seminars.

A third audience to which this publication has been geared consists of the teachers and students of law school courses on arbitration. At this writing, there are very few, if any, law student textbooks or handbooks available that provide detailed "hands on" instruction on the arbitrator function. This book seeks to fill that gap.

Finally, advocates in arbitration may indeed find this book quite useful. In particular, chapter three focuses on "Hearing Functions and Duties" of arbitrators, and may provide advocates insight as to what arbitrators expect of advocates during the arbitration proceeding. It also discusses how advocates should conduct themselves in order to maximize the likelihood that they will prevail on motions and objections and on the general merits of their cases. Appendix A presents possible grounds for arbitrator's rulings on objections and motions, and therefore provides possible grounds that advocates may advance in support of such objections and motions.

In creating this book, I have made every effort to use a personable and personalized writing style, as if I were having a face-to-face conversation with you. I hope you find this style to be friendly and engaging, as intended. Finally, I sincerely hope that this book will, in some significant way, enhance the quality of the arbitrator profession both nationally and internationally for many years to come.

John W. Cooley
2005

Acknowledgments of John W. Cooley

I am grateful for the people, both lawyers and nonlawyers, who taught me much about problem solving, lawyering, and life, and who unwittingly, have shaped the content of this book. The list would be endless, but I particularly want to recognize:

Angela Cooley, Joan and Ken Kottemann, Judge Thomas Fairchild, Collins Fitzpatrick, Judge Michael Mason, Howard Stone, Antoinette Saunders, Terry Tierney, John Buccheri, Michael Siegel, David McGuire, Lynn Gaffigan, John Huston, Nancy Peace, Jim Alfini, Leonard Schrager, Stephen Goldberg, Jeanne Brett, Lynn Cohn, Jamie Carey, Jim Faught, Tom Haney, Mitchel and Pam Byrne, Tom and Perlita Campbell, Jordan Margolis, Ray and Joyce Zeiss, Nancy and Bob Doyle, Nina Appel, Richard Salem, Jim Sullivan, Jim Bailey, Gino DiVito, Erwin Katz, Douglas Johnson (my "Beast Barracks" squad leader at West Point), Todd and Betty Musburger, Judge Morton Denlow, Dennis Coll, Judy and Bob Holstein, Bonnie and Neal Rubin, Bill O'Laughlin, Ron and Sarah Basso, Jeffrey Rogers, Dan Murray, Thomas Strubbe, Art and Sheila Kriemelman, Judge Marvin Aspen, Karen and Mike Tangen, Petronio Muniz and Keila Porto, Judge Frank McGarr, Bill Quinlan, Cheryl Niro, Paul and Diane Schultz, Tom Croak, David Hopkins, Tom Geraghty, Bob Burns, and Paul Lisnek.

Special acknowledgment is extended to my deceased wife, Maria, and to my children, John and Christina.

About the Author

John W. Cooley is a former United States Magistrate, Assistant United States Attorney, Senior Staff Attorney for the United States Court of Appeals for the Seventh Circuit, and a litigation partner in a Chicago law firm. He is a Fellow of the Chartered Institute of Arbitrators, London, England, of the American Bar Foundation, and the International Academy of Mediators. He is a member of the Council of the American Bar Association's Section of Dispute Resolution.

In private practice in the Chicago area, John is a founding member of Judicial Dispute Resolution, Inc. (JDR). He has served as a Special Master for federal judges and as an arbitrator and mediator in a wide variety of complex, multi-million dollar commercial disputes, both domestic and international in character.

An Adjunct Professor of Law at Northwestern University School of Law, John teaches a course in negotiation and mediation. In addition, he is the principal designer and instructor of a "Mediation Advocacy" cybercourse that was developed by Northern Illinois University in cooperation with the ABA's Section of Dispute Resolution.

John is the author of the first edition of this book, *The Arbitrator's Handbook* (NITA 1998, first edition). He co-authored *Arbitration Advocacy* 2d (NITA 2003) with Northwestern University Law Professor Steven Lubet. John authored *The Mediator's Handbook* (Advanced Practice Guide for Civil Litigation) (NITA 2000); *Mediation Advocacy* (NITA 1996, second edition 2002); Callaghan's *Appellate Advocacy Manual* (1989, supplemented through 1995); and more than fifty articles on litigation, judicial, and ADR topics. The first editions of *Arbitration Advocacy* and *Mediation Advocacy* have been published in the Portuguese language by the University of Brasilia in Brazil. His latest work, *The Creative Problem Solver's Handbook for Negotiators and Mediators*, jointly sponsored by the ABA Section of Dispute Resolution and the Association for Conflict Resolution, is scheduled for publication in late 2004.

John is a Vietnam War veteran. He is a graduate of the United States Military Academy at West Point and the University of Notre Dame Law School. He received a year of his legal training in international and comparative law at the Notre Dame Law School's Centre for Legal Studies in London, England.

Chapter One

General Description of the Arbitration Process

Equity is justice in that it goes beyond the written law. And it is equitable to prefer arbitration to the law court, for the arbitrator keeps equity in view, whereas the judge looks only to the law . . .
—Aristotle

❀ ❀ ❀ ❀

Arbitration has had a long history in the United States, going back to procedures carried over into the Colonies from mercantile England. William Penn arbitrated a dispute involving creditors' claims against a British owner of "West Jersey,"[1] and George Washington put an arbitration clause in his last will and testament to resolve disputes among his heirs. Abraham Lincoln urged lawyers to keep their clients out of court and he, himself, arbitrated many controversies, including a boundary dispute between two farmers.[2] Today, arbitration is being used to resolve a broad range of disputes in various industries and in myriad areas of law, both domestically and internationally.

This first chapter discusses topics very basic to a clear understanding of the arbitration process and the arbitrator's role in it. For readers uninitiated in arbitration, the discussion here will serve as a foundation for further learning; for the experienced arbitrator, it will provide a refresher module on arbitration fundamentals. In the next few pages, we will explore the stages of the arbitration process, its benefits and limitations, the various types of arbitration and their application to various types of disputes, the role of the arbitrator in the common law and civil law arbitration models, the role of the arbitrator in international disputes, the qualities of the effective arbitrator, and the ethical aspects of the arbitrator's function.

Welcome to the world of arbitration. Relax and enjoy the tour.[3]

---

1. Rodolphe J.A. deSeife, *Domke on Commercial Arbitration*, 1995 Supplement, §2:03, 15 (Clark Boardman Callaghan, 1995).
2. See John W. Cooley, *Arbitration vs. Mediation—Explaining the Differences*, 69 Judicature 263, 264 (Feb.–March 1986).
3. For an explanation of the advocate's role and function in arbitration, *see* John W. Cooley with Steven Lubet, *Arbitration Advocacy*, 2d ed., (NITA 2003).

The Arbitrator's Handbook

1.1   OVERVIEW OF THE ARBITRATION PROCESS

Arbitration is one process in a broad spectrum of means for resolving disputes, collectively called Alternative Dispute Resolution or "ADR."[4] It may be defined as a process in which one or more neutrals render a decision after hearing arguments and reviewing evidence. In arbitration, the parties to a dispute relinquish their decision-making right to the neutral party, or arbitrator, who renders a decision for them. By pre-agreement, the neutral's decision is either binding or nonbinding. If binding, the neutral's decision is final, and the winning party may enforce it against the losing party. If nonbinding, the neutral's decision is advisory in aid of settlement.

1.1.1   Stages of the arbitration process.

In arbitration practice in the United States, the process is adversarial and normally consists of six stages: initiation, preparation, prehearing conferences, hearing, decision-making, and award.[5] The arbitration proceeding itself, consists of three discrete segments: prehearing, hearing, and post-hearing—the first segment incorporating the first three stages of the process and the third segment incorporating the last two stages. A brief discussion of the six stages appears in this section, and a more detailed explanation supplements it in succeeding chapters. The arbitration process in civil law jurisdictions is often more inquisitorial in nature and its differences are discussed infra in Section 1.2.2.

Initiation. The three principal ways disputants may initiate an arbitration proceeding in U.S. arbitration practice are by a submission, by a "demand" or "notice" pursuant to a pre-dispute agreement, and, in the case of a court-annexed proceeding, by court rule or court order.

Disputants use initiation by submission where there is no prior agreement to arbitrate. First, both initial parties to the dispute need to decide whether other parties should be involved in the arbitration, and whether the entire dispute is appropriate for arbitration. If the entire dispute should not be arbitrated, the parties or advocates representing them must decide what aspects of the dispute will be arbitrated. Next, the parties must decide whether the arbitration will be administered by an agency or will be ad-hoc (non-administered). Parties can choose an arbitrator from a panel of a national dispute resolution organization, from a panel of a community center that deals in alternative dispute resolution, or they can agree to use an independent arbitrator. If the

---

4.   *See generally,* Stephen B. Goldberg, Frank E. A. Sander, Nancy H. Rogers, *Dispute Resolution: Negotiation, Mediation, and Other Processes* (Little Brown and Company, 1992); Leonard L. Riskin and James E. Westbrook, *Dispute Resolution and Lawyers* (West Publishing Co., 1987).

5.   Cooley, *supra* note 2 at 264–66.

arbitration is administered, the administering dispute resolution organization may schedule a conference to coordinate the exchange of information and to consider other matters that will expedite the arbitration process. If the arbitration is non-administered, the parties must decide how they will split up the administrative functions. Eventually, the submission must be signed by all parties to the dispute. At a minimum, it names the arbitrator(s) (or method of appointment), and describes the arbitrator's authority, the procedure to be used at the hearing, a statement of the matter in dispute, the amount of money in controversy, and the remedy sought. Initiating arbitration by submission is very difficult, because it often requires parties already in dispute to cooperate in the design of a process and procedures, in choosing the neutrals, and in administering the process. Because it is unrealistic to expect parties who are emotionally at odds to cooperate, many advocates avert these problems by incorporating an arbitration clause into a contract, which locks in these parameters before the fact, providing a vehicle through which arbitration can automatically be initiated by "demand" or "notice" as next described.

Where parties have agreed by virtue of a clause in a contract to arbitrate disputes arising out of the contract, one party may initiate arbitration unilaterally by serving upon the other party or parties a written "demand" or "notice" to arbitrate under the terms of that clause. When demanding arbitration pursuant to a contract clause, the party making the demand sends a copy of it to the administering agency, if the arbitration is being administered. In this regard, parties must be careful to comply with all procedural requirements in the arbitration clause in order to avoid losing arbitration rights on any issues. An opposing party may submit an answer to a demand. However, an answer is ordinarily not required, and a claim will usually be assumed to be denied in the absence of an answer. The demand and answer, if filed, will normally be read by the arbitrator at the beginning of the hearing and will often frame his or her ultimate decision in the dispute.

In court-annexed arbitration, the court initiates arbitration by order or rule. Such mandatory arbitration is usually nonbinding, unless the parties agree otherwise. Depending on the particular court-annexed system, either the parties choose or the judge or court administrator appoints an arbitrator or panel of arbitrators.

Preparation. Experienced and effective advocates take the preparation stage of arbitration seriously. They know that they must fully understand and thoroughly prepare their cases for arbitration as if they were proceeding to trial. Depending on the nature of the case, prehearing discovery may be necessary. The goals of simplicity and utility in arbitration often weigh against extensive discovery, so the arbitrator normally determines its permissible extent. During the preparation period, advocates often enter into fact stipulations, where possible. Ordinarily, in court-annexed arbitration, no discovery is permitted after the arbitration panel is assigned, though much may have occurred beforehand while the case was pending on the court's docket.

Prehearing conference. The arbitrator normally schedules a prehearing conference in more complex arbitration cases. The arbitrator conducts this conference. Its purposes are to clarify any pre-arbitration issues and to discuss scheduling, as well as to handle any procedural, discovery, or evidentiary issues. At this conference, advocates can make any necessary motions or objections, which can either be ruled upon during the conference or scheduled for briefing. All pertinent communication should take place at the preliminary conference, because in arbitration, unlike mediation, no ex parte conversations between the arbitrator and a party or party's counsel are permitted.

Hearing. Parties may waive oral hearing and have the dispute determined on the basis of documents only, but in virtually all cases, the arbitrator conducts an evidentiary-type hearing. Because arbitration is a private proceeding, absent a statutory or rule exception, the hearing is not open to the public. All persons having a direct interest in the case, however, are normally entitled to attend. Other persons may attend by agreement of the parties and with the arbitrator's permission. When a necessary party fails to appear in person or through counsel, a default award may be entered against that party.

A formal written record of the hearing is not usually necessary, and the use of a court reporter is the exception rather than the general practice. A party requiring an interpreter is responsible for arranging one. Witnesses appearing at the hearing are normally required to speak under oath.

The advocates customarily make an opening statement designed to acquaint the arbitrator with each party's view of what the dispute is about and what the party expects to prove by the evidence. Occasionally, a respondent may opt to make an opening statement immediately prior to presenting initial evidence.

The advocate for the complaining party normally presents his or her evidence first, and advocates may ordinarily introduce any evidence they choose, subject to procedural, fairness, relevance, and materiality objections. Unless otherwise agreed, advocates need not comply with the legal rules of evidence, though the arbitrator may rely on their principles for guidance when ruling on objections to evidence. Certain court-annexed arbitration programs, however, require that evidentiary rules be applied to some, if not all, the evidence to be introduced a hearing. Unlike the court setting, the arbitrator may direct that evidence be introduced which has not been previously advanced by either party. When authorized by rule or by law, the arbitrator may also subpoena witnesses or documents upon his or her own initiative or by request of counsel. In the appropriate case, an arbitrator may exercise his right to inspect the particular premises, accident location, or construction site in question.

Decision-making. When the issues are not complex, the arbitrator may render a decision immediately after the conclusion of the hearing, and normally no later than 30 days from the closing date of the hearing. However, when there are multiple arbitrators and the case has several issues, the more usual procedure is for the arbitrators to take the case under advisement, sometimes direct post-hearing memoranda to be filed, meet later to thoroughly discuss the issues in the case, reach their decision, and commit it to writing. In very complex cases, these tasks may require several weeks.

Award. The arbitrator renders his or her decision in the form of an award. It may be given orally, but more commonly it is in written form and signed by the arbitrator, or arbitrators, if there is an arbitration panel. Awards are normally short, definite, and final as to all matters under submission. Occasionally, particularly in labor cases, they are accompanied by a short, well-reasoned opinion. Depending on the parties' pre-arbitration agreement, the award will be binding or non-binding. If binding, it will be judicially enforceable, and to some extent, reviewable. In court-annexed arbitration, the award is usually non-binding, and if either party rejects it, the parties proceed to a trial de novo in court.

1.1.2 Benefits and limitations of arbitration.

Experience with dispute resolution processes over the centuries has ascribed certain benefits to the use of arbitration and has equally delineated its limitations. As to the benefits of arbitration, it is normally non-public, a trait advantageous to the resolution of certain types of disputes where the parties desire privacy regarding both the proceedings and the outcome. Furthermore, by mutual agreement the parties select qualified neutrals who sometimes have specific expertise relevant to the dispute. Such specific expertise is not always available by resort to the court system. Also, in arbitration, parties generally have more control over the resolution process. Representation by counsel is advisable but not necessary in some instances.

Arbitration, while having some of the evidential and procedural regularity of court adjudication, is conducted in a less formal and less rigorous setting, thereby enhancing the potential for a more expeditious resolution. Applying legal and equitable norms and creating remedies often tailor-made to the situation, arbitrators issue decisions as awards that can be enforced through the judicial process, bringing finality to the conflict. As to the cost of arbitration, parties usually share the expense of the neutrals' fees, as well as certain administrative costs. Depending on the nature of the dispute, however, the fees and costs associated with the arbitration process are normally much less than those associated with a case that traverses the course of the court adjudication process.

On the other hand, arbitration has its limitations. Private arbitration lacks quality control since the arbitrators are independently selected in individual cases and are not generally accountable to any supervisory authority. As a process, it is also becoming increasingly encumbered by "legalization." Its other drawbacks include the lack of public norms, the lack of binding precedent, insufficient opportunity for full discovery, relaxed rules of evidence, usually no written reasons for decision, no uniformity of decisions, and usually no opportunity for appeal. As to cost of the process, some complex arbitration hearings can last for weeks or months, costing the parties much more than they had initially projected. For your convenience and quick reference, the chart appearing below consolidates some of the benefits and limitations of arbitration.

BENEFITS	LIMITATIONS
Privacy	Lack of quality control
Parties control forum	Neutrals unaccountable
Special expertise of neutral	Increasingly encumbered by "legalization"
Parties select neutrals	Relaxed rules of evidence
Written procedures	Limited or no discovery
Reasonably expeditious	No public norms
Choice of applicable norms	No precedent
Achieves finality	No uniformity of decisions
Tailors remedy to situation	Usually no written reasons for decision
Enforceability	Usually no appeal
Relatively inexpensive	Limited subpoena power

Occasionally, in assisting advocates in selecting the resolution process appropriate for the dispute, neutrals are asked whether arbitration is an option. The following guide lists some situational indicators favorable to an arbitrated resolution of a dispute. The presence of only one of these indicators (and the absence of any unfavorable indicators) may be sufficient to trigger scheduling of arbitration.

FAVORABLE INDICATORS FOR ARBITRATION

- Parties and counsel agree to participate in the arbitration process and desire a prompt resolution.
- Pre-agreement exists to arbitrate disputes arising out of an underlying contract.
- Dispute is of the type qualifying for compulsory arbitration under local court rules.
- Legal issues predominate over factual issues.
- Parties will not have to maintain a direct or indirect relationship after resolution of a dispute.
- Sufficient discovery has occurred or information has been developed to permit counsel to cogently present their clients' claims and defenses.
- Parties desire to minimize litigation costs.
- Parties wish to avoid establishing a judicial precedent, or they wish to establish an arbitration precedent that will guide their future conduct.
- A significant power imbalance exists between parties.
- Information (testimony or documents) in the possession of third parties is crucial to a claim or defense, and the third parties will not provide the information unless subpoenaed.
- Parties are still deadlocked after an attempted negotiated and/or mediated settlement.
- Parties have dramatically differing appraisals of the facts of the case and the applicable law.
- Parties have a history of acting in bad faith in negotiations.
- Parties want the matter settled confidentially.
- An immediate decision by a third party neutral is needed to protect the interests of a disputant or the public.

The following guide lists some of the situational indicators unfavorable to the use of arbitration. The presence of one of these indicators could be sufficient reason to decline using arbitration to resolve a particular dispute.

UNFAVORABLE INDICATORS FOR ARBITRATION

- A party cannot effectively represent its best interests and will not be represented by counsel at the arbitration sessions.
- A party seeks an unusual remedy or creative resolution that is not available in arbitration.
- The resolution will require monitoring.
- Major constitutional issues are involved.
- The best resolution requires disclosure of information to the decision-maker, but such information cannot be disclosed to the other side.

- Substantial formal discovery is needed to provide a party with the information necessary to support a claim or defense.
- Stakes are too high to risk a binding, unappealable award.
- A judicial precedent is needed to explain application of a new or rarely construed statute.
- Case has some pivotal emotional aspects that would best be presented to and considered by a jury.
- Case is currently pending in court before a judge who is mutually acceptable to the parties and who could hear and decide the case sooner than arbitrators could be selected and an arbitration hearing held.

Sometimes the parties need to make a choice between using arbitration and mediation to resolve their dispute. Mediation, in contrast with arbitration, is a process in which a neutral assists the disputants in reaching a voluntary settlement of their differences through an agreement that defines their future behavior.[6] The essential distinction between the two processes lies in who makes a decision for the disputants. In arbitration, the disputants allow the neutral to make the resolution decision for them; in mediation, the disputants participate in a joint decision-making process, making the decision for themselves with the mediator's assistance. The following chart organizes and highlights some of the important criteria that should be considered when making a choice between mediation and arbitration to resolve a dispute.

IMPORTANT CRITERIA FOR SELECTING BETWEEN MEDIATION AND ARBITRATION

MEDIATION	ARBITRATION
Desire to preserve continuing relations	Need to offset power imbalance
Emphasis on future dealings	Need for decision on past events
Need to avoid win-lose decision	High volume of disputes
Disputants desire total control of process	Need to compel participation
Dispute has multiple parties and issues	Premium on speed and privacy
Absence of clear legal entitlement	Premium on closure

1.1.3 Mandatory vs. voluntary arbitration.

Traditionally, arbitration has been voluntary in the sense that the parties agree, either before or after the dispute arises, to submit such dispute to the process for resolution. However, in recent years there has been an increasing trend in the United States toward the creation of statutes and court rules providing for mandatory (also called court-annexed) arbitration and mediation, both as a means of easing the backlog of cases and as an attempt to reduce the

---

6. *See generally*, John W. Cooley, *Mediation Advocacy*, 2d ed., (NITA 2002).

amount of time and money spent by parties resolving their disputes. The rules governing these programs vary significantly from jurisdiction to jurisdiction, and arbitrators should take care to apprise themselves of the specific procedural requirements of the jurisdiction in which they are selected to arbitrate. For example, some mandatory arbitration programs require that notice of the introduction of certain types of documentary evidence be served on the opponent within a certain time frame and that the rules of evidence be applied by the arbitrators at the hearing. Some court rules impose penalties, in the form of court costs and fees, on parties who reject the mandatory arbitration award, opt for a trial de novo, and fare worse than they did in the arbitration proceeding. Many of these programs have been criticized for their coercive nature, pressuring parties, who are sometimes unrepresented, into forgoing substantial due process rights they would otherwise enjoy in the traditional trial proceeding. However, because a growing number of courts consider early settlement to be in the parties' and the court's best interests, tendency for the courts to employ mandatory arbitration and mediation is likely to expand rather than shrink.

1.1.4 Hybrid arbitration processes.

There are times when classic arbitration is not the most appropriate alternative for resolving a particular dispute. Advocates increasingly exercise creativity in selecting or designing an appropriate hybrid process to satisfy their clients' specific needs. As an arbitrator, you should be aware of the various alternatives and accommodate and facilitate the parties' use of them.

High-low arbitration. A form of arbitration widely used in personal injury and other types of disputes is high-low arbitration, also called bracketed arbitration. It is commonly used where liability is not an issue, though that condition is not a prerequisite. In this process, the parties negotiate to impasse, and then proceed to arbitration. Plaintiff's last settlement demand and defendant's last offer establish a bracket defining the limits of the arbitrator's award in the case. The arbitrator, however, conducts the arbitration without knowledge of the endpoints of the bracket. The parties are free to make any evidence-based arguments they wish regarding damages, and assuming that the arbitrator determines the defendant to be liable, he or she makes a decision on damages as if it were an ordinary arbitration. When the arbitrator renders an award, neither party will be liable for a figure outside the agreed-to bracket. For example, assume that in a particular case, the plaintiff's last demand was $100,000 and the defendant's last offer was $50,000. The parties then proceed to an arbitration hearing at which the plaintiff argues entitlement to damages in the amount of $150,000, and the defendant argues that plaintiff is entitled, at most, to

$25,000. If the arbitrator renders an award of $125,000, the defendant will pay no more than $100,000. If the arbitrator renders an award of $35,000, the plaintiff will receive $50,000. If the arbitrator renders an award of $75,000, the plaintiff will receive $75,000 because that figure falls within the pre-agreed bracket.

There are several advantages to using the high-low arbitration procedure. First, it reduces the parties' risk of allowing a third party to decide their fate. Going to the arbitration, both parties know the lower and upper limits on the award. Second, it encourages vigorous bargaining, the plaintiff wanting to establish the highest minimum award possible and the defendant seeking to fix the lowest maximum award possible. This situation usually forces the parties to find a reasonable settlement range and, at the same time, a reasonably narrow bracket. If the bracket is too large—$25,000 and $1,000,000—when the parties proceed to arbitration, there is very little advantage to high-low arbitration over ordinary arbitration unless, of course, one side or the other has thoroughly misjudged the value of the case. Finally, high-low arbitration can provide an economically favorable alternative to going to trial after an unsuccessful mediation. Typically, a skillful mediator helps the parties arrive at a reasonable settlement range which can serve as the bracket in a subsequent high-low arbitration conducted by another neutral.

Baseball arbitration. Baseball arbitration is a type of "last best offer" arbitration in which the disputing parties agree in writing to negotiate to only one position—their last and best offer—and then submit the dispute to arbitration. In baseball arbitration, the arbitrator must choose the last best offer of one of the parties and may not find a different result under any circumstance.

This type of last best offer arbitration had its origin in U.S. major league baseball player salary negotiations, but now is an ADR method adaptable to practically any type of dispute involving a monetary solution. A quick decision is a valuable feature of the classic version of baseball arbitration. The arbitrator must pick one figure or the other and is encouraged to render his or her decision within twenty-four hours. The decision is binding, and there can be no compromise. Also, the arbitrator need not explain the decision.

The rigidity of last-best offer arbitration is its main selling point. It is its own deterrent. Labor experts believe that a party's risk in having its offer rejected and the other side's offer selected, promotes good faith bargaining, encourages a narrow negotiated settlement bracket, and, in practice, provides an incentive for parties to resolve differences without an arbitration hearing.

Med-Arb. In Med-Arb, by pre-agreement of the parties, the neutral conducts a mediation to settle the entire dispute or part of it, after which the neutral arbitrates any unresolved issues. Usually, the same neutral performs the role of mediator and arbitrator, but different neutrals may serve in those roles.

Arb-Med. In this process, the parties first proceed to arbitration before an arbitrator who will render a binding decision. When the decision is made, it is not shown to the parties. Rather, the arbitrator places it in a sealed envelope. Thereafter, the parties can negotiate a resolution on their own, or they can involve the arbitrator as a mediator to help mediate a resolution. The arbitrator's decision, having already been made, will not be influenced by any confidential information of the parties. If the negotiations or mediation are unsuccessful, the parties open the sealed envelope and are bound by the award. Parties negotiating in the shadow of the sealed award tend to reach a joint decision for themselves rather than entrust their fate to an imposed solution of unknown value.

Co-Med-Arb. The ADR process called Co-Med-Arb has emerged in recent years as an antidote to many of the ills which plague the process of Med-Arb, described above. As explained above, Med-Arb is a combination of the mediation and arbitration processes in which a neutral serves in the role of mediator initially and attempts to settle the dispute. If mediation is unsuccessful, usually the same neutral serves in the role of arbitrator, hears evidence presented by the parties, and then renders an arbitral award. Med-Arb "has been praised for its efficiency gains and condemned for resulting in a 'confusion of roles' that jeopardizes both the effectiveness of mediation and the integrity of arbitral decision-making."[7]

The basic concept of Co-Med-Arb is to use two neutrals, one in the role of mediator and one as arbitrator, but to have them work as closely together as possible to maximize their efficiency while avoiding confusion of roles. Even though Co-Med-Arb employs two neutrals, the design of the process seeks to avoid duplicative expenses by saving time needed to bring the arbitrator "up to speed" should the mediation prove unsuccessful.

The parties select both the mediator and the arbitrator prior to the dispute or after the dispute arises. The two neutrals jointly tend to procedural matters such as conducting a prehearing conference, setting dates for meetings, and

---

7. Christian Buehring-Uhle, *Co-Med-Arb Technique Holds Promise for Getting Best of Both Worlds*, 3 World Arbitration and Mediation Report 21 (1992). See also, Bette J. Roth, Randall W. Wulff, & Charles A. Cooper, *The Alternative Dispute Resolution Guide* §37:12 (Lawyers Cooperative Publishing, 1995).

scheduling the filing of briefs. The mediator and arbitrator review all submitted documents prior to the hearing and, at the initial session of the hearing, they sit as a panel to hear the parties' opening statements in what is called the open phase of the hearing. During this open phase, the arbitrator presides. Both the arbitrator and mediator may ask clarifying questions of counsel, but the mediator withholds asking "sensitive" questions regarding the parties' needs and interests until the second, or confidential, phase of the process. After the close of the open phase of the process, the rules preclude the mediator from discussing the substance of the dispute with the arbitrator, though the two neutrals may usually confer on procedural matters.

In the confidential phase, the mediator attempts to mediate the dispute to resolution. If the parties reach impasse, they proceed to the third phase of the process and present their evidence to the arbitrator. When this occurs, the mediator is usually "on call" in the event that the parties desire to resume mediation at one or more points during the arbitration. If the parties resume mediation, the mediator sets strict time limits on the mediation conference.

Although mediation efforts may not be initially successful in resolving the entire dispute, they can lead to a variety of beneficial results, including streamlining the arbitration, achieving a stipulation of facts or agreed limitation of issues, and resolving several of the contested issues. The mediator may also be helpful after the conclusion of the arbitration hearing. If the parties desire, the arbitrator may withhold the award until after the parties have a limited-duration final session with the mediator to attempt to work out a mutually satisfactory settlement. If the mediation is successful, the parties agree that the award should not issue. If the mediation is unsuccessful, the arbitrator issues the award, and if the parties desire, they can request that the mediator conduct a post-award settlement conference.

Although the Co-Med-Arb process is generally more expensive than pure mediation or arbitration, use of the process can prove to be a wise investment. In complex, high-stakes disputes, the value of Co-Med-Arb's collateral benefits may far outweigh its cost in dollars. Because of the continuous availability of mediation, there is opportunity for settlement early in the Co-Med-Arb process, or at any number of points during the process. Moreover, the process may avoid damaging continuing relationships that the parties need to maintain. In short, the two-neutral Co-Med-Arb tandem process may allow disputants to extract the best of both the mediation and the arbitration processes, while minimizing the disadvantages associated with them or with their sequenced amalgam, Med-Arb.

1.1.5   Application of arbitration to various types of disputes.

Arbitration is used in a variety of dispute settings in various practice areas. As an arbitrator, you may be selected to perform the neutral function in any one of them. Several of these dispute settings and practice areas are described in this section.[8]

Business disputes. Arbitration clauses are increasingly being incorporated into business contracts and agreements. Corporate executives find that one of the advantages of including arbitration clauses in contracts and of arbitrating commercial disputes is the opportunity it allows them to choose arbitrators as neutral decision-makers who are knowledgeable about the specific industry and understand technical terms and subtle nuances of the dispute.

For example, technology disputes bring their own unique problems. These disputes often involve multiple parties and contain a number of difficult, technical or scientific issues that must be comprehended and decided. Decisions in such disputes also may impact a variety of other businesses, including publishing, cable, entertainment, telecommunications, and manufacturing. Arbitration can provide a useful, tailored mechanism to resolve these intricate problems and save parties both time and expense.

Another category of business disputes that is particularly well-suited for arbitration is that which produces a high volume of small to mid-size claims. One such dispute is the consumer complaint. The Better Business Bureau and other organizations have been very successful in administering arbitration programs that handle and resolve large volumes of such disputes efficiently and cost-effectively.

Construction disputes. Nearly without exception, business disputes of all types are amenable to resolution through arbitration. One category of business dispute—the construction dispute—warrants separate consideration, because it is particularly suited to arbitration (or arbitration after attempted mediation). Construction disputes are characteristically technically complex, involve a unique vocabulary, and require the testimony of numerous experts. Often, the number of documents associated with these disputes is formidable, but in the arbitration proceeding, discovery can usually be effected voluntarily and much more quickly than it could be if the case were to be litigated in court. Also, because the arbitration procedure is less formal and more flexible than a court proceeding, the arbitrators usually can accommodate the schedules of parties and witnesses more easily, take witnesses out of turn, and design

---

8. *See generally, Martindale-Hubbell Dispute Resolution Directory* 4–1 through 4–36 (Martindale-Hubbell, 1995).

the process to meet the sometimes unusual needs of the particular dispute and disputants.

Employment disputes. Since the 1940s, arbitration has been the leading mechanism apart from negotiation for resolving labor disputes involving unionized workers. In recent years, both arbitration and mediation have been used increasingly in resolving employment disputes not involving collective bargaining issues. For example, arbitration can be used in a variety of disputes which pit a non-union employee against an employer. These disputes include those regarding alleged discrimination based on race, sex, religion, sexual orientation, and physical and mental disabilities. They also include disputes which arise out of the terms and conditions of employment as contained in an employment contract. These contractual disputes sometimes concern wages, promotion, termination, benefits, covenants not to compete, confidentiality clauses, and scope of function. In many of these situations, arbitration is used after mediation proves unsuccessful.

Insurance disputes. Arbitration has been used for many years to resolve disputes that arise under insurance policies. These disputes can involve disagreements between insurance companies and their policyholders; between two or more insurance companies over liability; and between a third party claimant and an insurance company over that claimant's right to be reimbursed under another person's policy (e.g., uninsured or underinsured motorist coverage). Personal injury, medical malpractice, legal malpractice, and property damage claims are just a few of the many types of cases that fall into this insurance dispute category. Other types of routinely arbitrated insurance-related claims include: workers compensation; title insurance; toxic tort and other environmental claims; architect and engineer professional negligence claims; and flood, earthquake, and other natural disaster claims.

Securities disputes. Arbitration has been used in the securities industry since the early 1800s. Within the industry, there are ten self-regulatory organizations (SRO's) that administer arbitrations and provide arbitrators for disputes. In the past, many arbitration clauses in securities contracts mandated that arbitration be administered by the SRO's. However, due to customer complaints, many clauses now include a choice between several dispute resolution organizations for administration of the arbitration proceedings should a dispute arise. Because of overcrowding of the court system, as well as several opinions by the United States Supreme Court removing any barriers to resolving securities cases through arbitration, the use of arbitration has increased dramatically in this practice area during the last decade.

If a dispute arises under an investment agreement containing an arbitration clause, the arbitration must take place in the forum dictated by the clause. Each arbitration forum has specific rules describing how arbitrators are selected and how they should perform their function.

Real estate disputes. In the last decade, the use of ADR, including arbitration, has expanded in the real estate industry. Increased use of these processes has been motivated, in part, by a desire on the part of the disputants to save time and money and to preserve confidentiality. Types of real estate disputes commonly submitted to mediation and arbitration for resolution include home purchase and sale agreements, listing agreements, leases, real estate partnerships and joint ventures, and real estate valuation. It is important to note that ADR may not always satisfy the needs of real estate contract parties, particularly as those contracts pertain to foreclosure, enforcement of a deed of trust, mortgage, or land contract, and mechanics liens, all of which are more appropriately suited for resolution by judicial means. Thus, experienced advocates who draft buy/sell agreements normally exclude from arbitration these and other related procedures and remedies which the court system is better equipped to handle. As an arbitrator in a real estate dispute, you should be aware that there may be certain law-imposed limitations on your authority and effectiveness.

Family disputes. Because of the sheer number of disputes involving family laws, the courts and parties are increasingly turning to private dispute resolution organizations for administrative relief. Before beginning the arbitration process, both sides sign an arbitration agreement that sets out the issues to be arbitrated, names of the arbitrators, and that contains the understanding of the parties that the arbitrator's decision will be binding. Although mediation is normally the preferred process in family disputes—particularly with respect to custody and visitation issues—arbitration is often quite helpful with respect to property division issues where mediation has been ineffective and the parties desire a speedy, economical resolution. Many divorce settlement agreements include arbitration clauses to settle any post-divorce disputes. This helps to minimize the possibility that one party will attempt to harass the other through a prolonged court battle. The mere presence of arbitration clause in a divorce decree encourages the parties to negotiate settlement of post-decree disputes, rather than to submit them to the uncertainty of a decision by a neutral arbitrator.

Health care disputes. Although the health care industries have been slow to use ADR processes for resolving disputes, ADR, particularly arbitration, is well-suited for the types of conflicts that arise there. The industries define a broad spectrum of potential ADR users, including hospitals, physicians, health insurers, medical equipment manufacturers and distributors, pharmaceutical companies, nursing homes, various managed care and health maintenance organizations, dental clinics, independent laboratories, etc. Arbitration and other ADR processes have been used successfully to resolve disputes between health care institutions and providers, as well as intellectual property disputes, disputes between insurers and subscribers, and contract disputes between medical product manufacturers and medical providers.

Government disputes. In recent years, state and federal governments have been incorporating public and private dispute resolution into their systems. The Administrative Conference of the United States, a federal agency that researches and monitors federal agency procedures, has been the vanguard in this trend toward expanded use of ADR methods to resolve disputes in which an agency of the federal government is a party. The Administrative Conference sponsors educational workshops on ADR. One of its goals is to implement dispute resolution programs in every agency of the federal government. By 1994, twenty-four federal agencies had signed pledges to review existing contract disputes and to consider settling them with out-of-court dispute resolution procedures.

International disputes. Arbitration has been the preferred method for settling international disputes for decades. Companies doing international business routinely include arbitration or other ADR-type clauses in their contracts, in order to avoid problems that can arise when dealing with a foreign legal system. Also, many foreign companies feel more comfortable with the arbitration process than they do with litigation. Parties can choose non-administered arbitration, but pursuing international arbitration through an organization has several advantages, including the fact that these organizations have well-established rules and lists of highly qualified individuals to act as arbitrators. Besides the American Arbitration Association, JAMS-Endispute, and the International Chamber of Commerce (ICC), other organizations that administer international arbitration include the United Nations Commission on International Trade Relations and Law (UNCITRAL), the London Court of International Arbitration (LCIA), the CPR Institute for Dispute Resolution, the Chicago International Dispute Resolution Association (CIDRA), the International Bar Association, the International Centre for Settlement of Investment Disputes (ICSID), and the World Intellectual Property Organization (WIPO), which offers many arbitration services.

A recurring challenge for parties initiating international arbitration is agreeing with the opponents on a site to hold the arbitration proceedings. It is best to choose a neutral location and to take into account the availability of professional and technical support in that area, how politically stable the area is, how local laws might affect the enforcement of the arbitration clause, and the degree of difficulty in enforcing an arbitral award once obtained. Other important challenges include determining where the other party's assets are held and whether the host jurisdiction adheres to the 1958 New York Convention on the Recognition and Enforcement of Foreign Arbitral Awards.

1.2   THE ROLE AND AUTHORITY OF THE ARBITRATOR

1.2.1   The adversarial (common law) model.

Court litigation in common law system. Aside from the availability of a jury trial, two principal characteristics of common law civil litigation systems, such as those existing in the United States and England, are: (1) a case preparation process in which the respective parties and their lawyers are responsible for investigating and presenting their cases to judges (or juries); and (2) a judicial decision-making process in which judges must rely on prior judicial precedent, called stare decisis, in rendering their decisions. Proceedings are adversarial in nature in that each lawyer must persuade the court that its position on the law and the facts is the correct one—the one that the judge (or jury) should adopt. Thus, when a plaintiff's lawyer formulates theories for claims and when a defense lawyer formulates defense theories, each must carefully, and sometimes exhaustively, examine the existing case law of the pertinent jurisdiction and prepare appropriate pleadings. Claims and defenses may, of course, be based on statutory or Constitutional law, but the common law lawyer cannot merely cite the statutory or Constitutional provision in support of the claim or defense. Rather, he or she must cite case law, as close as possible to the facts of his or her own case, interpreting those provisions. If the statute or Constitutional provision has never been interpreted by a court, the lawyer is obliged to find prior case law which may be applied by analogy to aid in the proper interpretation of the provision at issue. Thus, for the common law lawyer to be effective, he or she must engage in a full investigation of the facts and a complete search of prior pertinent law, then present the most cogent and persuasive arguments to the judge or jury, as the case may be.

In common law civil litigation, pretrial testimonial and documentary discovery are routinely permitted. In fact, in some situations, they constitute, figuratively, the lengthy, very expensive tail that wags the shorter, less expensive dog—the trial. In larger cases, each side may produce thousands of documents, and the lawyers may take depositions of scores of witnesses, including experts. But even in the cases where much less in terms of dollars is at stake, lawyers generally have complete discretion to conduct detailed, non-oppressive discovery within the time limits set by the court.

At trial, whether before a jury or a judge sitting without a jury, counsel present opening statements. Afterwards, plaintiff's counsel presents plaintiff's case by calling witnesses, asking them questions on direct examination, and introducing documents as the testimony unfolds. The judge requires counsel to strictly comply with rules of evidence to protect the integrity of the truth-finding process. Defense counsel may cross-examine each witness after plaintiff's counsel completes the cross-examination of the witness. Redirect and recross-examination may follow. The judge may also ask questions of witnesses, but judicial questioning is the exception rather than the rule in the United States' common law litigation model. After counsel for plaintiff has completed introducing all the evidence in the plaintiff's direct case, the plaintiff "rests," and the defense counsel presents the defendant's evidence. When all the defense evidence has been introduced, the defense rests, and the plaintiff may be permitted to present rebuttal evidence. At the close of all evidence, counsel for the parties make final or closing arguments to the jury or the judge sitting without a jury, as the case may be.

In a jury case, after hearing the closing arguments, the judge instructs the jury on the law, the jury proceeds to deliberate, and it ultimately returns its verdict. Counsel may file post-trial motions (motion for judgment notwithstanding verdict, motion for new trial, etc.). The judge either grants the motion or denies it and enters a judgment on the jury's verdict. If the trial judge allows the verdict to stand, he or she enters judgment on it, and one or more parties may then appeal the judgment within a specified period of time.

In a case tried before a judge without jury, after the close of the evidence, the judge may require legal briefs or proposed findings of fact to be filed and subsequent oral arguments before rendering a decision and judgment. After the judgment is entered on the trial court docket, one or more parties may appeal.

Arbitration in common law system. Arbitration conducted in a common law system naturally has many of the characteristics of common law civil court litigation. While arbitration procedures and evidentiary requirements are, in some situations, significantly more relaxed than those prevailing in civil court litigation, many of the features of civil court litigation still find a well-defined image in the arbitration process. For example, common law arbitration is adversarial in that counsel for respective parties prepare their cases based on their perceptions of the facts and law and attempt to persuade the arbitrators to their point of view. Normally, arbitrators allow at least some discovery, consisting of document exchange and specified prehearing depositions. Occasionally, arbitrators will permit extensive prehearing discovery, depending on the nature and complexity of the case.

An arbitration conducted in a common law system proceeds much like the process described above relating to a common law trial. The primary difference is that evidentiary rules are relaxed or are not strictly enforced. Hearsay evidence is generally permitted. Counsel for the parties conduct the questioning of witnesses, but arbitrators usually do not take an active role in questioning witnesses. Arbitrators, however, normally take an active role in questioning counsel when they are making their closing arguments. Prior to hearing final arguments, it is not uncommon for arbitrators to require counsel to file briefs or proposed findings of fact and conclusions of law.

Customarily, common law arbitrators render their awards within a specified period of time after the close of the evidence, and unless the parties have agreed otherwise, the arbitrators' written award will succinctly state the award without providing supporting reasons. This tradition of the unexplained award has given rise to criticism that awards in common law arbitrations often have more of a basis in equity than in law. To avoid this problem, parties who want their disputes decided on the basis of law, rather than on the personal, equitable inclinations of the arbitrators, often provide a requirement in their arbitration agreement that the arbitrators reach their decision according to the applicable law. In addition, some parties agree to have the arbitrators provide a written opinion explaining the award, though in a complex case, such opinion may be quite lengthy and can add significantly to the cost of the arbitration. In common law arbitration, unless otherwise agreed by the parties, the award is final, binding, and judicially reviewable only on extremely narrow grounds.

1.2.2 The inquisitorial (civil law) model.

Court litigation in civil law system. Aside from the non-availability of a jury trial and the non-applicability of case precedent, two principal characteristics of civil law litigation systems, such as those existing in Germany and France, are: (1) the existence of a piecemeal series of written submissions with intermittent oral hearings in which the judge decides issues; and (2) the active role of the judge in shaping the issues for decision through a process of interrogation, hence the term inquisitorial system.[9] Procedures in civil law systems, while similar from country to country, vary in many technical respects.

---

9. *See* Peter Schlosser, *Lectures on Civil-Law Systems and American Cooperation With Those Systems,* 45 Kan L. Rev. 9 (1996); *see generally,* Charles Platto, *Pre-Trial and Pre-Hearing Procedures Worldwide* (Graham & Trotman, 1990).

In Germany, for example, an attorney commences litigation by filing with the court a very extensive, detailed written statement with numerous enclosures. The primary purpose of this document is not, as in the common law system, to apprise the defendant of the claims against it, but rather to convince the judge initially as to the merits of plaintiff's case. Plaintiff's initial document may anticipate the positions of the defendant and provide a response to them. As the case progresses, the files associated with a case may become extensive and complicated.

In contrast, the procedure for initiating a claim in the French court system is less critical and far less burdensome. In France, the purpose of the statement of claim is more like that of common law court systems—to inform the defendant of the allegations and claims being brought against him or her. The statement of claim must include the facts on which plaintiff relies, as well as copies of relevant written evidentiary materials. The text must draw conclusions from which the claimed remedy may be readily inferred.

Traditionally, there has been little or no common law style discovery permitted in civil law systems, though some countries are beginning to permit it, most notably France and the Canadian province of Quebec. In Germany, a judge has extremely restricted authority to order the production of documents, but when deciding a case, the judge may take into account a party's refusal to produce documents.

In Germany, between the initiation of proceedings and the final oral hearing, counsel are usually free to submit as many written statements to the court as they desire. These submissions describe factual allegations and the legal arguments based on statutory law. Judges read the submissions of both parties before entering the court hall.

A similar procedure prevails in France. A special judge is in charge of the French court's functions prior to the final oral hearing. This special judge collects the parties' materials, questions witnesses, appoints or suggests the appointment of experts, and performs many of the functions carried out by the parties' counsel in common law countries.

In civil law systems, the parties normally propose witnesses, but the judge decides which witnesses should be questioned and actually conducts the questioning. Lawyers may put questions to the witnesses after the judge has concluded the examination. In civil law systems, there is usually no cross-examination. Lawyers must pose questions that are non-argumentative and free from suggestive connotation. In many civil law systems, expert witnesses are appointed by the judge and paid by the state treasury. Customarily, the expert must submit a report. Parties seldom insist on questioning the expert at an oral hearing. Often the expert's report results in a settlement of the case.

Because much of the judicial work is accomplished by the judge's private reading of the submissions and through his or her conduct of the interim oral hearings, the final oral hearing is often quite brief and somewhat anti-climactic. Usually, the attorneys merely restate the requests for relief already contained in their written submissions. The judge makes a decision based upon his or her own conclusions as to what fairness requires considering the facts, the relevant statutory provisions, and without reference to what other judges have decided in similar fact and law situations.

Arbitration in civil law system. Many countries with civil law systems have different arbitration procedures depending on whether the dispute being arbitrated is domestic (or national—i.e., involving no foreign parties) or international (involving a foreign party or parties). The trend among civil law countries, however, seems to be toward removing the distinctions between national and international arbitration and providing arbitrators and parties wide powers to self-determine what procedures should govern any particular arbitration. The information in this subsection describes the kinds of arbitration procedures parties and arbitrators might design if the resulting arbitration process is to have predominantly civil law system attributes.[10]

In domestic civil law arbitration, parties have the burden of proof and must disclose documents in support of their claims or defenses. However, traditionally, parties have not been expected or compelled to reveal documents that are merely requested by the opponent but do not support their position. In arbitrations conducted in civil law countries, a party requesting an order to compel production of documents must do so before a judge.

In general, in domestic civil law arbitrations, documentary evidence is favored over oral evidence. Testimony of witnesses (as opposed to parties) is commonly under oath. Arbitrators take an active role in questioning parties and witnesses, sometimes only allowing parties to propose questions that the arbitrators then actually put to the witnesses. Arbitration proceedings are customarily recorded in writing or on audiotape. Arbitrators' appointment of an expert with technical knowledge is common in domestic civil law arbitration.

---

10. *See generally*, Peter Eijsvoogel, *Evidence in International Arbitration Proceedings* 21–27 (International Association of Young Lawyers, 1994).

1.2.3 The international arbitrator.

In international arbitration, the distinction between common law and civil law arbitration is fading with the passage of time. The general trend in international arbitration, as noted above, is self-determination of the arbitration procedures jointly by the arbitrators and the parties, applicable to any particular international case. Thus, as an international arbitrator, you may be required to take an active role in designing the process and procedures specifically appropriate to your case. This may require meshing both common law and civil law procedural customs within the framework of the arbitration rules, for example, with the International Chamber of Commerce, or some other provider of dispute resolution. Here are some design considerations to be taken into account when preparing for and performing that task.[11]

Statutory arbitration rules. Virtually every country has statutes which govern domestic arbitration. Some countries have statutes which additionally prescribe procedures for conducting international arbitrations. You should be aware of these sources of arbitration procedures when performing your design function. Note that some countries have set forth mandatory standards or principles under which an international arbitration must be conducted. Also, most countries permit their court procedural provisions to be applied to international arbitrations.

Non-statutory arbitration rules. Countries often prefer the use of particular institutional arbitration rules for international arbitrations. Rules most often used for international arbitrations are the Rules of Arbitration of the International Chamber of Commerce (ICC). On the South American continent, the rules of the Inter-American Commercial Arbitration Commission (IACAC) are widely used. Additionally, many local or national chambers of commerce have their own arbitration rules, as for example, the Zurich Chamber of Commerce (ZCC).

Discovery. Many countries have pre-complaint discovery procedures connected with their court systems. These procedures are also commonly used with respect to arbitrations. Many countries have procedures for court-ordered witness testimony, which may be applied for during an arbitration proceeding. Exchange of documents is common in most countries, but the authority of an arbitrator (and in some instances, even a court) to compel production of documents is generally limited.

Preparation of witnesses. Some countries have prohibitions against counsel contacting witnesses prior to an arbitration hearing. Other countries allow

---

11. *See generally,* Eijsvoogel, *supra* note 10 at 3–14

counsel to contact and prepare their own witnesses, but prohibit counsel from contacting an opponent's witnesses. Still other countries permit counsel to contact an opponent's witnesses with the consent of opposing counsel.

Examination of witnesses. Most countries, even civil law countries, allow counsel to ask questions of witnesses during the arbitration hearing, though some require that counsel only propose the questions and that the arbitrators ask them. Commonly, counsel question witnesses first, followed by the arbitrators, but in some countries (Austria, Germany, and the Netherlands), the arbitrators begin the questioning.

Documents. In many civil law countries, it is common to present documents with the initial pleading and to supplement them during the proceeding. Some countries still require original or certified copies to be submitted, though the trend is toward allowing photocopies of documents unless authenticity is questioned.

Testimonial evidence. Many civil law countries do not permit a party to testify as a witness in arbitration. Some countries do not permit parties or witnesses to testify under oath; other countries do not initially require a party to testify under oath but permit such party to request that the opposing party be placed under oath.

Experts. Expert testimony is widely used in civil law countries. Normally, the arbitrator may appoint an expert if the parties consent. In some countries, the parties may additionally retain their own experts. Experts render reports, and in some countries, testify and are subjected to examination by the arbitrators and counsel.

Legal arguments. Requirements for legal argument vary from country to country. In some countries, the emphasis is on written legal arguments, starting from the initiation of the arbitration. In other countries, the emphasis is on oral arguments with only citations to the relevant law. In most countries where foreign law is applicable, counsel file legal briefs with the arbitrators.

Evaluating evidence in decision-making. Customarily, countries permit the introduction of hearsay evidence in arbitration proceedings, but a few countries prohibit it altogether. There is a wide variation among countries regarding the relative weight to be given testimonial evidence vis-a-vis documentary evidence. Some countries require that the parties specifically elect to have the arbitrators decide the case either on an equitable basis or on a legal basis.

1.2.4 Qualities of an effective arbitrator.

Whether you are selected by the parties, an organization, the court, or other arbitrators, you will be expected to treat the disputants who come before you with neutrality and impartiality. In fact, neutrality and impartiality are the most important qualities of an arbitrator. Other important attributes that you, as an arbitrator, must possess and display include honesty, patience, intelligence, common sense, good listening and communication skills, an appropriate sense of humor, the ability to make a decision with an open mind, a firmness to control the proceedings, and good judgment. Being well-organized and punctual, as well as displaying respect for advocates, their clients, and their opposing viewpoints are also important arbitrator qualities. Your education, training, technical and scientific expertise, and arbitration experience are also important, but you need not be trained in every minute aspect of law. Indeed, many arbitrators are not lawyers. Functionally, it is much more important that an arbitrator is reasonable, flexible, and willing to conduct the proceeding so as to achieve a fair outcome.

If you want to be an effective arbitrator, you will be actively involved in the management of the disputes before you. If you are inclined to sit on the sidelines and let two parties fight it out, you may be called an "arbitrator," but you probably will not gain the reputation of being an effective one.

1.2.5 Maintaining neutrality and impartiality.

Parties are quick to forgive arbitrators for their foibles, idiosyncrasies, and petty character faults. What parties will not forgive or overlook is a perceived inclination that an arbitrator is overly and unjustifiably harsh on them or favors an opponent. Such conduct can evoke the perception that the arbitrator is partial to a party or has lost his or her neutrality. Consequently, arbitrators must be scrupulously careful to avoid even the appearance of partiality, prejudice, or bias throughout the arbitration proceeding. To ensure that you are maintaining your neutrality and impartiality, you may find it helpful to review from time to time the following list of "don'ts."[12]

Don't offer substantive legal advice. By suggesting a theory of claim or defense, or worse yet, by directing counsel to cases describing and supporting such claims or defense, you usurp the role of the advocate, and at the same time, disrupt the balance of your neutral role. The advocate whose legal position is weakened by your behavior might resent your "assistance" to the opposing party and might reasonably conclude that you are favoring the opponent,

---

12. *See generally* James L. Branton and Jim D. Lovett, *Alternative Dispute Resolution*, Vol. 10, Trial Lawyer Series, "Arbitration," 2–59 (Knowles Publishing, Inc., 1996).

that you have prejudged the matter, and that you are setting the stage for entering an award adverse to that advocate's own position.

An arbitrator's offering of advice on procedural matters is not as problematic. The arbitrator has a systemic interest in ensuring that the arbitration is conducted procedurally according to the rules and the pertinent law. Stating views on what the rules and laws require procedurally is an important aspect of the arbitrator's function. There is no harm in an arbitrator implying in advance how he or she might rule on a procedural motion, if filed. The implication may discourage the party from making or filing the motion, and thereby contribute positively to the overall efficiency of the proceeding.

Don't invite a perception of partiality. Avoid discussions of a person known in common with one of the advocates, witnesses, or parties in front of the opposing advocates, witnesses, or parties. Also, in joint sessions, avoid discussions of individuals that you and other advocates, witnesses, or parties know in common. Be careful not to control the proceeding in favor of one of the parties or to interject your own biases by volunteering unnecessary information in connection with your oral rulings. Avoid projecting too much agreement or disagreement with a party's position or argument. Never offer a tentative decision or express an opinion as to the merits of the case. Never accept evidence or testimony from a party without giving the opposing party the opportunity to see or consider the evidence and to comment or object.

Don't engage in behaviors indicating prejudgment or lack of interest. Refrain from commenting favorably or unfavorably regarding the testimony of any party or witness, and avoid summarizing the testimony of a witness for clarification of an advocate or party. Be conscious of your body language. Be careful not to communicate irritation, impatience, or lack of interest by rough or casual handling of hearing exhibits. Avoid sidebar discussions with panel members while an advocate is interrogating a witness.

Don't engage in behaviors outside the arbitration proceeding that might compromise your neutrality and impartiality. Do not participate in any settlement discussions of the parties, which might provide you with confidential, non-evidentiary information. An exception to this might occur when the parties formally request you to serve as a mediator and they sign an agreement regarding your post-mediation role, should the mediation prove unsuccessful. Never discuss the case with anyone but your fellow panel members outside the arbitration proceeding. Never independently visit or investigate the pertinent site or evidence scene without informing the parties and obtaining their agreement for you to do so.

The above discussion of behaviors to avoid to ensure your neutrality and impartiality as an arbitrator has conveniently taken us to the threshold of our next very important topic—arbitrator ethics.

1.3 ARBITRATOR ETHICS

In this chapter, we have discussed some of the considerations parties take into account when selecting an arbitrator. In this section, we wish to review briefly the ethical code which governs the conduct of arbitrators. It is important for you to be familiar with the ethical restraints on arbitrator behavior so that you will know how to conduct yourself ethically as an arbitration when it may be appropriate for you to disqualify or recuse yourself from a case.

The Code of Ethics for Arbitrators in Commercial Disputes—Revised 2004 (Code) (see Appendix K), prepared jointly by a special committee of the American Arbitration Association (AAA) and a Task Force of the American Bar Association (ABA), consists of ethical guidelines for many types of arbitration, but it does not apply to labor arbitration, which is generally conducted under the Code of Professional Responsibility for Arbitrators of Labor-Management Disputes. It addresses ethical norms applying to arbitrators whether they are: selected or designated by the parties or other individuals as "neutrals"; or appointed by the parties, acting alone, and then those two party-appointed arbitrators select a neutral arbitrator. In the discussion which follows, we will address the ethical norms which apply specifically and separately to neutral arbitrators and party-appointed arbitrators. It should be emphasized that party-appointed arbitrators are of two types: (1) neutral and (2) "Canon X arbitrators," defined as arbitrators who by agreement or understanding of the parties may be predisposed toward the party who appointed them, but in all other respects, are obligated to act in good faith and with integrity and fairness.

1.3.1 Canon I—Integrity and fairness of process.

Canon I of the Code provides: An arbitrator should uphold the integrity and fairness of the arbitration process.

Neutral arbitrators. An arbitrator has a responsibility not only to the parties, but also to the arbitration process itself. An arbitrator must observe high standards of conduct so that the integrity and fairness of the process will be preserved. Thus, an arbitrator should recognize a responsibility to the public, to the parties whose rights will be decided, and to all other participants in the proceeding.

A person should accept appointment as an arbitrator only if fully satisfied that he or she: (1) can serve impartially; (2) can serve independently from the parties, potential witnesses, and the other arbitrators; (3) is competent to serve; (4) can be available to commence the arbitration in accordance with the requirements of the proceeding; and (5) is able to devote the time and attention to its completion that the parties are reasonably entitled to expect. Arbitrators should conduct themselves in a way that is fair to all parties and should not be swayed by outside pressure, public clamor, and fear of criticism or self-interest. They must avoid conduct and statements that give the appearance of partiality toward or against any party. Arbitrators must also act within the parameters of the authority given them by the agreement of the parties, but arbitrators are not required ethically to comply with any agreement, procedures or rules that are unlawful or that, in the arbitrator's judgment, would be inconsistent with the Code. Arbitrators should not withdraw or abandon an appointment unless compelled to do so by unanticipated circumstances that would render it impossible or impracticable to continue. Arbitrators who are compelled to withdraw prior to the completion of an arbitration should take reasonable steps to protect the interests of the parties in the arbitration, including return of evidentiary materials and the protection of confidentiality.

Party-appointed arbitrators. A party-appointed arbitrator has an obligation under Canon IX to ascertain, as early as possible but not later than the first meeting of the arbitrators and parties, whether the parties have agreed that the party-appointed arbitrators will serve as neutrals or whether they shall be subject to Canon X, and to provide a timely report of their conclusions to the parties and other arbitrators. In making this determination, party-appointed arbitrators should review the agreement of the parties, the applicable rules and any applicable law bearing upon arbitrator neutrality. In reviewing the agreement of the parties, party-appointed arbitrators should consult any relevant express terms of the written or oral arbitration agreement. It may also be appropriate for them to inquire into agreements that have not been expressly set forth, but which may be implied from an established course of dealings of the parties or well-recognized custom and usage in their trade or profession. Where party-appointed arbitrators conclude that the parties intended for the party-appointed arbitrators not to serve as neutrals, after making their report as just described, they may act as provided in Canon X unless or until a different determination of their status is made by the parties, any administering institution or the arbitral panel. In addition, until party-appointed arbitrators conclude that the party-appointed arbitrators were not intended by the parties to serve as neutrals, or if the party-appointed arbitrators are unable to form a reasonable belief of their status from the foregoing sources and no decision in this regard has yet been made by the parties, any administering institution, or the arbitral panel, they should observe all of the obligations of neutral arbitrators set forth in the Code. Party-appointed arbitrators not governed by Canon X must observe all of the obligations of Canons I through VIII unless otherwise required by agreement of the parties, any applicable rules, or applicable law.

"Canon X Arbitrators" must observe all of the obligations of Canon I subject only to the following provisions: (1) they may, by agreement or understanding of all participants, be predisposed toward the party who appointed them but in all other respects they are obligated to act in good faith and with integrity and fairness. For example, Canon X arbitrators should not engage in delaying tactics or harassment of any party or witness and should not knowingly make untrue or misleading statements to the other arbitrators. The provisions of subparagraphs B(1), B(2), and paragraphs C and D of Canon I, insofar as they relate to partiality, relationships, and interests are not applicable to Canon X arbitrators.

1.3.2 Canon II—Disclosure of bias or conflicts of interest.

Canon II of the Code provides: An arbitrator should disclose any interest or relationship likely to affect impartiality or which might create an appearance of partiality or bias.

Neutral arbitrators. Persons who are requested to serve as arbitrators must, before accepting, make a reasonable effort to inform themselves of any pertinent interests or relationships, and disclose: (1) any known direct or indirect financial or personal interest in the outcome of the arbitration; (2) any known existing or past financial, business, professional or personal relationships which might reasonably affect impartiality or lack of independence in the eyes of any of the parties; (3) the nature and extent of any prior knowledge they may have of the dispute; and (4) any other matters, relationships, or interests which they are obligated to disclose by the agreement of the parties, the rules or practices of an institution, or applicable law regulating arbitrator disclosure. This obligation to disclose pertinent interests or relationships is a continuing duty and any doubt as to whether or not disclosure is to be made should be resolved in favor of disclosure. Disclosure is normally made to all parties unless the parties' agreement, the law, or rules direct otherwise. After the arbitrator's disclosure, if the parties desire that the person serve as the arbitrator, that person may properly serve.

If all parties request an arbitrator to withdraw, the arbitrator must do so. If less than all the parties request that the arbitrator withdraw because of alleged partiality, the arbitrator must withdraw unless: (1) an agreement of the parties, or arbitration rules agreed to by the parties, or applicable law establishes procedures for determining challenges to arbitrators, in which case those procedures should be followed; or (2) in the absence of applicable procedures, if the arbitrator, after carefully considering the matter, determines that the reason for the challenge is not substantial, and that he or she can nevertheless act and decide the case impartially and fairly.

If compliance by a prospective arbitrator with any provision of the Code would require disclosure of confidential or privileged information, the prospective arbitrator should either: (1) secure the consent to the disclosure from the person who furnished the information or the holder of the privilege; or (2) withdraw.

Party-appointed arbitrators. Canon X arbitrators have the obligation under Canon II to disclose to all parties, and to the other arbitrators, all interests and relationships which Canon II requires disclosed. They are not obliged to withdraw under Canon II for alleged partiality if requested to do so by a party or parties who did not appoint them.

1.3.3 Canon III—No improper communications with parties.

Canon III of the Code provides: *An arbitrator should avoid impropriety or the appearance of impropriety in communicating with parties.*

Neutral arbitrators. If the parties have entered into an arbitration agreement and it contains procedures regarding communications between the arbitrator(s) and the parties, those procedures govern. If the arbitration agreement does not have a provision regarding communications between arbitrators and parties, the following procedures apply.

An arbitrator or prospective arbitrator should not discuss a proceeding with any party in the absence of any other party, except in any of the following circumstances:

Prospective arbitrator: When the appointment of a prospective arbitrator is being considered, the prospective arbitrator:

(1) may ask about the identities of the parties, counsel, or witnesses and the general nature of the case; and

(2) may respond to inquiries from a party or its counsel designed to determine his or her suitability and availability for the appointment. In any such dialogue, the prospective arbitrator may receive information from a party or its counsel disclosing the general nature of the dispute but should not permit them to discuss the merits of the case.

(3) Unless otherwise provided in Canon III, in applicable arbitration rules or in an agreement of the parties, whenever an arbitrator communicates in writing with one party, the arbitrator should at the same time send a copy of the communication to every other party, and whenever the arbitrator receives any written communication concerning the case from one party which has not already been sent to every other party, the arbitrator should send or cause it to be sent to the other parties.

(4) Discussions may be had with a party concerning such logistical matters as setting the time and place of hearings or making other arrangements for the conduct of the proceedings. However, the arbitrator should promptly inform each other party of the discussion and should not make any final determination concerning the matter discussed before giving each absent party an opportunity to express the party's views.

(5) If a party fails to be present at a hearing after having been given due notice, or if all parties expressly consent, the arbitrator may discuss the case with any party who is present.

Party-appointed arbitrators. In an arbitration in which the two party-appointed arbitrators are expected to appoint the third arbitrator, each party-appointed arbitrator may consult with the party who appointed the arbitrator concerning the choice of the third arbitrator. In addition:

(1) In an arbitration involving party-appointed arbitrators, each party-appointed arbitrator may consult with the party who appointed the arbitrator concerning arrangements for any compensation to be paid to the party-appointed arbitrator. Submission of routine written requests for payment of compensation and expenses in accordance with such arrangements and written communications pertaining solely to such requests need not be sent to the other party.

(2) In an arbitration involving party-appointed arbitrators, each party-appointed arbitrator may consult with the party who appointed the arbitrator concerning the status of the arbitrator (i.e., neutral or non-neutral).

Canon X requires Canon X arbitrators to observe all of the obligations of Canon III, subject only to the following provisions:

(1) Like neutral party-appointed arbitrators, Canon X arbitrators may consult with the party who appointed them to the extent permitted in paragraph B of Canon III;

(2) Canon X arbitrators shall, at the earliest practicable time, disclose to the other arbitrators and to the parties whether or not they intend

to communicate with their appointing parties. If they have disclosed the intention to engage in such communications, they may thereafter communicate with their appointing parties concerning any other aspect of the case, except as provided in paragraph (3) below.

(3) If such communication occurred prior to the time they were appointed as arbitrators, or prior to the first hearing or other meeting of the parties with the arbitrators, the Canon X arbitrator should, at or before the first hearing or meeting of the arbitrators with the parties, disclose the fact that such communication has taken place. In complying with this requirement, it is sufficient that there be disclosure of the fact that such communication has occurred without disclosing the content of the communication. A single timely disclosure of the Canon X arbitrator's intention to participate in such communications in the future is sufficient;

Canon X arbitrators may not at any time during the arbitration:

(a) disclose any deliberations by the arbitrators on any matter or issue submitted to them for decision;

(b) communicate with the parties that appointed them concerning any matter or issue taken under consideration by the panel after the record is closed or such matter or issue has been submitted for decision; or

(c) disclose any final decision or interim decision in advance of the time that it is disclosed to all parties.

(5) Unless otherwise agreed by the arbitrators and the parties, a Canon X arbitrator may not communicate orally with the neutral arbitrator concerning any matter or issue arising or expected to arise in the arbitration in the absence of the other Canon X arbitrator. If a Canon X arbitrator communicates in writing with the neutral arbitrator, he or she shall simultaneously provide a copy of the written communication to the other Canon X arbitrator;

(6) When Canon X arbitrators communicate orally with the parties that appointed them concerning any matter on which communication is permitted under the Code, they are not obligated to disclose the contents of such oral communications to any other party or arbitrator; and

(7) When Canon X arbitrators communicate in writing with the party who appointed them concerning any matter on which communication is permitted under the Code, they are not required to send copies of any such written communication to any other party or arbitrator.

1.3.4 Canon IV—Fairness and diligence.

Canon IV of the Code provides: An arbitrator should conduct the proceedings fairly and diligently.

Neutral arbitrators. An arbitrator should conduct the proceedings in an even-handed manner. The arbitrator should be patient and courteous to the parties, their representatives, and the witnesses and should encourage similar conduct by all participants. In addition:

(1) The arbitrator should afford to all parties the right to be heard and due notice of the time and place of any hearing. The arbitrator should allow each party a fair opportunity to present its evidence and arguments.

(2) The arbitrator should not deny any party the opportunity to be represented by counsel or by any other person chosen by the party.

(3) If a party fails to appear after due notice, the arbitrator should proceed with the arbitration when authorized to do so, but only after receiving assurance that appropriate notice has been given to the absent party.

(4) When the arbitrator determines that more information than has been presented by the parties is required to decide the case, it is not improper for the arbitrator to ask questions, call witnesses, and request documents or other evidence, including expert testimony.

(5) Although it is not improper for an arbitrator to suggest to the parties that they discuss the possibility of settlement or the use of mediation, or other dispute resolution processes, an arbitrator should not exert pressure on any party to settle or to utilize other dispute resolution processes. An arbitrator should not be present or otherwise participate in settlement discussions or act as a mediator unless requested to do so by all parties.

(6) Co-arbitrators should afford each other full opportunity to participate in all aspects of the proceedings. Code provision is not intended to preclude one arbitrator from acting in limited circumstances (e.g., ruling on discovery issues) where authorized by the agreement of the parties, applicable rules or law, nor does it preclude a majority of the arbitrators from proceeding with any aspect of the arbitration if an arbitrator is unable or unwilling to participate and such action is authorized by the agreement of the parties or applicable rules or law.

Party-appointed arbitrators. Canon X arbitrators must observe all of the obligations of Canon IV .

1.3.5 Canon V—Just, independent, and deliberate decision making.

Canon V of the Code provides: An arbitrator should make decisions in a just, independent and deliberate manner.

Neutral arbitrators. The arbitrator should, after careful deliberation, decide all issues submitted for determination. An arbitrator should decide no other issues. In addition:

(1) An arbitrator should decide all matters justly, exercising independent judgment, and should not permit outside pressure to affect the decision.

(2) An arbitrator should not delegate the duty to decide to any other person.

(3) In the event that all parties agree upon a settlement of issues in dispute and request the arbitrator to embody that agreement in an award, the arbitrator may do so, but is not required to do so unless satisfied with the propriety of the terms of settlement. Whenever an arbitrator embodies a settlement by the parties in an award, the arbitrator should state in the award that it is based on an agreement of the parties.

Party-appointed arbitrators. Party-appointed arbitrators must observe all of the obligations of Canon V except that they are permitted to be predisposed toward deciding in favor of the party who appointed them.

1.3.6 Canon VI—Trust and confidentiality.

Canon VI of the Code provides: An arbitrator should be faithful to the relationship of trust and confidentiality inherent in that office.

Neutral arbitrators. An arbitrator is in a relationship of trust to the parties and should not, at any time, use confidential information acquired during the arbitration proceeding to gain personal advantage or advantage for others, or to affect adversely the interest of another. In addition:

(1) The arbitrator should keep confidential all matters relating to the arbitration proceedings and decision. An arbitrator may obtain help from an associate, a research assistant or other persons in connection with reaching his or her decision if the arbitrator informs the parties of the use of such assistance and such persons agree to be bound by the provisions of Canon VI.

(2) It is not proper at any time for an arbitrator to inform anyone of any decision in advance of the time it is given to all parties. In a proceeding in which there is more than one arbitrator, it is not proper at any time

for an arbitrator to inform anyone about the substance of the deliberations of the arbitrators. After an arbitration award has been made, it is not proper for an arbitrator to assist in proceedings to enforce or challenge the award.

(3) Unless the parties so request, an arbitrator should not appoint himself or herself to a separate office related to the subject matter of the dispute, such as receiver or trustee, nor should a panel of arbitrators appoint one of their number to such an office.

Party-appointed arbitrators. Cannon X arbitrators must observe all of the obligations of Canon VI.

1.3.7 Canon VII—Integrity and fairness in arrangements for compensation and expense reimbursement.

Canon VII of the Code provides: An arbitrator should adhere to standards of integrity and fairness when making arrangements for compensation and reimbursement of expenses.

Neutral arbitrators. Arbitrators who are to be compensated for their services or reimbursed for their expenses shall adhere to standards of integrity and fairness in making arrangements for such payments. In addition:

Certain practices relating to payments are generally recognized as tending to preserve the integrity and fairness of the arbitration process. These practices include:

(a) Before the arbitrator finally accepts appointment, the basis of payment, including any cancellation fee, compensation in the event of withdrawal and compensation for study and preparation time, and all other charges, should be established. Except for arrangements for the compensation of party-appointed arbitrators, all parties should be informed in writing of the terms established.

(b) In proceedings conducted under the rules or administration of an institution that is available to assist in making arrangements for payments, communication related to compensation should be made through the institution. In proceedings where no institution has been engaged by the parties to administer the arbitration, any communication with arbitrators (other than party appointed arbitrators) concerning payments should be in the presence of all parties; and

(c) Arbitrators should not, absent extraordinary circumstances, request increases in the basis of their compensation during the course of a proceeding.

Party-appointed arbitrators. Canon X arbitrators should observe all of the obligations of Canon VII.

1.3.8   Canon VIII—Truthful and accurate advertising.

Canon VIII of the Code provides: An arbitrator may engage in advertising or promotion of arbitral services which is truthful and accurate.

Neutral arbitrators. Advertising or promotion of an individual's willingness or availability to serve as an arbitrator must be accurate and unlikely to mislead. Any statements about the quality of the arbitrator's work or the success of the arbitrator's practice must be truthful. In addition:

(1) Advertising and promotion must not imply any willingness to accept an appointment otherwise than in accordance with the Code.

(2) Canon VIII does not preclude an arbitrator from printing, publishing, or disseminating advertisements conforming to these standards in any electronic or print medium, from making personal presentations to prospective users of arbitral services conforming to such standards or from responding to inquiries concerning the arbitrator's availability, qualifications, experience, or fee arrangements.

Party-appointed arbitrators. Canon X arbitrators should observe all of the obligations of Canon VIII.

1.3.9   Canon IX—Party-appointed arbitrators' duty to determine and to disclose their status.

Canon IX of the Code provides: Arbitrators appointed by one party have a duty to determine and disclose their status and to comply with this Code, except as exempted by Canon X.

Party-appointed arbitrators. Canon IX pertains to party-appointed arbitrators and imposes certain duties on them relating to determination, disclosure, and compliance of their neutral or non-neutral status. Explained in more detail:

(1) In some types of arbitration in which there are three arbitrators, it is customary for each party, acting alone, to appoint one arbitrator. The third arbitrator is then appointed by agreement either of the parties or of the two arbitrators, or failing such agreement, by an independent institution or individual. In tripartite arbitrations to which the Code applies, all three arbitrators are presumed to be neutral and are expected to observe the same standards as the third arbitrator.

(2) Notwithstanding this presumption, there are certain types of tripartite arbitration in which it is expected by all parties that the two arbitrators appointed by the parties may be predisposed toward the party appointing them. Those arbitrators, referred to in the Code as "Canon X arbitrators," are not to be held to the standards of neutrality and independence applicable to other arbitrators. Canon X describes the special ethical obligations of party-appointed arbitrators who are not expected to meet the standard of neutrality.

(3) Specific requirements imposed on party-appointed arbitrators are stated above under the heading "Party-appointed arbitrators" in the discussion related to Canon I.

(4) Canon X arbitrators must observe all of the obligations of Canon IX.

1.3.10 Canon X—Exemptions for non-neutral party-appointed arbitrators.

Canon X of the Code provides: Exemptions for arbitrators appointed by one party who are not subject to rules of neutrality.

Party-appointed arbitrators. Canon X applies only to party-appointed arbitrators who are not subject to the rules of neutrality. Their obligations under the Code are described above in relation to each of the Canons I through IX.

Chapter Two

The Arbitrator's Prehearing Functions and Duties

There are some things you learn best in calm, and some in storm.

—Willa Cather

❈ ❈ ❈ ❈

2.1 INITIATION OF ARBITRATION

2.1.1 Reviewing the arbitration clause, the demand and response, and pertinent rules.

After you have been appointed or selected as an arbitrator in a particular case, you should carefully review the parties' arbitration clause or submission agreement, the claimant's demand and the respondent's response to the demand (if available), and the pertinent arbitration rules. The principal purpose of this review is to acquaint yourself with the type of arbitration process and procedures the parties have designed and agreed to use, the nature of the dispute, whether the dispute (or any aspect of it) is not properly in arbitration before you, the existence of possible conflicts of interest that you will need to disclose, any time constraints under which the parties or the arbitrator must act, and the law and rules that will be applicable to the arbitration proceeding. Another important purpose of this review is to give yourself an early opportunity to anticipate procedural issues that need to be addressed by the partie s, and if necessary, decided by you, either before the preliminary hearing with the parties or during it.

Reviewing the arbitration clause. There are several items to which you should give careful attention when reviewing the parties' arbitration clause or submission agreement.

- **Intent to arbitrate.** Most arbitration clauses allow the parties equal access to arbitration—that is, each party has a separate right to invoke arbitration, and no party has a right to sue the other in court over disputes defined by the agreement as appropriate to arbitrate. Some arbitration clauses are drafted so as to reserve to one party (usually the drafter of the agreement) the option to sue in court. Presumably, such agreements are enforceable if the parties to the arbitration agreement had equal bargaining power when they entered into the agreement. However, if there is a bargaining power imbalance, as in the situation of a Fortune 500 company and an individual consumer, a court may find the consumer's obligation to arbitrate to be unenforceable, either because of duress or misunderstanding. If you are confronted with an arbitration clause that gives one party the option to sue in court, then you should immediately determine, by conference call or simultaneous communication to all parties, whether all the parties have separately agreed in writing to arbitrate rather than to proceed in court.

- **Disputes to be arbitrated.** Typically, future-dispute arbitration clauses contain language committing the parties to arbitrate "any controversy or claim arising out of or relating to this contract."

One would think that such broad language would include all possible disputes between the contracting parties within its sweep. This is not always so. Enterprising, creative lawyers who want to litigate in court always seem to find ways to argue that a particular dispute does not "arise out of or relate to" the contract in question. The present dispute, they might argue, arises out of a separate contract, not having an arbitration clause; or the dispute relates to a service related to the purchase of products, and therefore not to the product sales contract containing an arbitration clause. Thus, when you review an arbitration clause, regardless of how broad or general the dispute-identifying language appears to be, realize that the parties may have differing perceptions of what disputes were intended to be covered by it. Also realize that regardless of what the arbitration clause says, the parties may separately agree that certain issues be litigated. For example, as pointed out in Section 1.1.5, supra, certain types of disputes are customarily carved out of an agreement to arbitrate, particularly those relating to foreclosures and enforcement of mortgages, liens, etc. The principal point to be made here is that the more effort you, as arbitrator, expend early in the proceeding to identify which disputes are due arbitration under the contract, and which are not, the less time you will spend during the course of the arbitration entertaining advocates' arguments regarding which claims or issues are actually before the arbitrator and what evidence is relevant or irrelevant to the proceedings. See Section 2.2.1, infra, for more information on this topic.

- **Joinder of claims or parties.** Occasionally, an advocate will name as respondents in a demand a party or parties who have not agreed to arbitrate. For example, a guarantor of a contract, who signs a separate guarantor agreement not containing an arbitration clause, may have a legitimate basis for objecting to being named as a respondent in arbitration when the contract between the two parties goes sour. Similarly, an architect and a general contractor who sign separate agreements (containing an arbitration clause) with an owner may each have a legitimate basis for contending that each is entitled to a separate arbitration hearing on the claim. On the other hand, as an arbitrator reviewing the arbitration clause, you may see the possible efficiency of consolidating the two arbitrations, and may bring the matter to the attention of the parties early on for their consideration.

- **Location of arbitration.** If the parties to an arbitration agreement are located in different parts of the country or world, the location of the arbitration hearing itself may be an issue. If not dealt with early in the proceeding, the matter of the location of the arbitration can develop into a major issue, particularly if an inconvenienced party believes that the location suggested by the other party does not appropriately take into account the logistical and economical limitations of that inconvenienced party. Usually, by pre-selecting a particular office of a dispute resolution organization to administer the arbitration, the parties by implication are agreeing to the location of the arbitration. The selection of particular office presumably determines the region in which that particular organization's affiliated arbitrators live and perform their neutral services. In such situations, the dispute resolution organization can sometimes handle disputes over "where the arbitration is to be held" administratively. But if an arbitration is non-administered and the parties reside far apart geographically, it is important for the arbitrator to get the parties to agree in the initial stages of the proceedings as to where the arbitration will be held. Related issues of where depositions, if any, are to be held can be addressed simultaneously with the location of arbitration issue.

- **Time limits.** The typical arbitration clause contains a time limit within which a party must initiate arbitration. The period is usually 30 days and is measured from the date the parties reach an impasse in their negotiations to resolve a dispute. Some arbitration agreements—particularly submission agreements—contain a provision setting time limits within which each of the parties must present their respective case. The purpose of this type of provision is to attempt to set some reasonable limit on the length, and therefore the cost, of the entire arbitration process. This is a very important provision in arbitration situations involving multiple parties. Another common time limitation found in arbitration agreements is the time period within which the arbitration panel is to render its decision. Ordinarily, this period is 30 days after the close of the evidence. In especially complex cases, longer periods are, of course, specified. It is important for you, as arbitrator, to review the arbitration clause to ensure that you know the pertinent time limits to which the parties have agreed so that you can comply with any that apply to you and also monitor the parties compliance with those that apply to them.

• **Arbitrator selection procedures.** Unless otherwise specified, if a dispute resolution organization is designated in the arbitration agreement, that organization's procedure for selecting the arbitration panel will govern the selection of arbitrators. However, where the arbitration is non-administered or, perhaps more accurately, administered by the disputants, the responsibility may rest upon you to move the arbitrator selection process along. For example, one commonly used method for selecting arbitrators is to have each party select one arbitrator and then to have those two arbitrators mutually select a third or "neutral" arbitrator. If you are a party-appointed arbitrator, you should contact the other party-appointed arbitrator as soon as possible to discuss selection of the third arbitrator. In some arbitration agreements, the arbitrators are designated by name in the agreement itself. If you find yourself in this situation in a non-administered case, you should contact the other two arbitrators to discuss initial procedural matters, and if appropriate, determine which arbitrator will serve as chair of the panel.

• **Scope of arbitrator's authority and jurisdiction.** An important aspect of any agreement to arbitrate is the written understanding of the parties as to what the scope of the arbitrator's authority and jurisdiction will be. For example, some arbitration agreements include guidelines for the arbitrator regarding what action he or she is authorized to take if certain events occur, such as respondent or his counsel failing to appear at a hearing or a claimant failing to prosecute. Some, but not all, dispute resolution organizations have specific rules which provide guidance in such instances, but if your arbitration clause covers those matters, you should comply with the guidelines in the arbitration clause. Also, if the arbitration clause limits the arbitrator's jurisdiction in some way—for example, jurisdiction to hear or decide punitive damage claims or claims related to matters pending before a judge for decision—then your authority is limited by those restrictions.

• **Pleadings and discovery.** Normally, rules of dispute resolution organizations leave to the discretion of the arbitrator the nature and type of pleadings and discovery permissible in the particular arbitration proceedings. However, if your arbitration agreement specifies in advance of the arbitration, permissible pleadings and the nature and scope of discovery, then you will be obligated to honor that agreement. Usually, discovery is minimized in arbitration. Nevertheless, the arbitration clause may contain an agreement outlining the form and extent of discovery which each party may initiate. For example, the parties might pre-agree to a limited number of interrogatories, requests to produce, and depositions of a specified length. They might also agree to procedures governing discovery related to experts and their reports. Sometimes parties pre-agree to adopt the federal discovery rules for the arbitration of a future-dispute. When the dispute actually arises and proceeds to arbitration, this pre-agreement could prove to be unnecessarily costly and burdensome, producing a situation where a discovery tail is wagging the small dog of a dispute. In such a situation, early in the proceedings you might want to revisit the question of the form and scope of discovery actually needed to adequately prepare their cases for arbitration.

•   **Confidentiality.** In some arbitration clauses, but particularly in submission agreements, you may find confidentiality provisions. For example, if the nature of the dispute involves sensitive business, technological, or financial information, you may find specific prohibitory provisions, with associated automatic sanctions, precluding the disclosure of information exchanged in or introduced during the course of the arbitration proceeding. Such provisions may place limits on how the information is to be maintained during the arbitration proceedings. They may even require the return of all such confidential information to the producing party at the conclusion of the arbitration proceeding. As arbitrator, you must be aware of these provisions, comply with them yourself, and monitor the parties' compliance with them.

•   **Evidence.** Although rules of evidence apply in some court-annexed arbitration programs, they do not customarily apply in private arbitration. In the type of arbitration that is the subject of a U.S. arbitration clause, hearsay evidence is usually admissible. Other types of evidence ordinarily excluded in a court of law may be deemed admissible in arbitration, with the arbitrators' customary caveat that they "will give the evidence the weight they deem appropriate." The perceived advantage of not applying rules of evidence to private arbitration is that the number of evidence objections and related lawyer squabbling is greatly minimized, thereby reducing the number of interruptions in the flow of information and making the proceedings more efficient overall. Even when no evidence rules apply, advocates will still make objections regarding the relevance or materiality of the evidence, but you can normally rule on these very quickly without the need for extensive oral argument. On the other hand, some arbitration clauses specifically require that the rules of evidence apply to all the evidence in the case or certain types of evidence. As an arbitrator, you will want to be aware of this early on. First, you may want to "brush up" on the evidentiary rules and hearsay exceptions, as explained in Chapter 3, infra. Second, the fact that the parties have agreed to abide by specified rules of evidence might influence how the panel members go about selecting their chair. If a panel, for example, is composed of two non-lawyers and one lawyer, and the parties desire that the rules of evidence apply, it might make sense for the lawyer to chair the panel and make the rulings on the evidentiary motions and objections.

• **Designation of law governing the arbitration agreement.** The arbitration agreement will normally specify the jurisdiction whose law is to govern it. You want to know what law applies to the agreement, because you may have to decide issues relating to an interpretation of the arbitration agreement early in the proceedings. Realize that the jurisdiction whose law governs the arbitration agreement may be different from the jurisdiction whose law controls all or some of the legal issues in the underlying contract. For example, a state's law of contracts may govern several of the legal issues arising out of a contract for goods and services, but because interstate commerce is involved, the Federal Arbitration Act may govern some of the procedural and substantive issues related to the arbitration and arbitration clause. These choices of law and interpretational issues become even more thorny when one or more of the parties are incorporated or reside in foreign countries. Occasionally, in order to decide initial contract interpretational issues, you may require that the parties file legal briefs on the issue of which law or laws are to be applied.

• **Court to have jurisdiction to enforce agreement and award.** As noted supra, the jurisdiction whose law governs the underlying contract may be different from the one whose law will govern the proceedings or enforce an award. Because the circumstances of the parties may change significantly—even to the extent of relocation or reincorporation of companies—between the time that the arbitration clause becomes effective and the time that a dispute arises, advocates often make the language of the enforcement provision as broad as possible, permitting the filing of such motions or the enforcing of awards "in any court having jurisdiction" at the pertinent time. At the beginning of the proceeding, knowing the law that will apply to the enforcement of the agreement and the award may impact your rulings on motions throughout the proceeding, as they pertain to the application of substantive law.

• **Payment of arbitration fees and expenses.** How and when the parties will pay the arbitrator's fees and expenses are normally important issues to arbitrators, and ones which they normally like to have resolved early in the proceeding. In an arbitration administered by a dispute resolution organization, the arbitrator does not ordinarily discuss these matters with the parties directly, but instead leaves them to the staff of the organization to handle. However, in a non-administered case, the arbitrator must discuss these matters soon after selection or appointment, because his or her involvement in the case may accelerate and may require a substantial investment of time. Fee setting is personal to each arbitrator, but if the case is administered, the organization normally prescribes the nature and amount of the fees, and schedules their payment. In some organizations, the amount of such fees vary depending upon the number of parties to the dispute and the complexity of the claims. It is customary that the parties each pay an equal share of the arbitrators' fees and expenses.

Reviewing the demand and response. It is also important for you to review the arbitration demand and response, if any, shortly after you are selected or appointed as arbitrator. This will alert you to the complexity of the case, the amount of time it will likely take to hear and determine, and the existence of potential conflicts of interest for which you would have to recuse yourself or about which you would have to disclose immediately to the parties for their consideration of whether you should be disqualified from hearing the case.

- **Demand.** Although there is no set structure or format for a demand in U.S. arbitration practice, it usually contains, at a minimum, the following information: (1) the names of all parties involved in the dispute and the names, addresses, and telephone numbers of their counsel; (2) a succinct, straightforward statement of facts, in chronological order; (3) a quote containing the exact language of the arbitration clause, or an attachment with a copy of the clause; (4) a statement of the claim or claims, and how they relate to the contract and the arbitration clause; and (5) a statement of the relief sought. In complex cases, it is common for the claimant to attach to the demand a pleading in the form of a complaint that would be filed in court. Indeed, some dispute resolution organizations permit a court-filed complaint to serve as the demand and claims when the parties opt to have their dispute resolved through arbitration rather than in the court system. You should carefully review the names of the parties and counsel to determine whether you have any present or former relationship with them that would serve as a basis for you to recuse yourself or for you to put the question to the parties. As an aid in making this determination, you might want to review Section 1.3.2, supra and Section 2.1.2, infra. In addition to checking for conflicts of interest, you should also pay close attention to any time limitations appearing in the arbitration clause or in the rules of the dispute resolution organization within which the claimant was to present or file a demand. If a demand is not filed with a dispute resolution organization on time or served on the other parties on time, the claimant may lose the right to have claims adjudicated in any forum, public or private. If a claimant is late filing a demand, you can reasonably expect that the respondent will file a motion to dismiss the demand. Another issue that occasionally appears in a demand is a claimant's request for provisional relief—that is partial relief or a partial award in advance of a full hearing on the merits. This may occur in situations where a claimant needs to have the arbitrator enter an order to protect or preserve assets, where a claimant needs an order requiring the continued construction of a building, or an order directing a manufacturer to continue shipping products to a distributor. If you see this in a demand, you should schedule an emergency preliminary hearing.

- **Response.** In U.S. arbitration practice, once the claimant has filed a demand for arbitration, the respondent can normally choose to answer or otherwise respond to the demand. Unlike the litigation setting, respondents are not usually required to file an answer. In fact, lack of an answer will not be construed as an admission of guilt, but rather as a denial of the claim(s) presented in the demand. One important exception to these principles relates to securities cases. In recent years, dispute resolution organizations administering securities cases have promulgated rules requiring respondents to answer demands with specificity. Failure to be specific in an answer may prevent a respondent from introducing evidence as to defenses not disclosed in the answer. Thus, if a response in the form of an answer accompanies a demand that you receive, and the pertinent rules require the answer to be specific and it is not, you can expect that the claimant will seek to prevent the respondent from introducing evidence as to defenses not disclosed in the answer. The typical answer usually contains, at a minimum: (1) a general denial of all the claims, as appropriate; (2) a denial of each separate claim with a short explanation of the respondent's version of the facts, and if the allegations are true, an acknowledgment of the truth of the claims; (3) a protest of the relief being sought; and (4) if applicable, a particularized or unparticularized statement of the affirmative defenses, depending on what the pertinent rules require. Typical affirmative defenses appear in the following chart.

TYPICAL AFFIRMATIVE DEFENSES

Accord and Satisfaction	Estoppel	Nonarbitrable Issue
Assumption of Risk	Failure of Consideration	Privilege
Breach of Contract	Failure to Exhaust	Release
Collateral Estoppel	Failure to Mitigate	Res Judicata
Comparative Negligence	Damages	Set-off
Contributory Negligence	Failure to State a Claim	Statute of Frauds
Condition Precedent	Fraud	Statute of Limitations
Contractual Remedies	Frustration of Purpose	Unclean Hands
Duress	Illegality	Waiver
	Impossibility	

A review of the answer and the affirmative defenses will help you determine whether there will be an evidentiary hearing in the case, and if there is one, how long you can expect it to last. For example, if the respondent has asserted release or res judicata, these issues will probably be tested initially by the parties on motions and, if the respondent is successful, there may be no need for an evidentiary hearing at all. Sometimes the answer contains a request for a bill of particulars, the respondent contending that the demand contains insufficient information for the respondent to be able to prepare a defense. If you see this in the response, you should make note of it as an item that must be taken up with the parties at the preliminary hearing, or before.

- **Counterclaims.** In addition to answering the demand, a respondent may also file a counterclaim. A counterclaim is usually separate from the answer and any from affirmative defenses. It normally contains the same elements required in a demand. Often, filing a counterclaim is the only opportunity for a respondent to present a new claim in the matter to be arbitrated, unless the arbitrator on respondent's motion later authorizes it. If a counterclaim is filed, you should review it to make sure it does not arise out of a different and separate agreement that did not provide for arbitration. If the counterclaim does arise out of a separate agreement, you can expect that the claimant will move to dismiss it.

Reviewing the pertinent rules. Do not expect that the procedural rules applicable to a trial will automatically apply in an arbitration hearing. Hearing rules may vary from arbitration to arbitration depending upon the content of the arbitration clause, the rules of any administering dispute resolution organization, the needs or desires of counsel, and the preferences of individual arbitrators. If the case is non-administered, and the arbitration clause does not make reference to any applicable arbitration rules, you should immediately suggest to the advocates that they agree to adopt a set of procedural rules to govern the proceeding.

Thus, at the inception of the arbitration, or at least in advance the preliminary hearing, you should carefully read the applicable rules. If you note any unusual and undesirable requirements, you should raise these matters for discussion at the preliminary hearing, or sooner if necessary. Hearing rules drafted years before into an arbitration clause—and perhaps by advocates not currently involved in the arbitration—are sometimes inappropriate for application to the dispute as it actually evolved. You, along with the advocates, can work out modifications of such rules during the preliminary hearing.

The same holds true for the rules of administering organizations. On many occasions, their rules need to be clarified in relation to the idiosyncrasies of the particular dispute, or of the identity and configuration of the parties. Here are a few illustrative examples:

- **Application of the Federal Rules of Civil Procedure.** Your dispute resolution organization may require you to apply the Federal Rules of Civil Procedure to any procedural question that arises in the hearing. If you believe that the application of such rules will work a hardship on the parties, you should bring specific matters to the attention of the parties and discuss other rule options with them.

- **Testimony not required to be under oath.** The rules of some organizations require witnesses to testify under oath only if it is required by law or requested by party. Normally, you will want to clarify at the preliminary hearing that you want all witness statements made on the merits to be under oath. That will raise the question as to whether there will be someone at the hearing authorized to administer oaths. Ordinarily, by statute you will have such authority, but in some cases you may not. If not, the court reporter, if one is scheduled to attend, may have the authority. The point is, if you want witnesses to make statements under oath, be sure there is means available at the hearing to ensure that it happens.

- **Evidence by affidavit.** Also, some organizations' rules permit the arbitrators to consider affidavits of witnesses in lieu of their appearance and testimony at the hearing. If affidavit evidence is not acceptable to you, you should notify the parties early in the proceedings so that they do not go to the trouble of obtaining affidavits unnecessarily.

- **Authorized representative.** Ordinarily, organizations do not require parties to be represented by counsel during an arbitration hearing. Some rules permit a party to be represented by an "authorized representative," and notice of such representation must be given to the opponent a few days in advance of the hearing. Sometimes this can cause a problem which should be solved early in the proceeding. For example, suppose that one party gives notice that she intends to have a specified person be her authorized representative during the arbitration proceeding. Suppose further that the opposing party intends to call that person as a witness at the hearing on the merits. This raises an "independence" problem on the part of the representative. The arbitrator should raise and discuss this problem with the parties early, so that the first party may opt to enlist another authorized representative, who can better serve in the capacity of independent advisor.

• **Decision and award.** Arbitration rules normally require decisions of the arbitrators to be by a majority, unless a unanimous decision is required by the arbitration agreement or by law. Sometimes advocates for the parties desire that the liability determination be unanimous, and that any damage award be by a majority—or some other such variation. Such matters should be raised and clarified at the preliminary hearing or before. Also, rules rarely include a provision explaining what occurs if one of three arbitrators finds it necessary to withdraw during an arbitration hearing, (due to ill health or a discovered conflict of interest, etc.), and the remaining two arbitrators disagree on the result. As arbitration becomes widely used, this problem may become more prevalent, and the parties will have to deal with it by prehearing agreement. Some rules require the arbitrators to provide no reasons for the award, and others permit arbitrators to award pre-judgment interest. If parties prefer something different than what such rules allow, you should raise these matters in the prehearing stage, and perhaps ideally during the preliminary hearing.

Above all, you should keep in mind that the rules of dispute resolution organizations commonly have an automatic "waiver of rules" provision. Such provision usually states that any party who proceeds with an arbitration after knowledge that any provision or requirement of the rules has not been complied with, and who fails to state an objection in writing, is deemed to have waived the right to object. Thus, if counsel do not carefully review the pertinent arbitration rules, they may find that they have wandered into a procedural quagmire from which they cannot gracefully escape. Some of these avoidable traps could affect their client's substantive, as well as procedural, rights. You may want to suggest to counsel that an ounce of prevention in these situations, may, indeed, be worth a pound of cure.

2.1.2   Conflict check.

As soon as you are notified that you have been selected or appointed as an arbitrator in a case, you should immediately perform a self-assessment to determine whether any circumstance exists which is likely to create a presumption of bias or partiality. If there is an actual or apparent significant conflict of interest, it is usually wise to recuse yourself, rather than disclose it and place the parties in an awkward position of asking you to disqualify yourself. If the actual or apparent conflict is minor, and you believe that a party is moving to disqualify you only for purposes of delay or avoidance of the arbitration, you may, of course, deny the motion. When the arbitration is being administered by a dispute resolution organization, and a party moves to disqualify you as arbitrator and you believe that the motion is groundless, you may have the option under the organization's rules to have the organization conclusively determine whether you should be disqualified or reaffirmed. The answers to the following list of questions may help you decide whether you must: (1) make disclosures to the parties and their counsel; (2) ask the administering organization to make the disqualification determination; or (3) simply recuse yourself outright.[1] Read the word "you" in the following questions to include yourself, any other person in your law firm, or anyone else with whom you are professionally affiliated.

- Do you presently represent any person in a proceeding adverse to any party to the arbitration?
- Have you represented any other person against any party to the arbitration?
- Have you had any professional or social relationship with counsel for any party in this proceeding or the firms for which they work?
- Have you had any social or professional relationship of which you are aware with any relative of any of the parties to this proceeding, any relative of counsel to this proceeding, or any of the witnesses identified to date in this proceeding?
- Have you ever served as an arbitrator in a proceeding in which any of the identified witnesses or named individual parties gave testimony?
- Have you, any member of your immediate family, or any close social or business associate been involved in the last five years in a dispute involving the subject matter contained in the case to which you are assigned?

---

1.   These questions appear on form materials sent by the American Arbitration Association to arbitrators at the time of their appointment to serve on specific case.

- Have you had any social or professional relationship with any other arbitrator assigned to this case?
- Have you served as an expert witness or consultant to any party, attorney, witness, or other arbitrator identified in this case?
- Have any of the party representatives appeared before you in past arbitration cases?
- Are you a member of any organization that is not listed on your biographical sheet?
- Have you ever sued or been sued by either party or its representative?

You should take the matter of conflict of interest very seriously at the outset of the case and throughout the arbitration proceeding, because a party's post-award discovery of a significant conflict of interest on your part could jeopardize the validity or durability of the award. Your disclosure obligations apply to parties or counsel who intervene during the course of the proceedings and to expert or lay witnesses who are called to testify.

2.1.3 Arbitrator's oath.

Many state statutes, rules of administering organizations, court rules, and submissions of parties require the arbitrator(s) to take or sign an oath before performing their arbitrator services. An example of the form of a typical arbitrator's oath is as follows:[2]

> I, _____, being duly sworn, hereby accept this appointment, attest that the panel biography provided by the administering organization is accurate and complete, and will faithfully and fairly hear and examine the matter in controversy between parties in accordance with their arbitration agreement, the Code of Ethics for Arbitrators [identify], and the rules of the administering organization [identify], and will make an award according to the best of the Arbitrator's understanding.
>
> Dated: _____ Signed _____
> Sworn to before me this _____ day of (Mo.), (Year).
>
> _____
>
> Notary Public

---

2. This form of arbitrator's oath is adapted from that of the American Arbitration Association.

Parties, of course, may waive the arbitrator's taking of the oath. Such a waiver is expressly authorized by statutes in some states.

2.1.4 Choosing the third arbitrator.

If you are a party-appointed arbitrator on a three-arbitrator panel, two items should initially be high on your agenda. First, you should review the code of ethics for arbitrators (see Section 1.3 and Appendix K) to refresh yourself on the ethical obligations of "non-neutral" arbitrators. After doing that, you should immediately begin thinking about choosing the third arbitrator for the arbitration panel. Customarily, the third arbitrator will become the chair of the panel, although that is not always the case. (See Section 2.1.5.)

Regardless of whether the third arbitrator will become the chair of the panel, two basic tasks will confront you when choosing the third panel member: (1) developing a list of potential neutral arbitrators; and (2) contacting the other party-appointed arbitrator and collaborating with him or her to select an arbitrator from the candidates each of you propose. In performing these tasks you will have to take into account many of the arbitrator selection considerations that advocates employ in choosing a neutral arbitrator. A description of some of these considerations follows.

The most important attribute for an arbitrator to possess is impartiality. Other attributes an arbitrator should possess include patience, intelligence, common sense, the ability to make a decision with an open mind, and, if the arbitrator is to be the panel chair, the firmness to control the proceedings and not let things get out of control. Your selected panelist should have, at a minimum, these prerequisites.

One of the first selection decisions you and your co-panelist will have to make is whether you wish to have a lawyer or non-lawyer serve on the panel. If you want a lawyer to serve as the third arbitrator, you may already be aware of several potential candidates having the necessary qualifications. If you do not know of any lawyer-arbitrators, you can contact various dispute resolution organizations to obtain lists and biographical sketches of potential arbitrators. If a non-lawyer arbitrator is desired, the task may be a little more involved. Both of you may have to first determine what type of expert would be most helpful in making the type of decision(s) that the case requires. If the case involves commercial issues, you may need to determine, depending on the factual situation, whether an accountant, a logistics expert, an economist, a banker, a tax specialist, or securities expert would best serve the panel's decisional needs. Similarly, if the arbitration involves construction issues, you would have to first decide whether the third arbitrator should be a general contractor, an architect, an engineer, or an owner. After making that decision, you would have to determine which particular expert in a field of choices would best satisfy the panel's needs. It is also important for both of you to take into account the personality of the third arbitrator and his or her compatibility with the personalities of yourself and your co-panelist. You can develop such information by talking to other arbitrators who have served on panels with the arbitrator candidates, or by talking to advocates who have previously employed their services.

Another point to keep in mind when selecting the third arbitrator is the existence of obvious conflicts of interest which would preclude the candidate from serving on your panel. For example, if a lawyer-friend of yours would be an excellent selection for your panel, but that lawyer's law firm is pursuing a lawsuit against one of the parties or subsidiary of one of the parties involved in your arbitration, then it would be inadvisable to invite that lawyer to serve on your arbitration panel.

2.1.5 Selecting chair of arbitration panel.

Cases involving party-appointed arbitrators. As pointed out above, in situations where each side selects an arbitrator and those two arbitrators select a third, normally the third arbitrator becomes the chair of the panel. However, there may be exceptions to that rule in actual practice. For example, in a construction case, if one party selects a lawyer as an arbitrator and the other party selects a contractor, those two arbitrators may find it necessary to have an architect on the panel. Barring any prohibition in the pertinent arbitration clause, the arbitrators may further decide that the lawyer should serve as the panel chair so that he or she could rule on evidentiary issues and generally supervise the discovery and litigation aspects of the arbitration proceedings. In other situations, barring contract or rule prohibitions, practical considerations may govern the selection of the chair. For example, by agreement of the parties, a party-appointed arbitrator may be selected to be the panel chair when that arbitrator has full-time administrative help and the other two do not; or where such arbitrator is more conveniently located geographically to the parties, thereby facilitating filing and argument of discovery and other types of motions.

Cases involving three neutral arbitrators. Where an arbitration panel consists of three neutral arbitrators, the three arbitrators will jointly decide who the chair will be. Considerations to be taken into account when selecting the panel chair include:

- whether an arbitrator can effectively assume the role of the chair of the panel (see Section 2.1.6);
- whether a panel member desires to be the panel chair;
- the predictable demands on the selected arbitrator considering the nature of the case and the parties;
- whether an arbitrator is a lawyer (though this is not controlling);
- relative celebrity, prestige, or peer status of the arbitrators;
- relative age of the three arbitrators, giving preference usually to the most senior member of the panel;
- relative arbitration experience of the three arbitrators;
- relative availability of the arbitrators to respond to emergency motions or other requests of the parties;
- in a non-administered arbitration, the availability of the arbitrator's support staff to coordinate the rescheduling of hearing dates and to type and issue the panel's notices and prehearing rulings;
- in a non-administered arbitration, relative geographic location of the arbitrators in comparison to the locations of the parties, giving preference to the arbitrator most centrally or most proximately located.

2.1.6   Role of the chair of arbitration panel.

The role of the chair of a three or more member arbitration panel is an important, multi-faceted one. The panel chair must be, first and foremost, a leader—someone to whom the parties and their counsel, as well as other panel members, look for procedural guidance and direction, fairness in the exercise of judgment, and as an example of stability, courtesy, civility, and wisdom. The chair must be able to inspire high-quality advocacy and, if necessary, to deal quickly and effectively with improper attorney, party, or witness conduct, while retaining the respect and high regard of all concerned. He or she must also be able to provide a calming influence when emotions rather than reason prevail, to avoid interfering with an attorney's opportunity to fully and fairly present his or her client's case, and be cognizant of the needs of individual witnesses who may not be separately represented and who may feel apprehensive about testifying because of non-familiarity with arbitration procedures or fear of the consequences of their testimony.

The chair of an arbitration panel customarily performs specific functions, which include the following:

- Assignment of duties to the other panel members. Such duties might be: keeping the evidence log, completing the daily record of progress of the arbitration hearing, drafting interim rulings, and in large cases, writing the first draft of the opinion supporting an arbitration award;

- In administered proceedings, interacting with the case administrator on procedural matters, including payment of the arbitrators' fees and expenses;
- In non-administered proceedings, the chair is usually responsible for sending out notices and scheduling orders;
- Entering prehearing rulings on routine or uncontested motions;
- Setting the agenda for arbitrator meetings and preliminary or mid-hearing meetings with the parties and their counsel;
- Making the opening statement on behalf of the arbitration panel at the beginning of the hearing on the merits;
- Ruling on uncomplicated evidentiary objections or motions during the course of the hearing on the merits;
- Entering an order closing the evidence; and
- Ensuring that the award is timely prepared and issued on time.

2.1.7 The arbitrators' initial conference.

In most panel arbitrations, after the panel members have been selected, they hold an initial conference to discuss a variety of topics pertinent to the arbitration. In small cases, this conference may take ten to fifteen minutes and occur just prior to the hearing on the merits. It may cover topics such as selection of the chair, the extent of the authority of the chair to rule on evidentiary objections and motions, and the agreed extent of arbitrator questioning during the hearing. In larger cases, the arbitrators' initial conference may take several hours, will usually cover the topics just described and, in addition, address a variety of others. For example, the initial conference will normally occur prior to the first preliminary hearing with the parties and their counsel, and may involve discussion of one or more prehearing motions filed by a party or parties, some of which may address substantive issues. Some of these motions may require additional review of the pleadings or supplementary research, and may necessitate the scheduling of another arbitrators' conference. In the initial conference, the arbitrators will also ordinarily discuss topics to be included on the agenda for the preliminary hearing with the parties.

2.1.8 Complying with court orders compelling or staying arbitration.

It is essential that you are aware of and comply with any court orders compelling arbitration or staying arbitration proceedings. If the parties tell you that a court has entered an order compelling arbitration, make sure that you ask them to submit a copy of the order for your review. Often, the court order will contain specific directives identifying the precise issue that is being sent to arbitration and establishing time limits within which the arbitration is to be accomplished, as well as other parameters. Similarly, if the court has stayed the arbitration pending court action, a review of the court order may enlighten you as to the specific reasons for the stay and provide a basis for estimating how long the stay will be in effect. Occasionally, a court order may permit discovery to proceed on certain matters in arbitration that are unrelated to the issues to be decided by the court. If the court has retained some issues for judicial decision and referred others to arbitration, it may well be that after reading the order you are still unclear as to the precise scope of the referral. In such an instance, you would be well-advised to ask the advocates to go before the judge and ask for a clarification of the referral order.

2.2   CONDUCTING THE PRELIMINARY HEARING

A preliminary hearing or prehearing conference can be requested by the arbitrator or by either party. It can be conducted face-to-face or by telephone. In a large case with complex issues a preliminary hearing is indispensable. In other cases, you will have to weigh the necessity and cost-benefits of having one. A one-hour preliminary hearing might obviate two-hours of procedural arguments at the beginning of the actual hearing, and may avoid the possibility of multiple postponements because of discovery and other prehearing squabbles. Cases requiring little or no discovery and involving a few thousand dollars, would probably not warrant a preliminary hearing.

A preliminary hearing usually provides many benefits to the parties and to the arbitrator. It is an opportunity for the parties to discuss the exchange of documents and witness lists, to stipulate to uncontested facts, to estimate the length of the hearing, and, outside the presence of the arbitrator(s), to explore settlement possibilities. If issues arise during the preliminary hearing that require briefing, the arbitrator can set a briefing schedule on related motions. If the parties, working together with the arbitrator, can accomplish all of these tasks during the preliminary hearing, the case is likely to proceed more smoothly. They will be able to concentrate more on the preparation and presentation of the substantive aspects of the case ones and not have to worry so much about the procedural.

2.2.1   Covering all pertinent topics.

Customarily, the arbitrator will commence the preliminary hearing by explaining its purpose and then by discussing the necessary preparation of the case for hearing. The following topics, at a minimum, are ordinarily discussed at a preliminary hearing. Additional topics appropriate for discussion in preliminary hearings in more complex cases appear immediately infra in Section 2.2.2.

Expectation of civility and professionalism. One of the first items on the arbitrator's agenda at the preliminary hearing should be his or her statement of expectation that the advocates and parties will treat each other with the highest standards of civility and professionalism. Such a statement will communicate a theme of non-tolerance of petty squabbling and derisive behavior on the part of the participants, and it will set the tone for an efficient proceeding. (See the Appendix M for a copy of Standards of Civility).

Applicable rules and law governing the procedure in the particular arbitration. As pointed out in Section 2.1.1, it is important that you, the advocates, and the parties know what rules and laws govern the interpretation of the arbitration clause, the arbitration procedures, and the substantive law affecting the decision and the enforcement of the award in the case. As arbitrator, you should confirm these matters with the parties at the beginning of the preliminary hearing. If there is disagreement as to which rules or laws apply to the case, the matter should be argued or briefed, if necessary, and you should decide the matter as soon as possible.

Ability to arbitrate all issues. You should also determine whether there is any dispute as to the ability to arbitrate of all issues raised in the demand, the cross-claims, and counterclaims, if any. The burden is usually on the party opposing arbitration to establish that a particular claim, issue, or matter falls outside the scope of the arbitration agreement. Whether the arbitrator or a court must decide varies somewhat among jurisdictions. As a general principle, however, if parties submit a matter to arbitration, a court will defer to the arbitrator's decision on the appropriateness of arbitration if it appears that the parties intended for the arbitrator to decide the issue(s). If a court must decide whether the parties agreed to arbitrate a certain issue, it normally applies state-law principles governing contract formation. However, it should be noted that courts generally do not assume that parties agreed to arbitrate the appropriateness or legality of arbitration unless there is clear and unmistakable evidence that they did so. Thus, if the issue arises, before you decide the matter you should study the arbitration clause or submission agreement to determine whether there is clear and unmistakable evidence that the parties intended for the arbitrator to decide.

Realize also that questions of arbitrability are not always patent. Sometimes they are latent and intricate. Often, they can be raised with respect to various aspects of the validity of the underlying contracts containing arbitration clauses or of the clauses themselves, including aspects of fraud in the inducement, of lack of mutuality, or of contract termination. They can also involve issues of the power or authority of the arbitrator to grant certain kinds of relief or an appropriate remedy, such as an injunction, specific performance, or the awarding of consequential or punitive damages. Thus, in some situations, a question may arise as to whether a party has waived the right to object to the arbitration on grounds of non-arbitrability, if the objection was not made before or at the beginning of the hearing on the merits of the legal claims. Courts are split on how to properly decide waiver of arbitrability issues, and if such an issue arises in a case you are arbitrating, you would be well-advised to review the applicable case law of the pertinent jurisdiction.

Federal cases vary as to the appropriate action courts should take when arbitrable and non-arbitrable claims arise out of the same transaction, and are intertwined legally and factually. The decisions in these cases usually depend on the totality of the factual and procedural circumstances. Some cases hold that the court, in such circumstance, may hear and decide all of the claims; other cases hold that the court can stay the litigation of the non-arbitrable claims pending resolution of the arbitrable claims in arbitration; and still other cases hold that a court may sever a single claim to send part of it to arbitration. The best course for you to follow when an issue of arbitrability arises is to have the parties research the applicable law in your jurisdiction and brief the issue. After you read the briefs, you may see a need to conduct your own independent research if the arbitrability issues are complex.

Discovery. In smaller cases, any necessary informal discovery may have been completed prior to the preliminary hearing. In such cases where informal discovery has not occurred, advocates might exchange documents during the preliminary hearing itself. In either situation, the arbitrator may hear counsel's arguments regarding relevancy, which may have the advantage of clarifying the parties' claims and defenses in the arbitration.

In larger cases, advocates may have attempted more formal discovery prior to the preliminary hearing. If the advocates have disagreed about the range of discovery requested by one side, the preliminary hearing is an opportunity to discuss the issue with the arbitrator. For example, if one advocate has intentionally withheld certain documents as part of an arbitration strategy, the opponent will most probably orally ask you to direct the advocate to produce the withheld documents, if they are not subject to a privilege. Such oral motions obviate the time-consuming, costly practice of drafting motions to compel the other side to produce this discovery. The parties can present their respective arguments on the discovery issue and receive an immediate ruling on it. In complex cases where there are multiple parties, cabinets of relevant documents, and several witnesses to depose, you may want to require counsel to submit a discovery plan by a certain date. If that occurs, the advocates will have to get together and negotiate a schedule for the production of documents and the depositions of witnesses. Also, you should confirm with the advocates at the preliminary hearing which discovery rules will apply. If there is a dispute about which discovery rules will apply or about the nature and scope of the discovery that will be undertaken, you can rule on these matters before the advocates launch into discovery and waste time and money bickering over the rules of the game.

Normally, arbitrators permit parties to take depositions of experts prior to the hearing on the merits. Cut-off dates for taking such depositions are normally set during the preliminary hearing. If depositions of these experts are not taken in advance of the hearing on the merits, advocates may waste much time at the hearing conducting exploratory questioning. Commonly called a "fishing expedition," there is usually nothing expedient about it.

Prehearing motions and briefing schedules. In the ordinary arbitration, many of the parties' motions can be presented orally and decided by you during the preliminary hearing. However, in more complex cases, one or more parties may have a need to file written procedural or substantive prehearing motions, in order to obtain certain types of relief. You should set briefing schedules on such motions at the preliminary conference, and where appropriate, encourage parties to file joint briefs to reduce the amount of duplicative briefing. You may also determine that it would be appropriate to hear oral argument on some of the motions after the briefs are on file. At the preliminary hearing, you should set briefing and oral argument schedules on these motions, making sure to allocate enough time for you to decide the motions and for the advocates to react in advance of the scheduled date of the hearing on the merits of the parties' claims.

Amended pleadings. It may become apparent in discussing the state of the pleadings or the amount of needed discovery that a claim, answer, or counterclaim is not sufficiently detailed. In such an instance, an advocate may ask you to direct that a pleading be amended to include more details.

Addition or joinder of parties. It may also become apparent during the preliminary hearing that other parties need to be notified of the arbitration and of their opportunity for voluntary addition as parties, or that they need to be joined as additional parties because of the existence of multiple arbitration clauses making them named parties to the dispute.

Witness lists. The arbitrator normally sets a date by which the parties must exchange a list of witnesses when they reasonably expect to call at the hearing on the merits. This list should contain the name of each witness and a short summary of anticipated testimony (if necessary). It should have attached to it the curriculum vitae of any experts, as well as copies of any pertinent expert reports. If the advocates do not bring up the topic of witness lists at the preliminary hearing, you should do so. More arbitrations are stalled or interrupted because of complaints of "surprise witnesses" than for any other reason. You should require the advocates to exchange lists of witnesses at least two or three weeks in advance of the hearing on the merits, so they can adequately prepare cross-examinations of those witnesses and decide how to best prepare their own witnesses. After receiving the opponent's list of witnesses, the opposing advocate may seek leave to amend his own list, to add or delete witnesses. You should make it clear to advocates that they have a continuing obligation to update their witness lists as soon as such information becomes available. You should also remind the advocates that right before they submit their witness list, they should double-check the availability of their witnesses to appear at the hearing on the merits. It is also a good idea to require the advocates to indicate the order in which they intend to call witnesses at the hearing on the merits.

Observers and other attendees. In some cases, parties may wish to have persons present who are not actual parties or witnesses in the case. These observers or other attendees often have an interest in the proceeding and its outcome, or they simply want to be there to assist a party presenting its case efficiently. Sometimes a spouse may desire to accompany a party to provide moral support; sometimes a corporate representative may want to be present to coordinate the timing of the appearance of witnesses as the hearing progresses. It is within your discretion to allow observers to be present and/or to limit their number. If an observer will predictably cause a disruption in the hearing, you may decide to rule at the preliminary hearing that the person should not be permitted to be present.

Hearing exhibits. It is important for you to set a date by which the advocates are to exchange exhibit lists or actual copies of premarked exhibits that will be introduced at the hearing on the merits. You should also require them to provide you or the administering organization with a list of the exhibits or, if you prefer, a hard copy of each. In more complex cases, you should suggest that the advocates have the exhibits placed in binders and tabbed by exhibit number. You should emphasize that the term "exhibits" includes any schedules, diagrams, charts, audiotapes, videotapes, etc., which the advocates intend to show for your review and consideration in making your decision on the merits. It is also wise to require the advocates to meet before the hearing on the merits and to agree on a set of joint exhibits in order to avoid introducing duplicates.

Fact stipulations. It is always a wise practice to encourage counsel to submit a stipulation of uncontested facts and to set a date by which the filing of the stipulation should occur. The stipulation may greatly reduce the amount of testimony and the number of exhibits that otherwise would have to be introduced at the hearing on the merits. If the advocates submit such a stipulation, you may want one of the advocates to read the stipulation aloud when the hearing on the merits commences. This procedure, of course, will vary depending on the case and the preferences of the other arbitrators on your panel.

Order of evidence. In multiple party cases with counterclaims, crossclaims, etc., you must work out with the advocates the order in which the parties will proceed in the presentation of their evidence at the hearing on the merits. When you discuss these topics, it is often wise to consider setting time limits for opening statements and case presentations, if appropriate and the parties agree.

Sequestration of witnesses. The issue of whether witnesses will be permitted in the hearing room when other witnesses testify should be discussed and decided at the preliminary hearing. Usually, the advocates will agree that the witnesses on both sides should be sequestered—that is, kept out of the hearing room at least until after they testify, and usually even after they testify. The purpose of sequestering witnesses is to guarantee, to the extent possible, that witnesses will not conform their testimony to each other, but speak from their separate memories of the events as they occurred. If there is a dispute on the sequestration issue, you can decide the matter at the preliminary hearing. Keep in mind that in corporate cases, it is customary that the corporation's counsel be permitted to have at least one corporate representative present during all testimony, even if that person will be called to testify as a witness at some point in the case. If you decide to direct that the witnesses be sequestered, it is a good idea to remind advocates to advise witnesses to bring reading material with them on the hearing day in order to occupy themselves while they are waiting to testify.

Burden and standard of proof. Topics commonly omitted from the agenda of a preliminary hearing are the burden and standard of proof that will be applicable to the evidence adduced at the hearing on the merits. These are very important topics that deserve special attention, especially in multi-party cases or cases in which there are claims, counter-claims, cross-claims, and third-party claims. Which party has the burden of proof and the burden of going forward, and what standard of proof each party must satisfy in order to prove their separate claims are matters that will have a very definite impact on how each advocate will prepare his or her case for the hearing. For example, if these matters are not discussed at the preliminary hearing, an attorney might come to the hearing believing that the evidence supporting his affirmative claims will not have to be presented until the second or third day of the hearing. The attorney may, therefore, be unprepared to go forward, not having pertinent documents with him and not having his witnesses available. Also, if an attorney comes to the hearing believing that the applicable standard of proof relating to his claims is preponderance of the evidence, when in fact the proper standard is clear and convincing evidence, (which, if realized in advance of the hearing, could have been met), then the arbitrators will be deprived of the necessary evidence to fairly decide the case. These issues of burden and standard of proof can be discussed at the preliminary hearing in conjunction with the topic of order or sequence of proof to be presented at the hearing on the merits.

Position statements or prehearing briefs. In most cases, you should direct the advocates to submit prehearing position statements or prehearing briefs a few days in advance of the hearing on the merits. Position statements, also called prehearing or opening briefs, are usually filed simultaneously by all parties on a designated date, though you may have them filed sequentially. A position statement or brief is a short memorandum, five to ten double-spaced pages in the average case, which succinctly apprises the arbitrators of the significant facts, the separate claims, the contentions, and supporting law. It should also contain the advocate's views on the remedies being sought, monetary and otherwise. It should embody the blueprint of each party's case. If properly prepared, it will be the type of document that you will find yourself referring to from time to time during the course of the hearing to help put the party's evidence in context.

Stenographer. If either party desires a stenographic record of the arbitration hearing, this should be discussed and resolved at the preliminary hearing. Court reporters or stenographers are not automatically provided at an arbitration hearing, nor are they ordinarily required to be present. At some time before the preliminary hearing, you should check statutes governing the arbitration proceeding in your jurisdiction to see if a stenographic record is required. At the preliminary hearing, the parties may decide to secure the services of a court reporter to make a record of the hearing. Rules of some dispute resolution organizations require that a party desiring to arrange for a court reporter contact the court reporting firm directly, and send notice to all other parties involved. If all parties so desire, the cost will be equally split among them. If only one party wishes to have a reporter present, that party will bear the entire expense. Such rules further provide that if the transcript will be the official record of the proceedings, then both the arbitrator and the opposing parties are entitled to see a copy of the transcript to inspect for any errors. However, an opposing party who does not pay an apportioned share of the expense is not entitled to a copy of the transcript.

Each party must decide on its own whether this extra expense should be undertaken, depending on the particular circumstances. In large cases with several different issues, a stenographic record of the hearing will be beneficial, particularly in the preparation of post-hearing briefs. If daily copy is available during the course of the hearing, it may be helpful to the advocates in preparing the cross-examination of their opponent's witnesses.

Interpreter. Any party desiring an interpreter at the hearing must make arrangements for one, and unless otherwise agreed, must assume the costs of the service. If applicable, the need for an interpreter should be discussed at the preliminary hearing. Lack of an interpreter on the hearing date may cause a hearing to be postponed. Normally, it is not a good idea to have a family member or a fellow employee serve as an interpreter for a party or witness. Such persons may not have a good enough grasp of one of the two languages and may not be familiar with all figures of speech. Where an interpreter is needed, it is best for the parties to hire a person who is certified as an interpreter, and ideally, one who provides interpreter services in court.

Special needs of sight, hearing, or otherwise physically impaired parties, witnesses, or counsel. At the preliminary hearing, you should inquire whether any of the parties or witnesses, or even counsel, have special needs that will require services relating to sight, hearing, or other physical impairments. If there are such special needs, you should discuss with the advocates how these can be satisfied and accommodated.

Setting a hearing date. One of your important tasks at the preliminary hearing is to set a date for the hearing on the merits, taking into account the schedules of all advocates, and to the extent possible, the schedules of the parties and witnesses.

Designating the place of hearing; arrangement of hearing room. Another important task at the preliminary hearing is to designate the place where the hearing on the merits is to be conducted. If the arbitration is administered, the hearing will normally be held at the location of the administering organization. However, in a multi-party case or in a non-administered case, a larger hearing space may be required. You may also desire a particular arrangement of tables in the hearing room, depending on the number of parties, counsel, and observers. These matters should be discussed and decided at the preliminary hearing.

Estimate of the length of the hearing. You should also inquire as to the amount of time each side will need to present its case. Advocates have a tendency to underestimate their time needs. In fact, a standing joke among arbitrators is that to arrive at an accurate estimate of the hearing time required by any case, they take the separate estimates of the advocates for all parties, add them together, multiply by two, and then add an extra day. When estimating the time required to present their cases, advocates often fail to take into account the total time required for any preliminary matters, opening statements, direct examination of their witnesses, cross-examination of their witnesses by their opponents, redirect examinations of their witnesses, recross-examinations, arguments over evidence, extended lunch breaks to allow the advocates to tend to their other clients, "dead time" waiting for witnesses to arrive, delays caused by taking witnesses out of order, delays caused by unanticipated evidence, rebuttal evidence, surrebuttal evidence, closing arguments, answering questions of the arbitrators, and site visits. When you ask the advocates to estimate the length of time their cases will require, it might be helpful to recite this list of items so that their estimates will be realistic.

Subpoenas. In virtually all U.S. arbitrations, arbitrators have the authority to issue subpoenas requiring the parties and certain witnesses to attend the arbitration hearing and requiring the production of documents. It is a good idea to explain the pertinent subpoena procedure to the advocates at the preliminary hearing. In most arbitrations, advocates prefer to subpoena every witness that they intend to call to testify in the proceeding. In many situations they will need to call the opposing party as an adverse witness, as well as other witnesses who are employed by the opposing party or are under his or her control. These matters should be discussed at the preliminary hearing so that opposing counsel is not surprised when the subpoenas issue. Also, you should advise the advocates to submit the subpoenas to you for review and signature far in advance of the hearing, so that the witnesses are able to adjust their schedules accordingly and so that documents may be produced in a timely fashion for use by the advocates in preparing their cases. You will also want to ensure that subpoenas are submitted at a convenient place and time for you to sign them.

Prohibition against ex parte communications with arbitrators. It is vitally important that you remind the advocates that there should be no ex parte communication with you, with certain limited exceptions. In administered cases, advocates should normally send all pleadings to the administering organization, which in turn, sends the documents to the arbitrators. In emergency situations, advocates may have to send pleadings directly to the arbitrator, with simultaneous service on opposing counsel. Obviously, where there is no administering organization, advocates must send their pleadings directly to the arbitrator, but such transmittals should not contain any communication that is not also provided to the opposing advocate.

Site inspections. In some arbitrations, you or the parties may perceive a need to visit a particular site or accident scene. Site inspections are most common in construction and accident cases—particularly catastrophic accidents. The advocates will arrange the site visit. In most situations arbitrators, advocates, parties, and some of the testifying witnesses will attend. Occasionally, advocates may request that they be permitted to take photographs of the site during the arbitrators' site visit for use when the hearing resumes. These requests are usually granted. Photographs preserve the scene as the arbitrators saw it. They also serve as a valuable visual aid for the advocates when used with other evidence to demonstrate a view of the site which either the arbitrators did not see, or saw, but did not appreciate the relevance at the time.

Audio-visual aids. The use of demonstrative exhibits and audio-visual aids are important to the effective presentation of any case, but they are particularly important in cases where proof requires the demonstration of the condition of physical objects as they were at the time of, or immediately before or after, a particular event. At the preliminary hearing, you should inquire of the advocates as to whether they will be using audio-visual aids, so that they do not surprise opposing counsel on the morning the hearing begins.

Experts. In arbitration, expert opinions are necessary where the matter in question is highly technical, and only a person with specialized skills will be able to clarify the issue for the arbitrator(s). If one advocate intends to call an expert witness, the opposing advocate will most likely see a need to call an expert also. It is usually not prudent for an advocate to arrange for multiple experts to testify on the same technical issue. Rarely does cumulative expert evidence provide any tactical advantage to an advocate, and it only prolongs the hearing. You should inquire of the advocates as to whether they intend to introduce expert testimony at the hearing. If they do, you should have the parties agree to a deposition time frame—a date by which the depositions have to be taken—at the preliminary hearing. Another expert-related topic that often generates disagreement among advocates in arbitration is the timing of the exchange of the experts' curriculum vitae and their written opinions. These matters should also be discussed and decided at the preliminary hearing.

Need for final oral arguments; post-hearing proposed findings of fact and conclusions of law. Although it may seem premature to raise at the preliminary hearing, it does no harm to discuss the issue of the need for final oral arguments or post-hearing findings or conclusions. This topic may have a direct impact on the advocates' thinking about how they intend to present their cases and whether they might need to arrange for the services of a court reporter. If the parties wish to defer these matters for discussion until near the end of the hearing on the merits, you can easily accommodate them and move on to the next topic on the preliminary hearing agenda.

Nature and form of award. At the preliminary hearing, you should confirm the nature and form of the award that the parties desire—the customary short award without a statement of reasons or an award incorporating a reasoned opinion. Realize that if the parties opt for an award with a reasoned opinion, there will be a basis to challenge the award by way of a motion for reconsideration. Such motion may extend the proceedings, cause additional costly briefing, and delay the enforcement of the award. In rare cases, the reasoned opinion may even provide the basis for a court challenge on the grounds that the arbitrators exceeded their authority or jurisdiction or that the award was manifestly unjust—whether or not there is actual merit to such challenges. Thus, before the parties opt for an award with a reasoned opinion, they should be made aware of the disadvantages of requiring one.

Appeal procedures. In recent years, certain dispute resolution organizations have added to their ADR rules, provisions allowing parties to pre-select a second panel of arbitrators to hear any appeals from the first arbitration panel's decision. This appellate procedure is normally used in cases involving huge damage claims, where the stakes are so high that the parties are unwilling to risk having a single arbitration panel issue an unchallengeable, binding award. If you are the chosen arbitrator in such a case, you may want to raise the matter of a possible appeal procedure at the preliminary hearing, or suggestion that the administering organization raise the matter in a separate conference outside your presence.

Pre-arbitration mediation. If the parties' arbitration clause or submission agreement does not provide for pre-arbitration mediation, you may want to raise the possibility of that option at the preliminary hearing. You could also ask the administering organization to raise this matter with the advocates in a separate conference. If you raise the matter at the preliminary hearing, it is ethically more appropriate to suggest that a neutral, other than yourself, conduct the mediation. Many cases which would require days or weeks of arbitration can be resolved with the help of a skillful mediator in a matter of a few hours. Actually, in most situations, there are great benefits and little risk of harm in trying mediation first. Even if the mediation process is not successful in resolving the dispute, it might result in the informal disclosure of information which may obviate the need to take any discovery in connection with the subsequent arbitration. Mediation might also be beneficial in draining anger and hostility from the dispute, thus permitting the arbitration to proceed more efficiently, and guaranteeing a less costly arbitration.

Additional preliminary hearings. If any issues are unresolved at the end of the preliminary hearing and require a later status that report or briefing as well as oral argument by counsel, you should schedule another preliminary hearing.

2.2.2   Considering procedural alternatives.

Assuming that a dispute has arisen and arbitration is going forward with yourself as the chosen arbitrator, either by virtue of an arbitration clause or by a negotiated submission agreement, you should give careful consideration as to whether there are procedural alternatives available to help make the arbitration hearing process more efficient, less time consuming, and less expensive. Depending on the nature of the dispute and the configuration of the parties, you may want to consider, very early in the preliminary planning process, the usefulness of: (1) videotaped or telephone testimony; (2) bifurcated hearing; (3) consolidation of claims; (4) phasing the arbitration; or (5) a class action procedure.[3] Of course another procedural alternative might be to conduct the arbitration, in whole or in part, in cyberspace. See Chapter Five for some basic suggestions on conducting a cyberarbitration.

Videotaped or telephone testimony. In cases where the testimony of witnesses or experts will be unavailable at the arbitration hearing, the parties may arrange to have the testimony—both direct and cross-examination—videotaped in advance, then played back at the hearing. The disadvantage of this procedural alternative, is that you will not have the opportunity to ask questions of the videotaped witnesses. A remedy for this is to have the videotaped witnesses available on speaker phone after the showing of the video so the wit-

---

3.   *See generally*, Ian R. MacNeil, Richard E. Speidel, and Thomas J. Stipanowich, *Federal Arbitration Law*, (Vol II) §18.9 (Little, Brown and Company, 1995); C. Edward Fletcher, *Arbitrating Securities Disputes* §9.2[2] (Practising Law Institute 1990).

nesses can answer your questions. Also, where witnesses are unable at the last minute to be present for the hearing, by agreement of counsel and with your approval, they could be permitted to testify by speaker phone.

Bifurcation. First, you should consider whether it makes sense to bifurcate the hearing into two parts. In the initial part, the parties would present their respective evidence on the liability issues. After hearing the evidence and the arguments of counsel on liability, you would recess to decide the liability issues and then return and announce your decision. If you determined that there was no liability on the part of any respondent, you would enter an award to that effect, and the hearing would be adjourned. If you determined liability as to one or more of the respondents, then the hearing would proceed as to the damage issues in relation to only those respondents. This procedure can be very effective in reducing the length of a hearing.

However, in many situations, it is very difficult for advocates to separate evidence related to liability from that related to damages. Thus, they tend to err on the side of inclusiveness, so that where the apportionment of a witness's testimony is unclear, advocates tend to introduce all the testimony under a liability label. Also, where certain witnesses' testimony can clearly be apportioned between liability and damage issues, witnesses might have to testify once in the liability portion and then testify again in the damage portion. This can greatly inconvenience witnesses and cause considerable expense to the parties. In short, bifurcation is probably best suited to cases in which the damage evidence is in the testimony of expert witnesses, who need not be called to testify on liability issues.

Consolidation of claims. When at least one party is common to separate disputes, there may be several reasons why the parties might propose that claims be consolidated for arbitration before the same arbitration panel. These include: (1) reducing the risk of conflicting arbitration awards; (2) reducing the expense to the parties; and (3) minimizing the time spent by parties and witnesses in providing testimony. And, depending on the circumstances, there may be very good reasons for one party to object to consolidation, despite the fact that the opposing counsel favors it. For example, if a respondent party in your arbitration case has a minor dispute with the common party, but that common party has a number of disputes with a second respondent party in a separate but related dispute, the first party would probably not be happy about paying arbitration fees to observe the other two battle out their disputes if the disputes were to be consolidated for hearing. Also, the first respondent may not want to be tainted by what the arbitrators perceive as much more egregious conduct committed by the second respondent. If parties cannot agree to consolidation, the party desiring it may file an action in court to compel it. Although courts are not uniform in their decisions, it is safe to say that where the issues to be resolved are substantially the same and no party will be prejudiced, courts will usually order arbitrations to be consolidated.

Phasing the arbitration. Phasing the arbitration is a combination of consolidation and bifurcation. It can be quite useful in complex multi-party arbitrations. In this procedure, after several cases are consolidated for hearing, the arbitrators divide the proceedings into three parts: (1) determining the liability of the various parties; (2) awarding damages and interest; and (3) allocating arbitration costs among the parties. The key to the success of this procedure is the arbitrators' subdivision of the first part of the proceedings dealing with liability determinations into "phases." The hearings can be phased so that the principal parties present their cases in the first phase against each other. These may involve both claims and counterclaims. The second phase can consist of the hearings of the multiple-respondent claims against each other; and the third and fourth phases can consist of hearing the claims of a third group of claimants against the parties already described, as well as the third group's claims against each other. Although this procedure seems quite complicated when described, it actually expedites the procedure. What actually occurs is that the arbitrators' decisions in the liability phase have a direct impact on issues that were to be raised by the parties who would subsequently present their liability claims and defenses. As the arbitrators decide these issues, those parties are educated as to how the arbitrators would most likely rule on similar claims or defenses should they present them in their cases. This causes a streamlining of the subsequent cases, the dropping of certain claims by some parties, and even settlement of many of the claims.

Class action procedure. Some disputes may be amenable to application of a class action procedure. If the number of potential plaintiffs is known and finite and the potential damages reasonably predictable, a respondent or respondents in arbitration may agree to such a procedure. However, in many multiple-claimant situations, several arbitrations may be pending, but the class action procedure requires that notice be issued to individuals who have no present formal claim against respondents, but who may have such a claim. This could expose respondents to the possibility of defending themselves before a single arbitration panel with authority to impose an award of an unknown high value, and without the right to an appeal. Respondents, faced with such a prospect, will normally oppose the class action procedure, opting instead to take their chances in separate arbitrations before different panels. Nonetheless, it is possible that despite a respondent's objection, a court may order classwide arbitration if an arbitration clause can be construed to authorize it and/or if such procedure is authorized by state law.

2.2.3 Written order summarizing the results of the preliminary hearing.

After the preliminary hearing, the arbitrator or arbitration panel should issue a written order regarding each of the matters that were addressed and either agreed to or ruled upon during the course of that hearing. Typically, that order would contain the following information:

- Date of the preliminary hearing;
- Identity of the arbitrators;
- Identity of the parties and their respective counsel;
- Dates by which parties must amend/specify claims and counterclaims, or file any motions (e.g. to join additional parties);
- Date by which parties should file stipulation of uncontested facts;
- Date by which parties must serve and file a disclosure of witnesses reasonably expected to be called at the hearing on the merits;
- A description of the information that must be provided regarding each proposed witness (e.g., full name, short summary of anticipated testimony, copies of expert reports, and written curriculum vitae of experts);
- A directive that each party must update its witness information as it becomes available;
- A directive to counsel that they must schedule the attendance of witnesses so that the hearing can proceed without unnecessary delay;
- A directive that each party must notify the other party or parties of the sequence in which that party intends to call its witnesses;
- Date by which the parties must exchange (or make available for inspection) copies of all exhibits to be offered and all schedules, summaries, diagrams, and charts to be used at the hearing;
- A directive that each proposed exhibit must be premarked for identification with a prescribed designation;
- A directive urging the parties to attempt to agree upon and submit a jointly prepared, consolidated, and comprehensive set of joint exhibits;
- Date by which the exhibits must be filed with the arbitrators or the administering organization;

- Date on which the hearing on the merits will commence;
- A statement of the parties' estimates, disclosed at the preliminary hearing, as to the expected length of their respective cases;
- (In an administered case) a directive that no direct oral or written communication between the parties and the arbitrators will be allowed, except at the oral hearings;
- Date by which prehearing briefs must be served and filed, and a directive as to their required form and content;
- A statement as to the type of award that the parties agreed to during the preliminary conference;
- A statement as to whether the parties agreed to arranging for a court reporter for the hearing on the merits;
- Date by which any preliminary motions be filed or otherwise be waived; and
- Date for subsequent preliminary hearing, if needed.

2.3 SUPERVISING PREHEARING DISCOVERY

2.3.1 Deciding whether to permit discovery.

Historically, there has been no right to formal discovery in arbitration proceedings. The opponents of arbitration discovery argue that the discovery process is incompatible with speedy, economical resolution of disputes—which is one of the goals of arbitration. Of course, the argument on the other side of the coin is that the preclusion of discovery leads to unjust results. Without discovery, parties cannot uncover key information relevant to the arbitrator's decision, and therefore injustice occurs. Also without discovery, there is a high risk that surprise evidence will be offered for introduction at the hearing. The hearing will then be interrupted to permit counsel to argue the admissibility of such evidence or to allow counsel time to arrange for and introduce controverting evidence. These interruptions and delays, argue the discovery proponents, take up as much or more time and cause as much consternation as limited prehearing discovery.

The upshot of all this is that in recent years there has been a trend toward permitting at least limited discovery in arbitration proceedings. Most arbitrators, for example, will permit counsel to depose witnesses who will not be available for the hearing. Others will allow more extensive discovery, depending on the complexity of the case, and particularly where the parties can agree on the scope of discovery. When faced with a decision whether to permit discovery, you should ask yourself this question: "without discovery, will the arbitration hearing simply be a series of glorified depositions, supervised by arbitrators whose time must be compensated, and consisting largely of a search for proof instead of a showing of truth?" If you answer "yes," it is probably in the best interests of the parties and the arbitration process to permit a reasonable amount of discovery.

2.3.2 Deciding what kind of discovery to allow.

Once you decide to permit discovery, the next question becomes what kind of discovery to allow. Discovery in an arbitration proceeding, as in litigation, serves the purpose of allowing the advocates to gather information to support their various contentions at the arbitration hearing. However, unlike court litigation where a specific set of procedural rules governs the discovery process, absent a specific statutory provision or court rule, no uniform set of rules exists to govern arbitration discovery practice. Therefore, the manner of taking discovery in arbitration is left generally to the discretion and agreement of the advocates. When the advocates cannot agree, you will have to designate the type of discovery procedures they will follow. You may designate arbitration procedures of your own formulation, or you may direct the parties to use all or a portion of the federal discovery rules or the discovery rules of the local jurisdiction. You should discuss these matters with the advocates and parties at the preliminary hearing. Before you leave the preliminary hearing, all persons concerned should have a clear understanding as to the specific limitations that you have placed on various forms of discovery, including: (1) requests for production of documents; (2) depositions; (3) interrogatories; and (4) requests to admit.

2.3.3 Deciding how much discovery to allow.

Closely related to the question of what kind of discovery to allow is the issue of how much to allow. Production or exchange of documents occurs, with arbitrator supervision as needed, in almost all arbitration. As noted supra, most arbitrators will permit some deposition discovery in the ordinary case and may allow several depositions if the claims include requests for considerable damages. Usually, in the ordinary case, arbitrators will permit only depositions of the principal parties. In more complicated cases, arbitrators customarily permit depositions of principal parties, important witnesses—whether or not they will be available at the hearing—and expert witnesses. Some arbitrators permit no interrogatories at all, believing that they are a waste of time; other arbitrators permit a limited number (say 20), if they believe that the interrogatories seek basic, otherwise unobtainable information, or that the answers to the interrogatories will obviate the need to take one or more depositions. It is not uncommon for arbitrators to deny or strike the dreaded "contention" interrogatories, as difficult, if not impossible, to answer with any degree of confidence until all discovery is concluded and the opening statements are planned and solidified. With regard to requests to admit, most arbitrators will permit a specific number of them if it appears that the use of this discovery device will reduce the amount of other discovery and/or lead to stipulated facts, a stipulated settlement, or withdrawal of a claim or counterclaim.

2.3.4 Subpoenas.

Whether you can issue subpoenas during the prehearing discovery process will depend on the laws of the particular state or jurisdiction, the applicable arbitration rules which govern the arbitration proceeding, or the authority contained specifically in the arbitration clause. The laws of the vast majority of states permit the arbitrator, during the course of an arbitration hearing, to issue subpoenas to compel appearance of witnesses and the production of documents (subpoena duces tecum). Relying on this authority, courts have generally concluded that arbitrators may issue discovery subpoenas where their purpose is the same as hearing subpoenas—to obtain evidence on the issues to be arbitrated. It is customary for arbitrators to issue prehearing subpoenas for medical, hospital, police, and similar types of records. Even in situations where state law does not provide for subpoenas, you might be able to issue subpoenas if the United States Arbitration Act is applicable to the proceedings. Title 9 U.S.C. §7 permits arbitrators to issue subpoenas if the evidence sought is material to the proceedings. However, you should be aware that, by statute or court rule, your authority to issue subpoenas for documents or witnesses located outside of particular geographic boundaries may be nonexistent or significantly curtailed. You should consult the appropriate case law in your jurisdiction to determine the geographical limits of your subpoena power.

As a matter of practice, in an administered arbitration, an advocate desiring issuance of a subpoena completes a subpoena form and delivers it to the case administrator, who in turn, presents it to the arbitrator for review and signature. The arbitrator then signs and returns it to the case administrator, who releases it to the advocate for service. Sometimes an arbitrator will ask the case administrator to determine from the requesting advocate information regarding the exact purpose or need for the subpoena. This occurs routinely when the requesting advocate is seeking information from a person or entity not a party to the arbitration proceeding. If an arbitrator believes that production of documents pursuant to a subpoena served on an objecting nonparty is oppressive or burdensome, the arbitrator would be acting well within his or her discretion to quash or withdraw the subpoena, or as an alternative, to drastically reduce its scope to those documents of critical importance to the subpoenaing party.

Once a subpoena has been issued, and a party refuses to comply or objects to the subpoena on some ground, the matter is normally taken to court by the advocate seeking to enforce the subpoena, or by the subpoenaed but objecting person or entity seeking to have the subpoena vacated or quashed. When an arbitrator reasonably refuses to issue a particular subpoena, courts usually will not compel issuance.

2.3.5 Ruling on discovery motions.

When ruling on discovery motions and objections, you should use the same fair and evenhanded approach that you would use in relation to any motion, procedural or substantive, that comes before you. In almost every situation, the parties will have competing interests relating to the requested discovery. You will have to evaluate them and, depending on the circumstances, determine which party's interests should prevail or whether the parties' interests can be balanced in some way. The primary interest of the party seeking discovery is to obtain evidence to support his claim or defense or to find proof to undermine his opponent's claim or defense. The interests of the party objecting to the discovery may be singular or several, and may be varied in their nature and relative importance. Basic interests of objecting parties relate to matters of economy, time, privacy, privilege, confidentiality, relevance, materiality, convenience, burden of producing, form, format, location, legal rights, clarity, and custody, among others. Where possible, you should encourage the parties to settle discovery disputes through their negotiation of a mutually acceptable solution. Don't hesitate to suggest solutions if the parties seem to be unable or unwilling to find an acceptable compromise on their own. For example, if a party objects to producing documents on the grounds that a document request is overbroad, unreasonably burdensome, and that responding to it would be excessively expensive, you might suggest merely making them available to an agent of the requesting party for inspection and copying. If, in another situation, an advocate objects to producing his client's distant-located employee for deposition in the city of the subpoenaing advocate, you might suggest that the advocates arrange for a telephone or video deposition or that the requesting advocate's client pay the expense involved in bringing the employee to the city. Objections to discovery based on a party's need for protection of business secrets can often be resolved through a carefully crafted protective order, requiring in the extreme case production limited to "attorney's eyes only" review. Many discovery disputes can be resolved through discussion and compromise of this type. Of course, some disputes involving matters of attorney-client or other types of privilege cannot be easily compromised. In such situations you will have to make individual discovery determinations, perhaps on a document- by-document basis.

2.4 PREHEARING PROVISIONAL COURT REMEDIES AND INTERIM ARBITRATION AWARDS

2.4.1 Prehearing provisional court remedies.

A provisional remedy is a remedy provided by court order to protect the subject matter of an arbitration. It is a type of preliminary judicial relief sought by a party in aid of arbitration. Provisional remedies, such as examination before trial, attachment, or injunction, are rare and usually sought and allowed by a court only upon a showing of particular necessity or emergency. Where a party appropriately seeks a provisional court remedy, the party does not waive its right to arbitrate. Courts will generally grant attachments of property where preservation of intact assets within the court's jurisdiction will make an award meaningful. Federal courts have entered preliminary injunctions before deciding arbitrability issues and to preserve the status quo pending arbitration. Prior to arbitration, federal courts have enjoined a sale of valuable contract rights to technology and payment on letters of credit by a bank. Usually, if the court does enter a preliminary injunction, the injunction extends only to the point in time when the arbitrators are able to determine whether the injunction or temporary restraining order should remain in effect.

2.4.2 Interim arbitration awards.

Under the rules of many dispute resolution organizations, an arbitrator may issue such orders for interim relief as may be necessary to safeguard property that is the subject matter of the arbitration. Also, an arbitrator may grant any remedy or relief that he or she deems just, equitable, and within the scope of the agreement of the parties. Measures within an arbitrator's interim award authority include those which preserve the status quo, insure ultimate compliance with the award, or address specific problems which cannot await the final award in protracted arbitration proceedings. Interim awards may involve corrective measures such as environmental cleanup, or the awarding of damages on uncontested claims that are severable from other claims, or the preserving of assets, such as the freezing of bank accounts. Interim awards have also taken the form of directives: for the parties to pursue a buyout arrangement; appointing appraisers and temporary receivers; appointing a person to perform an accounting; defining procedures by which one software manufacturer could examine the programming materials of another software manufacturer. Usually interim awards are final and confirmable if they resolve with finality a self-contained, discrete, independent, separable issue according to the contract. In the appropriate case, such awards are subject to immediate judicial enforcement, prior to the completion of the arbitration.

2.5 PREPARING FOR THE ARBITRATION HEARING

2.5.1 Reading the prehearing briefs and materials.

Arbitrators who perform most effectively are those who conscientiously prepare for the arbitration. Such arbitrators read the materials, including any briefs and hearing exhibits, provided by the parties. In some arbitrations, there will be little to read in advance of the hearing; in other arbitrations of a more complex nature, you may be inundated with reading materials. This subsection provides some helpful tips on how to approach and successfully accomplish preparation in the more complex arbitration cases.

Tips for effective reading—general. Reading is the process by which one may mentally acquire vast amounts of information. In reality, it is seeing with the mind engaged. But it is a skill which is vital to the arbitrator function, and it can be developed, improved, and applied efficiently with a little effort on your part. Here are some helpful tips on how to enhance your effectiveness and productivity when you read in your arbitrator role.

- **Physical conditions conducive to reading.** You might be surprised to learn that room temperature is an important element contributing to effective reading. Most central heating systems in offices and libraries maintain a room temperature between 68 and 70 degrees Fahrenheit. You should know, however, that research has disclosed that this range of temperatures is a bit too warm for the brain to function at peak performance. The brain performs best when the surrounding air temperature is 65 degrees Fahrenheit. Thus, if you have a choice, you should opt to read in that part of an office or library that is a little chillier than you might like. Bundling up slightly to offset the cooler conditions may pay increased dividends in terms of mental clarity.

  With respect to lighting, research has shown that natural daylight is better for reading than artificial illumination. Natural daylight is more restful to the eyes because it contains a full range of the visible spectrum. Some fluorescent lighting is limited to a very narrow band of wavelengths and may put undue strain on the retinas. If possible, you should avoid reading directly in front of a window on a bright, sunny day. Eye strain can result when you look out the window periodically, forcing your eyes to make rapid accommodation to account for the change in light intensity.

- **Location and position.** When reading and writing near a window you should position yourself so that the shadow of your writing hand will not fall across the page of your document. Windows should be on your left if you are right-handed; and on the right, if you are left-handed. If artificial lighting is used, it is best that it be reflected from a ceiling or wall, rather than focused directly onto the paper. Focused lighting may generate reflections from shiny objects on the desk, causing eyes to become fatigued quickly. High intensity lighting (or spotlights) in a darkened room is also disadvantageous, for the same reasons that sitting in front of a window on a sunny day is not recommended. In a darkened room, every time you glance away from the high intensity lighted area, your eyes have to accommodate to a rapid change in intensity and thus become fatigued more quickly.

- **Seating and posture.** Apart from location and position, seating and posture play an important role in the efficiency of the reading effort. If you have a choice of seating, your chair should be sufficiently high so that the thigh is horizontal and the lower leg is at a right angle to it with the feet resting comfortably on the floor. Otherwise, the chair edge may exert pressure on the leg, obstructing blood circulation. Table height is also an important consideration. If the table is too low, you will slouch and feel tension and fatigue in your back. If too high, your arms will push up into your shoulders causing discomfort. Posture-wise, the least tiring reading position is an upright one with the back slightly bent forward. Unless you are used to it, sitting totally erect can add tension to the back muscles and cause attendant fatigue.

- **Goal to reduce fatigue.** Fatigue after an extended reading session is partly mind-related, partly eye-related, and partly muscle-related. Implementing the above suggestions will increase the efficiency of your reading session and help minimize your feelings of post-session fatigue and mental drain.

- **Reading briefs and materials for a general understanding.** Realize that when you read the materials initially provided by the parties, you may not understand them in detail. Your purpose for reading in advance is to give you some familiarity with the types of testimonial and documentary evidence you might expect and to give you some sense of the information supporting the claims and defenses of the parties. Your reading of the briefs will provide you with an overview of each side's perception of the facts and related law, if applicable. It will not, however, provide you with the same type of understanding of the case that you will have when all the evidence has been submitted you hear the parties' closing arguments. The initial reading will prepare your mind to learn.

2.5.2 Anticipating procedural and evidentiary problems.

When you examine the pleadings, prehearing briefs, witness lists, and exhibit binders in preparation for the arbitration hearing, be conscious of potential problems relating to procedures and evidence that may arise early in the proceedings. If the problems that you perceive are minor, you can address and resolve them with counsel at the beginning of the arbitration hearing. If, however, problems seem significant in that they have the likelihood of causing substantial delay mid-hearing, you may have to call for a special telephone or face-to-face prehearing conference to discuss these matters with counsel, so that these procedural or evidentiary disputes can be addressed and resolved before the hearing commences. An unexpected hiatus during an arbitration hearing can disrupt the schedules of the parties, lawyers, experts, and fact witnesses. It is often very expensive to reschedule and reassemble these people, and can cause the counsel and arbitrators to take additional time in preparation for the rescheduled hearing. Problems that you might perceive when reviewing the documents in advance of the hearing would include: counsel complaining that he or she has not received the written report of the opposing party's expert witness; counsel stating that his client may only be available by telephone during the hearing; counsel suggesting that a site visit be conducted before or during the hearing; counsel complaining that opposing counsel has not produced blueprints critical to a decision on the appropriateness of the ultimate construction; respondent's counsel's statement that the claimant's principal claim is not covered by the arbitration agreement and is therefore non-arbitrable; a comment by counsel that the proceeding should be consolidated for hearing with another arbitration case that is about to be filed; counsel's objection to prehearing production of documents containing "confidential business information"; and the like. If you can detect and deal with these types of issues in advance of a scheduled arbitration hearing, you will likely save yourself much inconvenience and stress later on.

2.5.3 Preparing lists of questions.

As you review the prehearing documents, you will likely think of points or questions that you will want to take up with counsel at the beginning of the arbitration hearing. It is helpful to make a list of such questions, rather than hope that they will come to mind at the time you are making your opening statement. One of the most important principles of being an effective arbitrator is not to assume that the parties' respective counsel have discussed hearing administration or organization of the proceedings prior to their arrival at the hearing site. Discussions you might assume lawyers would naturally and logically engage in prior to the hearing rarely occur, unless they have been prompted to discuss them by the arbitrator or the case administrator. Some of these administrative types of questions might include: if the hearing will extend across several days, the daily starting time; when morning, lunch, and afternoon breaks will occur; length of breaks; location of restrooms; where witnesses may wait prior to appearing to give testimony; whether witnesses will be sequestered; whether arrangements need to be made for audio-visual equipment; whether witnesses need to testify out of order because of their schedules; whether counsel have sufficient copies of documents to present to the arbitrators and opposing counsel; whether counsel will be able to stay after normal business hours, if necessary; and the like. Some of these matters, of course, may have been discussed in the preliminary hearing, but questions not covered at that time should be addressed at the beginning of the hearing. The former agreements regarding similar administrative matters should also be confirmed with counsel, with their clients present.

2.6   CONDUCTING A SITE VISIT

In certain cases, it is helpful for the arbitrators, counsel, and parties to actually visit the site or location at which the claim actually arose. Sometimes principal fact witnesses and expert witnesses also attend, and on occasion, the arbitration is conducted in the vicinity of the site so that the site may be re-visited at pertinent stages of the hearing. Site visits are commonly conducted in cases involving construction claims; heavy machinery patent claims; major tort or product liability claims; environmental claims; major vehicular, air-craft, or other catastrophic accident claims; major real estate claims; and major fire insurance claims, to name a few.

It must be emphasized that arbitrators who conduct site visits must be on their guard to preserve the integrity of the arbitration process and to avoid any appearance of bias or prejudice regarding the merits of the parties' claims or defenses. If at all possible, you should be careful to avoid being transported to or from the site by one party outside the presence of the other party or parties. If, because of distance, limited availability of transportation, or difficulty of terrain, you must accompany the parties to the site, you should make every attempt to ensure that a representative of each party is given the opportunity to travel with you. Once at the site, you should be careful not to make any statements about what you are shown that might indicate your inclinations regarding the positions of the parties. During explanations of counsel, even your facial expressions can communicate your agreement or disagreement with what he or she is saying. Thus, you should be conscious of your body language and endeavor to present a neutral affect. You should avoid making private comments to counsel for one or more of the parties as you move from one point to another during the course of your site visit.

If you and the other arbitrators on your panel need to discuss matters concerning your collective observations, you should move to an isolated location out of ear-shot of the other participants. You, of course, may ask questions of counsel, but you should avoid asking questions which would give any indication that you have prejudged factual or legal issues. As an arbitrator, your impartiality and neutrality are your most important assets. You should be constantly on your guard during a site visit to preserve them.

2.7 WITHDRAWAL, INCAPACITY, OR DEATH OF AN ARBITRATOR

Occasionally, on a three-arbitrator panel, an arbitrator may have to withdraw from the panel for personal or family reasons, or may become incapacitated due to a chronic or unanticipated health condition. In a rare situation, an arbitrator may die at some point during an arbitration proceeding. If the parties' arbitration agreement does not provide an agreed procedure for such an eventuality, absent the parties stipulation, the remaining arbitrators should look to the administering organization's rules or, if unavailing, to the applicable case law to determine the proper course of action. Your determination of whether or how to fill an arbitrator vacancy will probably, in large part, depend on the stage of the proceeding during which the vacancy has occurred. If the vacancy occurs in the prehearing stage, the parties may agree to select an individual to fill the vacancy. If the evidentiary portion of the hearing has commenced, the parties may agree to proceed with two arbitrators, stipulating as to the procedure to be followed if the arbitrators cannot reach a consensus as to the award to be entered in the case. Rule 20 of the American Arbitration Association's Commercial Arbitration Rules, for example, provide that "in the event of a vacancy in a panel of neutral arbitrators after the hearings have commenced, the remaining arbitrator or arbitrators may continue with the hearing and determination of the controversy, unless the parties agree otherwise." If the arbitration is being conducted pursuant to the Federal Arbitration Act, you should be aware that the Act (9 U.S.C. §5) provides for court appointment of an arbitrator in certain circumstances to fill a vacancy.

Chapter Three

The Arbitrator's Hearing Functions and Duties

The truth often does sound unconvincing.
—Agatha Christie

❄ ❄ ❄ ❄

3.1 ARBITRATORS' CONFERENCE

Prior to the arbitration hearing, and sometimes immediately before the scheduled beginning of it, the arbitrators customarily meet to discuss the hearing procedures. If a chair of the panel has not been previously selected or designated, the arbitrators will agree as to who is to serve as panel chair. Assuming that a preliminary hearing has already been held with the parties and the advocates, items which routinely appear on the arbitrators' conference agenda include: how evidentiary objections will be handled (e.g., by the chair ruling alone, by the chair after consultation with the other panel members, or by a combination of these two procedures); any changes in the schedules of the arbitrators; when breaks in the hearing will be taken; which panel member will record the admission or exclusion of exhibits; which panel member will complete the daily status form, if required to be submitted by the dispute resolution organization; how the arbitrators plan to conduct any questioning of witnesses; whether post-hearing briefs should be needed or anticipated; whether the question of the desirability of a written opinion should be discussed with the advocates initially; whether all or some of the witnesses should be sequestered; what form the witnesses' oaths or affirmation should take; whether the arbitrators have specific instructions on how documentary evidence, including stipulations, should be introduced; and other matters as the particular situation requires. Additionally, at the arbitrators' conference, the arbitrators might discuss how to rule on any prehearing motions and briefs which have been filed and whether to permit the advocates an opportunity to present short oral arguments on these motions. The more comprehensive the arbitrators' conference is, the less likely the arbitrators will have to take lengthy recesses early in the hearing to discuss matters related to procedures and the advocates' preliminary requests.

3.2 SEQUENCE OF HEARING—GENERAL

In arbitrations conducted domestically or involving predominantly U.S. parties, the sequence of events at the arbitration hearing of a two-party case is as follows:

- **Arbitrator or panel chair makes opening statement.**

- **Arbitrator handles any preliminary matters.**
- **Parties make respective opening statements.**
- **Claimant presents evidence of direct case.** Claimant's counsel conducts direct examination of each witness; respondent's counsel cross-examines each witness; counsel may conduct redirect and recross of each witness as arbitrator permits; arbitrator asks clarifying questions, as needed; counsel introduces documents during the testimony of witnesses, though the parties may agree, alternatively, to put most of the documents in evidence at the beginning of the hearing, or at the end of the hearing.
- **Claimant rests direct case.**
- **Respondent presents evidence of direct case.** Respondent's counsel conducts direct examination of each witness; claimant's counsel cross-examines each witness; counsel may conduct redirect and recross of each witness as arbitrator permits; arbitrator asks clarifying questions, as needed.
- **Respondent rests direct case.**
- **Claimant presents optional rebuttal evidence.**
- **Respondent presents surrebuttal evidence, as arbitrator permits.**
- **Parties rest their cases.**
- **Claimant presents final argument.**
- **Respondent presents final argument.**
- **Claimant presents rebuttal argument.**
- **Respondent presents surrebuttal argument, as permitted by arbitrator.**

Sometimes there are variations to this sequence of events. For example, a respondent may delay its opening statement until immediately before it begins presenting evidence in its direct case. Also, a claimant may waive its right to make a rebuttal argument and ask, instead, to delay its final argument until after respondent has made its final argument. Also, occasionally the parties may agree to examine witnesses out of order and even outside the period of its own direct case in order to accommodate the schedules of testifying witnesses, particularly expert witnesses.

Where there are multiple parties and/or multiple counterclaims and cross-claims, counsel and the arbitrators must discuss in advance of the hearing how the above-described basic hearing structure will have to be adjusted to accommodate the presenting and testing of the evidence of all parties on all of their claims.

3.3   ARBITRATOR'S OPENING STATEMENT

As a sole arbitrator in a case, or as a chair of an arbitration panel, you will be expected to make an opening statement. If there has been no preliminary hearing in the case, or if it has been held by telephone, this will be your first opportunity to build rapport with the parties and their clients, to gain their respect and

confidence, and to impress upon them how you expect to conduct the proceedings and how you expect parties and counsel to inter-relate as the proceedings
progress. The behavioral ground rules that you announce in your opening statement should be designed to set a positive tone for the hearing and serve as a guide
for the participants to proceed efficiently and expeditiously in the presentation of
their respective cases. Some topics you may consider including in your opening
statement are discussed immediately below.

3.3.1   Personal introductions.

Common courtesy dictates that at the beginning of the arbitration hearing,
if there has been no preliminary hearing, the arbitrator or the panel chair should
introduce the arbitrator(s) first. Then, the presiding arbitrator should ask each
participant to identify himself or herself by name and to state any job title and
organization and/or party with which the person is associated. Counsel should be
asked to state their names and the party or parties whom they are representing. If
several participants are in the hearing room, it is often a good idea for the presiding arbitrator to circulate a sheet of paper so that the participants can record their
identifying information for the benefit of the arbitrator(s). You should be aware
that some dispute resolution organizations require that at the end of the hearing
day the arbitrators record and submit, the names of the persons who attended
each hearing session.

3.3.2   Disclaimer of bias and partiality.

Next, the presiding arbitrator—and if there is a panel, all of the arbitrators—
should, if it is true, make a statement disclaiming any bias or partiality regarding
the participants, the claims, or defenses. You should realize, however, that during
the prehearing stage, it is not uncommon for an arbitrator to become aware of a
potential conflict of interest or a situation which might bring his impartiality into
question. After carefully reading through the proposed witness list of a party, for
example, an arbitrator may discover that he is a casual acquaintance of an expert
of that party—he and the expert belong to the same tennis club, and the arbitrator sees him there once in awhile and exchanges pleasantries. If the arbitrator
feels uncomfortable with this situation, he should disclose these facts and let the
parties decide whether to make a motion for recusal. In the example given, it is
unlikely that a party would move for recusal. It is usually advisable, however, for
an arbitrator to disclose such bases for perceived partiality up front in the hearing,
rather than wait until the appearance of the expert witness who, in front of all
arbitration participants, might unthinkingly make reference to "prior meetings"
at the tennis club.

3.3.3 Explanation of arbitration process and legal effect of award.

In the opening statement, the presiding arbitrator should also explain the arbitration process, the nature of the proceedings that the participants are about to encounter, and the legal effect of the award. In many situations, parties in an arbitration have never before experienced the process. An early explanation of what they should expect will usually relieve tensions and have a calming effect on the proceedings. Discussing the legal effect of an award will be, for you, a check on whether the parties and their counsel have consciously agreed to a particular type of end result. For example, you should state your understanding that the award is to be binding and non-appealable. If a party believed that she agreed to a non-binding advisory award, then the issue of the legal effect of the award can be clarified at the outset. If a party believed that she agreed to a baseball type or high-low arbitration, these issues can also be resolved so that a dispute over the nature of the award will not erupt at the conclusion of the arbitration hearing or after the award issues.

3.3.4 Procedural ground rules.

If not already addressed at a prior preliminary hearing or in written communications to counsel in advance of the hearing, the presiding arbitrator should also explain procedural ground rules that will govern the proceedings. These ground rules usually consist of the individual preferences of the arbitrator or arbitration panel and, as discussed above, may address such matters as: procedures for introducing documentary evidence (e.g. showing exhibit to opposing counsel first); swearing of witnesses; sequestration of witnesses; the timing and length of hearing breaks; order of presentations; location of counsel and witness in the hearing room to assist court reporter in making an accurate record; time limitations on opening statements or on segments of the hearing itself; and the like.

3.3.5 Arbitrator's instructions to testifying witnesses.

You may want to consider sharing the following "Dos and Don'ts" with clients and witnesses prior to their testimony in an arbitration hearing:[1]

The Dos of Testifying

- Do tell the truth.
- Do listen carefully to each question.
- Do ask for clarification if you don't understand a question.
- Do take your time when answering questions.
- Do allow the questioner to finish the question before answering.

---

1. Adapted from Thomas Oehmke, *Commercial Arbitration* 219–21 (The Lawyers Cooperative Publishing Co., 1987).

- Do testify politely—refrain from being hostile, defensive, or humorous.
- Do speak clearly, distinctly, and confidently when answering questions.
- Do keep your answers brief.

The Don'ts of Testifying

- Don't answer a question on cross-examination until the arbitrator rules on your counsel's objection to it.
- Don't let the other side pressure you into giving answers that you don't believe to be true.
- Don't be afraid to clarify any statements you make, or correct any mistakes in your testimony.
- Don't be afraid to answer "I don't know" or "I don't remember," if you don't know the answer to a question.
- Don't try to impress the arbitrator or opposing counsel with a large vocabulary.
- Don't testify about what you heard from someone else or about information which you cannot personally verify.

3.3.6 Answering questions of parties or counsel.

At the end of the presiding arbitrator's opening statement, he or she should invite counsel and the parties to ask any questions they might have regarding the described procedures or the proceedings which are about to commence. This allows counsel to think about unique or idiosyncratic problems associated with the proper presentation of his or her case. These are best discussed openly before the case begins, rather than at a point in the proceedings which will cause a stoppage or significant delay in the hearing. Such problems might include the need for a language interpreter and the proposed use of a party as the interpreter, the need to arrange to have special audio-visual equipment transported and set up in the hearing room, the need to have a witness testify by telephone, or the need to have high-paid expert witnesses "on call," requiring an hour's notice of the time of their testimony.

3.4 HANDLING PRELIMINARY MATTERS

3.4.1 Ruling on motions.

It is a rare circumstance when the parties do not have motions to present to the arbitrators at the beginning of the hearing. Typical among such motions are: motion to sequester witnesses; motion to call a witness out of order; motion in limine to preclude the introduction of certain evidence; motion to issue witness subpoenas; motion to require production of the originals of certain documents; and the like. Sometimes a party may make motions orally after the presiding arbitrator's opening statement. In other instances, a movant may submit written motions, and the other parties may respond in writing prior to the hearing.

Unless a motion is very simple to decide or is uncontested, the arbitrators should normally leave the hearing room to consider the motion or motions. If the arbitrators stay in the hearing room, it is often possible for the parties to overhear—or perceive through the arbitrators' body language—how the arbitrators come to their conclusions on a particular matter, thus compromising the integrity of their decision-making process. Witnessing how the arbitrators decided their motions may influence one or more parties to conclude—perhaps quite erroneously—that one or more of the arbitrators have prejudged the merits of their case.

3.4.2   Confirming the witness schedule.

A preliminary matter which frequently needs to be discussed is the witness schedule. Several weeks may elapse between the preliminary hearing and the filing of the witness lists, on the one hand, and the evidentiary hearing, on the other. During these interim periods, witnesses may become ill, may be subpoenaed for another arbitration or court case, or otherwise become unavailable. It is advisable for the presiding arbitrator to confirm at the beginning of the hearing that the witness schedule is still accurate and viable. If there has been a change in the identity of the witnesses or their expected order and time of testimony, these problems can be addressed before counsel becomes embroiled in a distrust-based dispute.

3.4.3   Swearing of witnesses.

It is common in U.S. arbitrations for witnesses to be sworn before they testify. Affirmation is also common. Either the presiding arbitrator swears witnesses, or the court reporter may do so. Sometimes, if several witnesses are present in the hearing room when the presiding arbitrator gives his or her opening statement, they can all raise their right hand and be sworn simultaneously. A commonly used model for swearing witnesses is as follows: DO YOU SOLEMNLY SWEAR OR AFFIRM THAT THE TESTIMONY THAT YOU ARE ABOUT TO GIVE IN THIS PROCEEDING IS THE TRUTH, THE WHOLE TRUTH, AND NOTHING BUT THE TRUTH (SO HELP YOU GOD)?

3.5   PARTIES' OPENING STATEMENTS

After you call the arbitration hearing to order, acknowledge your oath, give your opening statement, hear and rule on any preliminary matters, and swear the witnesses, you will normally request that the advocates proceed with their opening statements on behalf of the parties.[2] Both claimant and respondent—or if multiple parties, all parties—are entitled to an opportunity to present an opening statement. The claimant usually speaks first, followed by the respondent.

---

2. The material presented in Sections 3.5 through 3.16 is a condensed adaptation of material appearing in John W. Cooley and Steven Lubet, *Arbitration Advocacy*, Chapter 5 (NITA, 1997).

The purpose of the opening statement is to assist you in understanding the evidence that is about to be presented. Its structure presents an oral synopsis or prologue of the real-life human drama which is to follow. It should help you identify issues while your mind is still fresh and uncluttered by volumes of evidence. It should also alert you to questions of fact and law that you will have to decide later.

The parties' opening statements normally follows a simple format, as shown below:

- Introduction
- Summary of facts, law, and theories
- Presentation of facts
- Brief statement of any applicable law, as appropriate
- Comment on opposition's case
- Restatement of summary of facts, law, and theories
- Statement of any request for relief

We will explore each of these topics below, as well as, the topic of ruling on objections made during the opening statements. First, however, it is important that we review some fundamental differences between an opening statement in an arbitration and an opening statement in a trial.

3.5.1 Basic differences between arbitration and trial opening statements.

Normally, the opening statements presented by advocates in arbitration are very similar to those presented in court before a jury or judge. However, you should be aware that not all arbitrators conduct arbitration proceedings in the same way. Thus, you may serve on panels with arbitrators who prefer variations to the standard trial opening statements. A description of some of these variations follows:

Written opening statements. Arbitrators who tend to comprehend information more easily by reading than by listening may require counsel to submit written opening statements prior to the hearing, in lieu of presenting oral opening statements at the commencement of the hearing. Also, some arbitrators believe that oral opening statements are inefficient and a waste of time—time which can be better used by the parties in presenting their evidence and making closing arguments. If one or more arbitrators on your panel take that view, but you believe that an oral opening statement would be a better way for the advocates to lay the groundwork for their trial stories, you will have to evaluate the pros and cons of insisting on oral opening statements. You certainly would not want to antagonize one or more of your panel members over a matter that, in the long run, may turn out to be inconsequential to the ultimate decision making process.

Claimant may request to make opening statement after respondent. As pointed out, *supra*, in arbitration as in a court trial, it is customary for the claimant to make an opening statement first, followed by the respondent's. And, as is common knowledge, it is not unknown in a court trial for a defense counsel to wait until the beginning of his or her case to present an opening statement. That also occurs routinely in arbitrations. From time to time in arbitrations, however, a claimant might make a request to present an opening statement at the beginning of the hearing, but after the respondent. Realize that in arbitration, the parameters of the opening statement are entirely within the arbitrator's discretion. You can set limitations on the length and scope of the opening statement, its detail or brevity, and its general manner or character. You can also entertain requests for changing the sequence of the opening statements, and you may, in fact, permit the claimant to present an opening statement after respondent's. But before you do, you should satisfy yourself that the advocate who makes such a request will not receive an unfair advantage if you allow it.

For example, a claimant may have strategic or tactical reasons for presenting his opening statement second. Such a request can throw the respondent off-balance. A lawyer for respondent who has not conscientiously prepared an opening statement—waiting to hear claimant's opening statement first, in order to respond—may find himself stumbling and at a loss for words if the arbitrator requires him to proceed first. In addition, claimant's counsel may find it an advantage to proceed second in order to have the last word. In the appropriate case, however, there might be a clear benefit to the arbitrators and the process to have the claimant address points covered by respondent's opening statement, outline the claimant's position, and then quickly follow that up with claimant's testimony, while the pillars and framework of her trial story are still fresh in the arbitrators' mind. If the respondent objects to a claimant presenting his or her opening statement second, then you or your panel will have to determine what is fair under the specific circumstances presented.

Statements may be deemed to constitute admissions. Some arbitrators listen carefully to the advocates' statements, hoping to catch them in some type of admission against their clients' interest. Some arbitrators may hold advocates to these admissions of adverse facts—consciously or subconsciously—even though the advocates' evidence does not ultimately bear them out. Such matters need to be discussed and resolved by the arbitrators in their prehearing conference. To avoid these problems, many advocates, at the beginning of their opening statements, request the arbitration panel not to hold against their clients any inadvertent misstatement of fact that they might make in the opening statement.

Omissions may constitute waiver of claim or defense. Similar to admissions against interest, though to a much lesser extent, an arbitrator may assume that what an advocate says in his or her opening statement is a waiver of a claim or defense. This is another matter that needs to be addressed and resolved by the arbitrators in their prehearing conference. Some advocates attempt to avoid this problem by stating in their opening statement that their remarks are intentionally abbreviated in the interest of efficiency and economy and that, even though they do not specifically address a matter in their opening statement, they are not waiving any claim in their written demand or any defense in their written answer, as the case may be.

Stipulations may be read aloud. Some arbitrators prefer that stipulations be read aloud at the time of the opening statement, so you may want to cover this topic in your prehearing conference with your panel members. Normally, arbitrators prefer an oral reading of stipulations in more complex cases in which a stenographic record is taken and in which the award will contain a reasoned opinion. Some arbitrators like to have a clear understanding up front as to which facts are uncontested and which are not. Having the stipulations read at the beginning of the hearing allows arbitrators to truncate later testimony when they find that it refers to already stipulated matters. Also, when the arbitrators begin preparing a reasoned opinion, all the stipulated facts will be consolidated conveniently in the beginning of the transcript for use in drafting a statement of facts, and for occasional reference, as needed. If you desire to have fact stipulations read aloud at the time of opening statements, you should advise the advocates of this preference at the preliminary hearing.

Arbitrator may permit a reply and surely. Unlike a judge in a court proceeding, an arbitrator, on request of counsel, may permit a reply or a surely to an opening statement. Although rare, this may occur in cases where there are counterclaims and/or where several arbitrations have been consolidated. If confronted with a request of this sort, you will have to determine what is fair in light of all the circumstances.

3.5.2 Rule against argument.

Opening statements in court and in arbitration are aligned in the sense that, generally, argument is permitted in neither. However, argument is a relative concept, defined in the eye of the beholder. Thus, in arbitration, as in court proceedings, certain remarks by advocates in their opening statements would satisfy a "bright line" test for constituting argument; others would not. Examples of remarks falling into the "obviously prohibited argument" category might include: (1) urging the arbitrator to draw inferences from the facts and make certain conclusions; (2) explaining the importance of certain evidence; (3) suggesting how it should be weighed; (4) commenting directly on the credibility of witnesses; and (5) appealing overtly to a sense of mercy or justice.

As a general principle, impermissible argument occurs when an advocate seeks to tell the arbitrator *how* he or she should make his decision. Because this broad principle is difficult to apply, other more narrow tests have been developed to help make distinctions. They are the witness test, the verification test, and the "link" test. Under the witness test, one questions whether a witness will actually be called to testify to the information conveyed in the opening statement. If so, and if that witness is permitted to testify because he or she has been deemed to have factual information, then the opening statement would be considered proper. If the witness is called, but not be permitted to testify as to the information because it has been deemed a conclusion—not in the province of a witness—then the opening statement would be considered improper.

Under the verification test, one questions whether the content of the opening statement can be verified; the point being that facts can be verified, but argumentative conclusions cannot.

Finally, under the "link" test, remarks descend to the level of impermissible argument when an advocate must supply a non-evidence based explanation—a rhetorical embellishment to link independent evidence with the point he is trying to make. An arbitrator may apply other tests, related to counsel's delivery style, to determine whether he or she has engaged in an improper opening argument. Tone of voice, for example, can turn a simple factual statement into scornful argument. Rhetorical questions, even innocently formulated, can be piercingly argumentative and elicit anger. Finally, extreme repetition of facts can be deemed argumentative and even hostile during an opening statement.

The rule against argument does not mean that advocates can not make comments about the applicable law. In almost every opening statement, whether in court or in arbitration, there is a need to include some information about the law, to let the trier of fact know what information is relevant to his or her determination. It is improper, however, for an advocate, in an opening statement, to argue for a particular interpretation or construction of the law.

3.5.3   Introduction and summary.

An advocate's introduction and summary serve the purpose of orienting you to the disputants and the dispute. After introducing himself and the client that he represents, the advocate normally provides a summary of the more detailed story which is to follow. The summary usually contains a few sentences describing the factual contours of the dispute, the advocate's theories of claims and defenses, and any necessary law to put the dispute in context. Often, advocates begin with a statement of their theme—a single sentence which captures the moral force of their case. After that, they mold their introduction around the overall theory of their case by answering the questions: What happened? Why did it happen? Why is my client's version correct? How can we be sure? Why does all this make sense? These questions are then answered in more detail during the next stage of the opening statement—the presentation of facts.

3.5.4   Presentation of facts.

In their presentation of facts, effective advocates state facts which: (1) they will support with evidence; (2) they believe to be true; and (3) they believe to be admissible. They should not discuss facts which they can only partially prove, nor refer to facts for which they have no evidence. They should also not stray into collateral matters, nor refer to topics which are not admissible. These matters, of course, can be the basis for their opponent's objections on which you may be asked to rule. Effective advocates apply the following principles in presenting their opening statements. You should encourage the application of these principles whenever possible:

Brevity. A time-honored quality of an effective opening statement is brevity. However, brevity is a relative concept. If an advocate represents a claimant in a case against several respondents and has separate theories involving different facts for each one, a "brief" opening statement may take forty-five minutes or more. If an advocate represents the respondent in such a case, an opening statement may last only ten to fifteen minutes. Thus, an effective advocate tailors the time to the task and keeps the presentation interesting. You can assist the advocates in achieving brevity by setting reasonable time limits on their opening statements. This is a topic that may be discussed at the preliminary hearing.

The principle of primacy. Behavioral research has shown that arbitrators are more apt to remember information they heard first in an arbitration proceeding rather than information buried somewhere in its succeeding stages. That is why effective advocates often present first the information in their opening statements that they think will have the greatest impact on the arbitrator in decision-making and that incorporates facts concerning the most critical parts of their story.

Operative facts. Arbitrations are won or lost most often on their facts—not on the applicable law. Thus, effective advocates focus early in the proceeding on what they perceive to be the operative facts of the case. Operative facts include: action and key events; the physical scene; transactions and agreements, if any; relationship of the parties; business context, if any; and motives and motivations of the parties or key players. Effective advocates also clearly relate selected aspects of the evidence to the legal issues that the arbitrator must take into account when deciding the case. They also emphasize undisputed evidence, eliminate tangential facts, and, after disclosing all the favorable information, at least acknowledge any facts unfavorable to their position.

3.5.5   Brief statement of law.

In arbitration, as in a court trial, the bulk of the advocates' legal arguments are reserved for the closing argument. An arbitration in which the arbitrator is a lawyer, closely approximates a bench trial in court. And when advocates present an opening statement in a bench trial, they usually have much more latitude in discussing legal issues than they do in a jury trial. Thus, as mentioned supra, if advocates believe that arbitrators must understand the law in order to properly comprehend their opening statements, they might sparingly refer to pertinent cases or statutes. In the appropriate case, they may also find it necessary to refer to applicable administrative rules, regulations, or rulings. Still, arguing the proper interpretation or construction of the law or regulations in an opening statement is almost always inappropriate.

3.5.6 Comments on opposition's case.

It is not inappropriate for an advocate to comment on the opposition's case. Effective advocates representing claimants normally concentrate on their own case for the majority of the opening statement, and then address the affirmative defenses and counterclaims, if any, one by one. Advocates for respondents, similarly, make denials to each of the claimant's specific assertions, accusations, or claims. However, they do not simply list all the claimant's unpleasant accusations, denying each one in sequence. Rather, they sanitize the accusation by first distilling the hostility, and then answering it by drawing on the positive aspects of their own case. Effective advocates for respondents sometimes also point out what claimant has omitted from his opening statement if the omission comments on evidence harmful to the claimant's case and cannot be explained away easily or be controverted by him. It is inappropriate for an advocate of any party to be personally derisive of another advocate or party during an opening statement.

3.5.7 Summary and request for relief.

The beginning of an opening statement is a preview of the advocate's positions and supporting evidence. The closing of an opening statement is a recapitulation of the preview to remind you how the advocate wants you to perceive his or her story. The effective advocate will briefly summarize the facts he will present through evidence, restate facts to which the parties have stipulated or admitted, reiterate the factual issues and factual theories, and describe what evidence will disprove his opponent's theories. Finally, the effective advocate will state what you must find in order for his or her client to prevail and will conclude with a statement of the damages, remedies, or relief that he seeks, as appropriate. If, at the conclusion of the opening statements, the advocates do not state the appropriate standard of proof and burden of proof for the proceeding, you should make an inquiry about these matters to remind them what those requirements are and what their evidentiary responsibilities will be.

3.5.8 Ruling on objections and responses.

Objections made by one advocate during another advocate's opening statement can be disruptive, distracting, rude, and antagonistic. They may even give you the impression that the objector has something to hide. They can also draw attention to matters which you may not have fully comprehended had the objection not been made. Thus, objections can be self-defeating for the advocate making them in that they can accomplish the reverse of their intended purpose. However, there may be instances when an advocate may legitimately object during an opponent's opening statement, and you must be prepared to rule on them. Some of these instances are discussed briefly below.

Improper argument. If an advocate is essentially making a closing argument in the opening statement, it is appropriate for an opponent to object. Normally, you will find it unnecessary to sustain an objection to a few sentences that seem argumentative, but if an advocate is making extensive legal arguments—explaining the application of specific cases and attempting to draw legal conclusions based on evidence that has not yet been admitted—you could properly sustain an objection directed to such legal arguments.

Personal knowledge of facts. An advocate for a party is not permitted to testify in an arbitration hearing. An advocate is an independent advisor, not a witness in the case. As a non-witness, an advocate should not be giving his or her personal opinion in the opening statement, touting his or her own credibility, or asserting personal knowledge of the facts. This is irrelevant and improper. If such comments are extensive, you should sustain an objection directed to them.

Raising issues or matters outside the pleadings. If an advocate begins discussing claims or defenses not framed by the pleadings, an opponent may properly object. If an opponent does not object, you may want to question whether the advocate has veered outside the contours of the pleadings. You should, however, keep in mind that if the opponent does not object, he or she might be doing so for a tactical reason. For example, if a claimant's objectionable comments in an opening statement are brief, the respondent's advocate may not object immediately, opting instead to address them in his or her own opening statement.

Discussing excluded evidence. If an advocate discusses evidence ruled inadmissible by one of your prehearing rulings, the opponent could properly object, and you would most likely sustain the objection. In the extreme situation, an advocate's flouting of your prior evidentiary rulings might serve as a basis for an opponent requesting sanctions in the form of dismissal of a claim or defense, or precluding introduction of certain documents or testimony. If this occurs, you will have to decide what is fair under the specific circumstances of the facts and conduct before you.

Advocate's comments demeaning a party or witness. An advocate may make disparaging remarks about a party's character or motives. If an opponent objects, you will have to use your discretion in determining whether the advocate has overstepped the bounds of fair play.

Exceeding limits on opening statement. If you have set limits on the scope or duration of the opening statement, and an advocate exceeds them, you would be well within ambit of appropriate decision-making to sustain the opponent's objection.

3.6   UNDERSTANDING BASIC PRINCIPLES OF EVIDENCE

3.6.1   General considerations.

The procedural rules that govern an arbitration hearing are those to which the parties have agreed. The same is true of the rules of evidence. In arbitration, parties rarely agree to observe formal evidentiary rules, like the Federal Rules of Evidence. It is believed that application of such rules spawn time-consuming evidence arguments, which are antithetical to the goal of efficient dispute resolution. Also, most arbitrations are analogous to a bench trial in court. In most bench trials, the application of the rules of evidence are more relaxed than in a jury trial, because judges are presumably better able than a jury to sort reliable evidence from the unreliable. Thus, in arbitration, the criteria for precluding evidence are quite narrow, usually limited to irrelevancy and immateriality. Only occasionally do arbitrators consult formal rules of evidence for guidance, and those are normally unique situations where a party asserts extreme prejudice to his case if the evidence is admitted. Even in those situations, however, the arbitrators will have to know what the evidence is in order to make a determination whether to exclude it. This fact renders prejudice questionable as a basis for objecting to evidence, because the objector may have to bring to the attention of the arbitrators exactly the evidence he is trying to keep from their view.

Most arbitrators conduct arbitrations with a common sense notion of what is important to resolve a case. They apply a low threshold for admitting evidence, and they weigh the reliability and importance of the evidence as the hearing continues and issues evolve. Some arbitrators view the arbitration process as an opportunity for the parties to vent pent-up anger and frustration, as well as an arena to do legal combat. Also, many arbitrators liberally admit evidence in arbitration to obviate a later court challenge to their awards based on allegations of unfair preclusion of critical evidence.

By the same token, arbitrators quickly become skeptical of the merit of a party's case when an advocate consistently supports his or her positions with unreliable evidence. Effective advocates take a conservative approach with evidence that supports critical elements of their claims or defenses, and a less conservative one with evidence relating to background or peripheral matters. Thus, in relation to required elements of proof of claims or defenses, effective advocates lay proper foundations for testimonial and documentary evidence and endeavor to comply with the rule against hearsay evidence. In relation to evidence less central to their legal claims, they are less concerned with the technical requirements of foundations and hearsay evidence.

Also, you should be aware that effective advocates are constantly on guard to detect their opponent's abuses of formal rules of evidence—sometimes not so much to exclude the evidence on technical grounds, but rather to: (1) ensure that they respond to the objectionable evidence by later presentation of their own controverting or rehabilitating evidence; and/or (2) have a basis for reminding the arbitrator in later argument that the objectionable evidence would not be admissible in a court of law, is unreliable, and therefore should be given little or no weight in the arbitration proceeding.

In order to ensure that you make appropriate rulings on evidentiary objections, you must know and understand what the generally accepted evidence requirements are.[3] In this section, we will review some of the basic definitions, concepts, and customs of evidence applicable in arbitration hearings. Some of the approved techniques for introducing testimonial and documentary evidence within the constraints of generally accepted evidence requirements appear in Sections 3.7 through 3.12, *infra*. Some of the typical grounds for making and ruling on objections and motions related to evidence appear in Section 3.14.

3.6.2 Direct and circumstantial evidence.

There are two principal types of evidence, direct and circumstantial. Direct evidence takes several forms: oral testimony, written documents, and objects. Direct evidence directly proves the fact for which it is offered. Circumstantial evidence does not directly prove a fact, but it gives rise to an inference that a fact exists. For example, in a wrongful death case where a victim was killed by a hit and run driver, direct evidence would be eye witness testimony identifying the driver to be the defendant. Testimony identifying the make and model of the car that hit the victim, the color of the license plates, and that it was heading in the direction of defendant's home two blocks away, would be circumstantial evidence. While direct evidence is usually preferable over circumstantial evidence, the latter can be powerful if the inference it raises is closely connected to the fact it is offered to prove. Often, circumstantial evidence may be the only type of evidence available for proof of a particular fact. If an entire case is built solely on circumstantial evidence, however, it will enjoy a significantly lesser chance of succeeding.

Arbitrators generally give more weight to direct evidence than to circumstantial evidence, but there are limitations on each type. For example, direct evidence

---

3. See generally, Craig Peterson and Claire McCarthy, *Arbitration Strategy and Technique*, §7.2 (The Michie Company, 1986); Anthony J. Bocchino and David A. Sonenshein, *A Practical Guide to Federal Evidence* 37–38 (NITA, 1993).

may become less powerful when the credibility of a witness is questionable. Circumstantial evidence loses potency when its relevancy is questionable. As an arbitrator, it is important to know the limitations of each type of evidence so that unreliable or irrelevant evidence is not admitted during a hearing.

3.6.3 Relevance and materiality.

Relevance is the relationship between a piece of evidence and the probability of the existence of a fact pertinent to a case. Relevance is a broader concept than materiality. Relevance pertains to the case generally, and materiality pertains to specific propositions to be proved in the case. Although relevancy is one of the more common evidentiary objections in arbitration, arbitrators rarely sustain them, unless the proponent can make no plausible argument of its relatedness to a theory or fact in the case. Consequently, the only instance in which it may be sensible for an advocate to object to evidence on grounds of relevancy is where the proponent of the evidence is attempting to raise a wholly collateral issue—for example, a contract which has no connection whatsoever with the dispute in question.

Evidence is material if it is offered to prove a proposition pertaining to an issue before an arbitrator for decision. Evidence can be factually relevant to a dispute—for example, with regard to background information—but may not be material to a particular area of inquiry. Thus, you may sustain an objection to evidence on grounds of materiality where, although a line of questioning is tangentially relevant to a defense already presented and concluded, it is not material to the counterclaim issue with regard to which the witness was specifically called to testify.

3.6.4 Hearsay and exhibits.

Hearsay evidence is normally admissible in arbitration, unless the parties agree otherwise. Like other forms of evidence, arbitrators will normally receive hearsay evidence and give it the weight they deem appropriate in the context of all the circumstances. Exhibits can be offered by either party and are admissible at the discretion of the arbitrator, regardless of foundation. All parties have an opportunity to examine exhibits.

3.6.5 Affidavits.

Affidavits are admissible as evidence in an arbitration. An arbitrator will assign the affidavit the appropriate weight, taking into account that the testimony was not subject to cross-examination.

3.6.6 Admissions of fact.

Written admissions of fact may be introduced in an arbitration hearing. However, effective advocates are often able to achieve more dramatic impact if the evidence is admitted orally through the opposing party on cross-examination.

3.6.7 Stipulations of fact.

As discussed *supra* with respect to the preliminary hearing, stipulations of fact may be submitted to the arbitrator prior or during the course of the hearing. Arbitrators generally encourage the parties to stipulate to facts in order to shorten the length of the hearing. Sometimes advocates orally stipulate to facts in order to undermine the dramatic effect of their opponent's proffer of evidence.

3.6.8 Judicial notice.

Arbitrators, like judges, can take judicial notice of certain facts without the necessity of formal proof. Examples of facts appropriate for judicial notice include: laws, facts about government, geographical locations, history, language and abbreviations, dictionary definitions, natural phenomena, names of streets, and national holidays.

3.7 CUSTOMARY PROCEDURE AND ETHICS OF DIRECT EXAMINATION

Direct examination is the advocates' opportunity to present the substance of their cases, offering the evidence available to establish the facts that they need to prevail. Having planned their persuasive stories, they must then prove the facts upon which they rest by eliciting the testimony of witnesses. In this section we will review the goals and basic rules of direct examination, customary procedures governing adverse and hostile witnesses, customary procedure of redirect examination and rehabilitation, and certain ethical issues related to direct examination. If you have a clear understanding of these matters, you will be better prepared to rule on objections relating to them, when they arise.

3.7.1 Goals of direct examination.

Effective advocates customarily design their direct examinations to accomplish one or more of the following basic goals.

Introduce undisputed facts. In most arbitrations there will be many important facts that are not in dispute. Such undisputed facts will often be necessary to establish elements of a party's case. Nonetheless, such facts cannot be considered by the arbitrator, and will not be part of the record for any later challenge, until and unless they have been placed in evidence through a witness's testimony. Thus, if a party fails to include critical undisputed facts in direct examination, you may be required to find against that party.

Enhance the likelihood of disputed facts. The most important facts in an arbitration will normally be those in dispute. Direct examination is an advocate's opportunity to put forward his or her client's version of the disputed facts in a manner that will be most persuasive to the arbitrator. The true art of direct examination consists, in large part, of an advocate's ability to effectively establish the certainty of his or her own facts, despite the other side's claims that they seem uncertain or untrue.

Lay foundations for the introduction of exhibits. In arbitration, on most occasions the foundations for exhibits can be the subject of a stipulation. However, where particular exhibits, (such as documents, photographs, writings, tangible objects, or other forms of real evidence), are critical to an advocate's case, and the opponent questions their reliability and will not stipulate to their foundation, the advocate may have to call witnesses to lay appropriate foundations through direct examination.

Strengthen or weaken the credibility of witnesses. Effective advocates strengthen the credibility of their own witnesses by eliciting the basis of their knowledge, their ability to observe, or their lack of bias or interest in the outcome of the case. They also weaken the credibility of their opponent's witnesses by presenting direct testimony of bias or motive, providing the background for an impeaching document, or by advancing direct testimony contradicting the testimony of the opponent's witness.

3.7.2 Basic rules governing direct examination.

There are some very basic rules governing the manner and means by which testimony may be presented in an arbitration hearing. If advocates violate these rules, you must be prepared to decide on the related objections. Some of these rules are discussed below.

Competence of witnesses. Every witness called to testify on direct examination must be legally "competent" to do so. This is generally taken to mean that the witness possesses personal knowledge of some matter at issue in the case, is able to perceive and relate information, is capable of recognizing the difference between truth and falsity, and understands the seriousness of testifying under oath or on affirmation.

Non-leading questions. Similar to the rule applying to court trials, in arbitration a principal rule of direct examination is that an advocate may not "lead" the witness. A leading question is one that contains or suggests its own answer. Since the party calling a witness is presumed to have conducted an interview and to know what the testimony will be, leading questions are disallowed in order to insure that the testimony will come in the witness's own words.

There are, however, numerous exceptions to the rule against leading questions on direct examination. An advocate is generally permitted to lead a witness on preliminary matters or issues not in dispute, in order to direct the witness's attention to a specific topic, to expedite the testimony on non-essential points, and, in some jurisdictions, to refresh a witness's recollection. In addition, it is usually permissible to lead witnesses who are very young, very old, infirm, confused, or frightened. Finally, it is always within your discretion to permit leading questions in order to make the examination effective for the ascertainment of the truth, avoid needless consumption of time, protect the witness from undue embarrassment, or as is otherwise necessary, to develop the testimony.

Narrative testimony. Another general rule is that witnesses, other than experts, may not testify on direct examination in "narrative" form. The term narrative has no precise definition, but it is usually taken to mean an answer that goes beyond response to a single specific question. Open-ended questions that invite a lengthy or run-on reply are said to "call for a narrative answer." An example of a non-narrative question is, "What did you do next?" The objectionable, narrative version would be, "Tell us everything that you did that day."

The non-opinion rule. Witnesses are expected to testify as to their sensory observations. What did the witness see, hear, smell, touch, taste, or do? Witnesses other than experts generally are not allowed to offer opinions or to characterize events or testimony. A lay witness, however, is allowed to give opinions that are "rationally based upon the perception of the witness." Thus, they are usually permitted to draw conclusions on issues such as speed, distance, volume, time, weight, temperature, and weather conditions. Similarly, lay witnesses may characterize the behavior of others as angry, drunken, affectionate, busy, or even insane.

Refreshing recollection. Although witnesses are expected to testify in their own words, they are not expected to have perfect recall. It is permissible for the direct examiner to "refresh" the witness's recollection. It is common to rekindle a witness's memory through the use of a document, such as her prior deposition or report. It may also be permissible to use a photograph, an object, or even a leading question.

3.7.3 Customary procedure governing adverse and hostile witnesses.

From time to time it may be necessary for an advocate to call a witness, such as the opposing party, who will be hostile to his or her case. Because unfriendly witnesses cannot be expected to cooperate in preparation, most jurisdictions allow the use of leading questions for the direct examination of such witnesses. Unfriendly witnesses fall into two broad categories: adverse and hostile.

Adverse witnesses. Adverse witnesses include the opposing party and those identified with the opposing party. Examples of witnesses identified with the opposing party include employees, close relatives, business partners, and others who share a community of interest. There are limited situations in which it may be profitable for an advocate to call an adverse witness. The first is when the adverse witness is the only person who can supply an essential element of the advocate's case. For the same reason, an adverse witness might also be called to authenticate a necessary document or to lay the foundation for some other critical exhibit. Finally, and most perilously, an adverse or hostile witness might be called solely for the purpose of making a bad impression. Needless to say, this tactic has a strong potential to backfire. It is within your discretion to determine whether any particular witness is sufficiently identified with the opposition as to allow leading questions on direct examination. In order to signal his or her intent to ask leading questions it is important for an advocate to alert the arbitrators and opposing counsel to the fact that he or she is calling an adverse witness.

Hostile witnesses. A hostile witness is one who, while not technically adverse, displays actual hostility to the direct examiner or her client. The necessary characteristic may be manifested either through expressed antagonism or evident reluctance to testify. Additionally, a witness may be treated as hostile if his testimony legitimately surprises the advocate who called him to the stand. Whatever the circumstances, it is generally necessary for you to declare a witness to be hostile before an advocate can proceed with leading questions.

3.7.4   Customary procedure for redirect examination and rehabilitation.

Purpose of redirect. Redirect allows an advocate the opportunity to respond to the cross-examination, and it may be used for a number of purposes. The witness may be asked to explain points that were explored during the cross, to untangle seeming inconsistencies, to correct errors or misstatements, or to rebut new charges or inferences. In other words, the purpose of redirect is to minimize or undo the damage, if any, that was effected during the cross-examination.

Basic rules of redirect.

•   **Scope.** Because redirect is allowed for counteracting or responding to the cross-examination, the material that can be covered on redirect is technically limited to the scope of the cross. The interpretation of this rule varies among arbitrators; some are quite strict, and others are fairly lenient. Almost all arbitrators, however, insist that counsel is not free to introduce a wholly new matter on redirect. The redirect must always have some reasonable relationship to the cross-examination.

- **Some leading permitted.** Many arbitrators will allow a certain amount of latitude during redirect, especially with regard to leading questions. Even without indulgence, leading questions are always permissible to direct the witness's attention or to introduce an area of questioning. A certain amount of leading may be necessary on redirect, in order to focus on the segment of the cross-examination that the advocate wishes to explain or rebut.

- **Recross-examination and additional redirect.** Redirect examination may be followed by recross, which may be followed by additional redirect, and so on. Each additional examination is limited to the scope of the one that immediately preceded it. Thus, recross is restricted to the scope of the redirect, and a second redirect is confined to the scope of the recross. There is no right to continue an infinite regression of successive "re-examinations." Rather, it is within your discretion to allow or deny a request for, say, re-recross. Most arbitrators routinely allow at least one redirect and one recross.

- **Reopening direct examination.** Reopening direct examination is an alternative to redirect. It can be employed where an advocate needs to pursue a line of questioning that is beyond the scope of the cross-examination. It is strictly within your discretion to allow counsel to reopen a direct examination.

Procedure of redirect. The redirect should concentrate on a few significant points that definitely can be developed. These can typically include explanations or rehabilitation.

- **Explanations.** An advocate focuses the witness's attention on the pertinent area of the cross-examination and then simply asks her to give her explanation.

- **Rehabilitation.** Redirect can be used specifically for rehabilitation of a witness who has been impeached by a prior inconsistent statement. Redirect can also be used to rehabilitate a witness with the witness's own prior consistent statements.

  Rehabilitating after impeachment. The technique for rehabilitation is similar to that used for any other explanation. The advocate directs the witness's attention to the supposed impeachment and requests a clarification. It may be that the alleged inconsistency can be easily resolved, or that the earlier statement was the product of a misunderstanding or misinterpretation. Whatever the explanation, the effective advocate normally concludes the rehabilitation with an affirmative statement of the witness's current testimony.

  Rehabilitating through prior consistent statements. A witness can also be rehabilitated through the introduction of a prior consistent statement.

Although a witness's own prior-to-arbitration account would ordinarily be hearsay, a prior consistent statement is normally admissible to rebut an express or implied charge of recent fabrication or improper influence or motive. Accordingly, once the cross-examiner suggests that the witness has changed her story, the direct examiner may show that the witness's testimony is consistent with an earlier report or other statement. Note that in some jurisdictions a prior consistent statement is admissible only if it predates the inconsistent statement used for impeachment.

3.7.5   Ethics of direct examination.

Most of the ethical issues in direct examination involve the extent to which it is permissible for a lawyer to "assist" a witness in order to prepare or enhance her testimony, as well as the duty of the lawyer when he or she suspects that a client or witness may commit, or has committed, perjury.

Preparation of witnesses. A recurring question is the extent to which lawyers may "coach" witnesses in preparation for their testimony. In many countries it is considered unethical for a lawyer even to meet alone with a witness prior to the witness testifying, because of the possibility for contamination of the testimony. In the United States, however, we take a far different view. Here, it is generally considered incompetent for a lawyer to fail to meet with and prepare a witness in advance of offering her testimony. Difficult issues arise, however, when counsel attempts to refresh a witness's recollection, to fill in gaps in her story, or to suggest alternative possibilities. Again, this practice is usually justified on the ground that it is necessary to ensure that the truth emerges fully. Witnesses can be forgetful, especially when they are unaware of the legal importance of certain facts. The guiding principle here is that counsel must, explicitly and implicitly, prepare the witness to give his or her own testimony, and not the testimony that the lawyer would favor or prefer. Most efforts to assist or empower the witness are ethical. Efforts at substitution or fabrication, no matter how well-cloaked, are not.

Offering inadmissible evidence. When evidence is admissible only for a limited purpose, it is unethical for a lawyer to attempt to put it to further use. The obligation of zealous advocacy does not require counsel to ignore or evade the arbitrator's rulings with regard to the restricted admissibility of evidence. By the same token, it is not permissible for a lawyer to prepare a witness to interject clearly inadmissible evidence. Where a motion in limine has been granted, for example, counsel cannot suggest or encourage a witness to use a narrative answer to volunteer the excluded information.

Perjury. The appropriate response to witness and client perjury has endlessly perplexed the legal profession. While no ethical lawyer would willingly be a party to perjury, questions arise as how best to prevent it without damaging the principles of confidentiality and zealous advocacy. There is no doubt that a lawyer may not call a non-client witness who is going to testify falsely, and must "take reasonable remedial measures should non-client perjury occur despite counsel's efforts to avoid it."[4] The thorny problem, however, is the client. An attorney must certainly take all reasonable steps to dissuade a client from presenting untrue testimony. But what if the client insists on presenting a story that the lawyer firmly believes is false? Or what if the client's perjury on the stand takes the lawyer by surprise, and becomes a *fait accompli* before the lawyer can stop it? The ABA Model Rules of Professional Conduct provide that counsel, in both civil and criminal cases, must take reasonable steps to remedy client perjury, even at the cost of revealing a confidential communication.[5] Although there are not any easy solutions to these dilemmas, it is fair to say that the trend is toward diminished latitude for the client and increased disclosure by counsel.

3.8 CUSTOMARY PROCEDURE AND ETHICS OF CROSS-EXAMINATION

This section discusses the role of cross-examination, its basic rules, and procedure. Several more advanced aspects of cross-examination—such as impeachment and the use of character evidence—are treated separately in Section 3.9.

3.8.1 The role of cross-examination.

If direct examination is the advocate's opportunity to win your regard for her case, cross-examination presents a danger that she will lose it. Cross-examination is frequently dramatic, often exciting, and in many ways it defines the adversarial method of dispute resolution. It is the ultimate challenge for the arbitration advocate. It allows her to add to her case or detract from the opposition's case by extracting information from the other side's witnesses. Furthermore, cross-examination is inherently testy. The witness may argue with the advocate, requiring the arbitrator to intervene and exercise control through cautionary rulings.

3.8.2 Basic rules governing cross-examination.

Some rules of cross-examination vary depending on locality, but the following are nearly universal.

Leading questions permitted. The most obvious distinction between direct and cross-examination is the permissible use of leading questions. Because an adversary's witnesses will have little incentive to cooperate with the cross-examiner or to be interviewed by the cross-examiner in advance of the hearing, the cross-examiner is allowed to ask questions that contain their own answers. Moreover, the advocate's right to ask leading questions is usually understood to include the right to insist on a responsive answer.

---

4. *See* Rules 3.3(c) and 3.4(b), ABA Model Rules of Professional Conduct.
5. Rule 3.3(b), ABA Model Rules of Professional Conduct.

Limitations on scope. Cross-examination is limited to the scope of the direct. Since the purpose of cross-examination is to allow an advocate to inquire of his adversary's witnesses, the scope of the inquiry is restricted to those subjects that were raised during the direct examination. Note that the definition of scope may vary from arbitrator to arbitrator. A narrow application of this rule can limit the cross-examiner to the precise events and occurrences that the witness discussed on direct. A broader approach would allow questioning on related and similar events. For example, assume that the defendant in an auto collision case testified that his brakes had been inspected just a week before the accident. A strict approach to the "scope of direct" rule might limit the cross-examination to questioning on that particular inspection. A broader interpretation would allow inquiries into earlier brake inspections and other aspects of automobile maintenance. A more generous approach to the scope of cross-examination is definitely the modern trend.

There are two general exceptions to the "scope of direct" rule. First, the credibility of the witness is always an issue. An advocate may therefore always attempt to establish the bias, motive, interest, untruthfulness, or material prior inconsistency of a witness, without regard to the matters that were covered on direct examination. Second, an advocate may cross-examine beyond the scope of the direct once the witness herself has "opened the door" to additional matters. In other words, a witness who voluntarily injects a subject into an answer on cross-examination may thereafter be questioned as though the subject had been included in the direct.

Other restrictions. A variety of other rules, most of which involve the manner or nature of questioning, also limit cross-examinations.

- **Argumentative questions.** An advocate may ask a witness questions, suggest answers, and assert propositions. An advocate may not argue with the witness. The definition of an argumentative question is elusive. Much will depend on the advocate's demeanor; perhaps an argumentative question is one that is asked in an argumentative tone. The following is a reasonable working definition: An argumentative question insists that the witness agree with an opinion or characterization, as opposed to a statement of fact.

- **Intimidating behavior.** An advocate is entitled to elicit information on cross-examination by asking questions of the witness and insisting upon answers. An advocate is not allowed to loom over the witness, to shout, to make threatening gestures, or otherwise to intimidate, bully, or badger the witness.

- **Unfair characterizations.** An advocate's right to lead the witness does not include a right to mislead the witness. It is objectionable to attempt to mischaracterize a witness's testimony or to ask "trick" questions. If a witness has testified that it was dark outside, it would mischaracterize the testimony to begin a question, "So you admit that it was too dark to see anything …" Trick questions cannot be answered accurately. The most famous trick question is known as the "negative pregnant," as in Senator McCarthy's inquisitional, "Have you resigned from the Communist Party?"

• **Assuming facts.** A frequently heard objection is that "Counsel has assumed facts not in evidence." Of course, a cross-examiner is frequently allowed to inquire as to facts that are not yet in evidence. This objection should only be sustained when the question uses the non-record fact as a premise rather than as a separate subject of inquiry, thus denying the witness the opportunity to deny its validity. An example of a question containing an unfair assumption would be: "Since you had been drinking, you were on foot instead of in your car that morning?" That the witness was drinking is an assumed fact. The problem with this sort of bootstrapping is that it doesn't allow the witness a fair opportunity to deny having been drinking in the first place.

• **Compound and other defective questions.** Compound questions contain more than a single inquiry: "Are you related to the plaintiff, and were you wearing your glasses at the time of the accident?" The question is objectionable since any answer will necessarily be ambiguous. Cumulative or "asked and answered" questions are objectionable because they cover the same ground twice (or more). Vague questions are objectionable because they tend to elicit vague answers.

3.8.3 Customary questioning procedure.

The advocate's essential goal of cross-examination is witness control. Control can be either non-assertive or assertive. With a cooperative or tractable witness, control may mean nothing more than asking the right questions and getting the right answers. A hostile, evasive, or argumentative witness may require that an advocate employ more assertive means. When you, as an arbitrator, observe an effective cross-examination, it will have characteristics as described immediately below.

Procedure for effective control of witness. To control witnesses, effective advocates often apply the following techniques in their questioning procedure:

• **Short.** They keep questions on cross-examination short, in both execution and concept. They usually keep each question to ten words or less, and contain its scope to a single fact or implication.

- **Leading.** Every question on cross-examination is leading. The question includes the answer. A non-leading question invites the witness to wander away from the advocate's story.

- **Propositional.** The best questions on cross-examination are not questions at all. Rather, they are propositions of fact that the advocate puts to the witness in interrogative form. The advocate already knows the answer—she simply needs to produce it from the witness's mouth. Every question of an effective cross-examination contains a proposition that falls into one of these three categories: (1) the advocate already knows the answer; (2) the advocate can otherwise document or prove the answer; or (3) any answer will be helpful. An example of the latter sort of question would be the classic inquiry to a witness who must admit having previously given a false statement: "Were you lying then, or are you lying now?"

Ineffective control procedure. The pitfalls of cross-examination are well-known, and include refusals to answer, unexpected answers, argumentative witnesses, and evasive and slippery witnesses. Virtually all of these problems derive from the same basic error on the part of the cross-examiner—failure to control the testimony. When you, as an arbitrator, observe an ineffective cross-examination, it will have some or all of the characteristics described below.

- **Non-leading questions.** The cardinal rule on cross-examination is that the advocate should use leading questions. The cardinal sin is to abandon that tool. For some reason, some advocates seem impelled to drift into non-leading questions once an examination has begun.

- **"Why" or explanation questions.** There is virtually never a need for an advocate to ask a witness to explain something on cross-examination. If the advocate knows the explanation, then the advocate should use leading questions to get the witness to tell it. If the advocate does not already know the explanation, then cross-examination surely is not the time for the advocate to learn it.

- **"Fishing" questions.** Fishing questions are the ones that an advocate asks in the hope that he might catch something. The advocate should not ask questions for which he does not know the answers.

- **Long questions.** Long questions have an almost limitless capacity to deprive a cross-examiner of witness control. Long questions, by their very nature, multiply a witness's opportunity to find something with which to disagree. The more words that an advocate uses, the more chance there is that a witness will refuse to adopt them all. A second problem with long questions is that they are easily forgotten or misunderstood. The witness may insist on answering the question that she thought the advocate asked, rather than the one that an advocate meant to ask.

- **"Gap" questions.** "Gap" questions constitute an especially enticing subset of explanation questions. Gaps are found in direct testimony more often than one might expect. A witness may neglect to testify about one of a series of important events, or may omit testimony concerning a crucial document. Alternatively, a witness might leave out important evidence on damages, or may fail entirely to testify as to an element, such as proximate cause, of the opposition's case. Ineffective advocates ask for answers that fill in the gaps in their opponent's case, forgetting that everything their opponent leaves out works in their favor.

- **"You testified" questions.** Another common method of surrendering control to a witness is through the use of questions that challenge the witness to recall the content of her earlier direct testimony. These can be referred to as "you testified" questions, because they inevitably contain some variant on those words. The problem with "you testified" questions is that they invite the witness to quibble over the precise wording used on direct examination. The exact language of the witness's earlier answer is seldom essential, but the "you testified" format inflates its apparent importance, often almost to the point of picking a fight.

- **Characterizations and conclusions.** Another way that an advocate can risk losing control on cross-examination is to request that a witness agree with a characterization or conclusion. Assume that an advocate is cross-examining the complaining witness in a vehicle hit-and-run case. The witness testified on direct that the accident occurred at midnight on a seldom-traveled country road. The advocate's defense is misidentification. Wishing to take advantage of the time and place of the events, the advocate asks this question: "It was too dark to see very well, wasn't it?"—seeking to have the witness to agree with the characterization of the lighting conditions. The witness, being nobody's fool, answers: "I could see just fine." An effective advocate would have asked the witness about the facts that led to the characterization, like the sun had gone down, there was no moon that night, there were no street lamps, there were no house lights, and there were no illuminated signs. The advocate could thereby save the characterization for final argument.

3.8.4   Ethics of cross-examination.

Like all powerful rhetorical tools, cross-examination can be used to mislead and deceive. Accordingly, certain ethical principles have developed that circumscribe a lawyer's use of cross-examination.

Factual and legal basis for questioning. To protect against the unscrupulous use of cross-examination, a general rule establishes that every question should have a "good faith" basis in fact.[6] Ordinarily, in a court case subject to discovery, counsel is not free to make up assertions at trial, or even to fish for possibly incriminating material. Rather, as a predicate to any "propositional" question, counsel must be aware of specific facts that support the allegation. In arbitration, where little or no discovery has been authorized, the "good faith" basis in fact requirement is somewhat relaxed, because counsel may be examining a witness for the first time at the hearing itself.

Also, in a court trial, the "good faith" basis for a cross-examination question cannot be comprised solely of inadmissible evidence. Trial counsel cannot allude to any matter "that will not be supported by admissible evidence." Thus, in a court trial a good faith basis cannot be provided by rumors, uncorroborated hearsay, or pure speculation. In an arbitration, this rule is somewhat relaxed, because hearsay is normally permitted. However, allegations based on evidence deemed inadmissible by the arbitrator may lead to a sustained objection, an admonition by the arbitrator, or even sanctions.

Assertions of personal knowledge. The general rule in a court trial is that it is unethical for counsel to "assert personal knowledge of facts in issue . . . or state a personal opinion as to the justness of a cause, the credibility of a witness, the culpability of a civil litigant, or the guilt or innocence of an accused."[7] While this problem most frequently occurs during closing argument, it also arises during cross-examination. Cross-examination questions often take a "Do you know?" or "Didn't you tell me?" format. Both types of question are improper, because they put the lawyer's own credibility in issue. "Do you know?" questions suggest that the lawyer is aware of true facts which, while not appearing on the record, contradict the witness's testimony. "Didn't you tell me?" questions argue that the witness and the lawyer had a conversation, and that the lawyer's version is more believable. In either case, the questions amount to an assertion of personal knowledge. In the informal setting of arbitration, some arbitrators may relax the enforcement of this rule, but other arbitrators may strictly enforce it.

Derogatory questions. It is unethical for a lawyer to ask questions that are intended solely to harass, degrade, or humiliate a witness, or to discourage him from testifying.

Discrediting a truthful witness. In arbitration, a witness cannot be degraded or debased simply to cast doubt on otherwise unchallenged testimony. On the other hand, true factual information may be used by a lawyer to undermine the credibility of a witness whose testimony is legitimately controverted.

---

6. *See* Rule 3.4(e), ABA Model Rules of Professional Conduct.

7. *See* Rule 3.4(e), ABA Model Rules of Professional Conduct.

Misusing evidence. The same rules apply on cross as on direct with regard to misusing evidence that has been admitted for a limited purpose.

3.9   PERMISSIBLE IMPEACHMENT

While advocates often use cross-examination to demonstrate inaccuracies or to rebut a witness's testimony, they also use it to discredit the witness as a reliable source of information. Successful impeachment renders the witness less worthy of belief, as opposed to merely unobservant, mistaken, or otherwise subject to contradiction. There are three basic categories of witness impeachment, each of which provides a reason to place less credence on a witness's testimony.

The most common method of impeachment is the use of a prior inconsistent statement, action, or omission. The elicitation of a prior inconsistency demonstrates that the witness's current testimony is at odds with her own previous statements or actions. In essence, this examination says, "Do not believe this witness, because her story has changed."

A second method of impeachment is the use of character, or "characteristic" evidence. This form of impeachment is aimed at demonstrating that the witness possesses some inherent trait or characteristic, unrelated to the case at hand, that renders the testimony less credible. Perhaps the witness is a convicted felon or suffers a memory defect. This examination says, "This witness is not trustworthy on any matter, because of who he is."

The third method, "case data" impeachment, involves the establishment of facts that make the witness less reliable, although only within the context of the case in arbitration. The witness might have a financial interest in the outcome of the case, or might be prejudiced against one of the parties. In other words, this examination says, "Give less weight to the witness because of her relationship to the case."

Impeachment generally begins and ends during cross-examination. When a witness concedes the existence of the impeaching information, nothing further needs be done, and the cross-examiner may go on to other matters. If, however, the witness denies the truth of the impeaching matter, the cross-examiner may be required to perfect or complete the impeachment by offering extrinsic evidence, or evidence that is adduced through the testimony of someone other than the subject of impeachment. This can occur whether the original impeachment was based upon prior inconsistency, character, or case data.

3.9.1   Role of impeachment.

Impeachment is a powerful tool. Unlike "standard" cross-examination, which may rely on unspoken premises and subtle misdirection, there can be no mistaking or hiding the intended impact of impeachment. All three kinds of impeachment are inherently confrontational. They challenge the witness's believability, perhaps even his veracity. Effective advocates use the techniques of impeachment sparingly, both to preserve the potency of the method and to avoid crying wolf over unimportant details.

Only on significant matters. Effective advocates never impeach witnesses on irrelevant, trivial, or petty inconsistencies. The process of impeachment, particularly through the use of prior inconsistency, is generally so confrontational that there is a great risk of the advocate's creating an annoying dissonance between expectation and reward. If the "punch line" fails to justify the build-up, the result can alienate the arbitrator, can be embarrassing to the advocate, and can significantly damage the advocate's case.

Only on true inconsistencies. The purpose of impeachment through the use of a prior inconsistency is to show that the witness has made contradictory statements. The technique works only when the two statements cannot both be true. If the two statements can be harmonized, explained, or rationalized, the impeachment will fail.

Only when success is likely. Failed impeachment can be disastrous. An advocate who begins an assault that cannot be completed will look ineffective at best and foolishly overbearing at worst.

Favorable information. Impeachment is not like mountain climbing. It should not be undertaken simply because it is there. The purpose of impeachment is to cast doubt on the credibility of some or all of a witness's testimony. There is nothing to be gained from casting doubt on testimony that was helpful to an advocate's own case. Thus, if an opposing witness has given an inconsistent statement, an effective advocate would not use it to impeach favorable hearing testimony.

The "Rule of Completeness." The "Rule of Completeness" provides that once a witness has been impeached from a prior inconsistent statement, the opposing advocate may request the immediate reading of additional, explanatory portions of the same statement. Under the Federal Rules of Evidence, for example, the adverse party may introduce any other part of the statement "which ought in fairness to be considered contemporaneously with it." Thus, even a true gem of an impeaching statement may be immediately undercut if some other part of the impeaching document explains or negates the apparent contradiction.

Refreshing the witness's recollection. Not every gap or variation in a witness's testimony is the result of an intentional change. Witnesses often become confused or forgetful. A witness may have testified inconsistently with her prior statements quite innocently or inadvertently. In these circumstances, it will often be possible for an advocate to use the prior statement to refresh the witness's recollection, rather than to impeach his credibility. The technique for refreshing recollection is the same on cross-examination as it is on direct. Many arbitrators, however, will allow a cross-examiner to refresh a witness's recollection without first being required to establish that the witness's memory has been exhausted.

Evidentiary Considerations. Prior inconsistent statements that were given under oath are admissible as substantive evidence; they can be used to prove the truth of the original statement. Prior inconsistent statements that were not given under oath are generally admissible for the limited purpose of impeachment; they can be used only to reflect on the credibility of the witness.

3.9.2   Prior inconsistent statements.

Prior inconsistent statements damage a witness's credibility because they demonstrate that the witness has changed his story. Depending upon the nature and seriousness of the change, the witness may be shown to be evasive, opportunistic, error-prone, or even lying. To accomplish any of these goals, of course, it is necessary that the prior statement be clearly inconsistent with the current testimony, and that it be directed to a subject of true significance to the case. Semi-inconsistencies concerning tangential matters will have little or no impact.

There are three steps necessary to impeach a witness with a prior inconsistent statement: (1) recommit; (2) validate; and (3) confront. Each of the three steps will be treated in detail below.

Recommit the witness. The first step a cross examiner must take in impeaching a witness with a prior inconsistent statement is to recommit the witness to his current testimony:

> QUESTION: Mr. Kaye, you testified on direct examination
> that the light was green for the southbound
> traffic, correct?

This is an example of the traditional way to recommit the witness. The purpose of recommitting the witness is to underscore the gulf between the current testimony and the prior statement. There is no evidentiary requirement that the witness be allowed to repeat the direct testimony. On the other hand, it is difficult to imagine how the two statements could be effectively contrasted without restating the testimony that is about to be impeached.

There is an elegant alternative to the traditional approach to recommitting the witness by rephrasing the direct examination in language that is beneficial to the cross-examiner's own case. There is no strict rule of evidence that requires a cross-examiner to repeat verbatim the witness's about-to-be-impeached testimony. The purpose of recommitment is only to focus attention on the inconsistency between the hearing testimony and the prior statement. It is therefore possible to recommit the witness to the content of the current testimony without repeating it word for word. The content, in turn, can be phrased in a virtually unlimited number of ways. Consider the simple traffic light example above. The witness testified on direct examination that the light was green for the southbound traffic, but his statement to the police was just the opposite. It is the cross-examiner's theory that the light was red for the southbound traffic. Rather than repeat the direct testimony, the cross-examiner can recommit the witness as follows:

QUESTION: Mr. Kaye, the light was red for the southbound traffic, correct?

ANSWER: No, that is not true.

QUESTION: Mr. Kaye, I would like to show you the statement that you gave to Officer Berkeley.

The cross-examiner can now proceed to impeach the witness with his own prior statement. This format for recommittal avoids repetition of the direct testimony. It also allows the cross-examiner to describe his own case in affirmative language: "Wasn't the light red for the southbound traffic?" Since the cross-examiner's case rests on the proposition that the light was red for the southbound traffic, the cross-examiner can profit from stating that affirmative fact as often as possible.

Validate the prior statement. Once the witness has been recommitted, the next step the cross-examiner must take in the impeachment procedure is to validate the prior statement. The initial purpose of validation is to establish that the witness actually made the impeaching statement. Depending upon the circumstances of the case, further validation may be employed to accredit or demonstrate the accuracy of the earlier statement, as opposed to the witness's direct testimony.

The fact that a witness has made a prior inconsistent statement is impeaching, but it does not necessarily demonstrate that the witness's current testimony is false or inaccurate. After all, the earlier statement may have been erroneous and the direct testimony correct. It is therefore frequently advantageous to show that the first statement was made under circumstances that make it the more accurate of the two. Since the two statements are by definition mutually exclusive, there is a natural syllogism: if the earlier statement is true, then the current testimony must be wrong. Thus, the "accreditation" of the prior inconsistent statement can further detract from the witness's credibility. Of course, no witness is likely to admit that her pre-arbitration statement was more accurate than her sworn testimony. It is therefore usually necessary to accredit the prior statement through the use of circumstantial evidence. Many indicia of accuracy can be attributed to the witness's earlier statement, including importance, duty, and proximity in time.

Accreditation through importance. A witness's earlier statement can be accredited by showing that the witness had an important reason to be accurate when giving it.

Accreditation through duty. A prior statement can also be accredited by showing that the witness was under either a legal or business duty to be accurate. The most common example of a statement given under a legal duty is prior testimony, either at trial, arbitration, or deposition.

Accreditation through proximity in time. Because human memory inevitably fades, an earlier statement can be accredited because it was given closer in time to the events being described. This source of accreditation can be employed whether the impeaching material is a written statement, a deposition transcript, or a business document.

Confront the witness with the prior statement. The final stage of impeachment occurs when the cross-examiner confronts the witness with the prior statement. The purpose of this confrontation is to extract from the witness an admission that the earlier statement was indeed made; recall that it is the fact of the prior inconsistency that is admissible as impeachment. This confrontation need not be "confrontational." It is frequently sufficient merely for the cross-examiner to require the witness to admit making the impeaching statement, since most impeachment is based upon a witness's forgetfulness, confusion, or embellishment. An effective cross-examiner reserves hostility or accusation for those rare situations when the witness can be proven to be lying or acting out of some other ill motive. The effective confrontation must be accomplished in a clear and concise manner that leaves the witness no room for evasion or argument. The classic approach is for the cross-examiner to simply read the witness's own words. There are two cardinal rules that effective advocates apply in confronting a witness with a prior inconsistent statement: (1) they read the statement to the witness—they do not ask the witness herself to read the statement aloud; and (2) they do not ask the witness to explain the inconsistency.

Ethical concerns. Two primary ethical issues arise when an advocate impeaches a witness through the use of a prior inconsistent statement. The first issue occurs when the advocate attempts to use the statement for a purpose other than that for which it was admitted. It is unethical for a lawyer to "allude to any matter which the lawyer does not reasonably believe is . . . supported by admissible evidence."[8] Once an arbitrator has ruled that certain evidence is admissible only for a limited purpose, it is inadmissible on those issues for which it has been excluded. In light of a limiting instruction, no lawyer can reasonably believe otherwise. Thus, it is unethical for a lawyer to "allude" to a purely impeaching state-

---

8. Rule 3.4(e), ABA Model Rules of Professional Conduct.

ment as though it had been admitted as substantive evidence. The second ethical issue in impeachment involves the admonition not to allow a witness to explain the inconsistency. Assuming that there may be a perfectly reasonable explanation for the discrepancy between two statements, is it ethical to prevent the witness from explaining? The answer lies in the fact that it is not truly possible for a cross-examiner to prevent a witness from providing an explanation. It will always be possible for opposing counsel to ask the witness to elaborate during redirect examination. No admissible evidence can ultimately be excluded as the result of cross-examination tactics. Thus, the most that the cross-examiner can accomplish is to prevent the witness from explaining an inconsistency during cross-examination. As an advocate, it is the cross-examiner's task to present the evidence that is favorable to her client; the very purpose of redirect is to allow the other side to fill in gaps, remedy errors, and correct misperceptions. Thus, leaving potential explanations to redirect is perfectly permissible under the adversary system.

3.9.3   Other prior inconsistencies.

In addition to prior inconsistent statements, witnesses may also be impeached through the use of prior omissions or silence, as well as on the basis of prior inconsistent actions.

Impeachment by omission or silence. Impeachment by omission generally follows the same theory as impeachment with a prior inconsistent statement. The witness's current testimony is rendered less credible because when she told the same story earlier, it did not contain facts that she now claims are true. In essence, the impeachment is saying, "Do not believe this witness, because she is adding facts to her story." In other words, "If those things are true, why didn't you say them before?" To be impeachable, the witness's prior omission must be inconsistent with the current testimony. A prior omission is not impeaching, or even admissible, if it occurred in circumstances that do not render it incompatible with the witness's testimony at the hearing. Circumstances which create the necessary discontinuity between omission and testimony include opportunity, duty, and natural inclination.

Prior inconsistent actions. Finally, a witness may be impeached on the basis of prior inconsistent actions. The witness's current testimony is rendered less credible when the cross-examiner points out that she did not act in conformity with her own story on some previous occasion: "If what you are saying now is true, why did you act inconsistently in the past?" Unlike impeachment through prior inconsistent statements or omissions, no elaborate set-up is necessary for the use of prior inconsistent actions. It is sufficient for the cross-examiner simply to put the questions to the witness.

3.9.4 Character and "characteristic" impeachment.

Character impeachment refers to the cross-examiner's use of some inherent trait or particular characteristic of the witness, essentially unrelated to the case at hand, to render the testimony less credible. The thrust of the impeachment is to show that the witness, for some demonstrable reason, is simply not trustworthy. The most common forms of characteristic impeachment include conviction of a crime, past untruthfulness and other bad acts, and impaired perception or recollection.

Conviction of a crime. A witness may be impeached on the basis of his or her past conviction of certain crimes. While the specifics vary from state to state, under the Federal Rules of Evidence a conviction is admissible for impeachment only if the crime: (1) was punishable by death or imprisonment in excess of one year under the law under which the witness was convicted, and the arbitrator determines that the probative value of admitting this evidence outweighs its prejudicial effect to the defendant, or (2) involved dishonesty or a false statement, regardless of the punishment. In addition, Rule 609(b) of the Federal Rules of Evidence provides that convictions generally may not be used if they are more than ten years old, and that juvenile adjudications are inadmissible under most circumstances.

Past untruthfulness and other bad acts. We have discussed the rules governing impeachment on the basis of a criminal conviction. What if a witness's untruthfulness or bad acts were not the subject of a conviction? The Federal Rules of Evidence strike a balance by allowing the impeachment of witnesses on the basis of specific instances of past misconduct, apart from criminal convictions, only if they are probative of untruthfulness. Thus, a witness can be impeached with evidence that he has lied on a specific previous occasion, but not on the basis of previous violence. Moreover, an arbitrator maintains discretion to exclude evidence even of past untruthfulness. Finally, incidents of prior untruthfulness may not be proven by extrinsic evidence. The cross-examiner is stuck with the witness's answer. Impeachment on the basis of past untruthfulness is therefore a very tricky matter. The cross-examiner must be certain that the witness will "own up" to the charge, since they will be unable to prove it otherwise.

Impaired perception or recollection. A witness can also be impeached on the basis of an inability to perceive or recall events. Perception can be adversely affected by a wide variety of circumstances. The witness may have been distracted at the time of the events, or his vision may have been obscured. The witness may have been sleepy, frightened, or intoxicated. The witness may have poor eyesight, or may suffer from some other sensory deficit. Any of these, or similar, facts can be used to impeach the credibility of a witness's testimony. As with so much else in cross-examination, this form of impeachment is usually most effective when the cross-examiner refrains from asking the ultimate question.

3.9.5 "Case data" impeachment.

Some facts are impeaching only within the circumstances of a particular case. They would be innocuous, or perhaps even helpful, in any other context. The most common forms of case data impeachment are based on the witness's personal interest, motive, and bias or prejudice.

Personal interest. A witness who is personally interested in the outcome of a case may be inclined to testify with less than absolute candor. Whether consciously or subconsciously, it is a well-recognized human tendency to shape one's recollection in the direction of the desired outcome. Impeachment on the basis of personal interest is therefore geared to take advantage of this phenomenon, by pointing out just how the witness stands to gain or lose as a consequence of the resolution of the case. The cross-examiner may apply the technique to both party and non-party witnesses.

Motive. A witness's testimony may be affected by a motive other than financial interest. The witness may have a professional stake in the issues being litigated, or may have some other reason to prefer one outcome to another.

Bias or prejudice. Bias and prejudice generally refer to a witness's relationship to one of the parties. A witness may be well-disposed, or ill-inclined, toward either the plaintiff or the defendant. Sadly, some witnesses harbor prejudices against entire groups of people. Bias in favor of a party is often the consequence of friendship or affinity.

3.10 EXPERT TESTIMONY

Expert witnesses can be helpful in a wide variety of arbitration cases. They can be used in commercial cases to interpret complex financial data, in tort cases to explain the nature of injuries, and in legal or medical malpractice cases to establish the relevant standard of care. Given the extraordinarily broad scope of expert testimony, and its extreme potential for influencing the judgment of the trier of fact, certain rules have developed regarding its permissible use, extent, and nature.

3.10.1 Standards for expert testimony.

Areas of expertise. Rule 702 of the Federal Rules of Evidence provides that expert opinions are admissible where the expert's "scientific, technical, or other specialized knowledge will assist the arbitrator to understand the evidence or to determine a fact in issue." Thus, there are two threshold questions. Does the witness possess sufficient scientific, technical, or other specialized knowledge? And will that knowledge be helpful to the trier of fact?

Scope of opinion. Rule 704 of the Federal Rules of Evidence provides that expert testimony, if otherwise admissible, "is not objectionable because it embraces an ultimate issue to be decided by the trier of fact." Arbitrators vary on their interpretations of the "ultimate issue" rule. Some arbitrators will allow experts to opine on virtually any issue, including such case-breakers as whether the claimant in a personal injury case was contributorily negligent, or whether the respondent in a securities case violated exchange rules. Many arbitrators might also allow an expert in a medical malpractice case to testify that the failure to order the tests fell below the standard of care generally exercised by practitioners in the relevant community. However, most arbitrators would balk at permitting the expert to testify that the defendant's conduct constituted malpractice, on the theory that malpractice is a legal conclusion that is not within the specialized knowledge of a medical expert.

Bases for opinion. Under Rule 705 of the Federal Rules of Evidence, an expert can testify to her opinion with or without explaining the facts or data on which the opinion is based. In theory, then, an expert, once qualified, could simply state her opinion on direct examination, leaving the cross-examiner to search for its basis. In practice, of course, this approach is rarely followed, since the expert's opinion could hardly be persuasive until its foundation is explained. The practical effect of the rule is to allow the witness to state her opinion at the beginning of the examination, and follow with her explication, rather than having to set forth all of the data at the outset.

3.10.2 The expert's overview.

Just as a lawyer cannot succeed without developing a comprehensive theory of the case, neither will an expert be effective without a viable, articulated theory. An expert's theory is an overview or summary of the expert's entire position. The theory must not only state a conclusion, but must also explain, in commonsense terms, why the expert is correct. Why did she settle upon a certain methodology? Why did she review particular data? Why is her approach reliable? Why is the opposing expert wrong? In other words, the expert witness must tell a coherent story that provides the arbitrator with reasons for accepting, and, it is hoped, internalizing the expert's point of view.

The need for a theory is especially true in cases involving "dueling experts." It is common for each of the opposing parties in litigation to retain their own expert witnesses. The arbitrator is then faced with the task of sorting through the opinion testimony and choosing which witness to believe. It is likely that both experts will be amply qualified, and it is unlikely that either will make a glaring error in her analysis or commit an unpardonable faux pas in her testimony. The arbitrator will therefore be inclined to credit the expert whose theory is most believable.

The importance of theory extends to all types of expert testimony. It is generally considered necessary, but not sufficient, for an expert to be thorough, exacting, highly regarded, incisive, honorable, and well prepared. Her testimony will suffer if she cannot support her opinion with commonsense reasons.

3.10.3 Customary procedure for offering expert testimony.

There is a certain logic to the direct examination of most experts. While the particulars and details will vary, there are a limited number of possible patterns which advocates use in organizing the testimony. It is absolutely necessary, for example, that you require the advocate to qualify the expert before proceeding to her opinion. The following is a broad outline that can accommodate the specifics of most expert testimony.

Introduction and foreshadowing. The first step that the effective advocate takes is to introduce the expert and explain her involvement in the case. Since expert testimony is qualitatively different from lay testimony, the effective advocate clarifies its purposes so that you will understand what you are about to hear. The advocate will ask the witness how she came to be retained and why she is present at the arbitration. Technical requirements of presenting expert testimony often result in a considerable time gap between the introduction of the witness and the substantive high points of her testimony. Thus, it is customary for the advocate to foreshadow the expert's opinion at the very outset of the examination.

Qualification. To testify as an expert, a witness must be qualified by reason of knowledge, skill, experience, training, or education.[9] An expert's qualifications are a threshold question for the arbitrator, who must determine whether the witness is qualified before permitting her to give opinion testimony. The qualification of the witness, then, is a necessary predicate for all testimony to follow. The advocate must take care to qualify the expert in a manner that is technically adequate and persuasive.

- **Technical requirements.** The technical requirements for qualifying an expert witness are straightforward. It is usually adequate for the advocate to show that the witness possesses some specialized skill or knowledge, acquired through appropriate experience or education, and that the witness is able to apply that skill or knowledge in a manner relevant to the issues in the case. There are, of course, other areas of basic qualification beyond education and experience. Examples include specialized training, continuing education courses, teaching and lecturing positions, licenses and certifications, publications, consulting experience, professional memberships, awards, and other professional honors. The establishment of basic qualifications, however, should not be the advocate's entire objective. It is equally, if not more, important to qualify the witness as persuasively as possible.

---

9. Rule 702, Federal Rules of Evidence.

- **Persuasive qualification.** The technical qualification of an expert merely allows the witness to testify in the form of an opinion. The advocate's ultimate goal is to ensure that the opinion is accepted by you. Persuasive qualification is particularly important in cases involving competing experts, since their relative qualifications may be one basis on which you will decide which one to believe. It is a mistake, however, for an advocate to think that more qualifications are necessarily more persuasive. An endless repetition of degrees, publications, awards, and appointments may easily overload any arbitrator's ability, not to mention desire, to pay careful attention to the witness. It is often better for the advocate to introduce the witness's detailed resumé or curriculum vitae, and to use the qualification portion of the actual examination to focus in on several salient points. Experience is often more impressive than academic background. So, for example, a medical expert may be more impressive if she has actually practiced in the applicable specialty, as opposed to possessing knowledge that is strictly theoretical. When presenting such a witness, then, an effective advocate typically dwells on her experience, pointing out details such as the number of procedures she has performed, the hospitals where she is on staff, and the numbers of other physicians who have consulted her. Finally, an effective advocate emphasizes areas of qualification where she knows the opposing expert to be lacking. If her expert has a superior academic background, she will use the direct examination to point out why academic training is important. If her expert holds a certification that the opposing expert lacks, she will have the expert explain how difficult it is to become certified.

- **Tendering the expert witness.** It is customary that, once qualifications have been concluded, the advocate must tender the witness as an expert in a specified field. The purpose of the tender is to inform you that qualification has been completed, and to give opposing counsel an opportunity either to conduct a voir dire of the witness or to object to the tender. The opposing advocate may use voir dire examination to attempt to develop deficiencies in the witness's qualifications. This is done in the midst of the direct examination for two reasons. First, if it can be shown that the witness truly is not qualified, there will be no reason to continue the direct examination. Second, objections raised as a consequence of voir dire can often be cured through additional direct examination. Note that voir dire on qualifications, as with all voir dire examination, is usually limited to the eventual admissibility of the expert testimony and is not normally used as a substitute for cross-examination regarding weight or credibility.

Opinion and theory.

- **Statement of opinion.** Under Rule 705 of the Federal Rules of Evidence, once the witness has been qualified and accepted as an expert, she may proceed to express her opinion without additional foundation. In other words, she may state her conclusions without first detailing the nature or extent of her background work or investigation. Many advocates believe strongly in taking advantage of the "opinion first" provision. Expert testimony tends to be long, arcane, and boring. The intricate details of an expert's preparation are unlikely to be interesting, or even particularly understandable. They will be even less captivating if they are offered in a void, without any advance notice of where the details are leading or why they are being explained. On the other hand, a clear statement of the expert's conclusion can provide the arbitrators with a context for the balance of the explanatory testimony.

- **Statement of theory.** Once the expert's opinion has been stated, immediately provide the underlying theory. The theory should furnish the nexus between the expert's conclusion and the data used to support the conclusion. In other words, the examination should follow this pattern: (1) here is my opinion; (2) here are the principles that support my opinion; and (3) here is what I did to reach my final conclusion.

Explanation and support. Having stated and supported her theory choice, the expert can now detail the nature of her investigation and calculations. Arbitrators cannot be expected to take the expert at her word, so the validity and accuracy of her data and assumptions must be established.

- **Data.** The effective advocate will ask the expert how she chose and obtained her data. The expert will explain why her information is reliable. The advocate will also ask her to describe any tests or computations that she performed. The treatment of underlying data is one of the trickiest aspects of expert testimony. Many experts are in love with their data, and anxious to lay it out in excruciating detail. Unfortunately, most arbitrators have little tolerance for lengthy descriptions of enigmatic scientific or technical processes. Effective advocates usually try to strike a balance, eliciting a sufficiently detailed treatment of the data to persuade the arbitrator of its reliability, but stopping before his or her attention span is exhausted. It is not sufficient for the expert simply to relate the nature of the data. Rather, she should go on to explain how and why the data support her conclusions.

- **Assumptions.** Most experts rely upon assumptions. They do not necessarily explain or outline every hypothesis they use, but they usually note and support their more important assumptions.

- **Theory differentiation.** In cases involving dueling experts there will be competing theories. Properly prepared and presented, each expert will attempt to persuade you that her theory ought to be accepted. It is customary for an advocate to ask his expert to comment on the opposing expert's work. This technique is called theory differentiation. The timing of theory differentiation can be important. Claimant's counsel generally will want to establish her own theory, before proceeding to criticize the respondent's expert. Depending upon the circumstances of the case, claimant's counsel might even want to forego theory differentiation entirely during his case in chief, but recall his expert for that purpose on rebuttal. The respondent, on the other hand, should address the claimant's expert's theory at some point during the direct examination of the respondent's own expert. This is usually done early in the examination (in order to rebut the claimant's expert immediately and forcefully), or toward the end of the testimony (in order to allow the respondent's expert to build up the positive aspects of her own theory before turning her attention to the opposition).

- **Conclusion.** An expert's direct examination customarily ends with a powerful restatement of her most important conclusions.

3.10.4 Customary procedure for cross-examination of expert witnesses.

Most of the basic approaches to cross-examination discussed in Section 3.8 can also be adapted to expert testimony. Effective advocates may use additional techniques for cross-examining experts, as explained below.

Research, as much as technique, lies at the heart of expert witness cross-examination. Advocates cannot conduct an adequate cross-examination without first thoroughly investigating all of the technical aspects of the expected testimony. The type and extent of the research that the advocates conduct will vary from case to case. Apart from conducting careful research and applying the results in questioning, other procedures generally used when cross-examining experts are as follows:

Challenging the witness's credentials. An expert witness's credentials are subject to challenge either on voir dire or during cross-examination. Voir dire may be used to object to the legal sufficiency of the expert's qualifications, while cross-examination is the time to attack their weight.

- *Voir dire* **on credentials.** Once the proponent of an expert has concluded the qualification segment of the direct examination, the opposing advocate is entitled to conduct a voir dire of the witness. A voir dire examination temporarily suspends the direct so that the opponent of the proffered evidence can inquire as to its evidentiary sufficiency. With regard to the qualification of experts, this means that the opposing advocate can interrupt the direct examination in order to conduct a mini-cross limited to the issue of the witness's credentials. It is frequently an uphill battle to persuade an arbitrator that a proffered witness should not be allowed to testify as an expert. Arbitrators often respond to such objections by ruling that they go only to the weight, and not the admissibility, of the expert testimony. Nonetheless, it is possible for an advocate, through the use of voir dire, to create a sufficient basis for an arbitrator to disqualify an expert. Grounds for disqualifying purported experts include remoteness of their credentials, the inapplicability of their specialties, the lack of general acceptance of their purported expertise, or the unreliability of their data.

- **Cross-examination on credentials.** The arbitrator's ruling that a witness may testify as an expert means only that the witness possesses sufficient credentials to pass the evidentiary threshold. It still may be possible for the advocate to diminish the weight of the witness's qualifications during cross-examination. There are three basic methods by which advocates attempt to diminish the weight of the testimony of their opponent's experts:

Scope of the witness's expertise. Although a witness may be well-qualified in a certain area or sub-specialty, it may be possible for an advocate to recast the issues of the case in such a way as to place them beyond the witness's competence.

Missing credentials. An expert witness may be minimally qualified to testify, but still lack certain important certifications, degrees, or licenses.

Relative credentials. An effective advocate will point out an adverse witness's missing credentials when their absence can be contrasted with his own expert's superior qualifications. Experts' credentials can be contrasted on the bases of certification and other matters. It is fair game for an advocate to point out his own witness's greater or more specific experience, teaching, publication record, or any other disparity that will enhance his expert and diminish the opposition. All of the rules of basic cross-examination apply here as well. Contrary to the belief of many lawyers, judges, and arbitrators, it is not necessary for a cross-examiner to establish that the witness has relied on the particular treatise, or even that the witness acknowledge it as authoritative. Under the Federal Rules, the reliability of a learned treatise may be established either by admission of the witness, by other expert testimony, or by judicial notice. Once the reliability of the treatise is confirmed, the impeachment may proceed in one of two ways. The cross-examiner may read a passage from the treatise into evidence without asking the expert any questions about it; the

Federal Rules require only that the passage be called to the witness's attention. The more traditional approach is for the cross-examiner to ask the witness whether she agrees with the particular quotation. At that point the witness must either accede or disagree. If she accepts the statement, the advocate's job is done. If she disagrees, the advocate may argue later that she is out of step with recognized authority. This rule allows an excerpt from a learned treatise to be read into evidence, but the treatise itself may not be received as an exhibit.

Challenging the witness's impartiality. Expert witnesses are supposed to be independent analysts, not advocates. The worst thing that can be said about an expert witness is that she has altered her opinion to fit a party's needs. Accordingly, effective advocates often cross-examine an expert on the issue of bias, if the material is there to be exploited. Cross-examination on bias falls into three basic categories.

- **Fees.** In arbitration, effective advocates will usually cross-examine an expert concerning her fee, only in fairly limited circumstances. For example, an advocate may be able to demonstrate bias if the fee is extraordinarily large. Similarly, it may be evidence of something less than objectivity if the witness has a large unpaid fee outstanding at the time that she testifies.

- **Relationship with party or counsel.** An expert's relationship with a party or counsel may also indicate a lack of impartiality. Some witnesses seem to work hand in glove with certain law firms, testifying to similar conclusions in case after case. While such an ongoing relationship is not proof of bias, it does suggest that the association may have been sustained for a reason. It can become questionable when a firm has engaged the same expert on a dozen or more occasions. While there may be a perfectly innocent explanation for this constancy, it is certainly reasonable for an advocate to bring it out during cross-examination. The same analysis obtains to witnesses who have testified repeatedly for the same party, although retained by different law firms. Finally, some cases may involve testimony by in-house experts, perhaps a company's own accountant or engineer. In most cases, such experts are susceptible to no more suggestion of bias than would be any other employee. In some situations, however, the in-house expert's judgment will be at issue in the case. An accountant, for example, may have failed to see that a debt was under-collateralized; an engineer may not have foreseen the need for more exacting tolerances. In these circumstances the cross-examination will most likely bring out the witness's personal stake in the outcome of the litigation.

- **Positional bias.** With or without regard to past retention, some experts seem wedded to certain professional, scientific, or intellectual positions.

Experts frequently will only testify for plaintiffs or only for defendants. Others reach only one range of conclusions. Some psychiatrists, for example, have been known never to find criminal defendants to be sane or competent. Where they exist, these rigidly held positional biases can be exploited effectively on cross-examination.

Pointing out omissions. Effective advocates know that an expert may be vulnerable on cross-examination if she has failed to conduct essential tests or procedures, or if she has neglected to consider all significant factors. The question of neglected tests or experiments will depend upon the unique factors of each case. Other sorts of omissions are more commonplace. Witnesses are frequently asked to give evaluations concerning the validity or accuracy of other experts' work. A consulting pathologist, for example, might be asked to re-evaluate the protocol of an autopsy conducted by the local medical examiner. No matter how prominent, a "second-opinion" witness can almost always be undermined by the fact that she did not conduct the primary investigation.

Substituting information.

• **Changed assumptions.** Almost all experts must use assumptions of one sort or another in the course of formulating their opinions. An expert's assumptions, however, might be unrealistic, unreliable, or unreasonably favorable to the retaining party. Effective advocates, therefore, sometimes ask the expert witness to alter an assumption, substituting one that the advocate believes to be more in keeping with the evidence in the case.

• **Varying the facts.** A related technique is for the advocate to vary the facts upon which the expert has relied, or to suggest additional facts.

• **Degree of certainty.** It is also possible for the advocate to challenge an expert's degree of certainty by suggesting alternative scenarios or explanations.

• **Dependence on other testimony.** The opinion of an expert witness often depends upon facts to be established by other witnesses. Thus, the expert's testimony may be undermined, not by anything an advocate asks the expert directly, but rather by challenging its factual underpinnings during the cross-examination of the fact witnesses. The effective advocate accomplishes this by obtaining the expert's concession that the other witness's facts are essential to her opinion.

Challenging technique or theory. The most difficult form of expert cross-examination occurs when the cross-examiner challenges the witness's method, theory, or logic. It is possible, but extremely unlikely, that an expert will admit she made a mistake or that her reasoning was faulty. In most cases an advocate will have little to gain by confronting an expert with any but the most glaring flaws, since that will only afford her an opportunity to explain. It is usually far more effective for an advocate to use his own expert to point out the opposition's errors, and then to draw his own conclusions during closing argument.

3.10.5 Ethics of expert examination.

Fees. Unlike other witnesses who can be reimbursed only for expenses, an expert may be paid a fee for preparing and testifying in an arbitration.[10] There is authority that an expert's fee must be "reasonable," but that limit has never been well defined. In any event, an unreasonably large fee would render the witness extremely vulnerable on cross-examination. A more salient restriction, found in virtually every jurisdiction, is the rule against paying contingent fees to expert witnesses. Contingent fees are prohibited because they provide the expert with an unacceptable incentive to tailor her opinion to the interests of the party retaining her.

Influencing testimony. Lawyers typically retain experts for one reason only: to help win the case. Given the expense involved, there may be a temptation to view the expert as simply another member of the team, who can be enlisted to provide whatever advocacy is necessary. Thus, it is not unheard of for attorneys to attempt to persuade experts to alter the content of their opinions. This is wrong. It is no more acceptable to attempt to persuade an expert to change her opinion than it would be to try to convince a percipient witness to change his account of the facts. The entire system of expert testimony rests upon the assumption that experts are independent of the retaining attorneys. Counsel must take care not to attempt or appear to use the fee relationship to corrupt the expert's autonomy.[11] As with other witnesses, however, it is not unethical in U.S. arbitration practice for counsel to assist an expert in preparing for trial. Counsel may inform the witness of the questions to be asked on direct examination, and may alert the witness to potential cross-examination. An expert may be advised to use powerful language, to avoid jargon, to use analogies, to refrain from long narratives, or to use other means that will help her convey her opinion accurately.

Disclosure and discovery. In arbitration, where discovery is usually the exception and not the rule, testifying experts are generally subject to discovery. Purely consulting experts, other than in extreme circumstances, are usually exempt from discovery. The question that arises is whether it is ethical for a lawyer to attempt to interview an opposing party's consulting witness, from whom formal discovery is not available. Needless to say, counsel must take care to determine the relevant jurisdiction's law on this issue—or better yet, obtain the arbitrator's permission—before attempting to interview the opposition's non-testifying expert.

---

10. Rule 3.4(b) comment 3, ABA Model Rules of Professional Conduct.
11. Rule 3.4(b), ABA Model Rules of Professional Conduct.

3.11 FOUNDATIONS FOR EVIDENCE

Before any evidence can be considered in a court trial, there must be some basis for believing it to be relevant and admissible. This basis is called the foundation for the evidence. In an arbitration hearing in which the parties have agreed that rules of evidence do not apply, the requirement for foundations is relaxed. But in hearings where a piece of evidence is critical to the case, the arbitrator will usually require counsel to lay a proper foundation. Where the arbitration agreement or the rules of a court mandatory arbitration program require the application of the rules of evidence, you will be required to ensure that the advocates comply with them and lay appropriate foundations for the evidence they wish to introduce. This section will prepare you for situations where you must make rulings as to whether evidentiary foundations, whether required or simply well-advised, have been properly laid.

3.11.1 Evidentiary foundations—general.

Components of foundation. There are three aspects to virtually all evidentiary foundations. To be received, evidence must be shown to be (1) relevant, (2) authentic, and (3) admissible under the applicable laws of evidence. While the discrete elements of foundation will differ according to the nature of the evidence and the purpose for which it is offered, these three considerations must always apply.

- **Relevance.** Relevance defines the relationship between the proffered evidence and some fact that is at issue in the case. Evidence should not be admitted simply because it is interesting or imaginative. Rather, it must be shown to be probative in the sense that it makes some disputed fact either more or less likely. The relevance of most evidence is generally made apparent from the context of the case, but occasionally it must be demonstrated by the establishment of foundational facts.

- **Authenticity.** The concept of authenticity refers to the requirement of proof that the evidence actually is what the proponent claims it to be. In other words, evidence is not to be admitted until there has been a threshold showing that it is "the real thing." The arbitrator decides whether an item of evidence has been sufficiently authenticated, and the criteria vary according to the nature of the evidence involved. The requirement of authenticity is not limited to tangible objects. It also applies to certain testimonial evidence. For example, a witness generally may not testify to a telephone conversation without first establishing her basis for recognizing the voice of the person on the other end of the line. That is, the identity of the other speaker must be authenticated.

- **Specific admissibility.** While evidence should generally be received if it is relevant and authentic, the law of evidence contains a host of specific provisions that govern the admissibility of various sorts of proof. In many cases evidence can be admitted only following the establishment of foundational facts. Most exceptions to the hearsay rule, for example, require such a preliminary showing. Similarly, a foundation must be laid for the admission of evidence of habit or routine practice, or for the admission of evidence of subsequent remedial measures.

Establishing Foundations.

- **Single or multiple witnesses.** The effective advocate's most common approach to the establishment of a foundation is simply to call a witness who can provide the necessary facts, and then to offer the evidence after that testimony has been elicited. Some foundations cannot be laid by a single witness. In such cases, the advocate must establish each part of the foundation from each of several witnesses before offering the evidence.

- **Conditional admissibility.** It is not always possible for the advocate to complete a foundation during the testimony of a single witness. However, a witness who is responsible for part of the foundation will in many cases have other important information concerning the exhibit. Rule 104(b) of the Federal Rules of Evidence embodies the doctrine of conditional admissibility, which allows the temporary or conditional admission of evidence based upon counsel's representation that the foundation will be completed through the testimony of a subsequent witness.

- **Using adverse witnesses.** Potentially complex foundations can often be simplified through the advocate's use of adverse examination. In a case where executed contracts have been exchanged through the mail, for example, it may be extremely difficult for one party to authenticate the other party's signature. This problem can be completely alleviated, however, simply by calling the opposing party as an adverse witness.

- **Cross-examination.** Foundation requirements apply equally during cross and direct examinations. Testimonial foundations must be laid on cross-examination for personal knowledge, voice identification, hearsay exceptions, and in every other circumstance where a foundation would be necessary on direct examination. In addition, there are special foundations for certain cross-examination techniques, such as impeachment by past omission or prior inconsistent statement. It is also often necessary for an advocate to use cross-examination to lay the foundation for the admission of exhibits. Respondent's counsel in particular can avoid calling adverse witnesses by attempting to establish foundations for her own exhibits while cross-examining a claimant's witness.

3.11.2 Customary foundations for testimonial evidence.

Personal knowledge. Witnesses are expected to testify from personal knowledge. The most common sort of personal knowledge is direct sensory perception: information gained through sight, hearing, touch, taste, and smell. Witnesses may also have personal knowledge of more subjective information, such as their own intentions or emotions, or the reputation of another person.

Special foundations for certain testimonial evidence. While most testimony requires a showing of personal knowledge, certain testimony calls for the establishment of additional foundational facts.

- **Conversations.** Witnesses are often called upon to testify to conversations between two or more parties. In order to authenticate the conversation, and thereby allow opposing counsel to conduct a meaningful cross-examination, effective advocates lay a foundation establishing the date, time, and place of the conversation, as well as the persons present at the time.

- **Telephone conversations and voice identification.** The foundation for a telephone conversation includes the additional element of voice identification, or a reasonable circumstantial substitute. In the absence of a basis for voice identification, circumstantial evidence can be used as the foundation for a telephone conversation. A telephone call placed by the witness can be authenticated by showing that the call was made to a listed number. Numerous other circumstances can be used to authenticate telephone conversations. For example, subsequent verifying events can form the foundation for telephone calls either placed or received by the witness.

- **Prior identification.** Under Rule 801(d)(1)(C) of the Federal Rules of Evidence, a witness may testify to his or her previous, out-of-court identification of an individual. This rule applies to both criminal and civil matters. The foundation for this testimony is that the out-of-court identification was made by the witness after perceiving the person identified.

- **Habit and routine.** To lay the foundation for evidence of habit or routine practice, the advocate must call a witness with personal knowledge of the regular conduct of the person or organization involved. Furthermore, the advocate must establish that the asserted conduct was, in fact, of a consistently repeated nature. This can be accomplished through proof of either extended observation or of the existence of a formal policy or procedure.

Individual habit. The most common foundation for an individual's habit is through evidence of a pattern of conduct repeated over a substantial period of time. The alleged habit must be clearly differentiated from independent or distinct activities.

Business practice. The routine practice of a business or organization may be established either through direct observation or through evidence of an existing policy or practice.

Foundations for hearsay statements. The rule against hearsay excludes evidence of out-of-court statements if offered to prove the truth of the matter asserted.[12] Numerous exceptions to the hearsay rule allow for the admissibility of out-of-court statements, provided that the necessary foundation is established. The foundations for exceptions that apply primarily to testimonial evidence are discussed below. Foundations for hearsay exceptions typically applying to documentary evidence are discussed in a later section. The following sub-sections are intended only as an abbreviated outline of foundations for the various hearsay exceptions for arbitrations in which the hearsay rule applies.

- **Party admissions.** Out-of-court statements made by the opposing party are generally admissible to prove the truth of the matter asserted. In brief, the previous statements of the opposing party are admissible if: (1) the witness can authenticate the statement, (2) the statement was made by the party against whom it is offered, and (3) the statement is adverse to the opposing party's claim or defense. The party admission exception also applies to statements made by the agent or employee of a party.[13] In such situations there are two additional elements to the foundation: (1) the declarant was an agent or employee of the opposing party at the time that the statement was made, and (2) the statement concerned a matter that was within the scope of the agency or employment.

- **Present sense impression.** The present sense impression exception allows the admission of out-of-court statements "describing or explaining an event or condition made while the declarant was perceiving the event or condition, or immediately thereafter."[14] The foundation for the exception is that (1) the declarant perceived an event; (2) the declarant described the event; and (3) the description was given while the event occurred, or immediately afterwards. A witness may testify as to her own present sense impression statement or that of another. It is generally necessary for the statement to have been

---

12. Rule 801, Federal Rules of Evidence.
13. Rule 801(d)(2)(D), Federal Rules of Evidence.
14. Rule 803(1), Federal Rules of Evidence.

made in the witness's presence, in order to satisfy the foundational requirement of personal knowledge.

- **Excited utterance.** The excited utterance exception is quite similar to the present sense impression rule, allowing for the admission of hearsay when the statement relates "to a startling event or condition made while the declarant was under the stress of excitement caused by the event or condition."[15] The foundation for an excited utterance is that (1) the declarant perceived a startling event or experienced a stressful condition; (2) the declarant made a statement concerning the event or condition; and (3) the statement was made while the declarant was under the stress of the event or condition. As with present sense impressions, a witness may testify to her own excited utterance or to that of another.

- **State of mind.** "State of mind" provides one of the broadest exceptions to the hearsay rule, as it allows the admission of statements concerning the declarant's "then existing state of mind, emotion, sensation, or physical condition" (such as intent, plan, motive, design, mental feeling, pain, and bodily health).[16] The foundation for this exception is that the statement actually be probative of the declarant's mental, emotional, or physical condition. This can best be demonstrated by the content of the statement itself. Apart from the content of the statement, there is no special foundation for the state of mind exception. However, the witness still must establish the authenticity of the statement by testifying as to (1) when the statement was made, (2) where it was made, (3) who was present, and (4) what was said. Note also that the statement must have been made during the existence of the mental, emotional, or physical condition that it describes.

- **Statement made for medical treatment.** The foundation for this exception is that the declarant made a statement for the purpose of obtaining medical care or diagnosis. The statement may be made to a physician, medical worker, or other person, so long as its purpose was to obtain or facilitate treatment. The statement may include medical history or past symptoms, but it must relate to a present bodily condition.[17]

- **Dying declaration.** The hearsay exception for dying declarations requires the following foundation: (1) the declarant made a statement while believing that his or her death was imminent, and (2) the statement concerned what he or she believed to be the cause of death.[18]

---

15. Rule 803(2), Federal Rules of Evidence.
16. Rule 803(3), Federal Rules of Evidence.
17. Rule 803(4), Federal Rules of Evidence.
18. Rule 804(b)(2), Federal Rules of Evidence.

3.11.3 Customary foundations for documents.

In addition to the usual issues of relevance and authenticity, the foundation for a document usually includes two other elements. Because documents invariably contain out-of-court statements, they must be brought within an exception or exclusion to the hearsay rule. Additionally, the proffer must comply with the "best evidence" or "original writing" rule.

Authentication. The authentication of documents typically requires proof of authorship or origin, and may also call for proof of transmission or receipt.

- **Handwriting and signature.** The signature or other handwriting on a document can be authenticated through a variety of means. A witness may recognize a signature based on past observation or may authenticate it on the basis of circumstantial evidence. Other possibilities include expert testimony and in-arbitration comparison by the arbitrator. A witness may always authenticate her own handwriting or signature. A witness may also authenticate the handwriting of another, if sufficient familiarity can be shown.

- **Circumstantial evidence of authorship or origin.** Many documents are printed or typewritten, and do not contain signatures or other handwriting. Unless such a document is uniquely marked, it will need to be authenticated via circumstantial evidence. Such evidence can be in the form of a letterhead, seal, stamp, or can be provided by the context of the case.

- **Mailing or transmission.** The admissibility of a document will often depend upon its receipt by, or at least transmission to, another party. This is an authenticity issue, since the document is made admissible only by its status as one that was actually or constructively *received*. In other words, proof of mailing authenticates the document as truly having been sent to the other party. Mailing can be proven either directly or through evidence of a routine business practice. Direct proof of mailing can be given in a single sentence: "I placed the document in an envelope, with the correct address, and I deposited it in the United States mail with sufficient postage."

The original writing ("best evidence") rule. The so-called "best evidence" rule was once a formidable obstacle to the admission of documentary evidence. In its harshest form, the rule excluded all but the original copy of any writing, unless certain conditions could be met. Today, the rule has been softened considerably, and now allows for the easy admissibility of most copies.[19] The rule constitutes an authenticity requirement, but its terms are sufficiently unique so as to call for separate treatment. The essence of the "original writing" rule is that the content of a document can be proved only by producing the original, or an

---

19. Rule 1002, Federal Rules of Evidence.

acceptable duplicate, unless the original is lost, destroyed, or unavailable. Under most circumstances today, a duplicate is admissible on the same terms as the original, so the rule now operates primarily to exclude testimonial summaries or paraphrases of a document. Note also that the original writing rule applies only to proof of a document's content, not its signing, acknowledgment, or delivery.

Foundations for hearsay exceptions. The offer of a document inevitably sets the hearsay bell ringing in opposing counsel's mind. While writings may be admissible for non-hearsay purposes, such as proof of notice or acceptance, they are frequently submitted precisely to prove that their contents are true. Various exceptions are available to allow the use of such documents, each requiring its own foundation. The more common exceptions are discussed in the following sections.

- **Business records.** Business records can include ledgers, accounts, calendar entries, memoranda, notices, reports, statements, and similar writings. All such documents constitute hearsay if they are offered to prove that their contents are true. Under the Federal Rules, the records of any regularly conducted activity are admissible if they (1) were made at or near the time of a transaction or event; (2) were made by, or based on information transmitted from, a person with knowledge; (3) were kept in the course of a regularly conducted business activity; and (4) were made as a part of the regular practice of that business activity.[20]

- **Computer print-outs.** Computer-generated print-outs have become a common form of business record. In the early days of computing it was considered necessary to prove that computer data entry and retrieval systems were reliable means for storing information, but this is no longer the case. The Federal Rules specifically recognize "data compilations" as an acceptable form of business record. Thus, the foundation for a computer print-out is basically the same as that for any other business record.

- **Summaries.** Many business records or other sets of data are so lengthy and ponderous that they cannot be conveniently produced in an arbitration hearing. Even if they could be produced, they may be so extensive and technical as to be impenetrable. In these circumstances it is permissible for advocates to substitute a "chart, summary, or calculation" that fairly presents the relevant information in a usable or understandable form.[21] The foundation for such a summary includes these elements: (1) the original documents are so voluminous that they cannot be conveniently examined in the arbitration

---

20. Rule 803(6), Federal Rules of Evidence.
21. Rule 1006, Federal Rules of Evidence.

hearing; (2) the witness has examined the original data; (3) the witness is qualified to produce a summary of the information; and (4) the exhibit is a fair and accurate summary of the underlying information.

- **Recorded recollection.** A witness's written notes, or other recorded recollection, may be admitted into evidence only if the witness "has insufficient recollection to enable him to testify fully and accurately at the time of trial."[22] The foundation for this exception to the hearsay rule comprises these elements: (1) the witness once had personal knowledge of the relevant facts or events; (2) the witness cannot currently recall the events fully and accurately; (3) the witness previously made an accurate memorandum or record of the facts; and (4) the memorandum or record was made at a time when the events were fresh in his or her memory.

- **Public records.** There are a number of hearsay exceptions that allow for the admissibility of public records, statistics, and reports. Such records are generally admissible if they were made by a public office or agency, and they set forth (1) the activities of the office or agency; or (2) matters observed pursuant to a duty imposed by law; or (3) in limited circumstances, certain investigative findings; or (4) officially required records of vital statistics.[23] Because most government records are "self-authenticating," it is not usually necessary for an advocate to call a witness to testify to their authenticity.[24]

- **Absence of public record.** Public records may also be used to show the non-occurrence of events. The foundation for this evidence is (1) that such events, occurrences, or matters were regularly recorded in some form; (2) that they were recorded by a public office or agency; and (3) that a diligent search has failed to disclose a record of a particular fact or event. This evidence may be offered by certification from the appropriate official, in which case no witness needs to be called. The evidence may also be offered via testimony.

- **Previous testimony.** The transcript of a person's previous testimony may be admitted into evidence if (1) the declarant is currently "unavailable" to testify; (2) the testimony was given under oath in court or at a deposition; and (3) the party against whom the testimony is being offered had a fair opportunity to examine the witness when the testimony was originally given.[25] Note that this exception allows the admission of the earlier statement as a substitute for current testimony. Unlike the use of prior testimony for impeachment,

---

22. Rule 803(5), Federal Rules of Evidence.
23. Rules 803(8) and 803(9), Federal Rules of Evidence.
24. Rule 902, Federal Rules of Evidence.
25. Rule 804(b)(1), Federal Rules of Evidence.

there is no requirement that the previous testimony be inconsistent with the declarant's current position. Under the Federal Rule, a witness can be deemed "unavailable" for a variety of reasons, including: (1) the valid assertion of a privilege; (2) persistent refusal to testify; (3) inability to attend the hearing due to illness; (4) death; (5) failure of memory; or (6) absence from the hearing notwithstanding the efforts of the proponent of the testimony to procure attendance.

- **Party admissions.** The party admission exception applies to documents as well as to oral statements. A party admission can be contained in a letter, report, memorandum, journal, progress chart, or virtually any other form of writing. Once the exhibit has been authenticated, the only remaining foundation is that it was made or adopted by a party against whom it is being offered, or by an agent, servant, or employee of such a party.

3.11.4 Customary foundations for real and demonstrative evidence.

Real evidence/tangible objects. Real evidence must be shown to be relevant and authentic. The relevance of real evidence is typically established by the context of the case, and often requires no additional attention when it comes to laying the foundation. Advocates must carefully establish authenticity, as it is the fact of authenticity that qualifies the exhibit as real evidence. In many cases the authenticity of real evidence can be shown by a witness's recognition of the exhibit. Other cases require a more detailed and complex foundation, usually referred to as chain of custody.

- **Recognition of the exhibit.** The authenticity of real evidence can be established through the testimony of a witness who is able to recognize the item in question. Many objects can be identified by virtue of their unique features. Others may have been given some identifying mark in anticipation of litigation. In either case, the witness must testify (1) that she was familiar with the object at the time of the underlying events, and (2) that she is able to recognize the exhibit in the arbitration hearing as that very same object.

- **Chain of custody.** A chain of custody establishes the location, handling, and care of an object between the time of its recovery and the time of trial. A chain of custody must be shown whenever (1) the exhibit is not uniquely recognizable and has not been marked, or (2) when the exhibit's physical properties are in issue.

Photography and other recording devices. Photographs and other recordings bridge the gap between real and demonstrative evidence. While a visual or audio recording of any sort is, strictly speaking, an illustration of a past event, its capacity to portray a scene with accuracy is so great that many arbitrators treat photographs and other recordings as tantamount to real evidence.

- **Still photographs.** The basic foundation for the admission of a still photograph is that it "fairly and accurately" portrays the scene shown. In all but a few situations it is not necessary to call the photographer to testify. It is generally possible to introduce a photograph through the testimony of any witness familiar with the scene as it appeared at a relevant time.

- **Motion pictures and videotapes.** As with photographs, a motion picture or videotape may be authenticated by any witness familiar with the scene or scenes portrayed. It is necessary to call the operator of the camera only if special features were employed, or if the date of the filming is in issue. A more difficult problem arises in the case of remote taping, when no person actually observed the events as they were recorded. In these circumstances the foundation must include additional information on operating procedures, as well as the condition of the equipment.

- **Audiotapes.** The foundation for an audiotape recording depends upon the purpose for which it is offered. A tape recording that is submitted merely as a voice exemplar, for example, may be authenticated by any witness who is able to recognize the voices of the various speakers. The same holds true for recorded music, as might be offered in a copyright dispute. The foundation can be laid by any witness familiar with the material recorded.

- **X rays and similar images.** X rays and images produced by such means as computerized axial tomography (CAT scans) and magnetic resonance imaging (MRIs), are essentially photographs of the body's internal composition. To lay a foundation a physician or other qualified person must testify that an x ray, CAT scan, or MRI is a fair representation of the internal structure of a given patient's body. The identifying marks on the film (which allow the physician to recognize which x ray belongs to which patient) are usually considered to be business records of the hospital or clinic.

Demonstrative evidence. Demonstrative evidence is used to illustrate, clarify, or explain other testimony or real evidence. When such an exhibit is sufficiently accurate or probative, it may be admitted into evidence.

- **Admissible demonstrative evidence.** The foundation for a map, chart, blueprint, or other diagram is essentially the same as that for a photograph. The witness must be familiar with the scene, location, or structure as it appeared at a relevant time, and must testify that the exhibit constitutes a fair representation. Additional foundation is necessary if the exhibit is drawn to scale.

- **Models and reproductions.** The foundation for a model or reproduction is also similar to that for a photograph. The witness must be familiar with the real location or object, and must testify to the model's accuracy. Issues regarding scale are identical to those concerning maps and diagrams.

- **Illustrative aids.** Exhibits that are insufficiently accurate to be allowed into evidence may often still be used for illustrative purposes. The foundation includes a witness's testimony that the exhibit will assist in explaining her testimony, as well as a general explanation or description of the inaccuracy.

3.12 HEARING EXHIBITS

In a trial held in court, the advocate is constantly concerned with preserving the record for appeal. The advocate must ensure that the record is complete, accurate, and that all appeal issues have been preserved in the record by rulings on appropriate motions or objections. In an arbitration, the advocate is not usually concerned with preserving the record for appeal. Rather, much like a sculptor, he or she is actively engaged in shaping the process toward a favorable decision by the arbitrator. Similarly, the arbitrator has a special interest to ensure that the record is as complete as possible, so that he or she will have a proper basis for rendering a fair decision for according appropriate relief to the parties. Thus, in an arbitration, the arbitrator and advocates are concerned with ensuring that all pertinent evidence is introduced and that the exhibits are properly used and handled.

3.12.1 Ensuring introduction of all pertinent evidence.

One would hardly think of maintaining a checking account at a bank without keeping a record or log of deposits and withdrawals. Such a record allows one to know the balance of the account (i.e. usable or available cash), what was deposited and when, what was withdrawn and when, what checks and deposits eventually cleared (i.e. actually admitted or acknowledged by the bank), and which were rejected for insufficient funds or other reasons. So too, one would hardly consider arbitrating a case, particularly one involving multiple documentary and other physical exhibits, without keeping a log or record of which exhibits were admitted (i.e. cleared), rejected (for insufficient foundation, irrelevancy, etc.), or offered and withdrawn.

During the course of an arbitration hearing, effective advocates keep an exhibit log for the exhibits that they seek to introduce into evidence. They also log the exhibits that the other party or parties seek to introduce. Normally the arbitrator, or one arbitrator on the panel, maintains similar logs. An example of an exhibit log format appears on the next page.

Date	Ex #	Dscrp	ID	Off	Off of Prf	Adm	Rul Resvd	Reason	Party Ad. Agn

There are several advantages which flow from arbitrators' use of exhibit logs during an arbitration. In arbitrations involving the use of many exhibits, having several parties, and/or lasting over the period of several days, an exhibit log of the type shown above assists in determining what evidence the advocates may properly refer to in closing arguments. Evidence not admitted cannot be the basis of any assertion in closing argument. Thus, a quick reference to the exhibit log can give you an instant picture of the parameters governing the scope of an advocate's argument. Such a log will also assist you in ruling on objections that the evidence being argued (or later in connection with post-hearing motions) was not admitted into evidence (or was withdrawn, as the case may be). Similarly, the exhibit log can be of significant assistance as a reference source when you begin to refamiliarize yourself with the evidence in connection with reviewing post-hearing briefs, deciding the case, and drafting the award. In performing such a task, it may serve as your overview document indicating which piece of evidence was rejected, when it was rejected during the proceedings (pointing you to the appropriate date of transcript), and your reason for rejecting the evidence. In a multi-party case, the log will assist you in remembering which exhibits were admitted against which parties.

In addition to these post close-of-evidence uses of the exhibit log, there are several benefits which accrue to its users *during* the course of an arbitration hearing. The exhibit log can be reviewed prior to the close of each side's case and to the close of all the evidence, so you and the advocates can satisfy yourselves that all critical pieces of evidence have been offered and admitted (or that there is a record of rejection). Also, the exhibit log can be reviewed to ensure that all objections to an opponent's exhibits have been clearly and comprehensively presented. Sometimes additional reasons for an advocate's objection to certain evidence will become apparent to the advocate during the course of the hearing. In such an instance, an advocate may wish to have you reconsider your previous ruling in light of the additional basis for objections. Normally, you should accommodate an advocate in this regard, particularly with respect to a critical piece of evidence whose admissibility is in dispute.

Occasionally, you will reserve ruling on the admissibility of certain exhibits, pending additional evidence "connecting them up" and establishing their relevance or materiality. The exhibit log assists you by serving as a reminder to which exhibits require a ruling. Also, you may decide to reject certain evidence, but on request, permit counsel to make an offer of proof immediately or later during the course of proceedings. The exhibit log can remind you which exhibits need to be supported by an offer of proof prior to the close of the evidence.

In summary, keeping an exhibit log ensures that an accurate record of the hearing evidence is properly preserved for later use in connection with reserved evidentiary rulings, decision-making, and drafting the award.

3.12.2 Ensuring advocates' proper handling and use of exhibits.

The role of exhibits. Exhibits are the tangible objects, documents, photographs, video and audio tapes, and other items that are offered for your consideration. Exhibits are the only form, apart from the testimony of witnesses, in which evidence can be received. In an arbitration hearing, exhibits enhance or supplement the testimony of the witnesses. Exhibits can make information clearer, more concrete, more understandable, and more reliable. The sub-sections immediately following will discuss the general procedures for the handling, introduction, and use of exhibits.

Types of exhibits. While the categories tend to overlap, and the lines cannot be drawn with precision, it is often helpful to think of exhibits as falling into these three categories: (1) real evidence, (2) demonstrative evidence, and (3) documentary evidence.

- **Real evidence.** The term "real evidence" generally refers to tangible objects that played an actual role in the events at issue in the hearing. Photographs, while obviously different from tangible objects, are so close to reality that they are also often treated as real evidence. Documents, such as contracts, memoranda, letters, and other primary writings, can also be considered real evidence, although the special rules that apply to out-of-court writings generally make it more convenient to treat "documentary evidence" as a separate category.

- **Demonstrative evidence.** The term "demonstrative evidence" refers to exhibits that did not play an actual role in the events underlying the case, but that are used to illustrate or clarify a witness's testimony. As compared with real evidence—which exists by virtue of the activities of the parties and witnesses in the case—demonstrative evidence is lawyer-generated. Demonstrative evidence can take the form of models, graphs, diagrams, charts, drawings, or any other objects that can explain or illustrate issues in the case.

- **Documentary evidence.** "Documentary evidence" refers to virtually all writings, including letters, contracts, leases, memoranda, reports, and business records. Written documents, almost by definition, contain out-of-court statements, and they are typically offered because their contents are relevant to the case. Thus, most documents face hearsay hurdles in a way that real and demonstrative exhibits do not. Tangible objects are admitted into evidence because of what they *are;* documentary exhibits are admitted because of what they *say.* The value of documentary evidence cannot be overstated. Intrinsic writings can provide proof of past events in a way that mere testimony cannot.

Prehearing procedures for the admission of exhibits. In arbitration, you can deal with and rule upon contested exhibits in a preliminary hearing. Advocates may file motions *in limine* (Latin for "at the threshold") prior to the hearing to exclude evidence or to obtain a ruling declaring certain evidence admissible. You can rule on such motions in a preliminary hearing. Stipulations and requests to admit can also be worked out in such a hearing.

Offering exhibits during the hearing. Whether they consist of real, demonstrative, or documentary evidence, there is one basic protocol by which effective advocates offer hearing exhibits. Although the details vary somewhat from one arbitration setting to another, the following steps form a nearly universal procedure.

- **Mark the exhibit for identification.** An advocate marks each exhibit for identification *before* it is offered into evidence, or even referred to in the course of a hearing. Marking the exhibit identifies it for the record so that it will be uniquely recognizable to anyone who later reads a transcript of the proceedings. References to "this letter" or "the first broken fastener" may be understood in the hearing room, but they will be meaningless to a reader of the transcript. "Respondent's exhibit three," on the other hand, can mean only one thing, assuming that the exhibit was appropriately marked and identified. Exhibits are generally marked sequentially, and further identified according to the designation of the party who first offered them. Thus, the exhibits in a two-party arbitration will be called claimant's exhibit one, claimant's exhibit two, respondent's exhibit one, respondent's exhibit two, and so forth. In multiple-party hearings it is necessary to identify an exhibit by the name, and not merely the designation, of the party who offers it. Accordingly, you will see references to claimant Bennett exhibit one, or Weber exhibit two.

In some arbitrations, claimants may be expected to use sequential numbers for their exhibits, while respondents are requested to use letters. Hence, claimant's exhibit one and respondent's exhibit A. The details of the particular marking system are unimportant, so long as it produces a clear and understandable indication of which exhibit is which. The "mark" itself usually takes the form of a sticker placed directly on the object or document. Stickers are available in a variety of forms. Many advocates use color-coded sets that already contain the words plaintiff or defendant, with a space left blank for the number assigned to each exhibit. The procedure of requiring the court reporter to mark exhibits has been widely replaced by the attorneys' premarking of exhibits, either at a prehearing conference or in the attorney's office. The term "marked for identification" means that the exhibit has been marked and can be referred to in arbitration, but has not yet been admitted into evidence. Exhibits that have been marked for identification may be shown to witnesses and may be the subject of limited examinations for the purpose of establishing a foundation. Many arbitrators shun "for identification" notation as redundant. All exhibits need to be marked, and the record will show which have been allowed into evidence, even in the absence of a special inscription.

- **Identify the exhibit for opposing counsel.** Advocates identify exhibits for opposing counsel before they are shown to the witness. This may be done by an advocate's referring to the exhibit number or by indicating its designation in the prehearing order, if one has been prepared. Most arbitrators expect an advocate to hand or display the exhibit to opposing counsel before proceeding.

Examine the witness on the exhibit's foundation. Having identified the exhibit, an advocate may then proceed to lay the foundation for its admission.

Show the exhibit to the witness. The first step is for the advocate to show the exhibit to the witness. This is typically done by handing it to the witness. If the exhibit is something as large as a life-size model or an enlarged photograph, the advocate will normally point to it and direct the witness's attention. In either case, the advocate will usually announce for the record what he is doing, using a shorthand description of the exhibit, as well as its identification number:

> COUNSEL: Ms. Bowman, I am handing you respondent's exhibit eleven, which is a letter dated July 26.

Such description ensures clarity and should be scrupulously neutral. While advocates are allowed to ask a leading question on preliminary matters, they are not allowed to begin arguing their case under the pretext of laying a foundation. Thus, they cannot say:

COUNSEL:	Ms. Bowman, I am handing you respondent's exhibit eleven, which is the letter in which the claimant agreed to provide repair service at no additional cost.

Identify the exhibit. The advocate's next step is to have the witness identify the exhibit. The witness should state the basis for her familiarity with the exhibit, and then describe it in some detail:

QUESTION:	Have you ever seen claimant's exhibit seven before?
ANSWER:	Yes, I have seen it many times.
QUESTION:	What is claimant's exhibit seven?
ANSWER:	It is a piece of the stationery that I received when my order was delivered from Quickset Printing.
QUESTION:	How is it that you recognize it?
ANSWER:	I remember how it looked when I took it out of the box.

Complete the foundation. In some situations, particularly those involving real evidence, the identification of the exhibit will provide a sufficient foundation for admission. In other circumstances, the foundation will be much more elaborate, perhaps calling for chain of custody or the establishment of a hearsay exception. These and other foundations for the introduction of real, demonstrative, and documentary evidence are discussed at length in other sections of this chapter.

- **Offer the exhibit into evidence.** Once the foundation has been completed, the advocate can offer the exhibit into evidence. Jurisdictions vary as to the formality with which this must be done. In the simplest version:

COUNSEL:	Mr. Arbitrator, we offer claimant's exhibit three.

In any case, the exhibit must be shown to the arbitrator, who will then ask opposing counsel if there are any objections to its admission. If there are no objections, the arbitrator will receive the exhibit into evidence.

- **Use of the exhibit.** Once an exhibit has been admitted into evidence, a witness can testify about its contents, and it can be used by an advocate to illustrate or amplify a witness's testimony. Tangible objects can be used in demonstrations.

3.13 ENSURING COMPLETENESS AND ACCURACY OF TRANSCRIPTS

Being courteous to your court reporter will be a small investment that will reap huge returns. The court reporter is part of the team—the team consisting of yourself and the advocates—whose goal is to produce a complete and accurate record of events as they occur in the hearing. As a team, you must help the court reporter achieve that end.

Ensure completeness of transcripts. Ways in which you, as an arbitrator, can help the court reporter make a complete record are:

- Avoid speaking when the court reporter is changing paper, marking exhibits, etc. Important statements may be unintentionally excluded.

- Avoid speaking simultaneously with advocates or other arbitrators—or worse yet—speaking before the witness is finished answering a question. Even the most competent court reporters are sometimes unable to completely unscramble simultaneous oral statements, and important information may be omitted from the subsequently prepared transcript.

- When appropriate, describe off-the-record trial events on the record, and invite other counsel and the arbitrator to clarify your characterization as they perceived the events or discussion.

- Orally (and accurately) describe gestures of witnesses if it is important to the clear understanding of what the witnesses are saying.

- Be aware that witnesses are not usually experienced at telling their stories in anything other than everyday language. Sometimes details are omitted because witnesses assume that they are communicating only with people in the hearing room. Thus, you must ask the advocates to fill in the omitted details through additional questioning. For example, a witness who describes the distance between herself and the point of impact of two automobiles as the distance between the witness and the rear wall of the hearing room would have little meaning to a reader of the transcript who was not present in the hearing room.

- Clearly indicate when you wish to go off the record and when you wish to resume on the record.

Ensure accuracy of transcripts.

Aside from ensuring that there will be no unintentional omissions in the testimony, colloquies, or oral descriptions on the record, you must ensure that the printed words ultimately appearing in the transcript will be accurate. Ways in which you can help the court reporter produce an accurate transcript are:

- Take reasonable measures to acquaint the court reporter with the nature of the case. Provide the court reporter with a pleading or order which contains an accurate case caption and the names of the arbitrator(s) and advocates. If the pleading briefly encapsulates the nature of the case and stage of the proceedings, that is even more helpful. Physically identify the advocates present, and other persons (parties, interpreters, paralegals, etc.) present at the hearing.

- If the proceedings involve complicated terminology and spellings (medical malpractice case, environmental case, etc.), ask the advocates to provide the court reporter with a glossary of terms in advance of the proceeding.

- Also, it is helpful for advocates to provide the court reporter with passages from text of complicated material or a list of case citations that they will be referring to in an oral argument before you.

- Ensure that advocates avoid blocking the court reporter's view of the witness when questioning the witness in the hearing room.

- If a witness uses a figure of speech or metaphor ("the claimant appeared to be 'knee high to a grasshopper' next to the towering respondent"), make sure through questioning that the record is clarified regarding the height of the claimant in relation to the respondent.

- Make sure that the spellings of persons' names, street names, etc. are accurate. Ask the witness to spell them if they are the least bit unusual.

- Be careful how a witness uses pronouns (he, she, they, etc.). Sometimes, when testifying about several individuals, it is necessary that the witness minimize the use of pronouns, and attribute conduct to named persons.

- Have the advocates and witnesses refer to documents by exhibit number (and page) at all times.

- Markings made by witnesses on a photograph or large demonstrative exhibit should be designated by the witness's initials or designated number or letter.

3.14 RULING ON OBJECTIONS AND OFFERS OF PROOF

3.14.1 Ruling on objections.

Objections are the means by which evidentiary disputes are raised and resolved. An advocate may make an objection to another advocate's questions, to a witness's testimony, to the introduction or use of exhibits, to an advocate's demeanor or behavior, and even to the conduct of the arbitrator. In many arbitrations, particularly those that are not recorded by a court reporter, very few objections are made. However, in some arbitrations which involve high stakes and a court reporter is present, and/or when the parties have agreed that rules of evidence will apply, objections are made as if proceeding in court. Because objections are really the exception and not the rule in most arbitrations, this subsection is intentionally abbreviated, consisting of only a short list of common objections, some typical responses, and some ethical considerations related to objections.

Form of question objections. The following list and descriptions of some frequently made objections (and responses) is intended only as a reference or guide, not as a substitute for thorough knowledge of evidence and procedure.

- **Leading question.** A leading question suggests or contains its own answer. Leading questions are objectionable on direct examination. They are permitted on cross-examination. See FRE 611.

  Typical Responses. The question is preliminary, foundational, directing the witness's attention, or refreshing the witness's recollection. The witness is elderly, very young, infirm, adverse, or hostile. Leading questions can most often be rephrased in non-leading form.

- **Compound question.** A compound question contains two separate inquiries that are not necessarily susceptible of a single answer. For example, "Wasn't the fire engine driving in the left lane and flashing its lights?"

  Typical Responses. Dual inquiries are permissible if the question seeks to establish a relationship between two facts or events. For example, "Didn't he move forward and then reach into his pocket?" Other than to establish a relationship, compound questions are objectionable and should be rephrased.

- **Vague question.** A question is vague if it is incomprehensible, incomplete, or if any answer will necessarily be ambiguous. For example, the question, "When do you leave your house in the morning?" is vague, since it does not specify the day of the week to which it refers.

  Typical Responses. A question is not vague if the arbitrator understands it. Many arbitrators will ask the witness whether he or she understands the question. Unless the precise wording is important, it is often easiest to rephrase a "vague" question.

- **Argumentative question.** An argumentative question asks the witness to accept the examiner's summary, inference, or conclusion, rather than to agree with the existence (or non-existence) of a fact. Questions can be made more or less argumentative depending upon the examiner's tone of voice.

  Typical Responses. The objection is a relevance issue, and its probative value can be explained: "Mr. Arbitrator, it goes to prove ..."

- **Narratives.** Witnesses are required to testify in the form of question and answer. This requirement insures that the opposing advocate will have the opportunity to frame objections to questions before the answer is given. A narrative answer is one which proceeds at some length in the absence of questions. An answer that is more than a few sentences long can usually be classified as a narrative. A narrative question is one that calls for a narrative answer, such as, "Tell us everything that you did on July 14." Objections can be made to narrative questions and narrative answers.

Typical Responses. An advocate's best response is usually to ask another question that will break up the narrative. Note that expert witnesses are often allowed to testify in narrative fashion, since technical explanations cannot be given easily in question-and-answer format. Even then, however, it is usually more persuasive for the advocate to interject questions in order to break up big answers.

• **Asked and answered.** An advocate is not entitled to repeat questions and answers. Once an inquiry has been "asked and answered," further repetition is objectionable.

Typical Responses. If the question has not been asked and answered, an advocate may point out to you the manner in which it differs from the earlier testimony. Otherwise, an advocate may rephrase the question so as to vary the exact information sought.

• **Assuming facts not in evidence.** A question, usually on cross-examination, is objectionable if it includes as a predicate a statement of fact that has not been proven. The reason for this objection is that the question is unfair; it cannot be answered without conceding the unproven assumption.

Typical Responses. A question assumes facts not in evidence only when it utilizes an introductory predicate as the basis for another inquiry. Simple, one-part cross-examination questions do not need to be based upon facts already in evidence. For example, it would be proper for an advocate to ask a witness, "Didn't you leave home late that morning?" whether or not there had already been evidence as to the time of the witness's departure. As a consequence of misunderstanding this distinction, "facts not in evidence" objections are often erroneously made to perfectly good cross-examination questions. If the objection is well taken, most questions can easily be divided in two.

• **Non-responsive answers.** It was once hornbook law that only the advocate who asked the question could object to a non-responsive answer. The theory for this limitation was that the opposing advocate had no valid objection so long as the content of the answer complied with the rules of evidence. The more modern view is that the opposing advocate can object if all, or part, of an answer is unresponsive to the question, since any advocate—or the arbitrator—is entitled to insist that the examination proceed in question-and-answer format.

Typical Responses. The advocate asks another question.

Substantive objections.

• **Hearsay objections.** Depending upon the agreed procedures, hearsay may or may not be admissible in arbitrations. The Federal Rules of Evidence define hearsay as "[a] statement, other than one made by the declarant while testifying at the trial or hearing, offered in evidence to prove the truth of the matter asserted." FRE 801(c). Thus, any out-of-arbitration statement, including the witness's own previous statement, is potentially hearsay. Whenever a witness testifies, or is asked to testify, about what she or someone else said in the past, the statement should be subjected to hearsay analysis. Statements are not hearsay if they are offered for a purpose other than to "prove the truth of the matter asserted." For example, consider the statement, "I warned him that his brakes needed work." This statement would be hearsay if offered to prove that the brakes were indeed defective. On the other hand, it would not be hearsay if offered to prove that the driver had notice of the condition of the brakes, and was therefore negligent in not having them repaired. There are also numerous exceptions to the hearsay rule.

Typical Responses. Out-of-arbitration statements are admissible if they are not hearsay, or if they fall within one of the exceptions to the hearsay rule. In addition to statements that are not offered for their truth, the Federal Rules of Evidence define two other types of statements as non-hearsay. The witness's own previous statement is not hearsay if (A) it was given under oath, and it is inconsistent with the current testimony; or (B) it is consistent with the current testimony, and it is offered to rebut a charge of recent fabrication; or (C) it is a statement of past identification. See FRE 801(d)(1). In addition, an admission of a party opponent is defined as non-hearsay, if offered against that party. FRE 801(d)(2). Some of the more frequently encountered exceptions to the hearsay rule are as follows:

> *Present sense impression.* A statement describing an event while the declarant is observing it. For example, "Look, there goes the President." FRE 803(1).

> *Excited utterance.* A statement relating to a startling event made while under the stress of excitement caused by the event. For example, "A piece of plaster fell from the roof, and it just missed me." FRE 803(2).

State of mind. A statement of the declarant's mental state or condition. For example, "He said that he was so mad he couldn't see straight." FRE 803(3).

Past recollection recorded. A memorandum or record of a matter about which the witness once had knowledge, but which she has since forgotten. The record must have been made by the witness when the events were fresh in the witness's mind, and must be shown to have been accurate when made. FRE 803(5).

Business records. The business records exception applies to the records of any regularly conducted activity. To qualify as an exception to the hearsay rule, the record must have been made at or near the time of the transaction, by a person with knowledge or transmitted from a person with knowledge. It must have been made and kept in the ordinary course of business. The foundation for a business record must be laid by the custodian of the record, or by some other qualified witness. FRE 803(6).

Reputation as to character. Evidence of a person's reputation for truth and veracity is an exception to the hearsay rule. Note that there are restrictions other than hearsay on the admissibility of character evidence. FRE 803(21). See also FRE 404; 405.

Prior testimony. Testimony given at a different proceeding, or in deposition, qualifies for this exception if (1) the testimony was given under oath; (2) the adverse party had an opportunity to cross-examine; and (3) the witness is currently unavailable. FRE 804(b)(1).

Dying declaration. A statement by a dying person as to the cause or circumstances of what he or she believed to be impending death. Admissible only in homicide prosecutions or civil cases. FRE 804(b)(2).

Statement against interest. A statement so contrary to the declarant's pecuniary, proprietary, or penal interest, that no reasonable person would have made it unless it were true. The declarant must be unavailable, and certain other limitations apply in criminal cases. FRE 804(b)(3).

Catch-all exception. Other hearsay statements may be admitted if they contain sufficient circumstantial guarantees of trustworthiness. The declarant must be unavailable, and advance notice must be given to the adverse party. FRE 807.

- **Irrelevant.** Evidence is irrelevant if it does not make more or less probable any fact of consequence to the case. Evidence can be irrelevant if it proves nothing, or if it tends to prove something that does not matter. FRE 401, 402.

Typical Responses. An advocate explains the relevance of the testimony.

• **Unfair prejudice.** Relevant evidence may be excluded if its probative value is substantially outweighed by the danger of unfair prejudice. Note that evidence cannot be excluded merely because it is prejudicial; by definition, all relevant evidence must be prejudicial to some party. Rather, the objection only obtains if the testimony has little probative value and is unfairly prejudicial. FRE 403.

Typical Responses. Most arbitrators are hesitant to exclude evidence on this basis. A measured explanation of the probative value of the testimony is the best response.

• **Improper character evidence, generally.** Character evidence is generally not admissible to prove that a person acted in conformity with his or her character. For example, a driver's past accidents cannot be offered as proof of current negligence. FRE 404(a).

Typical Responses. Past crimes and bad acts may be offered to prove motive, opportunity, intent, preparation, plan, knowledge, identity, or absence of mistake. FRE 404(b).

• **Improper character evidence, conviction of crime.** As noted above, the commission and even conviction of past crimes is not admissible to prove current guilt. The credibility of a witness who takes the stand and testifies may be impeached on the basis of a prior criminal conviction, but only if the following requirements are satisfied. The crime must have been either (1) a felony, or (2) one which involved dishonesty or false statement, regardless of punishment. With certain exceptions, the evidence is not admissible unless it occurred within the last ten years. Juvenile adjudications are generally not admissible. FRE 609.

Typical Responses. If the crime was not a felony, the conviction may still be admissible if it involved dishonesty. If the conviction is more than ten years old, it may still be admissible if you determine that its probative value, supported by specific facts and circumstances, substantially outweighs its prejudicial effect. FRE 609.

• **Improper character evidence, untruthfulness.** As noted above, the past bad acts of a person may not be offered as proof that he or she committed similar acts. Specific instances of conduct are admissible for the limited purpose of attacking or supporting credibility. A witness may therefore be cross-examined concerning past bad acts only if they reflect upon truthfulness or untruthfulness. Note, however, that such bad acts (other than conviction of a crime) may not be proved by extrinsic evidence. The cross-examiner is stuck with the witness's answer. FRE 608(b).

Typical Responses. An advocate may explain the manner in which the witness's past bad acts are probative of untruthfulness.

• **Improper character evidence, reputation.** Reputation evidence is admissible only with regard to an individual's character for truthfulness or untruthfulness. Moreover, evidence of a truthful character is admissible only after the character of the witness has been attacked. FRE 608(a).

Typical Responses. Explain the manner in which the reputation evidence is probative of truthfulness or untruthfulness.

• **Lack of personal knowledge.** Witnesses (other than experts) must testify from personal knowledge, which is generally defined as sensory perception. A witness's lack of personal knowledge may be obvious from the questioning, may be inherent in the testimony, or may be developed by questioning on voir dire. FRE 602.

Typical Responses. An advocate may ask further questions that establish the witness's personal knowledge.

• **Improper lay opinion.** Lay witnesses (non-experts) are generally precluded from testifying as to opinions, conclusions, or inferences. FRE 701.

Typical Responses. Lay witnesses may testify to opinions or inferences if they are rationally based upon the perception of the witness. Common lay opinions include estimates of speed, distance, value, height, time, duration, and temperature. Lay witnesses are also commonly allowed to testify as to the mood, sanity, demeanor, sobriety, or tone of voice of another person.

• **Speculation or conjecture.** Witnesses may not be asked to speculate or guess. Such questions are often phrased as hypotheticals in a form such as, "What would have happened if ..."

Typical Responses. Witnesses are permitted to make reasonable estimates rationally based upon perception.

• **Authenticity.** Exhibits must be authenticated before they are admitted. Authenticity refers to adequate proof that the exhibit actually is what it seems or purports to be. Virtually all documents and tangible objects must be authenticated. Since exhibits are authenticated by laying a foundation, objections may be raised on the ground of either authenticity or foundation.

Typical Responses. An advocate may ask additional questions that establish authenticity.

- **Lack of foundation.** Nearly all evidence, other than a witness's direct observation of events, requires some sort of predicate foundation for admissibility. An objection to lack of foundation requires the arbitrator to make a preliminary ruling as to the admissibility of the evidence. FRE 104. The evidentiary foundations vary widely.

  Typical Responses. An advocate explains the foundation or attempts to lay a proper foundation.

- **Best evidence.** The "best evidence" or "original document" rule refers to the common law requirement that copies or secondary evidence of writings could not be admitted into evidence, unless the absence of the original could be explained. Under modern practice, most jurisdictions have significantly expanded upon the circumstances in which duplicates and other secondary evidence may be admitted. FRE 1001-1003.

  Typical Responses. Ask additional questions demonstrating either that the item offered is a duplicate, or that the original is unavailable.

- **Privilege.** Numerous privileges may operate to exclude otherwise admissible evidence. Among the most common are attorney-client, physician-patient, marital, clergy, psychotherapist-patient, and a number of others that exist either by statute or at common law. Each privilege has its own foundation and its own set of exceptions. FRE 501 did not change the common law privileges, but state statutory privileges may not stand in arbitrations governed by federal rules.

  Typical Responses. Virtually all privileges are subject to some exceptions, which vary from jurisdiction to jurisdiction.

- **Subsequent remedial measures.** Evidence of subsequent repair or other remedial measures is not admissible to prove negligence or other culpable conduct. FRE 407. The primary rationale for this rule is that parties should not be discouraged from remedying dangerous conditions, and should not have to choose between undertaking repairs and creating proof of their own liability.

  Typical Responses. Subsequent remedial measures may be offered to prove ownership, control, or feasibility of precautionary measures, if controverted. FRE 407. Evidence of subsequent repair may also be admissible in strict liability cases, as opposed to negligence cases.

- **Settlement offers.** Offers of compromise or settlement are not admissible to prove or disprove liability. Statements made during settlement negotiations are also inadmissible. FRE 408.

Typical Responses. Statements made during settlement discussions may be admissible to prove bias or prejudice of a witness, or to negate a contention of undue delay. FRE 408.

Ethics and objections. Ethical issues frequently arise in the context of making and meeting objections. Because the objecting process is one of the most confrontational aspects of the arbitration hearing, it often tests counsels' reserves of good will, civility, restraint, and sense of fair play. The three most common problems are discussed below.

- **Asking objectionable questions.** It is unethical for an advocate to attempt to use information contained in questions as a substitute for unobtainable testimony. Some lawyers believe that the idea of zealous advocacy allows them to slip information before an arbitrator by asserting it in a question, knowing full well that the witness will not be allowed to answer. The usual scenario is as follows:

LAWYER:	Isn't it true that you were once fired from a job for being drunk?
OBJECTION:	Objection, relevance.
LAWYER:	I withdraw the question. (Sotto voce: Who cares about the ruling? I never expected to get it in, but now the arbitrator knows that the witness is a drunk.)

This conduct, even if the information is true, is absolutely unethical. Testimony is to come from witnesses, with admissibility ruled upon by the arbitrator. It subverts the very purpose of an adversary hearing when lawyers abuse their right to question witnesses in order to slip inadmissible evidence before the arbitrator.

- **Making questionable objections.** The same general analysis applies to the use of objections as it does to the offer of evidence. Counsel need not be positive that an objection will be sustained, but must only believe that there is a reasonable basis for making it. Again, in arbitration it is up to the arbitrator to decide whether to admit the evidence.

- **Making "tactical" objections.** Many lawyers, and more than a few trial advocacy texts, tout the use of so-called "tactical" objections. Since an objection is the only means by which one lawyer can interrupt the examination of another, it is suggested that objections should occasionally be made to "break up" the flow of a successful examination. An objection can throw the opposing lawyer off stride, or give the witness a rest, or distract the arbitrator from the content of the testimony. This advice is usually tempered with the admonition that there must always be some evidentiary basis for the objection. The real message, however, is that an objection may be used for any purpose whatsoever, so long as you can make it with a straight face. This view is unfortunate. It amounts to nothing more than the sneaky use of objections for a wholly improper purpose. No arbitrator would allow a lawyer to object on the ground that the opposition's examination is going too well. The fact that disruption can be accomplished *sub silentio* does not justify it. The same is true of other "tactical" uses of objections, such as suggesting testimony to a witness.

3.14.2 Ruling on offers of proof.

An offer of proof consists of actual evidence (testimonial or documentary), or of a statement of counsel (oral or written) demonstrating what evidence counsel would seek to introduce if the arbitrator had not sustained opposing counsel's objection. It is important to note that an advocate makes an offer of proof only after the arbitrator has sustained an objection to a question propounded to a witness or an objection to a proffered exhibit. Its primary purpose is to preserve the record so that if judicial review becomes necessary, the reviewing court will have a basis for determining whether or not the arbitrator properly excluded the evidence. A secondary purpose of an offer of proof is to serve as a basis for having the arbitrator reconsider a ruling, excluding the evidence.

As implied *supra*, an offer of proof may be made in one of two forms: formally, through tendering the actual evidence (testimony or exhibits); or informally, through statement of counsel on the record. A formal offer of proof is generally preferred. Usually, testimonial offers of proof occur during an advocate's direct examination of a witness. The advocate should make clear on the record which portion of the offer of proof is being submitted.

In responding to an offer of proof, an effective advocate will state her objections clearly and succinctly on the record. The advocate will normally also seek to cross-examine the witness who is the vehicle for a testimonial offer of proof, in order to further buttress her position that the evidence has been properly excluded by the arbitrator. The opposing advocate should be allowed to state all grounds for his opposition to the proposed evidence when the offer of proof is made. Otherwise, grounds not stated may be deemed waived on later court review.

3.15 ARBITRATOR'S PREROGATIVE TO CALL WITNESSES AND DIRECT INTRODUCTION OF OTHER EVIDENCE

In civil law countries, where the arbitrator's role is inquisitorial, it is common for arbitrators to determine which of the witnesses proposed by the parties will testify at the arbitration hearing. In some countries, the arbitrators conduct most, if not all, of the questioning of witnesses. Civil law arbitrators also frequently appoint independent experts to advise them on technical matters. In the United States, arbitrators rarely call witnesses on their own motion or direct the introduction of other evidence. In the United States, the collective philosophy holds that the advocates, as the masters of their respective cases, have the responsibility to bring forward the evidence supporting their claims and defenses.

3.16 ENTERTAINING FINAL ARGUMENTS

3.16.1 Deciding whether to permit final argument.

It would be an unusual situation if an arbitrator did not hear final argument, however short, in an arbitration. Exceptions include instances when the evidentiary hearing is extremely brief and the parties have filed detailed prehearing briefs, or when the parties and arbitrators agree that the issues in arbitration can be decided on the basis of the pleadings, the stipulated exhibits, and the briefs without oral argument.

3.16.2 Role and function of the final argument.

The whole story. Final or closing argument in arbitration is the advocate's only opportunity to tell the story of the case in its entirety, without interruption, free from most constraining formalities. Unlike witness examinations, the final argument is delivered in counsel's own words, without the need intermittently to cede the stage to the opposition. Unlike the opening statement, it is not bound by strict rules governing proper and improper content. In other words, final argument is the moment for pure advocacy, when all of the lawyer's organizational, analytic, interpretive, and forensic skills are brought to bear on the task of persuading you and your colleagues on the arbitration panel. The final argument cannot be fully successful unless the preceding stages of the arbitration hearing were also successful. The opening statement's mental image will not stay with the arbitrator unless it is sustained by evidence from the witness stand. More to the point, the final argument cannot paint a picture that is contrary to, or unsupported by, the evidence. While the final argument can and should be the capstone of a well-tried case, it is unlikely to be the saving grace of a poorly-tried one. You can expect that an advocate's well-planned, well-executed final argument will have the following characteristics.

Use of theory and theme.

- **Theory.** The final argument communicates the advocate's theory of the case. Some witnesses can be disregarded, some details omitted, some legal issues overlooked, but the theory of the case is absolutely essential. A simple

151

recitation of facts is not sufficient. Rather, the argument brings together information from the various witnesses and exhibits in a way that creates only one result. A successful presentation of theory in the final argument is logical, believable, and legally sufficient.

- **Theme.** An effective advocate makes the theme a constant presence throughout the final argument. Unlike opening statement and witness examinations, where a theme can only be used intermittently, the effective advocate organizes the entire final argument to emphasize the theme. She begins with a statement of the theme and constantly returns to it in each segment of the argument.

What makes it argument. Recall the cardinal rule of opening statements that advocates may not argue. In final argument, on the other hand, advocates may and should argue, if they are serious about winning their case. The gloves are off and the limitations removed, but what precisely distinguishes argument from mere presentation of the facts? The following are some of the most useful elements of "argument" that you can expect to experience in a well-presented final argument.

- **Conclusions.** The advocate in final argument is free to draw and urge conclusions based upon the evidence. A conclusion is a result, consequence, or repercussion that follows from the evidence in the case. It is not sufficient for an advocate to draw, or even urge, conclusions. An effective advocate goes on to explain why the desired conclusions are the correct ones.

- **Inferences.** While a final argument can and should include broad conclusions, it may also include narrow conclusions commonly known as inferences. An inference is a deduction drawn from the existence of a known fact. In other words, the inferred fact need not be proven, so long as it is a common-sense consequence of some established fact. An inference should be accepted by you only if it is well-grounded in common understanding. For example, everyone will be willing to infer a child's age from knowledge of her grade in school. There is no need to explain that third graders are typically eight or nine years old. Other inferences, however, may be more complicated.

- **Details and circumstantial evidence.** Final argument is an advocate's only opportunity to explain the relevance and consequences of circumstantial evidence. Much of the art of direct and cross-examination consists of the accumulation of details that lead to a certain conclusion or result. The splintered knowledge of the individual witnesses, not to mention the deliberate strategy of advocates, may result in the scattering of such details throughout the arbitration hearing. During final argument, the advocate can reassemble the details so that you have a clear understanding of the evidence.

- **Analogies, allusions, and stories.** Advocates may use analogies, allusions, and stories in final argument. Analogies are used to explain human conduct through reference to everyday human behavior. A witness's testimony can be strengthened or diminished by comparing her version of events to some widely understood experience or activity. While analogies can be very powerful, there is always danger that they can be inverted and exploited by the other side. Claimant's counsel, therefore, often reserves the use of analogies until rebuttal, when the respondent will no longer be able to reply.

An allusion is a literary or similar reference that adds persuasive force to an argument. In earlier days, before the advent of mass culture, trial lawyers' allusions were most commonly drawn from Shakespeare or the Bible. Today, permissible references are just as likely to be taken from motion pictures, television, popular songs, fairy tales, or even advertisements. It is permissible for advocates to use stories, in the form of either hypotheticals or anecdotes, so long as the story is based on facts in evidence.

- **Credibility and motive.** Advocates may also use the final argument to comment on and compare the motive and credibility of witnesses. Most arbitrations involve competing renditions of past events, which you must resolve in order to reach a decision. Final argument is the only time when the advocate may directly confront the character of the witnesses, and explain why some should be believed and others discounted. Witness examinations can bring out impeaching facts, and the opening statement can use apposition to contrast the credibility of different witnesses. Only in final argument can counsel make direct comparisons. Finally, advocates can argue motive on the basis of proven facts or logical inferences. Advocates may tell you why a witness would exaggerate, waffle, conceal information, quibble, or lie. The suggested reasons need not be based on outright admissions, so long as they follow rationally from the testimony in the case.

- **Weight of the evidence.** While the opening statement is limited to a recitation of the expected evidence, effective advocates use the final argument to assert the weight of the evidence. Why is one version preferable to another? Why should some facts be accepted and others rejected? Why is one case stronger than the other?

- **Demeanor.** It is fair game in final argument for an advocate to comment on a witness's demeanor. Demeanor arguments are usually negative in nature, since it is easier to characterize untrustworthy conduct.

- **Refutation.** Another distinguishing feature of argument is refutation of opposing positions. Opening statements and witness examinations may recite and elicit facts that are contrary to the opposition, case, but final argument can refute it directly by pointing out errors, inconsistencies, implausibilities, and contradictions.

- **Application of law.** Final argument provides the advocate an occasion to apply the law to the facts of the case. Discussion of law is extremely limited during the opening statement and all but forbidden during witness examinations, but it is a staple of the final argument.

- **Moral appeal.** It is permissible in final argument for an advocate to elaborate on the moral theme of the case. Recall that a theme states, usually in a single sentence, a compelling moral basis for a verdict in a client's favor. The theme invokes shared values, civic virtues, or common motivations. Effective advocates state the theme during the opening statement, allude to it in witness examinations, and hammer it home in the final argument.

3.16.3 Typical format, structure, and content, and delivery of final argument.

Format. In most arbitrations, the parties' final arguments are divided into three distinct segments, which are presented in the following order: the claimant's argument in chief, the respondent's argument in chief, and claimant's rebuttal. In some arbitrations, the claimant will be allowed to opt to argue second. Thus, there are only two components: the respondent's argument and the claimant's rebuttal.

Structure. Effective advocates structure the final argument for maximum persuasive weight. For them, the central thrust of the final argument is always to provide reasons—logical, moral, legal, emotional—for the issuance of an award in their client's favor. Every aspect of the final argument contributes in some way to the completion of the sentence, "We win because ..." The desired conclusion should simply follow from the facts and law of the case. Few cases, however, will go to arbitration unless the facts are capable of multiple interpretations. Effective argument therefore places a premium on arrangement and explanation.

The use of topical organization is the guiding principle in the structure of final arguments. One of the simplest and most effective forms of organization is for the advocate to divide the case into a series of discrete factual or legal issues. Large issues, such as liability and damages, are obvious, but they are also too broad to provide help in ordering an argument. It is more useful to think of issues as narrower propositions of fact or law. A second form of topical organization revolves around elements and claims. Every legal cause or defense is composed of various discrete elements. A claim of negligence, for instance, must be supported by proof of duty, breach of duty, cause in fact, proximate cause, and damages. A claimant can therefore develop her final argument by discussing the evidence as it supports each of the distinct elements of her cause of action. A respondent, who needs to challenge only a single element in order to win, will use the same form of organization, but will truncate it by focusing only on those elements that are likely to be negated. An advocate can also persuade an arbitrator by identifying the key turning points in the hearing and explaining them in a way that comports with the arbitrator's life experience and sense of reality.

Alternative organizational structures for final argument include chronology and witness listing. While chronology can certainly play an important role in final argument, it is usually not the best approach to overall structure. The difficulty with chronology is that events are unlikely to have occurred in the most persuasive sequence. Early events can frequently be illuminated by their subsequent consequences. Aside from chronology, some lawyers persist in presenting final argument as a series of witness descriptions and accounts, essentially recapitulating the testimony of each witness. This approach diminishes the argument's logical coherence and force. Where topical organization focuses on the importance of issues and chronological organization focuses on the real-life sequence of events, witness listing depends on nothing more than the serendipity of which witness said what. It is a lazy, and usually ineffective, method of organization. While it will often be necessary to compare witness accounts in the course of a final argument, effective advocates would not use them as the primary focus of their argument.

Content. The specific content of any final argument will obviously be determined by the facts and issues in the case. You should expect, however, the following kinds of information to be present in every effective final argument.

- **Tells a persuasive story.** Virtually every final argument should contain all of the elements of a persuasive story. The argument should detail the evidentiary support for the advocate's theory of the case and consistently invoke the trial theme. A persuasive story has four basic elements, each of which answers an important question: What happened? Why did it happen? How can we be sure? Is it plausible?

- **Ties up cross-examinations.** Final argument is the time when the advocate ties up issues intentionally left unaddressed during cross-examination. Recall the questions that are forbidden to the prudent cross-examiner. The effective advocate never asks a witness to explain; never asks a witness to fill in a gap; never asks a witness to agree with a characterization or conclusion. By asking these questions and others like them, the advocate risks losing control of the witness. All authorities agree that it is better for an advocate to refrain from asking the ultimate question, and to make the point instead during the final argument. Thus, the effective advocate will spend some portion of the final argument drawing the previously unspoken conclusions.

- **Comment on promises.** Advocates on both sides of a case will inevitably make various promises and commitments to you during the course of the hearing. These promises may be overt, as is often the case during opening statements: "We will produce a series of documents and work records that prove that the respondent was nowhere near the scene of the accident." Or the commitments may be implicit in the theory of the case. When a claimant seeks damages for personal injury, there is obviously an implied promise of certain proof. Whatever the case, final argument is the time for advocates to comment on promises made, kept, or broken.

- **Resolve problems and weaknesses.** Effective advocates use final argument to solve problems and confront weaknesses. No matter how well the evidentiary phase of the hearing proceeded, advocates are sure to be left with a number of difficult or troublesome issues. Once identified, these issues can be addressed and resolved in the course of final argument.

- **Discuss damages.** An arbitration can often be divided into the conceptual areas of liability and damages. Although liability is the threshold issue, the issue of damages is critical to your decision-making and award. If the advocates fail to address the issue of damages, make sure you raise the issue and have them discuss it.

Delivery. As an arbitrator, you will witness a broad range of quality among advocates in their delivery of final argument. When you experience one that is particularly effective and persuasive, you can reasonably expect that the advocate has used many of the following techniques.

- **No reading.** Effective advocates do not read their opening statements or final arguments. They make their presentations from an outline.

- **Simple, straightforward language.** Their presentations are reasonably straightforward and direct. They know that in final arguments, simple, active language may be applied in argumentative form.

- **Verbal pacing.** They also know that the speed, tone, inflection, and volume of their speech can be important persuasive tools. Changes in speed, tone, inflection and volume can be used to signal transitions and maintain the arbitrator's attention. They avoid speaking too quickly or too loudly. The pacing of their speech can be used to convey perceptions of time, distance, and intensity. If they describe an event rapidly, it will seem to have taken place very quickly. If they describe it at a more leisurely pace, the time frame will expand. In similar fashion, rapid speech tends to magnify intensity and reduce distance. Slower delivery reduces intensity and increases distance.

- **Movement for emphasis and transition.** Effective advocates also know that a certain amount of body and hand movement enlivens their final argument and increases the attentiveness of the arbitrator. They use gestures to emphasize important points or to accent differences between their case and the opposition's. They also use body movement for emphasis or transition. Pausing and taking a step or two alerts the arbitrator that they are about to change subjects. Moving toward the arbitrator underscores the importance of what they are about to say. Moving away from the arbitrator signals the conclusion of a line of argument. Constant movement, however, is distracting to the arbitrator.

- **Visuals and exhibits.** Effective advocates know that their final argument need not be confined to words alone. They use visual aids and exhibits to enhance the value of their presentations.

- **Use of emotion.** Effective advocates know that the best approach to emotion is to save it for the times when they are discussing the moral dimension of their case. They will avoid waxing passionate over the date on which a contract was signed, but they will show appropriate outrage or resentment toward a party who intentionally breached a contract, knowing that it would cause great harm to another. They also know that the absence of emotion may be taken as a lack of their belief in the righteousness of their case. What reasonable person would be unmoved when discussing crippling injuries to a child or perjury by the opposing party? There are points in many arbitrations that call out for an outward display of feeling, and a flat presentation in such instances is likely to communicate the absence of conviction on the part of an advocate.

3.16.4 Ethics of final argument.

The rules of ethics, evidence, and procedure combine to place a number of very real, though definitely manageable, limits on what advocates can say during final argument. You should know and understand these limitations so that you can properly caution advocates appearing before you or properly rule on pertinent objections regarding perceived unethical behavior, when raised.

Impermissible argument.

- **Statements of personal belief.** It is improper and unethical for an attorney to "assert personal knowledge of facts in issue … or state a personal opinion as to the justness of a cause, the credibility of a witness, the culpability of a civil litigant …"[26] The purpose of this rule is twofold. First, it prevents

---

26. Rule 3.4(e), ABA Model Rules of Professional Conduct..

lawyers from putting their own credibility at issue in a case. The arbitrator is required to decide a case on the basis of the law and evidence, not on their affinity for or faith in a particular lawyer. While advocates strive to be trusted and believed, they subvert the adversary system if they make an overt, personal pitch. Moreover, if they make a statement of personal belief, they inevitably suggest that the they have access to off-the-record information, and therefore they invite the arbitrator to decide the case on the basis of non-record evidence.

- **Appeals to prejudice or bigotry.** It is unethical for an advocate to attempt to persuade an arbitrator through appeals to racial, religious, ethnic, gender, or other forms of prejudice. People—including arbitrators—can be swayed by their own biases, but lawyers cannot and should not seek to take advantage of this unfortunate phenomenon. An appeal to prejudice asks the arbitrator to disregard the evidence, and to substitute an unreasonable stereotype or preconception. Thus, such arguments violate the rule prohibiting an advocate from alluding to "any matter the lawyer does not reasonably believe is relevant or that will not be supported by admissible evidence."[27] However, the advocate's mention of race, gender, or ethnicity is not always improper. It may, for example, be permissible for an advocate to refer to a party's race if it is relevant to identification by an eyewitness. On the other hand, it is definitely unethical for an advocate to make racial or similar appeals implicitly or through the use of code words. An argument based on bigotry cannot be saved through subtle language.

- **Misstating the evidence.** While advocates are permitted to draw inferences and conclusions, it is improper for them intentionally to misstate or mischaracterize evidence in the course of final argument.

- **Misstating the law.** In most jurisdictions attorneys may use final argument to explain the relevant law and to apply the law to the facts of the case. Counsel may not, however, misstate the law or argue for legal interpretations that are contrary to the court's decisions.

- **Misusing evidence.** When evidence has been admitted only for a limited or restricted use, it is improper for an advocate to attempt to use it for any other purpose.

- **Exceeding the scope of rebuttal.** It is objectionable for an advocate to attempt to argue new matters on rebuttal.

---

27. Id

3.16.5 Ruling on objections during final argument.

The protocol of objections.

• **Making objections.** Objections during final argument follow the same general pattern as objections during witness examinations. Counsel should state succinctly the ground for the objection. There is usually no need to present argument unless requested by the arbitrator. Most attorneys, however, avoid objecting during opposing counsel's final argument. It is considered a common courtesy to allow opposing counsel to speak uninterrupted. Moreover, the overuse of objections may result in the interruption of one's own final argument. It is unethical to make spurious objections simply for the purpose of interfering with opposing counsel's argument. This does not mean, of course, that seriously improper arguments should be tolerated.

• **Responding to objections.** The best response to an objection is often no response. An objection disrupts the flow of final argument, and an extended colloquy with the arbitrator will only prolong the interruption. A dignified silence will usually be sufficient to allow the arbitrator to rule. Once the arbitrator rules, whether favorably, unfavorably, or inscrutably, counsel should simply proceed by adapting the argument to the arbitrator's ruling.

3.16.6 Arbitrator's questioning of advocates during final argument.

Prior to the final argument, the sole arbitrator or members of an arbitration panel should decide what initial questions to put to counsel, if any, in closing argument. Arbitrators vary on how much questioning they conduct during the final argument, but, where the hearing is lengthy, the issues are difficult, and/ or the law is complex, most arbitrators do not hesitate to conduct extensive questioning. It is important for arbitrators not to "tip their hand" as to their leanings on the merits by the nature and manner of their questioning. After receiving answers to their questions, the presiding arbitrator should ask whether any parties present have statements to make in response to the arbitrator's questions or to statements made by other parties in response to them.

3.17 CONCLUDING THE HEARING

3.17.1 Determining when evidence will be "closed."

The rules of most dispute resolution organizations require the arbitrator or arbitrators to make a specific determination as to when the evidence is formally "closed." The date of the closing of the evidence may be set after the arbitrator or panel members have reviewed the briefs and determined that the evidence is complete, that no additional documents need to be filed, and that they do not need to call any witnesses on their own in order to decide the case. Customarily and often by rule, the date on which the evidence is closed is the date from which the time period begins running for the arbitrator(s) to issue the award.

3.17.2 Determining whether parties should file post-hearing briefs.

Occasionally, you or the advocates will see a need for the advocates to submit post-hearing briefs. You may direct such briefs to be filed in lieu of closing arguments or in addition to them. Usually, you will request such briefs in complex factual cases where it is not completely clear, even from the advocates' oral arguments, whether there is sufficient evidence to sustain particular elements of claims or defenses. However, there may be other reasons for requesting briefs. For example, there might be very difficult legal questions which you must decide and which require citations to the particular cases supporting the parties' respective positions. In other situations, you may need the parties' respective views on how scientific or highly technical testimony of expert witnesses supports their legal positions. Thus, it is very important, before leaving the hearing room for the last time, that you decide for yourself and make clear to the advocates whether you want them to focus on any particular topics covered by the evidence submitted and the arguments heard.

If you do not request that post-hearing briefs be filed, the advocates may request permission to file them. Occasionally, there are evidence situations that are so delicate, so intricate, or so fraught with the potential for misunderstanding, that the only way the advocates feel they can handle them effectively is through a meticulous review and marshalling of the evidence. There may be other reasons why they might conclude that post-hearing briefs are necessary. For example, in a high stakes case, where defeat would mean substantial monetary loss to their client, advocates often request permission to file briefs.

You should expect the advocates to draft post-hearing briefs with the same care they would take in drafting a good appellate brief. When requesting that briefs be filed, you should emphasize how important it is that their briefs possess qualities of brevity, clarity, succinctness. If you think it necessary or appropriate, you should set page limitations for the briefs. You should also remind them that you expect thorough referencing and citation to the hearing transcript, if there is one, and to any pertinent exhibits introduced during the hearing.

3.17.3 Setting post-hearing briefing or oral argument schedule.

In cases where the parties desire post-hearing briefing an oral argument, you will need to set a schedule for these events.

You should remember to allot time, as appropriate, for the court reporter to complete and distribute the transcript of proceedings. When scheduling the filing of briefs in the ordinary case, it is advisable for you to set specific dates when the briefs are to be filed and served, rather than merely saying "two weeks" or "the week after next." Also, include time for filing reply briefs. If time is of the essence, you may consider having the parties file simultaneous main briefs and simultaneous reply briefs. In multiple party cases in which some parties are aligned, you may want to suggest that the parties submit joint briefs or divide the briefing in order to avoid duplication of effort to reduce the expense of the parties.

In setting the briefing schedule, you may also want to consider the form in which you wish the briefs to be filed. Most arbitrators prefer double-spaced briefs bound so that they lie flat on a table. You may also request briefs in a form conforming to local trial or appellate court rules. In recent years, it has become common practice for arbitrators to request counsel to file their briefs in hard copy and data disk form. Of course, if you wish briefs to be filed in data disk form, you should specify the software operating system and the word-processing software desired. In the near future, assuming appropriate security measures have been devised to ensure confidentiality, it is predictable that all post-hearing submissions will be cyberbriefs "filed" and "served" through use of the Internet. The same is predictable for the awards and opinions of arbitrators.

Having briefs filed in data disk form can be very helpful to the arbitrators, particularly in complex cases where briefs or the proposed findings of fact and conclusions of law are extensive, and the arbitrators need to prepare a comprehensive, detailed opinion supporting their award. While the data on the disks is not ordinarily used word for word in the arbitrator's opinion, use of the data can facilitate the arbitrator's drafting of stipulated facts; quotations from contracts, statutes, and case law; and other matters and descriptions in the brief, as to which the parties agree and/or with which the arbitrator is in complete agreement.

In many situations, the filing of post-hearing briefs is a substitute for oral argument. In some complex arbitrations, however, the parties will request, and/or you will desire to have, oral argument in addition to post-hearing briefs. You may delay determining whether there will be a need for oral argument until after reading the briefs. In any event, when scheduling oral argument, it is important to allow sufficient time between the date set for the filing of the final briefs and the date for oral argument, so that you or the panel can properly review the briefs and prepare questions for oral argument. It is also advisable to set specific time limits for each party to present its argument, including any rebuttal arguments. Where several parties are aligned and there is lead counsel, you might suggest or direct that the oral argument time be divided among the aligned parties so that lead counsel is allotted the majority of the time, with the remainder distributed among the remaining aligned parties so that each can make specific points on behalf of their respective clients.

It is very important to the integrity of the arbitration process and to the accept-ability of the later-issued arbitration award that, if oral argument is scheduled, each party's counsel be permitted an opportunity to be heard orally—even if the time allotted is limited, and even if counsel does not take advantage of the opportunity. If there is to be a questioning period by the arbitrators, there should also be a final period allotted to each party to give its own response to the arbitrators' questions or to make any statements regarding the answers given by any party in response to the arbitrators' questions.

3.17.4 Arbitrator's final remarks.

As a sole arbitrator or chair of an arbitration panel, it is customary to make concluding remarks in the final hearing of the case, prior to adjournment for deliberation and decision-making. In these remarks, traditionally the arbitrator thanks the parties for their presentations and compliments counsel, as appropriate, on the competence, civility, and professionalism they have demonstrated in representing the interests of their clients. It is not uncommon for counsel to thank the arbitrator or arbitrators for their services in conducting the proceedings. The arbitrator usually sets the date by which the parties can expect the award to be issued.

Chapter Four

The Arbitrator's Post-Hearing Functions and Duties

General propositions do not decide concrete cases The decision will depend on a judgment or intuition more subtle than any articulate major premise.

—*Oliver Wendell Holmes, Jr.*

✳ ✳ ✳ ✳

4.1 RULING ON POST-HEARING MOTIONS

After the hearing has concluded, advocates may sense a need to file motions before or after issuance of your award. These motions fall into two general categories: motions to reopen the hearing and motions to modify or correct the award.

Motion to reopen hearing. Normally, you may reopen the hearing on your own motion or on the motion of any party.[1] Reasons why you might want to reopen a hearing might include apparent insufficient evidence on an aspect of the case; doubt as to applicable law; or additional briefing is needed. Customarily, if reopening the hearing would delay your issuance of the award beyond the time limitation specified in the arbitration agreement, you should not reopen the hearing without the consent of all parties. Ordinarily, you should not reopen the hearing after the award is issued.

If a party moves to reopen the hearing, the party must demonstrate good cause. Satisfactory "good cause" customarily includes newly-discovered evidence which could not have been known or presented at the time of the hearing. The moving party must show that the evidence was unavailable at the time of the hearing or that there is a reasonable explanation for its non-production. The movant must also demonstrate that the reopening will not seriously affect a substantial right of the other party.

Motion to modify or correct the award. A motion to modify or correct the award is in the nature of a motion for reconsideration, but normally reconsideration does not permit any material modification of the award. Advocates may file a motion to modify or correct an award where:[2]

- there is an evident material mistake in the figures referred to in the award

---

1. *See generally* Oehmke, *Commercial Arbitration* (Revised Edition), Chapter 125 (Clark Boardman Callaghan, 1995).
2. Id. at §128:04.

- there is an evident material mistake in the description of any person, thing, or property referred to in the award
- the arbitrators have issued an award concerning a matter not submitted to them
- the form of the award is incorrect
- information needs to be added or deleted to effect the intent of the award
- clarification is needed to promote justice between the parties

A motion for modification or clarification must demonstrate indefiniteness or confusion in the interpretation of the award. A sufficient basis for such a motion might be a movant's assertion of an incapability to understand and/or to comply with the award.

4.2 REVIEWING POST-HEARING BRIEFS

If the parties have filed post-hearing briefs or proposed findings of fact and conclusions of law, you should read through them carefully, making notes as you do so. Taking notes has several purposes. First, they provide a running record of points you do not understand and for which you will need to find an explanation in the other side's brief, at oral argument (if one is scheduled), or in later discussions with your other panel members. Second, they can preserve questions that you have about the evidence or the law, which you can check out when you have completed reviewing all of the briefs. Third, they can highlight what you believe to be the pivotal aspects of the case that are crucial to your decision-making, and on which you wish to rely in reaching your conclusions and/or in discussing the case with your other panel members.

4.3 DECIDING THE MERITS OF THE CLAIMS AND DEFENSES

4.3.1 The decision-making process—general.

When an arbitrator or a panel of arbitrators decides a case, they engage in a process that has a core of elements common to all types of decision-making. Those elements are: (1) defining the problem; (2) establishing the boundary conditions for a tentative solution; (3) finding a tentative solution that satisfies all of the boundary conditions and yields a reasonable and fair result; (4) ensuring self-implementation of the tentative solution by providing clear instructions as to how the decision is to be carried out; and (5) trouble-shooting the tentative solution by testing its validity and appropriateness through hypotheticals before finalizing and converting it to a final decision.

Defining the problem. It is a common phenomenon among judges and arbitrators to have one view of a case after they read the briefs and hear the evidence, and then to have quite a different view after they have had an opportunity to read all of the exhibits and applicable case law, and sit down to actually write the decision in the case. Often, the arguments of the parties are not fully crystallized in their minds until the time comes to make a decision. It is at that moment that they, as decision-makers, must define the problem or problems to be solved—which may even be perceived by them to be somewhat different than the problems framed by the parties. In arbitration, the problems that the arbitrators must define are the factual and legal issues, that need to be decided. Carefully defining all the issues is the first important step in the arbitrator's decision-making process.

Establishing the boundary conditions. Arbitrators must be particularly vigilant to establish boundary conditions for their tentative solutions and for their final decision. They should not define an issue which is beyond their authority to resolve, nor should they arrive at a tentative solution or a final decision which grants relief that is illegal or inappropriate. Arbitrators' authority is not plenary. In decision-making, they must be constantly mindful that they derive their authority from the contract of the parties and from any applicable statutory or common law. The problems they define and the decisions they reach must reflect and acknowledge the limitations and restrictions imposed by those sources.

Finding a satisfactory and fair tentative solution. Arbitrators must not only find a tentative solution that satisfies the boundary conditions, but they must also arrive at a solution which is objectively fair and reasonable. This stage of the process requires the arbitrators to analyze and weigh the evidence; interpret and analyze contract provisions; evaluate the respective rights and duties of the parties; and find, interpret, analyze, and apply the appropriate case law, statutes, and/or regulations to reach a fair and reasonable result. That commonly vindicates and compensates the wronged person or entity, and exposes the wrongdoer.

Ensuring self-implementation of the tentative solution. Arbitrators also must ensure that the tentative solution is understandable and that it provides sufficient explanation, so that its directives can be fully implemented without further comment or elaboration.

Trouble-shooting and finalizing a decision. Where a final decision will contain several directives regarding distribution of funds or complicated instructions regarding non-monetary matters, the arbitrators should trouble-shoot the proposed final decision by thinking of hypothetical situations in which their decision would be effectuated. Then they think of ways in which the decision's objectives might be thwarted because of incomplete instructions to the parties. The arbitrators can then amend the tentative solution to include instructions to obviate those problems.

4.3.2 The decision-making procedure.

Typically, a single arbitrator will want to decide a case as soon after the hearing as possible, while the information is still fresh in his or her mind. The decision-making procedure may vary somewhat from individual to individual, but usually it consists of reading notes taken during the evidentiary hearing, reviewing the hearing exhibits, reviewing the transcript, reading the pertinent case law, analyzing and deciding the various issues in the case, and drafting the award and opinion, if appropriate.

Where there is a three-arbitrator panel, the decision-making procedure may vary. Usually, soon after the evidentiary hearing, the arbitrators will meet to discuss their tentative reactions to the evidence and the arguments. This normally occurs even before the parties' post-hearing briefs are received. The chair of the panel leads the discussion. After the parties file their briefs, the arbitrators will meet once again, either in person or by telephone, to discuss their tentative conclusions about the case. In that meeting they will normally reach a decision, and one of the panel members will volunteer to draft the award, which will later be circulated to the panel members, signed by each of them, and issued.

If the award is to be accompanied by an opinion, the chair of the panel will designate one of the three panel members to write a draft award and opinion. The opinion author will then circulate a draft award and opinion to the other two panel members, after which another meeting or telephone conference is held. Final adjustments or corrections are made, the award and opinion is circulated for signature, and then issued.

4.3.3 Customary standards for interpreting contract language.

In many arbitrations in which you will be involved, you will be required to interpret contract language in connection with your deciding the case and entering an award. This subsection describes some of the customary standards you should apply when performing this arbitrator function.[3]

Ambiguity. If words of a contract are plain and clear, there is no need to resort to technical rules of interpretation. If the contract language is ambiguous—that is, capable of more than one meaning—then the technical interpretational rules must be applied. Even though both parties contend that a contract provision is ambiguous, you might find it plain and clear, based on your application of the technical rules of construction.

Intent of the parties. When interpreting contract language, you should take into account the intent of the parties, relying where possible, on the construction

---

3. *See generally*, Elkouri & Elkouri, *How Arbitration Works Fifth Edition* (BNA), Chapter 9.

favoring the purpose and aims of the particular contract provision under scrutiny. You can normally determine the intent of the parties from the express language of the agreement, the parties' statements made during pre-contract negotiations, the parties' bargaining history, and the past practice of the parties under this or previous contracts.

Mutual mistake. A mutual mistake occurs when parties sign a contract that contains terms or provisions which do not comport with their actual agreement. This sometimes occurs when the parties are mutually mistaken about the definition of a word or the use of punctuation. In such a circumstance, you may reform the contract to reflect the true intent of the parties. If a mistake is unilateral, rather than mutual, you would ordinarily lack a sufficient basis to reform the contract.

Legal validity. Normally, where two interpretations of contract language are possible, one making the contract provision lawful and the other making it unlawful, you should opt for the interpretation that makes the provision valid and lawful. Unless there is evidence to the contrary, it is reasonable for you to presume that the parties intended to conclude a valid contract.

Normal and technical word usage. In the absence of evidence showing that words were used in a different or colloquial meaning, you should give them their ordinary and popularly accepted meaning. Thus, you should give the word "may" its ordinary permissive meaning, unless there is convincing evidence that the parties intended a mandatory meaning. You should interpret trade or technical terms in their usual trade or technical sense. If a word is used by the parties in one sense in a contract or series of contracts, you should interpret it similarly throughout the contract or contracts, unless a party presents a convincing basis for not doing so. If you determine that the definition of a term in a contract is unclear, you can resort to a dictionary definition. If the parties have defined a contested term in their contract, however, you should ordinarily not look outside the contract to find a definition of the term. If you do resort to a dictionary definition, you should consider using a dictionary compiled for use by the relevant industry.

Construing the agreement as a whole. Ordinarily, you should determine the meaning of words or phrases, not in their isolated context, but rather in relation to the various parts and provisions of the document as a whole. You should treat words or phrases as surplusage only if you are unable to glean their reasonable meaning from the agreement as a whole. If necessary, you may imply the existence of words where the absence of them renders a passage nonsensical, meaningless, or does not comport with the reasonable intent of the parties.

Avoiding absurd, harsh, or ludicrous results. If meanings proposed by the parties would produce absurd, harsh, or ludicrous results, you may substitute your own interpretation that leads to a just and reasonable one. Generally speaking, you should interpret an ambiguous contract provision so as to yield a meaning that is reasonable and equitable to all parties, rather than a meaning that would give one party an unfair or unreasonable advantage that could never have been within the contemplation of the other parties.

Expressing one matter precludes another. A common interpretational principle of legislation is "expressing one matter precludes another." This principle also applies to interpreting contracts in arbitration. Thus, in the absence of contrary evidence, if a contract expressly states a series of requirements, it is presumed that there are no other requirements. Similarly, if a contract expressly states a series of exceptions, it is presumed that the parties intended no other exceptions.

General category determined by specific examples. Another common legislation interpretational aid is that "a general category is determined by specific examples." This principle can also be used in contract interpretation. Thus, when you are interpreting a contract provision, where general words follow enumerated specific terms, you should interpret the general words to include only items of the same general nature or class as those contained in the enumeration, unless there is evidence that the parties intended a broader sense.

Specific versus general language. Similarly, the meaning of a general contract provision should be restricted by more specific provisions. Where two contract provisions concern the same subject matter, you should give precedence to the more specific provision.

Avoidance of forfeiture. If you are in a position where one reasonable interpretation of a contract provision will work a forfeiture—say a loss of right for lack of timeliness—and another reasonable interpretation will prevent forfeiture, you should ordinarily adopt the latter interpretation. This follows the principle that the law (or equity) abhors a forfeiture.

Pre-contract negotiations. If you must interpret an ambiguous contract clause, sometimes you will be able to glean the intent of the parties from their written communications in pre-contract negotiations. Both communication and lack of communication regarding a particular subject matter can provide an indication of the parties' intent regarding language which ultimately appears in a contract. If an agreement is not ambiguous, you should not examine the record of pre-contract negotiations to determine the meaning of an agreement's provisions.

Compromise offers not to be considered. In determining the meaning of contract provisions, you should give no weight whatsoever to concessions or compromise offers made by the parties in their pre-arbitration attempts to settle the controversy.

Experience or training of parties or their agents. If untrained laypersons drafted the contract provisions, you may be less inclined to apply a strict construction to them. On the other hand, if the drafters were sophisticated and experienced in drafting contracts, then you may properly apply a more strict construction to the fruits of their labor.

Custom and past practice of the parties. There are four standards for contract interpretation that relate to custom and past practice of the parties. They are: industry practice; prior settlements; interpretation against the drafter of the provision in question; and handbook and manual standards.

- **Industry practice.** Where a party has contracted with several entities and used the same provisions, you may take into account the practice of such pairs of parties in determining the intended meaning of the contract at issue before you. Also, if an industry practice or interpretation is firmly established, you may follow the industry's definition preference.

- **Prior settlements.** If the parties have previously resolved a dispute over the interpretation of a particular contract provision, either orally or in writing, you may use such prior agreement of the parties in determining the meaning of the same contractual provision.

- **Interpretation against drafter of provision.** A common rule of contract interpretation is to interpret a contested provision against its drafter. This rule places the burden on the drafter to ensure that there is a mutual understanding of the obligated parties as to what the drafter intended. You should apply this rule only as a last resort, in the event that you are unable to resolve ambiguity by any other standard of interpretation. You should not enforce the rule if the final version of a contested provision is significantly different from the one initially proposed by the drafter. Also, if the complaining party was not in fact misled, you need not apply the rule against the drafting party.

- **Handbooks and manuals.** Handbooks or manuals used by the parties pursuant to a contract may provide a basis for interpreting ambiguous contract terms. However, handbooks or manuals drafted and distributed by only one of the parties should not be relied on as evidence to bind another party to a particular definition or interpretation.

Implications of insurance policy. You may consider the implications of the meanings of an insurance policy in interpreting contract provisions, if the terms of the policy have been incorporated into the contract or have otherwise been agreed upon by the parties.

4.3.4 Customary application of the rules of substantive law.

The general rule in both statutory and common law arbitration is that arbitrators need not follow otherwise applicable substantive law in reaching their decisions, unless the arbitration agreement requires it.[4] The Uniform Arbitration Act, the Federal Arbitration Act, and the state statutes are silent on the subject of use or application of law to decide issues before them. This statutory silence reflects the universal understanding that arbitrators who are not lawyers generally are expected to reach their decisions on the basis of their experience, knowledge of the customs of the pertinent industry, fair and good sense for equitable relief, and their sense of the justice of the case.

If, however, the arbitration clause in the case before you requires the application of substantive law as a predicate to your reaching a decision, your first step in the decision process is to ascertain, conclusively, what body of substantive law should be applied. This is not always a simple task. Some arbitration clauses will not specifically dictate what substantive law the parties desire to have you apply to the facts of a dispute arising under the clause. If this happens, you might consider having the parties decide whether they want a legal or equitable resolution of their dispute. If they opt for a legal one, then you should ask them to agree as to the body of substantive law they want you to apply. If they disagree, then you will have to select an appropriate body of law yourself. Your selection might reasonably be guided by the location of the arbitration hearing selected by the parties or by the specific law under which the parties agreed to have the main contract interpreted. Where the parties cannot agree as to the applicable body of substantive law, you can also be guided by the settled principle that in absence of an express contrary direction in the contract or submission, arbitrators are not bound by rules of law in determining issues submitted to them.

4.3.5 Application of basic contract, tort, and equity principles.

If you serve as an arbitrator regularly, you will find that in making your decisions, you are repeatedly called upon to know and apply some basic principles of contract and tort law. Below appear twelve basic principles of contract and tort law for your quick-reference use, as a template for placing the parties' arguments in a logical context for analysis and decision-making and as a starting point for researching the law of the pertinent jurisdiction. Twelve principal maxims of equity are also provided in the event that you are asked to base your decision on equitable principles, rather than on strict legal authority.

---

4. *See generally,* Martin Domke, *Domke on Commercial Arbitration,* §§ 25:00 - 25:04 (Rev. Ed.)(Clark Boardman Callaghan, 1995).

Contract. Twelve basic principles of contract law are described below.[5]

- A contract consists of an offer and an acceptance.
- An offer is a communication in the form of a promise by which an offeror creates in the offeree the power to form a contract by accepting the offer in an authorized manner.
- An acceptance is a communication by which the offeree makes a return promise that unequivocally manifests his or her intent to be bound by that promise.
- For a contract to be enforceable, the parties' promises must: (1) be made for valid consideration; (2) reasonably induce the promisee to detrimentally rely on the promise; or (3) come within the provisions of a statute that does not require consideration (e.g. agreements to modify contracts).
- Usually, an offeror may revoke an offer prior to the time of acceptance.
- Usually, an offeree's rejection of an offer terminates the offer, and the offeree cannot revive the offer by a belated attempt to accept it.
- Certain contracts must, by statute, be in writing in order to be enforceable.
- Promises are asserted by a plaintiff to show the duty that a defendant breached with respect to the contract; conditions are asserted by a defendant to show that his or her duty to perform never arose; promises may also be enforced under a theory of quasi-contract where the promisor has been unjustly enriched.
- There are three broad types of conditions: express, implied, and constructive. Conditions may be legally excused in at least six situations: offeree's rejection of a proper offer; failure of a prior condition; anticipatory repudiation of a promise by the other party; waiver; estoppel; and impossibility of performance of a condition.
- Defenses to contract enforceability that affect the assent to be bound include: (1) capacity to contract (minority, mental defects or illness, under influence of drugs or intoxicants); (2) undue influence; (3) duress; (4) third party inducement; (5) mistake; or (6) misrepresentation and fraud.
- Defenses to contract enforceability that are based upon policy include: (1) unconscionability; (2) public policy; (3) illegality; (4) exculpatory clauses; and (5) contracts violating licensing requirements.
- Remedies available for breach of contract include: (1) compensatory or expectation damages; (2) reliance damages; (3) restitution; (4) stipulated (liquidated) damages; (5) interest; (6) punitive damages; (7) specific

---

5. *See generally* Claude D. Rohwer and Gordon S. Schaber, *Contracts in a Nutshell* (West Publishing, 1997).

performance; (8) rescission; (9) reformation; and (10) statutory damages and attorney's fees.

Tort. Twelve basic principles of tort law are described below.[6]

- The elements of a cause of action for negligence are: (1) a duty owed by defendant to plaintiff; (2) a breach of that duty by defendant's failure to conform to the required standard of conduct; (3) a sufficient causal connection between the defendant's negligent conduct and the resulting harm; and (4) actual loss or damage of a recognized kind.

- Usually, in determining whether conduct is negligent, the law applies an objective standard of reasonableness, commonly called the reasonable person standard.

- To prove a charge of negligence, a plaintiff must advance sufficient evidence to tip the scales of probability in his favor with respect to each element of the cause of action—duty, breach, causation, and damages.

- The scope of one's legal duty is a question of law.

- With respect to the cause element, conduct can be classified as negligent only if it involves a foreseeable and unreasonable risk of harm. If there is an intervening cause subsequent to the tortious conduct of defendant, the defendant will remain liable if he ought to have foreseen the intervening cause and taken it into account in his conduct.

- Defenses to negligence liability include: plaintiff's contributory negligence; plaintiff's comparative negligence; plaintiff's imputed contributory negligence; assumption of risk; plaintiff's failure to mitigate damages; plaintiff's failure to avoid consequences; and statutes of limitations and repose.

- An intentional tort is an act committed with a desire to cause certain immediate consequences; an actor's motive for his conduct—revenge, protest, punishment, theft, self-defense, may in appropriate cases aggravate, mitigate, or excuse the actor's wrong.

- Typical intentional torts include battery, assault, false imprisonment, intentional or reckless infliction of emotional distress, trespass to land, trespass to chattels, and conversion.

- Defenses to liability for intentional misconduct include consent, self-defense, defense of others, defense of property, forcible repossession of land, necessity, authority of law, and privileged discipline.

- In most jurisdictions, a product liability claim may be based on one or more of these theories: negligence; breach of warranty; strict tort liability.

---

6. *See generally* Edward J. Kionka, *Torts in a Nutshell* (West Publishing Co. 1992).

- Ordinarily, an employer is not vicariously liable for harm caused by an employee's use of an instrumentality (e.g. automobile) entrusted by the employer to the custody of the employee, when the instrumentality is not then being used by the employee in the scope of the employment.

- The general rule is that a principal is not vicariously liable for the torts of an independent contractor, unless the principal was negligent in selecting, instructing, or supervising the independent contractor; principal has a duty to perform for which he cannot escape responsibility by hiring an independent contractor; or the work to be performed is particularly or inherently dangerous.

Equity. There are twelve principal "maxims of equity."[7] While these twelve maxims do not comprise the only foundations on which equitable jurisprudence has been built, they have proven considerably important over the centuries to aid in the understanding of equity as a concept whose primary characteristics are fairness, flexibility, and morality. They are presented here, together with a brief explanation, as a practical aid for you when you, as arbitrator, must arrive at a decision on an equitable basis.

- **Equity will not suffer a wrong to be without a remedy.**
  In early times, equity was thought to be a court of conscience, and a plaintiff invoked that conscience when he or she was suffering a misfortune for which there was no remedy possible at law. Thus, injunctions to restrain torts came into existence when the common law only offered monetary damages as a remedy.

- **Equity follows the law.**
  Equity must recognize the predominance of legal estates, rights, interests, and titles. Equity can never declare that a fee simple estate is not a fee simple estate. It can, however, prevent a legal owner of a fee simple estate from wrongfully or harmfully using its legal rights.

- **Where the equities are equal, the first in time will prevail.**
  Where there is a conflict between the rights of two equitable claimants, the general rule is that the claims rank in the order of temporal priority.

- **Where the equities are equal, the law will prevail.**
  Where an equitable interest is acquired earlier in time than a legal interest against which it is asserted, the legal interest will prevail. Thus, a person holding an equitable interest in an estate will not prevail against a bona fide purchaser of the legal estate for value, without notice of the prior equitable interest.

---

7. *See generally*, R. P. Meagher, W. M. C. Gummow, and J.R. F. Lehane, *Equity Doctrines and Remedies* Butterworths, 1975); Dan B. Dobbs, *Law of Remedies* (2d Ed.) Vol. 1 (West Publishing, 1993).

- **One who seeks equity must do equity.**
  Any plaintiff desiring an equitable remedy can only do so on the condition that he or she fulfills his or her own legal and equitable obligations arising out of the dispute. Thus, a plaintiff is entitled to specific performance of a contract only if the plaintiff has performed all of the obligations which he has agreed to perform under that contract.

- **One who comes into equity must come with clean hands.**
  If a plaintiff whose conduct in a transaction has been improper (e.g. fraudulent) seeks relief in equity, such relief will be denied.

- **Equity aids the diligent, not the tardy.**
  One who seeks relief in equity may not delay, lest he or she be denied equitable relief on grounds of laches, acquiescence, or the like.

- **Equity is equality.**
  In this maxim, "equality" means proportionate equality. Thus, the maxim generally expresses the objective of both law and equity, namely, to effect a distribution of profits and losses proportionate to the several claims or to the several liabilities of the parties to the dispute.

- **Equity looks to the intent (or substance), rather than to form.**
  This maxim finds its example in situations where an equity court infers a trust although no trust language is used or, as in the case of an "illusory trust," determines no trust to exist although the words of a trust are used.

- **Equity regards as done that which ought to be done.**
  Often equity treats a contract to do something as if the thing were already done. Thus, equity will treat a person who, for valuable consideration, agreed to take a lease as if he were the lessee.

- **Equity abhors a forfeiture.**
  Under this maxim, a court may relieve a party from the consequences of some limited and technical default. Thus, if a tenant made a late rent payment, the equity court could prevent forfeiture of the lease by allowing the tenant to make the late rent payment.

- **Equitable remedies are given as a matter of grace or discretion, not of right.**
  This maxim focuses on the fairness, flexibility, and morality aspects of equity, and emphasizes its subjective quality.

4.3.6 Determining liability.

Deciding an arbitration case is normally a two-step process. The first step requires you to decide liability on each claim; the second requires you to decide the appropriate damages to be awarded on that claim. If liability is not found on a claim, then of course, the damages are zero, and the award on that claim is zero.

If liability is found as to a particular claim, then you must determine the type and amount of damages and other appropriate relief to be awarded on that claim. Sometimes this is a very difficult task. The total monetary award for a claimant, then, is the sum of the individual monetary awards calculated with respect to his or her separate claims.

In determining whether a claimant has proved liability on a particular claim, you should separately consider whether the claimant has met its burden with respect to that claim and whether the respondent has successfully defended the claim. The following series of questions is designed to assist you in making your liability determination on each claim.

Claimant's Theory of Claim and Related Evidence

- What were the elements of claimant's claim?
- Did the claimant satisfy its burden to prove *each element* of its claim?
- Did the parties stipulate to the existence of any element of claimant's claim?
- Did respondent admit to an element of claimant's claim either in pleadings or during the arbitration hearing?
- Was any item of evidence, critical to the proof of an element of claimant's claim, deemed inadmissible by the arbitrator?
- Was the testimony of claimant's witnesses credible?
  —What motivations were operating to influence witnesses to **exaggerate** material and relevant facts or events?

  —What motivations were operating to influence witnesses to **misrepresent** material and relevant facts or events?

  —What motivations were operating to influence witnesses to omit material and relevant facts and events?
- Was the testimony of claimant's witnesses reliable?
  —What portion of testimony consisted of direct evidence?

  —What portion of testimony consisted of circumstantial evidence?

  —What portion of testimony consisted of unreliable hearsay?
- Was the claimant's documentary evidence credible?
- Was the claimant's documentary evidence reliable?
- What weight, if any, should be given to claimant's affidavits?
- Was the respondent able to impeach the veracity of claimant's critical testimonial evidence?

- Was the respondent able to impeach the veracity of claimant's critical documentary evidence?

Respondent's Theory of Defense and Related Evidence

- What were the elements of respondent's defense?
- Did the respondent satisfy its burden to prove *each element* of its defense?
- Did the parties stipulate to the existence of any element of respondent's defense?
- Did claimant admit to an element of respondent's defense either in pleadings or during the arbitration hearing?
- Was any item of evidence, critical to the proof of an element of respondent's defense, deemed inadmissible by the arbitrator?
- Was the testimony of respondent's witnesses credible?
- What motivations were operating to influence witnesses to **exaggerate** material and relevant facts or events?

    —What motivations were operating to influence witnesses to **misrepresent** material and relevant facts or events?

    —What motivations were operating to influence witnesses to omit material and relevant facts and events?

- Was the testimony of respondent's witnesses reliable?
    —What portion of testimony consisted of direct evidence?

    —What portion of testimony consisted of circumstantial evidence?

    —What portion of testimony consisted of unreliable hearsay?

- Was the respondent's documentary evidence credible?
- Was the respondent's documentary evidence reliable?
- What weight, if any, should be given to respondent's affidavits?
- Was the claimant able to impeach the veracity of respondent's critical testimonial evidence?
- Was the claimant able to impeach the veracity of respondent's critical documentary evidence?

Determination of Liability on Claim

- If the parties' lay testimonial evidence was in direct conflict, which testimony was more believable?
- If the parties' expert testimonial evidence was in direct conflict, which testimony was more convincing.
- If the parties' documentary evidence was conflicting, which documentary evidence was more believable?

- Was the claimant's evidence sufficient overall?
- Was the claimant's evidence sufficient as to a portion of its claim?
- Has the claimant satisfied the overall standard of proof as to this claim or a portion of it—preponderance of the evidence, clear and convincing evidence, etc?
- Was the respondent's theory of defense and related evidence sufficient to defeat claimant's claim?
- Was the respondent's theory of defense and related evidence sufficient to defeat a portion of claimant's claim?

If you find liability on one or more claims, cross-claims, or counterclaims, the next step is to determine the type and amount of damages, or other types of relief to award.

4.3.7 Determining compensatory damages.

The arbitrator's authority to award compensatory damages is ordinarily plenary, so long as liability has been properly determined and such damages do no more than make the claimant whole.[8] That having been said, however, you should realize that your authority to award compensatory damages in a specific instance may be limited by a liquidated damages clause in a contract between the parties or by specific provisions of applicable statutes or rules. If you award excess compensatory damages in an arbitration, a court may consider the excess amount to be punitive in nature and vacate that part of the award, or remand the whole award amount for your reconsideration.

You should take great care when awarding consequential damages—for example, loss of business reputation, loss of business opportunity, loss due to delayed completion of a construction project. Before awarding consequential damages, you should be satisfied that there exists a basis for doing so under a reasonable interpretation of the applicable arbitration statute, rules, or agreement of the parties.

4.3.8   Considering appropriateness of awarding punitive damages.

If you determine that punitive damages might be appropriate in the particular circumstances of the case before you, and if you are conducting an arbitration under a state arbitration act, you should consult the law of the particular state to determine whether awarding punitive damages is within the scope of your authority.[9] You should be aware that some states forbid an arbitrator to award punitive damages, even if the parties' arbitration agreement permits it. The Federal

---

8. *See generally*, Domke, *supra* note 4 at §30:02.

9. Id. at § 30:05.

Arbitration Act, on the other hand, has been construed to permit arbitrators to award punitive damages in circumstances where the arbitration agreement authorizes such an award, despite the fact that the applicable state law prohibits punitive damage relief in arbitration. The rationale leading to this result is that the choice-of-law clause in an arbitration agreement relates to law regarding substantive rights of the parties as applied by state courts, whereas the other provisions in the agreement, some incorporating arbitration rules, govern procedures and relief or remedies available in the arbitration proceeding. In short, unless parties proceeding under the Federal Arbitration Act specifically agree in a pre-dispute or present-dispute arbitration clause that the arbitrator may not award punitive damages, the arbitrator may entertain a party's request to award them. You should also be aware that if in a particular arbitration punitive damages are not awardable, and the arbitrator awards excessive compensatory damages, a court may deem a portion of the award to be punitive and vacate it.

4.3.9   Determining equitable and other remedies.

You must consult the law of your individual jurisdiction to determine whether you can grant equitable relief as part of your final award in a particular case.[10] While the current state of the law and applicable federal and state policies tend to authorize arbitrators to impose final equitable relief—particularly when proceeding under the Federal Arbitration Act—courts are divided over whether an arbitrator has the authority to order a respondent to provide security, during the course of the arbitration, to ensure the availability of relief to a claimant should there be a final decision in claimant's favor. Sometimes the rules governing the arbitration proceeding, incorporated by reference into the arbitration clause, clearly permit the arbitrator to grant equitable remedies, such as specific performance.

4.3.10 Considering appropriateness of awarding attorneys' fees, costs, and interest.

Of course, the American rule regarding the award of attorney's fees is that, in the absence of a party's bad faith conduct, attorney's fees may not be awarded to a winning party automatically as of right, but rather such award must have a statutory, rule, or contract basis.[11] Before awarding attorney's fees in a U.S. arbitration, you should have an articulable and justifiable factual and legal basis for doing so, since such award is the exception rather than the rule in the United States.

While it is unusual for attorney's fees to be awarded in arbitration proceedings, the same is not true for costs. The rules of dispute resolution organizations

---

10. Id. at § 30:04.

11. *See generally*, Elkouri & Elkouri, *How Arbitration Works*, (5th Ed.) 591 (BNA); Domke, *supra* note 4 at §30:03. Rodolphe J.A. DeSeife, *Solving Disputes Through Commercial Arbitration* §3:43 (Callaghan, 1987).

ordinarily provide for the award of costs by the arbitrator to a prevailing party. Such costs include the arbitrator's fees, the administrative fees, expenses related to stenographic services, among others. However, the award of such costs to a prevailing party is not automatic. Where the parties have timely proceeded through the arbitration process with legitimate claims and defenses and have supported such positions in good faith with proper evidence and arguments, it is usually not appropriate to award costs against the losing party.

Unless a statute, rule, or contract provision provides otherwise, you may ordinarily include interest as a component of the arbitration award, even though the entitled party does not request it. Also, you are usually free to determine the date from which the interest should run, so long as the amount of damages against which the interest is computed is reasonably ascertainable on the date you choose. If the pre-award amount due is not ascertainable in a particular case, you may determine that the interest should run from the date of the award. The percent interest to be applied is that which is required by the parties' contract, and failing that, by statute, regulation, rule, or custom in the particular jurisdiction in which you are arbitrating.

4.4   DRAFTING THE AWARD

4.4.1   Considering the nature and purpose of the award.

An award may be either binding or non-binding, depending on the parties' pre-arbitration agreement or the rules governing the particular arbitration. Binding awards are enforceable under applicable breach of contract laws. In most jurisdictions, a binding arbitration award has the same effect as a court judgment, except that it is not usually subject to appeal in any court of law. A non-binding award has no legal effect, but of course, the parties can still agree to accept it. Even if the non-binding award is not accepted by the parties, it can still be used by the parties to facilitate settlement. In some jurisdictions, a party who rejects the result of a court-annexed arbitration may in some circumstances be liable for the opponent's costs and attorney's fees. Sometimes it is helpful in non-binding award situations for the arbitrator to accompany the award with a brief explanation as to his or her reasoning. This written explanation can be helpful to a mediator who conducts a settlement conference in the case after the non-binding award has been rendered.

Also, parties to an arbitration sometimes reach a settlement of their dispute prior to, during the course of, or after the arbitration hearing.[12] If this occurs in a case where you are an arbitrator, the parties may ask you to enter an award which incorporates the settlement terms. The purpose of such an award is to discourage a party from backing out of a settlement. You have discretion to enter such an

---

12. *See generally*, Domke, *supra* note 4 at §28:03.

award. Ethically, you are not required to do so if you are not satisfied with the propriety of the terms of the settlement. If you do decide to enter such an award, you will guard against a successful court challenge of the award if you ensure that the award contains: (1) a stipulation signed by the parties describing the terms of the settlement, the stage of the proceedings when the settlement occurred, and the allocations of fees and expenses in the arbitration; and (2) the parties' agreement that you are authorized to render such consent award.

Arbitrators are expected to maintain their awards and hearing notes in confidence and not disclose them to anyone but the parties or the administering organization without the consent of the parties.[13]

4.4.2 Knowing the jurisdictional requisites of a binding award.

Before you draft a binding award it is very important for you to review the requisites for such an award, as established by the jurisdiction in which you are rendering it, the procedural rules which govern the particular arbitration, and the arbitration agreement. Ordinarily, you may grant any just and equitable relief within the scope of your authority as defined by statutes and rules. However, the parties by agreement may have limited the scope of the allowable remedies or relief available to them in the proceeding. You should definitely be aware of these limitations before you begin to draft a binding award.

The formal requisites of a binding award are typically as follows. The award:

- should always be in writing, signed by you and the other arbitrators on the panel, and, if required by rules or the parties' agreement, notarized and witnessed.
- should be clear and concise.
- normally does not include a written opinion explaining the arbitrator's reasoning.
- must contain a ruling on all claims (principal claims, counter-claims, cross-claims, third-party claims, etc.) and damage requests (compensatory, consequential, punitive, etc.) in issue.
- must name the winning party on each claim, and the party against whom the award is rendered.
- must specify the precise dollar amount of the award on each claim.
- must apportion all administrative fees and expenses for the hearing and assess the arbitrator's fees and attorney's fees, if appropriate.
- fix interest rate on award, as appropriate.

---

13. *See generally*, Domke, *supra* note 4 at §24:07.

4.4.3 Complying with time limits.

It is imperative that the arbitrator comply with time limits governing issuance of the award. If you fail to comply with such time limits, you may be providing the losing party with a basis, regardless of merit, to contest the enforcement of the award in court on a technical ground. Normally, the parties will fix the time period within which the arbitrator must render the award. They may do this through the pre-arbitration agreement or in the arbitration clause of the original contract. Time periods may also be fixed by dispute resolution organization rules, local court rules, judge's guidelines, or statute. Dispute resolution organizations commonly have rules allowing thirty days for an arbitrator to issue an award. If the time limit in the parties' agreement conflicts with that set by rule or statute, the agreement controls. In the ordinary situation, an experienced arbitrator with knowledge of the subject matter should, however, be able to render an award (without an opinion) almost immediately after an arbitration hearing.

4.5 DRAFTING THE OPINION SUPPORTING THE AWARD —GENERAL

As noted above, except in labor cases, arbitrators are ordinarily not required to state reasons for their awards or draft written opinions setting forth their reasoning.[14] Nor are they required to make separate findings on each issue submitted for determination. If, however, the parties agree that the award should be accompanied by a written opinion or by findings of fact and conclusions of law, then the advice contained in this section should be of considerable assistance to you.

4.5.1 Reading the record of proceedings.

Reading techniques for enhancing comprehension and retention of information. There are several measures that you can take as an arbitrator to enhance your comprehension and retention of information in your reading of the record of proceedings.

- **Plan the reading session(s).** If possible, you should set aside blocks of time (three to five hours or more) to read the record of proceedings. However, if you are a busy attorney with an active law practice, you may have to read a record piecemeal, devoting one hour or less at a time. In either event, you should plan the reading session and have with you the necessary documents from the record to make your efforts meaningful.

- **Review your current knowledge of the case.** You should spend a few minutes thinking about the case, and then decide which portions of the record might be more efficient to read first.

---

14. *See generally*, Domke, *supra* note 4 at §29:06.

- **Overview the material.** Before you begin reading the record (or parts of it), you should determine whether the record is complete. It is possible, of course, that one of your fellow panelists used a hearing exhibit to draft a mid-hearing ruling and inadvertently put it with his case file. Usually, where the parties have introduced many exhibits into evidence, they will have provided you with a list of the exhibits in evidence. Perhaps you or a panelist prepared such a list. In any event, it is always a good idea to check your exhibits against that list before you begin reading the record.

- **Place materials in chronological order.** In most cases, the record should be read in the chronological order in which the information or evidence was introduced at the hearing.

- **Read in-depth.** Overall, you should read the record carefully and with focused concentration. Reading of certain parts of the record (for example subpoenas, notices of hearing, etc.) can be rapid and inspectional in nature. You should make notes as you go along, as appropriate.

- **Use visual guides.** Some readers find that use of a pointer, such as the blunt end of a pencil or a fingertip moved along underneath a line of print, can actually accelerate their reading rate and improve their comprehension of the material. You may want to experiment with this technique. It is claimed to improve reading effectiveness in these ways: (1) it helps to eliminate unnecessary back-skipping by the eyes; (2) it encourages the eyes to move faster across the page; and (3) it encourages the eye to take in more words with each fixation, which increases the content and improves comprehension.

- **Photocopying and highlighting.** It is sometimes an effective technique for the reader to make copies of crucial parts of the record and underline or highlight important words contained in them for later use in issue formulating and drafting the body of the opinion.

- **Reject unneeded, irrelevant information.** Do not waste your time reading through documents that were deemed to be inadmissible evidence. The information contained in them cannot be used when drafting your opinion.

- **Take regular breaks.** Research has shown that taking a five minute break every thirty to forty minutes during a reading session increases the reader's retention of the material and reduces the possibility of mental fatigue.

- **Review your notes.** If you are reading a record piecemeal in short (or long) reading sessions over a period of days, it is helpful toward achieving continuity of comprehension to review your last session notes prior to commencing the new reading session. It also is a check against duplicating your previous efforts (reading what you have already read) or mistakenly omitting review of an important aspect of the record of proceedings.

Reading post-hearing submissions. If the parties have filed post-hearing briefs or proposed findings of fact and conclusions of law, you should read those before you begin your detailed review of the record of proceedings. This will imprint on your mind the perspectives of the parties regarding the merits of their respective claims and defenses, as well as the quantity and quality of evidence supporting them. As you later carefully read through the pleadings, transcripts, and exhibits, you will be able to evaluate for yourself whether the parties' perceptions mesh with yours.

Reading pleadings and rulings. In an arbitration lasting several days, weeks, or months, the parties may have filed many pleadings, and you may have entered many rulings. You should review these pleadings and rulings prior to drafting your opinion. You will want to do this because you may want to note some of these pleadings and rulings in your opinion, and you will not want to contradict any prior ruling by what you say in your opinion. It is also advisable to take notes while you read the pleadings and rulings. In taking such notes, you might find it beneficial to have two yellow pads, side by side, or a split-screen personal computer. You can use one of the pads or screens for your "chronicle notes," and the other for "editorial notes." In the left margin of the "chronicle notes," identify the document by number or abbreviated description and by internal page number, as appropriate. Then to the right of the document number, describe the nature of the document and any pertinent information in its contents. If the document suggests matters that need to be investigated in other parts of the record, identify the document in the left margin of the "editorial notes," and jot down your present thoughts regarding the possible implications of the document with the other parts of the record you might want to check. As you review the entire record, look back at the "editorial notes" from time to time, and focus on parts of the record that they suggest need further investigation. At the end of the entire record review, inspect the "editorial notes" once again to insure that all the questions you had about the record have been answered.

Reading transcripts and exhibits. After reading the pleadings, you should to read the transcripts and exhibits. "Chronicle notes" and "editorial notes" should be made as when you reviewed the pleadings. Start a new page for each witness, and indicate in your "chronicle notes" the stage of the examination (direct, cross, redirect, recross). The transcript volume and page numbers should be placed in the left margin. Only short phrases should be used to capture the witnesses' testimony. When exhibits are discussed (and received into evidence) in the transcript, note this fact by transcript page number and exhibit number in the left margin. Do not simply rewrite the transcript. That would defeat the purpose of note-taking, which is to provide a handy tool in the nature of an expanded index to facilitate your use of and citation to the record, when you later conduct your analysis of the evidence and your "evidence matrix."

It is important that as you progress through the transcript, you read the complete exhibits in the sequence they appear. This will enable you to appreciate the meaning and full implications of the parties' "stories" in their full context. Often this will be your first opportunity to review the documentary exhibits carefully and thoroughly. This is particularly true of the lengthier exhibits. A detailed review of lengthy critical documents in the transcript review process will greatly assist your understanding of the transcript that follows. Such documents sometimes contain diagrams, illustrations, numerical analyses, and other information which will help you define and clarify the contours of the case. They should also assist you in placing the transcript and exhibits in their proper context. As you read through the transcript, you may also wish to refer to notes you took during the arbitration hearing itself regarding the evidence, credibility of witnesses, etc.

4.5.2   The five parts of an opinion.

The form, format, and length of your opinion supporting an award will normally be governed largely by its purpose, the agreement of the parties, the applicable rules, and the nature of the case. If the rules require, or the parties agree, that findings of fact or conclusions of law must accompany an award, then you must satisfy that requirement. If the parties have pre-agreed to an "equitable decision," then the opinion can simply describe your reasoning leading to the award, without citing or analyzing case law. If the parties desire you to provide an opinion in a simple personal injury case, the opinion might consist of a very short explanation—one to three pages—communicating factual findings, liability determinations, and how you arrived at the damage amount. However, when you must draft a comprehensive legal opinion in an arbitration case, the opinion should resemble a court opinion in form, content, and style. If you are sitting as a hearing arbitrator in the ordinary evidentiary-type arbitration, then your opinion should resemble a trial judge's opinion. If you are sitting as an appellate arbitrator in an arbitration case, then your opinion should resemble an appellate judge's opinion.

The structure of a hearing arbitrator's opinion consists of five separate elements:[15]

- opening or orientation;
- summary of claims and defenses and other issues;
- statement of facts;

---

15. *See* Ruggero Aldisert, *Opinion Writing* 151-63 (West Publishing, 1990).

- discussion, analysis, and application of the relevant law or equitable principles;
- a disposition.

An appellate arbitration panel's opinion has a similar structure, as follows:[16]

- the nature of the action, and how it reached appellate tribunal;
- the questions to be decided;
- the material or adjudicative facts;
- the determination of the questions of law;
- the disposition of the case.

The five separate elements of the hearing arbitrator's opinion are discussed in detail below, in relation to the drafting of a hearing arbitrator's opinion. Where there are significant differences between this type of opinion and an appellate arbitrator's opinion, they will be noted. As a side note, you will find that many of the principles applicable to good brief writing also apply to good opinion writing.

4.6   THE OPENING

Similar to a trial court opinion,[17] the opening or orientation paragraph of an arbitration opinion should begin with the identification of the parties. It should then continue with a description of the type of case being brought, the relief sought, and the principal issue presented. This will set the stage for the next part of the opinion structure, the summary of all claims, defenses, and other issues in the case.

If you are sitting as an appellate arbitrator, you should consider the following questions when drafting the opening paragraph of your appellate opinion:[18]

- **What:** What is the specific nature of the principal issues and the areas of law implicated in the appeal?
- **Who:** Who is taking the appeal? Who won at the evidentiary level of the arbitration?
- **When:** When was the alleged error committed in relation to the arbitration proceedings? Is the appeal based on insufficiency of evidence? Did the alleged error occur during the pleadings stage, or at the prehearing, hearing, or post-hearing stage?

---

16. *See* Aldisert, *supra* note 15 at 71.

17. *See* Aldisert, *supra* note 15 at 153.

18. Aldisert, *supra* note 15 at 75.

- **How:** How did the arbitration award arise? Was the award issued as a result of summary judgment, a directed finding, or a full evidentiary hearing? Did the arbitrator render an opinion?

- **Where:** Where does the appeal come from—a single arbitrator; a panel of arbitrators; is a governmental agency involved?

4.7 SUMMARY OF CLAIMS AND DEFENSES AND OTHER ISSUES

The next step in drafting the arbitration opinion is to succinctly set forth a summary of the claims and defenses of the parties, as well as other pertinent issues that your opinion will address. This summary serves the very important purpose of letting the reader know at the outset what the road map of your opinion will be—what kind of journey to expect. In a simple two-party case, where there are no cross-claims or counterclaims, this summary will be brief. However, in complex cases with multiple parties and multiple claims, the summary of claims and defenses conceivably could be quite extensive. Apart from a statement of the legal and equitable claims of the parties (including related requests for various types of relief) and the corresponding defenses or responses, this summary should also contain a statement of the issues which you must address prior to exploring and deciding the merits of the claims and defenses of the parties. Issues of this type consist of questions arising from or relating to: arbitrability of the case as a whole; arbitrability of particular issues in the case; motions to recuse an arbitrator; motions to disqualify counsel; motions to dismiss certain claims or parties; motions to sever claims or parties; motions to consolidate claims; motions to exclude categories of evidence; motions to bifurcate; motions for directed findings; and the like.

4.8 STATEMENT OF FACTS

4.8.1 Introduction.

The medium with which the arbitrator works permits practically an infinite number of design opportunities, from no facts at all on one end of the spectrum, to every factual detail in the record on the other. The master opinion writer earns his or her reputation by knowing which factual details to select, how to state them as facts, and where to arrange them in the opinion. The post-hearing briefs or the proposed findings of facts submitted by the parties may provide a basis for you to begin thinking about the facts and how you wish to determine them and present them. You should keep in mind, however, that the fact-finding function is yours as the arbitrator. You should approach it independently, looking only to the parties' submissions for ideas or suggested approaches. This subsection will provide guidance on the time-tested mechanics of drafting a statement of facts that properly supports the legal conclusions of your opinion.

Additionally, there are two separate and equally important design considerations to take into account when drafting a statement of facts for an arbitration opinion: form and content. For example, three varieties of form which immediately come to mind are:

1. Full, initial statement of facts at the beginning of the opinion.
2. Partial initial statement of facts, with supplemental facts in the opinion sections.
3. Full initial statement of facts as to some issues; partial initial statement of facts as to other issues, with supplemental facts in the opinion sections.

The form which the facts ultimately take may, in large measure, depend on the type of issues you have framed—fact, law, process, or mixed. Usually the form will vary from case to case. For example, if the parties have stipulated to the facts, and only legal issues are being raised, then form no. 1 *supra*, (full initial statement of facts) would be appropriate. However, if in another case, the parties have raised law, fact, and process issues, you may see the need to use form no. 3, *supra*, in presenting your statement of facts. As a novice opinion writer, much thought should go into selecting the form for presenting your facts; as you gain experience you will find that selection of form will be almost instinctive.

Content considerations also present almost limitless opportunities for creativity in your opinion writing. For the most part, you are limited only by the extent of factual detail in the record. Thus, the "story" you ultimately tell as your "statement of facts" (after evaluation and verification) is only one of an infinite variety of potential stories. As an arbitrator, you want to tell the story that is the most reasonable and compelling one in support of your award. As we shall see *infra*, such a story must be accurate, objective, and persuasive.

4.8.2   Mechanics of drafting a statement of facts.

There are a number of conventions which have developed over the years with respect to drafting a statement of facts for arbitration opinions. The principal conventions include: (1) rules or contract provisions; (2) story development; (3) headings and subheadings; (4) references to the record; and (5) quotations and footnotes. These are discussed separately, infra.

Rules or contract provisions. Some dispute resolution organizations have requirements concerning opinion drafting. Also, the parties' arbitration agreement may contain specific provisions regarding the form or format of the opinion that may relate to the statement of facts. You should read such rules or contract provisions prior to beginning your opinion.

Story development. The aim in drafting a narrative statement of facts is to produce one that reads like a novel (or short story), but is not fiction. A good facts statement is a hybrid of a novel and a chronicle (whose principal elements are factual precision and chronology). The fiction characteristic aside, the other aspects of a novel provide a useful structure within which to discuss how the story of the facts statement should be developed. Modern criticism on novel and fiction writing identifies six basic elements or aspects of writing an interesting story: organization; background; chronology; direction; synthesis; and closure.

- **Organization.** A novel is a story written as a narrative of events arranged in their time-sequence.[19] The keystone of such a story is the scene. As one author has observed, "[L]ife does not come to us packaged in a series of scenes. It is up to the writer to package it."[20] Some novelists have only a very vague notion of a story line or theme when they begin to write, allowing the story's contours to emerge from their imagination as they move through chapter-drafting from the inside-out, so to speak. Other novelists have a sketch outline of where they are going, and they permit their creativity and imagination to flesh out the details within the context of the overall plan. Still other novelists externally impose organization on story development through a more detailed outline, including important scenes or situations, character and event interaction, and an ending. The arbitrator's approach to writing a statement of facts more closely equates to this last type of novelist—but in an even more exaggerated way. Organization or "packaging" of the facts statement is facilitated, because the story's scene development is preordained by the prior selection of legal issues and by the legal arguments which have been intellectualized, to be formalized later. It is important when drafting the statement of facts that the arbitrator knows where he/she is going every step of the way. He or she must display the art of a novelist and the organization of a scientist. One way to prepare effectively for the fact drafting task is to read the parties' closing arguments immediately before you begin outlining the facts. This reading will refresh you on the parties' story structure and will assist your own structuring of the facts.

The first step in facts drafting is to make a topical outline. Though subject to change, this initial outline permits the arbitrator to think through the "scenes" needed to develop the story that best supports the ultimate conclusion presented in the legal argument. The topics in the outline will vary, depending on the case and the number and types of problem-designs (legal issues). An example of a topic outline appears *infra*. In this hypothetical case, a bank has sued three former members of its board of directors for conspiracy, fraud, self-dealing, and breach of fiduciary duty in connection with certain loan transactions. As the arbitrator, you might prepare this topic outline after reviewing the record:

---

19. E.M. Forster, "Aspects of the Novel," in J. Hersey (ed.), *The Writer's Craft* 75 (Alfred A. Knopf, 1974).
20. W. Sloane, *The Craft of Writing* 69 (W.W. Norton & Company, 1979).

I. BACKGROUND

   A. Description of Plaintiff Bank

   B. Description of Defendants Parker and Mallory

   C. Description of Loan Procedures

   D. Description of Functioning of Board of Directors

II. DEFENDANTS' MEETINGS

   A. Meeting at Director Parker's Summer Home

   B. Meeting at Colorado Ski Resort

   C. Meeting at Fireside Restaurant

III. FORMER DIRECTOR PARKER'S TRANSACTIONS

   A. The Tierney Transaction

   B. The Squires Transaction

   C. The Campbell Transaction

IV. FORMER DIRECTOR MALLORY'S TRANSACTIONS

   A. The Zeiss Transaction

   B. The Kriemelman Transaction

   C. The Tangen Transaction

V. DISCOVERY OF THE ALLEGED CONSPIRACY

   A. Complaint by Mr. Tangen

   B. Complaint by Mrs. Tierney

   C. Investigation by CPA Firm

VI. RESIGNATIONS FROM BOARD OF DIRECTORS AND EVENTS SUBSEQUENT

   A. Events Surrounding Resignations

   B. Former Directors' Written Explanations

   C. Former Directors' Statements to Government Auditors

After the topic outline is prepared, you are ready to reorganize the information in the record a format more suitable for story writing. This is commonly called "marshalling the evidence," and it consists of two separate levels of information structuring. Marshalling the evidence is analogous to what a card dealer would do with a shuffled deck of cards, if the hypothetical game required that the deck be divided into the four separate suits. The dealer, by going through the deck card by card, could easily divide it into four separate "topic" stacks of spades, hearts, diamonds, and clubs. This would constitute the first-level information structure. A second-level structure could be achieved by ordering the cards in each of the four stacks from deuce through ace. Other substructuring could also be achieved as necessary. Applying this analogy to drafting a facts statement, the topic outline discussed *supra* becomes an "evidence matrix." The evidence matrix is created by reviewing the abstract you prepared when reading the record and by transcribing each pertinent item of evidence (together with its transcript page, pleading, or exhibit) onto your evidence matrix under the appropriate topic heading (i.e. spades, hearts, diamonds, clubs, in the cards analogy). Include both favorable and unfavorable items of evidence, and beside each item, give a brief description of the evidence. When that is completed, you will have achieved first-level structuring of factual information. In the bank fraud example used *supra*, the first-level evidence structuring might appear (partially completed) as follows:

I. BACKGROUND

    A.   Description of Plaintiff Bank

        Vol. I,   Tr.   5–8   (Location, years established)
                       Tr.   9–12 (No. of employees; subsidiaries)
                       Tr. 15–20 (No. of directors and officers)

        P. Ex.   5A (Member, FDIC)

        P. Ex.   15 (Bank charter)

        P. Ex.   20 (Articles of Incorporation)

    B.   Description of Defendants

        Vol. VI,   Tr. 85–96 (Defendant Parker)
        Vol. VII,   Tr. 20–30 (Defendant Mallory)

    C.   Description of Loan Procedures

        Vol. V,   Tr. 50–75 (Supervision of Loan Accounts)
        P. Ex.   50, 66, 70 (Loan Application Forms)
        P. Ex.   25 (Standard Operating Procedures)
        P. Ex.   10 (State Banking Guidelines)
        P. Ex.   30 (American Bank Institute Guidelines)

    D.   Description of the Functioning of Board of Directors

        Vol. III,   Tr. 35–59 (Testimony of Chairman of Board)
        P. Ex.   6A (Operating Procedures, 1998–99)
        P. Ex.   6B (Operating Procedures, 1996–97)

| P. Ex. | 6C (Operating Procedures, 1994–95 |
| Vol. III, | Tr. 1–34 (Testimony of Bank President) |

II. DEFENDANTS' MEETINGS

A.   Meeting at Director Parker's Summer Home

Vol VIII,	Tr. 66–86 (Testimony of Parker's Neighbor)
P. Ex.	55 (Phone Log)
Vol VIII,	Tr. 87–100 (Testimony of Housekeeper)

After completing the first-level evidence structuring, you will be ready to perform second-level structuring in your evidence matrix. This does not have to be performed at once as to all topics. You may perform second-level evidence structuring just prior to drafting the facts, relating to the particular topical section of your outline. Second-level structuring is accomplished by placing the evidence items contained in each topical section in numerical order as they will be discussed to produce a logical story flow. (This is analogous to putting cards together by suit in numerical order). A partial example of second-level evidence structuring, showing the sequence of the facts by the numbers in the brackets on the left, appears *infra*.

I. BACKGROUND

A. Description of Plaintiff Bank

[4]	Vol. I,	Tr. 5–8 (Location, years established)
[5]		Tr. 9–12 (No. of employees; subsidiaries)
[6]		Tr. 15–20 (No. of directors and officers)
[3]	P. Ex.	5A (Member, FDIC)
[1]	P. Ex.	15 (Bank charter)
[2]	P. Ex.	20 (Articles of Incorporation)

B. Description of Defendants

| [2] | Vol. VI, | Tr. 85–96 (Defendant Parker) |
| [1] | Vol. VII, | Tr. 20–30 (Defendant Mallory) |

C. Description of Loan Procedures

[4]	Vol. V,	Tr. 50–75 (Supervision of Loan Accounts)
[5]	P. Ex.	50, 66, 70 (Loan Application Forms)
[1]	P. Ex.	25 (Standard Operating Procedures)
[2]	P. Ex.	10 (State Banking Guidelines)
[3]	P. Ex.	30 (American Bank Institute Guidelines)

D. Description of the Functioning of Board of Directors

[1]	Vol. III,	Tr. 35–59 (Testimony of Chairman of Board)
[4]	P. Ex.	6A (Operating Procedures, 1998–99)
[3]	P. Ex.	6B (Operating Procedures, 1996–97)
[2]	P. Ex.	6C (Operating Procedures, 1994–95)
[5]	Vol. III,	Tr. 1–34 (Testimony of Bank President)

II.   DEFENDANTS' MEETINGS

A. Meeting at Director Parker's Summer Home

[2]	Vol VIII,	Tr. 66–86 (Testimony of Parker's Neighbor)
[3]	P. Ex.	55 (Phone Log)
[1]	Vol VIII,	Tr. 87–100 (Testimony of Housekeeper)

By using the evidence matrix, you can begin drafting the facts of the topical sections, assured that you have all the evidence pertinent to that topic in front of you. You may decide not to use all of the information, for one reason or another. There is no question, however, that if you include or exclude information in your facts statement, you will be doing so on the basis of an informed decision. The evidence matrix will also permit you to detect immediately which elements of a claim or defense have been supported by sufficient evidence and which have not. Your analysis of the evidence matrix may even cause you to change your mind about legal conclusion you intended to make later in the opinion, or add another one that the evidence matrix generates.

- **Background.** Every statement of facts has a beginning, a middle, and an end. For our purposes, the "beginning" is the "background," the "middle" is "synthesis," and the "end" is "closure." In the background sections of the statement of facts you should identify, early on, the principal characters—the parties—and explain their interrelationships. If the plaintiff is a corporation with many subsidiaries, and knowledge of the subsidiary structure is important to an understanding of your legal conclusions, then that structure should be described in detail. You should also explain in detail the events precipitating the dispute(s) between the parties and prepare the reader by identifying the "scenes" to follow in your facts statement. If you do not include a separate "statement of the case" section in your opinion, then your background section to the statement of facts should describe the procedural history of the case, at least briefly.

You should include a "statement of the case" section of an opinion when the procedural history of the arbitration will aid readers' full understanding of your later legal analysis and conclusions. An extensive "statement of the case" is normally reserved for complex arbitration proceedings involving court-referred arbitration, multiple parties, multiple claims, and active prehearing motion practice with rulings affecting the nature and/or quantity of the hearing evidence. Ordinarily, the statement of the case includes an explanation of the nature of the parties and the dispute, the circumstances under which the case has come before the arbitration panel, and the procedural events occurring prior to the arbitration hearing. You should draft the statement of the case in the chronological order of pertinent prehearing events. The question of how much detail to include in a statement of the case is often troublesome to the novice opinion writer. It shouldn't be. First, include procedural information that will place your ultimate result in its proper context; and second, wait to draft the statement of the case until all the other parts of the opinion have been drafted. In this way, your knowledge of the case will be seasoned, and you will have a better feel for what your readers need to know, initially, about the nature of the prehearing or hearing events. Certain items should almost always be included in the statement of the case: identification of the parties, description of their respective claims, and the relief sought by the parties. Which prehearing procedural events should be included will depend largely on the issues you plan to address in your opinion. If discovery and other prehearing rulings are the subject of your opinion, you should include a discussion of those items. If prehearing and hearing evidentiary rulings are important in the shaping your decision in the case, then you should discuss the nature and details of those rulings. Dates of procedural events should be included if they are significant in relation to your later analysis.

- **Chronology.** Your statement of facts should normally chronicle events in the time sequence of their occurrence. However, if no relevant "events" occurred (e.g. arbitration concerns only the interpretation of a contract provision), no chronology may be necessary.

- **Synthesis.** Synthesis involves integrating characters, dialogue, and events into something called a plot. A storyteller would define a plot as an arrangement of related events establishing a situation, with anticipation, suspense, emotion, and satisfaction in a dramatic form.[21] As one storyteller put it, "'The king died and then the queen died' is a story. 'The king died, and then the

---

21. H. and W. Burnett, *Fiction Writer's Handbook* 34 (Harper & Row, 1975).

queen died of grief' is a plot. The time sequence is perceived, but the sense of causality overshadows it."[22]

You should keep in mind that the way evidence comes into the record at the arbitration hearing has little or nothing to do with the way information should be presented in the arbitration opinion. The order of evidence at the hearing is dictated by many variables, including the availability of witnesses at particular times, the reduction of certain evidence to stipulations, the use of summaries of documentary evidence introduced at the beginning or end of a hearing, the use of audiotapes and transcripts, etc. Sometimes the order of the evidence makes little or no sense at all. That is why the closing argument is such an important aspect of arbitration. That is the moment when the advocates synthesize for the arbitrators all the bits and pieces of evidence that have come before them in various forms and sequence, in order to communicate an organized, logical, credible story. The arbitrator does something very similar when he/she writes a statement of facts, but the arbitrator has the advantage of time—time to analyze, reflect, and craft words and sentences. Toward this end, as noted *supra*, the arbitrator's review of the transcript of the closing argument in a case prior to fact drafting is very helpful to the arbitrator. It greatly facilitates the synthesis task. In a statement of facts, the sense of causality of a "plot," which emerges from the evidence synthesis, must arise from a relationship of words and ideas. It should not be overtly communicated, however. Save causality statements for the section of the opinion in which you discuss, analyze, and apply the law to the facts of your case.

• **Direction.** A story must move the reader in some direction. There must be some underlying theme, message, moral, or perceivable pattern with which the reader can identify. The direction of the statement of facts is toward the legal conclusions to be made later. The arbitrator must never lose sight of them when he/she is drafting the facts statement. Every word must count in the overall plan. Nothing is right until all is done, and a total unity between facts and legal conclusions has been accomplished.

• **Closure.** A statement of facts must give a sense of permanence, as well as a sense of life. Each fact statement shares with the reader a glimpse of life, offering a peek through a keyhole to view a segment of humanity in a given frame of time. In that sense, each is a discrete set of scenes, with has a beginning and an end. A statement of facts must have closure; but it can be subtle. The ending must give the reader the feeling of having gone full-circle through

---

22. E.M. Forster, *supra* note 19 at 72.

a story with a return to the starting point—to await the "meta-story," or critique, the legal conclusions confirming who the villains and heroes are, and why.

In summary, in drafting a statement of facts, you are, in part, creating the overall background for the legal conclusions and disposition which will follow. In some respects, the simpler a background is, the better the figure in front of it will be. "Simple" does not mean short. It means clear, direct language presented mostly in the active voice, void of any legalisms (hereinbefore, thereinafter, etc.) or other similar gobbledygook. The statement of facts must also be thorough. It should not include every detail of the record, but rather those items necessary to support, complement, and harmonize with the legal conclusions. Many an arbitrator has fussed for hours over a legal conclusion, never getting it right because the defect is an omission in the statement of facts, which he has neglected. Finally, the facts statement must be credible. That is, it must be accurate and must communicate characters, relationships, and events in such a way that the reader can identify with it and believe that they could have rationally existed or occurred in the ordinary course of human interaction and involvement.

Headings and subheadings. The text of the statement of facts should be interspersed with topical headings and subheadings in order to communicate organization and development of context and to enhance readability. These, of course, can be borrowed directly (or modified) from the topic headings of the evidence matrix discussed supra. Also see Section 4.9.3, *infra*.

References to the record. It is advisable for you to provide references to the record in your statement of facts. This is particularly true where you know that your arbitration opinion is subject to review by a government agency or an appellate arbitration panel. If within a paragraph of the statement of facts, sentences are derived from facts contained in different parts of the record (transcript, pleadings, exhibits), or if several parts of the record support the information contained in a particular sentence or sentences, each sentence should be separately referenced to the record. If an entire paragraph is grounded on one or more pages of the record, then the record reference(s) may appear at the end of the paragraph. Customary designation symbols are "Tr." for transcript and "Ex." for exhibits. If you have the least concern that the parties or any reviewing tribunal will not understand what part of the record your symbol refers to, you should explain the meaning of your symbols early in your brief, usually in a footnote.

Quotations and footnotes. The general convention about quotations and footnotes is to use them sparingly and tastefully. The same guidelines applicable to use of quotations and footnotes in drafting legal conclusions is also pertinent in a statement of facts (see Sections 4.10.7 and 4.10.8 *infra*).

4.8.3 Writing with accuracy.

The validity of a legal conclusion, like the conclusion of a syllogism, is critically dependent upon the truth of the factual premises from which it derives. Although part of the validity of the reasoning in an arbitration opinion derives from proper selection of case precedent, a good share of its validity hinges on the truth and accuracy of its factual predicates. Thus, to ensure the soundness and legitimacy of your arbitration opinions, you should take exceptional care to ensure that they are factually accurate.

In order to guard against making unintentional misstatements of the record in drafting your statement of facts, you should apply three basic rules of factual accuracy:

Ensure that each fact is supported by the record. You must be able to document every sentence in your facts statement. It's not enough to "feel certain" about a fact—that's certitude. You must be certain. You may not need to physically reference each sentence to the record, but you must be fully satisfied that you could provide record references if asked. Never present matters outside the record as fact, unless an exception applies, such as judicial notice.

Take care not to modify content of the record. Do not paraphrase quotations of colloquy or testimony. Never quote out of context where it will alter the plain meaning of the text in the record.

Be careful not to omit material facts. Misstatement of the record is possible through commission or omission. Omitting crucial, material facts can be as serious an error as actively misstating the record.

Use the correct words. Another aspect of writing with accuracy is using the correct words to convey your intended meaning. This involves correct selection and spelling of words. When writing an arbitration opinion, don't hesitate to use a dictionary or thesaurus. Choosing the wrong word can blur written communication and perhaps cause you embarrassment. Here are a few pairs and groups of words which warrant careful attention:[23]

adapt:	to adjust, to make suitable
adept:	apt, skilled, proficient
adopt:	to accept or take as one's own
affect:	to influence; to cause a response (always a verb)
effect:	result (noun); to cause (verb)

---

23. Definitions extracted from H. Shaw, *Dictionary of Problem Words and Expressions* (McGraw-Hill, 1975).

allusion: indirect mention or reference
elusion: escape
illusion: something strongly supposed to exist

ambiguous: having several possible meanings
equivocal: not determined; of doubtful nature

biannual: twice a year; semi-annual
biennial: once in two years or lasting two years

censer: incense burner
censor: to examine
censure: to condemn or to find fault

ceremonial: used to describe a formal act or deed (custom) in relation to things
ceremonious: same, but in relation to persons

consecutive: uninterrupted succession
successive: following in a regular (but not necessarily uninterrupted) sequence

consistently: steadfastly, without change
constantly: perpetually, unceasingly

discreet: prudent, cautious, careful
discrete: separate, distinct, apart
disregardless: not a word—use regardless
irregardless: not a word—use regardless

effective: something that has power to produce, or which does produce, an effect or result
efficient: use of energy, skill, or industry to produce a desired result
effectual: refers to any agency or force that produces an intended or desired result

emerge: to come forth
immerge: to plunge into; to disappear

exceedingly: to an unusual degree, extremely
excessively: too much; beyond normal limits

exceptionable:	objectionable
exceptional:	extraordinary, unusual
factitious:	artificial; contrived—applied to things
fictitious:	not real, applied to works of the imagination
farther:	refers to measurable distance in space
further:	greater in quantity, time, and degree; also means moreover
feasible:	capable of being done
possible:	able to happen
ferment:	excitement, commotion, tumult, in a state of unrest (used as a noun)
foment:	to incite; to arouse; to inflame (a verb only)
flaunt:	to show off; to make a boastful display
flout:	to scoff at; to scorn
forbear:	to desist, to keep back (verb)
forebear:	an ancestor; forefather (noun)
forego:	to go before; precede
forgo:	to give up; to abstain
foreword:	preface, introductory statement
forward:	in front; located in advance
gantlet:	kind of military punishment ("running the gantlet")
gauntlet:	kind of glove ("taking up the gauntlet")
gamut:	series of musical notes; the whole range of anything
illicit:	unlawful
elicit:	to bring out; to draw forth
immanent:	inherent
imminent:	impending
eminent:	prominent; respected
imply:	to suggest a meaning only hinted, not explicitly stated
infer:	to draw a conclusion from statements, evidence, or circumstances

ordinance:	regulation, rule, law
ordnance:	artillery; military weapons of any kind
perspective:	mental point of view (noun)
prospective:	expected; potential (adjective)
precede:	to come before; to go in advance of
proceed:	to go forward; to carry on
presumptuous:	arrogant; taking too much for granted
presumptive:	based on inference; not fully established
principal:	main, foremost
principle:	a governing rule or truth
rebound:	to spring back
redound:	to have an effect or result; to accrue
simplified:	made less complex and complicated
simplistic:	overly simplified
tortuous:	winding; crooked
torturous:	full of or causing pain or torture

As to spelling accuracy, below are listed some of the words arbitrators frequently misspell when writing opinions. If this list does not contain a word you are having trouble spelling, please consult a dictionary. Don't risk guessing incorrectly.

Words Ending in IBLE

accessible
admissible
comprehensible
corruptible
destructible
discernible
divisible
imperceptible
incompatible
indefensible
infallible
permissible

Words Ending in ANT

claimant
complainant
conversant
exorbitant
extravagant
intolerant
irrelevant
preponderant
redundant
vigilant

Words Ending in ENT

correspondent
eminent
immanent
imminent
improvident
imprudent
independent
inexpedient
insolvent
intermittent
irreverent
preeminent
transcendent
translucent

Words Ending in ER

accuser
adviser or advisor
assayer
extortioner

Words Ending in OR

adjudicator
ancestor
assessor
benefactor
collaborator
contractor
distributor

grantor
guarantor
interlocutor
investigator
investor
malefactor
mediator
narrator
operator
originator
perpetrator
possessor
precursor
predecessor
procrastinator
progenitor
proprietor
purveyor
spectator
speculator
stipulator
successor
supervisor
testator
warrantor

Words Ending in CEDE

accede
concede
intercede
precede
recede
secede

Words Ending in CEED

exceed
proceed
succeed

Words Ending in SEDE

supersede

4.8.4   Writing objectively.

Inexperienced arbitrators often have difficulty differentiating between "stating the facts" and "arguing the facts." With a little instruction and a few examples, however, they can quickly grasp the differences. "Stating the facts" means writing the facts objectively, yet appealingly. The persuasive effect of "stating the facts" arises almost exclusively from selection and juxtaposition of pieces of evidence in the record. Qualifying or modifying adjectives and adverbs are used with the utmost conservatism—and only if they are wholly justified and documented in the record. "Arguing the facts" in connection with forming legal conclusions, on the other hand, permits much more latitude. It allows characterization of facts and inferences, so long as they are reasonable and not strained or misleading. Qualifying and/or modifying adjectives and adverbs are welcome guests. However, one principle must be etched in your memory. Facts may never be argued in the "statement of facts" section of the opinion. The statement of facts must be written in a totally objective manner. In order to aid you in understanding the distinction between stating the facts and arguing the facts, consider this example:

Excerpt from Statement of Facts:

> John Smith, a young man who spoke Polish fluently but very little English, applied for employment with EZ Janitorial Service ("EZ") on July 5, 1989. EZ hired him on July 6, 1989. Mr. Wilson, a supervisor at EZ, spent less than 15 minutes interviewing him. In making the hiring decision, Mr. Wilson, himself hired without being interviewed, relied mostly on a recommendation from Mr. Falcon, whom Wilson had known for some years. Wilson did not ask anyone whether Smith had ever been arrested and convicted of a crime. Wilson did not check with the police department, Federal Bureau of Investigation, or any other person or entity about Smith's possible criminal record. Wilson accepted Smith's denial that he was ever arrested, and he checked no further into the information contained in Smith's employment application. A bank employee later identified Mr. Smith as the rapist. (Tr. 20-24; 43-45)

Note that in this excerpt the opinion writer uses reasonably short declarative sentences without editorializing. To the extent possible, the writer uses the actual words contained in the transcript. The writer avoids using connecting words (however, moreover, therefore, accordingly, consequently, etc.) because they naturally induce an argumentative tone.

Excerpt from the Legal Conclusions Concerning Same Facts:

> The conduct of EZ Janitorial service here was negligent and confirms the need for a liberal interpretation of the scope of the "Security

Guard Act." At the time of the rape, EZ had been performing janitorial and security services for the Bank Building for approximately eight years. During this period and at the time of the hiring of Smith, EZ's hiring procedures were extremely lax. Mr. Wilson, the security and janitorial supervisor of the Bank Building, had been hired in 1983 without an interview. EZ hired Smith after a 15-minute interview, and EZ performed no follow-up background check. Yet, EZ later assigned Smith to perform sensitive security duties at the Bank Building, and a bank employee later identified Smith as her rapist. This is precisely the type of situation that the craftsmen of the Security Guard Act sought to obviate.

Note that in this example, the statement of facts portion simply recounts the testimony in the record, but the argument "labels" the conduct of EZ as negligent and ties in the statute, implying that it was this conduct that the legislature specifically intended to prevent.

4.8.5 Writing to persuade.

To be effective, your statement of facts must persuade. The persuasion referred to here is much different from that found in the legal analysis section of the opinion. Here, facts are subconsciously compelling to the reader; there, facts are consciously compelling. Persuasion is that quality of the statement of facts that makes facts "live and bear fruit." It is not a natural quality of facts; it is a quality acquired by facts only through the opinion writer's artful selection, crafting, and juxtaposition of factual information in the record.

Selecting evidence for fact sentences. By creating an evidence matrix (described *supra*), a good deal of the facts selection task is accomplished. During that sorting process, you have already, consciously or unconsciously, eliminated, that evidence which is not usable in the statement of facts. The bases for your decision to eliminate evidence may have been relevance, credibility, redundancy, authenticity, or others. The evidence contained in your evidence matrix, however, represents information you have selected for conversion into "facts." Figuratively, you have put all the information in the record through an imaginary colander. What remains in the colander is now the medium for your art, but the selection process is not yet complete. You must next determine, under each heading or subheading of your evidence matrix, the evidence that is specifically usable as facts. In making this selection you must keep the following criteria in mind.

(1) The factual information selected must:
    a. be credible
    b. relevant to your story
    c. generally support your legal conclusions, or
    d. show the impossibility of the losing party's story or legal theory

(2) Relevant factual information unfavorable to the winning party should always be selected and dealt with as described infra in this section.

Having accomplished this secondary colander process (and having put the factual items in numerical order for story telling), you are ready to begin crafting fact sentences.

Crafting fact sentences. The statement of facts is composed of a series of fact sentences. These fact sentences should, where possible, take the form of simple, declarative sentences in the active voice. They are often composed of several fact phrases. It should be emphasized that the words or fact phrases used as persuasion enhancers must appear in the record in the precise form that they are used in the statement of facts (if the word "prominently" was used by the witness, the word "prominently" should appear in the facts statement, not a synonym). Characterizing the facts (using words not contained in the record) can be done later when you are presenting the facts and their inferences in connection with your legal analysis and conclusions.

Juxtaposing fact sentences. By positioning or juxtaposing fact sentences, you can achieve enhancement of their overall persuasive quality. Juxtaposition of fact sentences may yield either emphasis of facts favorable to the winning party or dilution of facts unfavorable to that party, depending on what the objective telling of the story allows.

4.9 DISCUSSING, ANALYZING, AND APPLYING RELEVANT LAW OR EQUITABLE PRINCIPLES—GENERAL CONSIDERATIONS

You should consider the following matters when drafting the section of your arbitration opinion in which you discuss, analyze, and apply the law in stating your legal conclusions: (1) complying with rules or contract provisions; (2) selecting and sequencing topics; (3) designing headings and subheadings; and (4) using a simple, direct writing style.

4.9.1 Rules or contract provisions.

Some dispute resolution organizations may have requirements concerning opinion drafting. Also, the parties' arbitration agreement may contain specific provisions regarding the form or format of the opinion that may relate to legal analysis and legal conclusions. You should read any such rules or contract provisions prior to beginning your opinion.

4.9.2 Selecting and sequencing topics.

If you have designed and organized the issues and sub-issues according to the instructions given in Section 4.7, supra, then selecting and sequencing of topics is all but complete. The effectiveness of the layout of your legal analysis and legal conclusions is directly dependent on the layout you designed for your issues. If your legal conclusions appear not to fit together and flow neatly and logically, then it is time to do some tinkering with your issue identification, evaluation, and organization process. Do not hesitate to return to the design of the problem when you are having difficulty designing the solution.

4.9.3 Designing headings and subheadings.

You must strive to paint for your readers a picture that they can perceive in their minds' eye; and the picture must be simple. This theme must permeate all phases of your opinion writing, and its application has special significance in the design and arrangement of the headings and subheadings in your legal analysis and conclusions. Headings and subheadings in the argument help paint the total picture of your logic and reasoning for your readers. Your headings and subheadings must have characteristics of color and interest, on the one hand, and organization and structure on the other. They must also be simple and direct in style and communicative content. In short, they should be succinct, simple, declarative sentences. Rarely should they contain complex clauses. To achieve color, you should tie the separate point headings to the facts of the case. They should not appear to be merely bland truisms, incontrovertible generalizations, or as one commentator has stated "blind headnotes" which might fit any number of cases. Another aspect of color in point headings is the form in which they are presented. It is customary for the point headings to appear in "all caps" or "initial caps." Also, underscoring or bolding is helpful to emphasize them so they catch the reader's eye.

Color and interest are closely connected. If you add color to a point heading you also make it more interesting. Take care not to make the point heading too long. A long, complex point heading defeats its purpose of being a quick picture—a snapshot. Readers soon lose interest in headings that are overly specific. Another option to enhance interest is to use the name of the party in the point heading, rather than a general label of "plaintiff" or "defendant." This option should be employed particularly where there are several parties to the arbitration proceeding. If you choose to use the names of the parties in your point headings, be consistent. Don't use "plaintiff" in one point heading, "complainant" in another, and "Mr. Smith" in yet another. This can be very confusing to your reader.

Aside from color and interest, point headings viewed holistically, must have organization and structure. To effectively list point headings in a table of contents in the front of the opinion, their organization and structure must appear to be (or, in fact, be) an inverted syllogism or series of inverted syllogisms with the headings being the conclusions and the subheadings being the conjunctive or disjunctive premises. Of course, in many cases the syllogisms may have many premises and subpremises, and subheadings might be used for other communicative purposes, including: dividing legal issues from factual issues; discussion of issues relating to particular parties; discussion of various lines of case authority; and interrupting expanse of printed matter. Overall, however, the structure of the point headings should give a crisp, clear picture of your legal conclusions as a whole, and also communicate a feeling of inevitability, credibility, logic, and truth.

4.9.4 Use charts, diagrams, and graphic illustrations where appropriate.

To synthesize large quantities of information, it is often helpful to readers of your opinion to incorporate charts and diagrams. Graphic illustrations, particularly in construction cases, patent cases, cases involving tracts of land, or cases involving abstract concepts, are also useful tools. All of these tools, when tastefully employed, can enhance the persuasive effect of the arguments contained in your ratio decidendi.

4.9.5 Using a simple and direct writing style.

Various commentators concerned with the topic of effective legal writing have used, among others, these terms to describe its characteristics: accuracy, brevity, clarity,[24] conciseness, precision, simplicity, and forcefulness.[25] William Strunk's, Elements of Style, the diminutive treatise which has been acclaimed for decades as the "last word" on effective writing, declares that writing must be simple and direct.[26] An eager editor could perhaps whisk away the "simple" as superfluous and leave "direct," which alone implies all the other characteristics. However, for organizational purposes, the two-word model nicely serves a discussion of legal writing style.

- **Employ a simple writing style.** The rules and examples displayed below are instructive on the elements of a simple writing style.

Omit unnecessary words. Strive for vigorous writing. Vigorous writing is concise. A sentence should contain no unnecessary words; a paragraph no unnecessary sentences.

Examples[27]

Wordy Version	Suggested
at the time	when
by means of	by
cause it to be done	have it done

---

24. E. Re, *Briefwriting and Oral Argument*, 6th ed., 8 (Occarra Publications, 1987).
25. H. Weihofen, *Legal Writing Style* (West, 1980), p. 4.
26. W. Strunk and E.B. White, the *Elements of Style*, 2d ed. (Macmillan Co., 1972), pp. vii-xii.
27. R. Leflar, *Appellate Judicial Opinions* 197 (West, 1974).

does not operate to	does not
during such time as	while
during the course of	during
for the reason that	because
give consideration to	consider
have a need of	need
in cases in which	when, where, if
in order to	to
in the event that, in case	if
in the interest of	for
is able to	can
is applicable	applies
is binding upon	binds
is unable to	cannot
is directed, is the duty	shall
it shall be lawful	may
make application	apply
on the part of	by
period of time	period, time
provided that	if, however
provisions of law	law
pursuant to	under
subsequent to	after
to the effect that	that
until such time as	until
under the provisions of	under

Do not use stilted, archaic, or overly intellectual language. Opt for simple words over formal ones:

Instead of:	Use:
consummate	complete
elucidate	explain
endeavor	try
expiration	end
utilize	use
interpose an objection	object
raise the question	ask

Avoid latinisms (a fortiori, sui generis, sine qua non, etc.) and legalisms (hereinbefore, thereinafter, etc.). Lighten style by removing weighty nouns.

Instead of:	Use:
We initiated the practice of looking up the law on the computer.	We started to use computerized legal research.

Favor focused words over unfocused; concrete over abstract.

Instead of:	Use:
He demonstrated satisfaction as he took possession of his well-earned opinion writing	He grinned broadly as he clutched his opinion writing award. award.

The position of words in a sentence can cause ambiguity. Concentrate on bringing together words and groups of words that are related in thought, and keep apart those that are not so related.

Instead of:	Use:
He only found two mistakes in the opinion.	He found only two mistakes in the opinion.
An arbitrator, if you fail to train him, does not progress professionally.	Unless trained, an arbitrator stagnates professionally.

Use correct transitional words. Using the correct transitional words assists the flow of communication. Here are some examples of transitional words and their uses:[28]

Words and phrases that signal a shift of topic from paragraph to paragraph within a document:

> moving now to a related point
> on the other hand
> associated but not precisely the same as
> another topic worthy of treatment here is
> analogously

Words and phrases linking one paragraph (or sentence) to another within a section (subdivided according to context):

Words that signal the addition of ideas:

similarly	too	in the same way
furthermore	in addition	nor

---

28. R. Weisberg, *When Lawyers Write* 163 (Little, Brown & Co., 1987).

moreover	next	and
likewise	besides	last

Words that signal the contrast of ideas or the concession of a point:

but	although	still
in contrast	however	conversely
on the contrary	yet	nevertheless
granted	even though	in spite of
notwithstanding		

Words that signal the introduction of an example:

for example	for instance	to illustrate
as proof	specifically	

Words that signal a cause and effect relationship:

as a result	since	thus
accordingly	so	then
therefore	consequently	because

Words that signal emphasis:

certainly	truly	surely
in fact	indeed	undoubtedly

Words that signal a summary or a conclusion:

thus	to sum up	therefore
accordingly	finally	in short
in conclusion	in summation	consequently

• **Employ a direct writing style.** The rules and examples displayed below are instructive on the elements of a direct writing style.

Use the active voice. The passive voice is often ambiguous and usually less forceful.

"I shall always remember my first arbitration hearing."

This is a much better version than:

"My first arbitration hearing will always be remembered by me."

The latter sentence is less direct, less bold, less concise. If the writer tries to make it more concise by omitting "by me," the sentence becomes indefinite:

"My first arbitration hearing will be remembered."

This version leaves open the question of who will remember it—the writer, some undisclosed person, the world at large?

Draft sentences in a positive form. Make definite, affirmative assertions. Avoid couching sentences in negative, receding, or noncommittal language.

Instead of:	Use:
Did not pay attention to	Ignored
Did not have much confidence	Distrusted

Use verbs to strengthen content. Use more direct transitive verbs, not merely the corollary "to be" intransitive ones.

Instead of:	Use:
Made the decision	Decided
Is binding on	Binds

Pay attention to arrangement of words and parallel construction. At the beginning of a sentence, avoid weak words and phrases or clauses initiated by the word "not." Make sure that verbs agree with subjects and that pronouns have appropriate antecedents. Strive for parallel construction in phrasing and constructing clauses.

Instead of:	Use:
Parallel sentence structures are not difficult to achieve and consist of patterns or arrangements of words so as to obtain balance and accent.	Parallel sentence structure consists of pattern arrangement of words to achieve balance and accent.

Punctuate properly.

- In a series of three or more terms with a single conjunction, use a comma after each term before the last term.

She stayed up late that night to read the record, to review the briefs, and to write her opinion.

- Enclose parenthetical expressions with commas.

The arbitrator, in his mid-eighties, sprightly entered the room and called the hearing to order.

- Use a comma to set off an independent clause.

  The court reporter was a friendly chap, and he enjoyed a great reputation among the arbitrators.

- Use a comma to set off a nonrestrictive clause (nonrestrictive clauses usually begin with "which"; restrictive clauses begin with "that").

Please get the claimant's brief, which is in the bottom drawer of the file cabinet (nonrestrictive).

Please get the claimant's brief that is in the bottom drawer of the file cabinet (restrictive).

Now that you have had a short refresher course in composition, you may wish to test your knowledge and proficiency on the subject. There is at least one grammatical or compositional error in each of the 28 sentences below (and even in the title).[29] The sentences themselves, provide clues to detecting the errors. Good luck.

28 MATTERS THAT WRITERS OUGHT TO BE APPRAISED OF

1. Subjects and verb always has to agree.
2. Make each pronoun agree with their antecedent.
3. Just between you and I, case is important too.
4. Being bad grammar, the writer will not use dangling participles.
5. Parallel construction with coordinate conjunctions is not only an aid to clarity but also the mark of a good writer.
6. Join clauses good, like a conjunction should.
7. Don't write run-on sentences they are hard to read, you should punctuate.
8. Don't use no double negatives. Not never.
9. Mixed metaphors are a pain in the neck and ought to be thrown out the window.
10. A truly good writer is always especially careful to practically eliminate the too-frequent use of adverbs.
11. In my opinion, I think that an author when he is writing something should not get accustomed to the habit of making use of too many redundant unnecessary words that he does not actually really need in order to put his message across to the reader of what he has written.
12. About them sentence fragments. Sometimes all right.
13. Try to not ever split infinitives.

---

29. R. Leflar, *Appellate Judicial Opinions* 195 (West, 1974).

14. Its important to use your apostrophe's correctly.

15. Do not use a foreign term when there is an adequate English quid pro quo.

16. If you must use a foreign term, it is de rigor to use it correctly.

17. It behooves the writer to avoid archaic expressions.

18. Do not use hyperbole; not one writer in a million can use it effectively.

19. But, don't use commas, which are not necessary.

20. Placing a comma between subject and predicate, is not correct.

21. Parenthetical words however should be enclosed in commas.

22. Use a comma before nonrestrictive clauses which are a common source of difficulty.

23. About repetition, the repetition of a word is not usually an effective kind of repetition.

24. Consult the dictionary frequently to avoid mispelling. "Corect speling is esential [sic]."

25. In scholarly writing, don't use contractions.

27. Proofread your writing to see if you any words out.

28. Last but not least, knock off the cliches. Avoid cliches like the plague.

In summary, your written opinion should be well-organized and divided by headings and subheadings where appropriate. Your writing style should be simple and direct. Use of unnecessary words and legalese, archaic, or intellectual language is always inappropriate. Words should be chosen carefully, and appropriate conventions of style, grammar, construction, and punctuation should be heeded. Do not repeat yourself. Avoid bluster and a self-important style with a passion. Keep your writing simple and unpretentious and its greatness will shine through.

4.10   DRAFTING THE RATIO DECIDENDI

4.10.1 Introduction.

Ratio decidendi is the Latin expression that describes the process of stating the reasons for a decision.[30] In arbitration, it describes the portion of an arbitrator's written opinion that discusses, analyzes, and applies legal principles. It involves the construction of a legal "argument" or a series of legal "arguments." Many of the same principles applicable to writing legal arguments for a court-filed brief also apply to writing the legal arguments contained in the ratio decidendi of an arbitration opinion. Persuasion, not merely logic, is the ultimate goal of such legal arguments. "Logic" and "persuasion" are not synonymous. Logic is merely one component of persuasion; granted a very important one. What is persua-

---

30. Aldisert, *supra* note 15 at 105-49.

sion? What are its elements? Besides its logical component, persuasion also has emotional and ethical (or value) components. In essence, a persuasive argument appeals to reason, emotions, and moral values. In order to maximize the overall persuasive effect of the arguments in your arbitration opinion you need to achieve a balance among those three elements.

There are five techniques for achieving this balance when discussing, analyzing, and applying the law in your arbitration opinion. They are: (1) think like a judge; (2) use an effective argument format; (3) know and apply the skills of legal analysis; (4) use charts, diagrams, and graphic illustrations where appropriate; and (5) avoid certain types of arguments. These techniques will be discussed separately in the next five subsections.

4.10.2 Thinking like a judge.

"Thinking like a judge" has been a recurring theme throughout this work. However, this skill or technique takes on special significance when you begin to draft the ratio decidendi of your arbitration opinion. At that moment, you must "crawl inside the judges' universe" and view the world through their eyes. You must ask yourself the question—if I were a judge, how would I view these facts and this law? Putting aside my own personal biases and prejudices, what would be persuasive to the average judge? You must ask and answer this question against the background of what a judge's role is in society and the specific judicial duties accompanying that role.

After assuming a judicial mind-set, take time to appreciate the judge's view of the world. You will first realize that, as judge, your role in society is quite simple to say, much more difficult to do. Simply stated, your primary role is to decide who's right and who's wrong in the disputes assigned to you, and to provide reasons supporting your decision. As a judge, your decisions and reasons will be conveyed through the vehicle of a judicial opinion. In drafting this opinion, you will have to differentiate between and apply the five separate aspects of legal precepts, which are:

(1) *Rules.* These are precepts attaching a definite, detailed consequence to a definite, detailed state of facts. A rule is usually the holding—the rule of law of a case.

(2) *Principles.* These are authoritative starting points for legal reasoning, employed continually and legitimately where cases are not covered or are not fully or obviously covered by rules in a narrower sense. Very often these authoritative starting points compete.

(3) *Legal Conception.* These are authoritative categories to which types or classes of transactions, cases, or situations are referred, in consequence of

which a series of rules, principles, and standards become applicable. They are chiefly the work of law teachers and law writers.

(4) *Doctrines.* These are systematic syntheses of rules, principles, and conceptions with respect to particular situations or types of cases or fields of the legal order. They are organized in logically interdependent schemes, whereby reasoning may proceed on the basis of the scheme and its logical implications. Doctrines are sometimes more or less embedded in legislation, and to some extent, in the course of judicial decision. They are the work of writers and teachers, and in the end and on the whole, their influence is exerted through the textbooks. As a rule, they have no formal authorities.

(5) *Standards.* These are general limits of permissible conduct to be applied according to the circumstances of each case. No definite, detailed set of facts is provided for. No definite pattern is laid down. No threat is attached to any defined situation. These are sometimes created by legislation, sometimes by doctrinal writers, and sometimes by judicial decision.

In most cases, the audience for your arbitration opinion will be limited to the parties and counsel in the case before you. However, if your arbitration opinion is issued under circumstances which require or allow it to be published, then your audience will be similar to the variety of audiences applicable to a published judicial opinion. Those audiences traditionally include:

1. judges (and arbitrators);
2. litigants in similar cases and their counsel;
3. the court or agency in which the litigation originates;
4. the general public;
5. the media;
6. the bar of your and other states;
7. law schools, faculties, and editors of law reviews;
8. societies whose goals are to improve or advance the law in specific topical areas;
9. Congress, state legislatures, and their committees; and
10. publishers of specialized reports.[31]

When applying the five aspects of legal precepts and considering the various potential audiences, the judge also has to take into account style and content considerations of judicial opinion writing, as follows:[32]

---

31. R. Leflar, *Some Observations Concerning Judicial Opinions*, 61 Colum L Rev 819 (1961).
32. Adapted from J. Hopkins, *Notes on Style in Judicial Opinions*, 8 Trial Judges Jour 49 (1969).

1. The approach of the opinion writer should be measured, temperate, and objective.
2. Usually facts should be stated at the outset; in some cases, facts are best discussed with their related issue(s).
3. Write simple declarative sentences.
4. Use active voice.
5. Use footnotes and quotations tastefully.
6. Use appropriate grammatical construction, sentence and paragraph structure, and choice of words.
7. Avoid reiteration.
8. Be careful of cliches, metaphors, and humor. Irony can be effective, if used sparingly.
9. Be clear and concise in language.
10. Do not over-cite.
11. Usually, a decision should be made on a major ground; avoid having decision rest on alternative grounds.
12. Ensure that precedent distinguished is truly distinguishable.
13. When interpreting a statute give effect to its spirit and intent.
14. Relief should be sharply defined.

Now, let's revert to the perception of the arbitrator and reflect on what we have learned from seeing the world through the eyes of judges. First, we learned that judges know and apply certain aspects of precept. As arbitrators, in order to communicate effectively with our audiences, we must also be able to distinguish between these aspects of precept and demonstrate our ability to do so in the design of our *ratio decidendi*. Moreover, we must be aware of the social interests involved in our particular case, and if appropriate, suggest the manner in which they must be balanced, when applying aspects of precept, to achieve justice. We must also keep in mind the audiences to which judges communicate in their judicial opinions. In some cases, those will also be our audiences.

Finally, when you study the structure, style, and content requirements of a judicial opinion, you quickly realize that the differences between a well-written judicial opinion, on the one hand, and a well-written arbitrator's opinion, on the other, are minuscule. The five part structure of the judicial opinion corresponds neatly with the five basic parts of an arbitrator's opinion. The closer your arbitration opinion approximates the requirements of a well-written judicial opinion, the better chance you will have that it be perceived as cogent, persuasive, and compelling by the parties, their counsel, and by any judges who might be required to review it.

Thinking like a judge is an important aspect of achieving a persuasive quality in your *ratio decidendi*. There is perhaps no greater honor for an arbitrator than to have the opinion of a reviewing tribunal track closely the reasoning and analysis of the *ratio decidendi* contained in his or her arbitration opinion. Arbitrators should have as their continuing goal to be students of the judicial mind and of the judicial role throughout their careers.

4.10.3 Using an effective analysis format.

Actually, designing an effective analysis format follows simple common sense dictates. Your *ratio decidendi* will normally contain several segments, each separately addressing a theory of claim being advanced by the claimant or plaintiff. As to each segment, keep this simple organizational strategy in mind" (1) tell 'em what you're going to tell 'em; (2) tell 'em; and (3) tell 'em what you told 'em. The steps of this simple format are further explained in the chart below.

---

(1) The heading of each segment should communicate the claimant's theory of recovery.
(The first paragraph of a segment should consist of a "set up" paragraph, letting the reader know what is coming in that segment—what to expect.)

(2) The first sentence or two of the first paragraph should concisely describe the claim of the claimant; the next couple of sentences should briefly describe the respondent's response or defense; and the next sentence or two should describe what your conclusion is with respect to that claim for recovery, and should point out that your reasons will be explained in the succeeding paragraphs.

(3) Then, analyze facts and relevant authorities (common law, statutory, and doctrinal analyses usually precede policy analysis) pertinent to the claim being discussed in the segment.

(4) State your conclusions regarding the merit of the claim and, if appropriate, describe the nature of relief or recovery to which the claimant is entitled, and the reasons supporting it.
(Provide a paragraph summarizing your conclusions as to that segment of the opinion.)

4.10.4 Knowing and applying the skills of legal analysis.

You can be analytical in communicating and explaining your *ratio decidendi* only if you know and apply the skills of legal analysis. These skills include: (1) applying the correct burden and standard of proof; (2) selecting and using case authority; (3) selecting and using statutory authority; (4) selecting and using other authorities; (5) applying techniques for using and arguing facts; (6) blending facts and authorities; and (7) arguing public policy.

Applying the correct burden and standard of proof. When you are reasoning to a conclusion in determining the merits of any claim or defense, it is very important to keep in mind which party has the burden of proof, and what standard of proof must be applied to the evidence adduced. Realize that the burden of proof may shift from party to party on certain issues, depending on the area of law or particular statutes involved. Also realize that even though one party may have the burden on a particular issue, another party may have the burden of proof overall. Ordinarily, the standard of proof in civil cases is "preponderance of the evidence." However, be careful to recognize circumstances where statutes, rules, or common law require "clear and convincing" evidence, "substantial evidence," or some other more stringent measure to be applied.

If you are sitting as an appellate arbitrator, you will be concerned with applying the appropriate scope and standard of review applicable in the first-level appellate court in the pertinent jurisdiction. "Scope of review" refers to the issues or matters: (1) the appellate panel has authority to hear and decide; and (2) the parties have properly preserved at the arbitration hearing for argument on appeal. The "standard of review" is a different concept. In federal civil practice, for example, there are four principal types of standards of review for issues raised on appeal. They are de novo, clearly erroneous, reasonable and rational, and abuse of discretion. They correspond to four principal types of errors—law, fact, mixed law-fact, process or procedure. Each issue raised on appeal could have a different standard of review, and you would have to apply the appropriate standard to each issue.[33]

Selecting and using case authorities. During your review of the parties' briefs and your own legal research, you no doubt will turn up many cases to support the main proposition of your ratio decidendi. The questions then become: which case authorities should you use; and how should you arrange and interrelate them with themselves and other types of authorities? These questions are answered in the succeeding subsections.

---

33. *See generally* John W. Cooley, *Callaghan's Appellate Advocacy Manual* (1995 Supp.) §8:02.50 (Clark Boardman Callaghan, 1989).

Cardozo taught that three types of cases confront judges,[34] and by direct analogy, these three types also confront arbitrators. They are: (1) where the rule of law is clear and its application to the facts is equally clear; (2) where the rule of law is clear, and the sole question is how it should be applied to the facts at bar; and (3) where neither the rule nor its application is clear. It is the third type that causes arbitrators the most difficulty in selecting and applying case authorities.

First, when selecting case authorities, you should be aware of the distinction between those cases needed to *set up* the main proposition (general principles, standards, doctrines, etc.) and cases directly supporting the main proposition. As to the latter cases, selection must be more precise. For example, if a party has requested that summary judgment be entered on one of its claims, you will probably be aware of many cases in your jurisdiction setting forth the standards for entry of summary judgment. Citing a case or cases in support of such a test does not require precise selection, although it is prudent to cite precedent that is recent and that generally supports the standards that you are applying. However, the selection of cases supporting your main propositions regarding the merits of the parties' claims or defenses, requires much more thought and analysis.

For main proposition support, your first concern should be to find a case which is on "all fours" (or as closely as possible) with your facts and consistent with your desired result. If you are addressing a federal claim, an "all fours" (or nearly so) federal court decision should be used as a precedent centerpiece in this order of priority: (1) United States Supreme Court; (2) the applicable Circuit Court of Appeals; (3) other federal Circuit Courts of Appeals; (4) federal district courts in the applicable Circuit; (5) other federal district courts; (6) supreme court of the applicable state; (7) supreme court of other states; (8) appellate courts in the applicable state; and (9) other state appellate court decisions. If you are addressing a state law claim, the priority of decisions for selection is: (1), (6), (9) (the applicable state jurisdiction's first, then others), (2) (construing law), (4) (construing applicable state's law), (7), (3), (5), and (9). If you have found a U.S. Supreme Court case that substantially supports your main proposition, you should use it. However, be careful of cases (U.S. Supreme Court and otherwise) which support your main proposition only marginally. Such cases might detract more from your conclusion than they support it. Also, rarely should a court's concurring opinion serve as your centerpiece decision. A court's concurring opinion, however, can be used effectively to add additional support to your centerpiece decision. Dissenting opinions of court decisions should be used with great caution.

Selection of appropriate case authorities to support your main proposition is important. Identifying the appropriate *portions* of them to rely on is equally

---

34. Aldisert, *supra* note 15 at 35.

important. You must be able to distinguish between a holding of a case and a dictum contained in that case. Black's Law Dictionary defines a "holding" as "a conclusion of law reached by the court as to the legal effect of the facts disclosed"; it defines "dictum" as an opinion of a judge "which does not embody the resolution or determination of the court." *Obiter dictum* is a type of dictum which is even less relevant to the issues of the case in which it appears, and commands less respect than ordinary dictum. There is nothing wrong with relying on or quoting dicta in support of an argument, so long as you know it is dicta, and you let the readers of your opinion know that you perceive it as such. If, however, you use dicta, believing it to be the holding of the case, you will weaken your *ratio decidendi*.

Selecting and using statutory authorities. In some of your arbitrations, the correct interpretation or application of a statute may be the subject of the legal dispute. The issue usually centers on whether the statute prohibits or permits certain conduct. When dealing with statutes in the parties' legal arguments, you should be mindful that there are many judicially sanctioned aids, both intrinsic and extrinsic, available to assist in their correct interpretation. Intrinsic aids include the following:[35]

> Textual construction.
> The pertinent context.
>
> Titles.
> Preambles.
> Enacting clauses.
> Purview provisions.
> Definition provisions.
> Provisos
> > – Strict construction.
> > – Sections to which applicable.
> > – Construction in regard to indictments.
>
> Exceptions.
> Saving clauses.
> General saving statutes.
> Heading and marginal notes.
> Punctuation.
> Associated words (noscitur a sociis).
> Ejusdem Generis.
> Expressio unius est exclusio alterius.
> Reddendo singula singulis.

---

35. *See* N. Singer, *Sutherland Statutes and Statutory Construction*, Vol 2A (Callaghan, 4th Ed), p. 117.

Common, technical, legal, trade, or commercial terms.
Gender.
Referential and qualifying words.
Singular and plural numbers.
Transposition of words or phrases.
Substitution of words and phrases.

The intrinsic aids with Latin labels in the above list perhaps need further explanation. Noscitur a sociis (literally, "it is known from its associates") applies when the legislative intent or meaning of a statute is unclear and permits determination of the meaning of doubtful words by reference to their relationship with other associated words and phrases. Thus, when two or more words are combined or grouped together, and they ordinarily have similar meaning, but are not equally comprehensive, the general word (or phrase) is deemed limited and qualified by the special word. For example, the term "farm laborer" could be deemed not included in the statutory language "no tradesman, artificer, workman, or other person whatsoever," because the phrase "other person whatsoever" is qualified or limited by the special words preceding it.

The intrinsic aid ejusdem generis (literally, "the same kind, class, or nature") applies when the following conditions exist: (1) the statute contains an enumeration of specific words; (2) the enumerated words suggest a class; (3) the class is not exhausted by the enumeration; (4) a general reference supplements the enumeration; and (5) there is not clearly manifested an intent that the general term be give a broader meaning than necessary.

When the aid expressio unius est exclusio alterius (literally, "expression of one thing is the exclusion of another") is applied to a statute designating a form of conduct, the manner of its performance and operation, and the persons and things to which it refers, there is an inference that all omissions should be understood to be intentional exclusions. Under application of this aid, a dismissed fireman could be held not allowed to recover contributions to a pension fund under statute allowing such recovery to one who "voluntarily resigns."

In applying reddendo singula singulis (literally, "referring each to each"), where a sentence of a statute contains several antecedents and several consequents, they are read distributively. Thus, where several words granting power, authority, and obligation are found at the beginning of a clause, it is not necessary that *each* of the words apply to the several branches of the clause. The words giving power and authority may be limited to particular subjects and those of obligation applied to others.

---

36. *See* N. Singer, *Sutherland Statutes and Statutory Construction*, Vol 2A (Callaghan, 4th Ed), p. 277.

Aside from intrinsic aids, extrinsic aids may also be used in statutory interpretation. Extrinsic aids include:[36]

> Legislative history.
> Preenactment history.
> History of enactment process.
> > – Messages of the executive.
> > – Reports of standing committees.
> > – Reports of special committees.
> > – Reports of conference committees.
> Reports of commissions to revise statutes.
> Statements at committee hearings.
> Reports of committees, commissions, and other sources connected with the legislature.
> – Views of draftsmen.
> Legislative debates.
> > – Statements of committeeman in charge of the bill.
> > – Statements of the sponsor of the bill.
> Testimony of members of the legislature.
> Motives of members of the legislature.
> Legislative action on proposed amendments to a bill.
>
> Explanations of initiative and referendum measures.
> Post-enactment history.

Of course, when interpreting statutes, reference can be made to related statutes or prior or subsequent versions of them. Case authority interpreting the statutory language in question is, by far, the most persuasive authority. However, when the statute is new, or the particular provision in question has not yet been judicially interpreted, you may have to resort to these intrinsic and extrinsic interpretational aids.

Selecting and using other authorities. Where possible, "mandatory primary authority" existing within the five law source areas should be used to support your *ratio decidendi*. These five law source areas are: constitutions; statutes and treaties; judicial decisions; court rules; and administrative and executive rules, decisions, and actions. However, secondary authorities may be used to supplement them, and in an unusual situation, may comprise your only source of authority. These secondary or "other" authorities consist, in part, of legal periodicals (including law review articles), legal treatises, attorney general opinions, restatements of the law, commission reports, reports and studies of governmental agencies, as well as American Bar Association and American Law Institute reports. These secondary authorities can be used effectively to buttress your mandatory primary authority, particularly where the trend in the law is not clearly defined in the cases, or the cases conflict on the point in question. The theory that secondary authority can be persuasive is supported by the many appellate court decisions which cite and quote from such material.

Applying techniques for using and arguing facts. In designing the arguments of your ratio decidendi, you should employ four techniques of using and arguing facts. They are: (1) using facts to set up arguments; (2) distinguishing cases; (3) reconciling apparent factual differences in cases; (4) mirroring facts; and (5) arguing by analogy.

- **Using facts to set up arguments.** Unless the issue is solely one of law, in which case all of the pertinent facts might appear in the Statement of Facts, you probably will have to use facts to set up your argument. In many cases, these facts will not be elaborate. Usually, you will only need a succinct, objective summary of facts specifically related to your argument to segue into your discussion of the case law. This may be comprised of only a few sentences. Normally, this factual set-up for what follows is not argumentative, though this may vary from situation to situation. It should contain references to the record as appropriate.

- **Distinguishing cases.** The process by which you show that a party's cases have little or no applicability to the determination of the specific issue(s) at bar is called distinguishing cases. The applicability of precedent to a case at bar can be distinguished on many grounds, including: (1) nature of the courts involved (federal vs. state; trial vs. appellate); (2) nature of issues involved; (3) age of precedent; (4) intervening precedent; and (5) intervening statutes nullifying the effect of the precedent. More often, however, a party's cases, while in every other way applicable in law, may be distinguishable on their facts.

When distinguishing cases on their facts, first mentally compare the facts the party is relying on to the facts of the case at bar. Note major differences in the nature of the parties, the background setting, pre-dispute events, the event precipitating the dispute, and post-dispute events. Then note lesser differences.

- **Reconciling apparent contradictions between cases.** The process of reconciling apparent contradictions between the case relied on by a party and the case at bar is an extension of the process of distinguishing cases. Its purpose is to show that the party's precedent fails to apply to the case at bar, and that the precedent, when its facts and holding are properly construed, describes a policy supportive of *your* proposition in the case at bar. Thus, reconciling apparent contradictions is a three-step process:

(1) Facts of a party's precedent and case at bar are distinguished. First, show facts are similar, but they differ in significant respects.

(2) Next show that the party's precedent reflects some larger policy, not necessarily apparent when it is first read.

(3) Finally, show that the larger policy, when applied to the case at bar produces a result consistent with your desired conclusion.

- **Mirroring facts.** Another effective use of facts in drafting arguments of your *ratio decidendi* is to demonstrate how the facts of controlling precedent in your favor are mirrored in the case at bar. This is done by first explaining the controlling precedent in detail, emphasizing all the facts reflected in the case at bar. There, immediately following, the facts and your desired result of the case at bar are described, using language and characterizations used by the court in the controlling precedent. If done artistically, your facts and desired result will seem almost identical to the controlling precedent.

- **Arguing by analogy.** In arguing by analogy, the specific objectives of the arbitrator are to find another situation that is as closely similar as possible to the subject situation, to point out the similarities, and to argue that the result of that situation should be applied to the subject situation. The skill of using analogies is in the ability to demonstrate that a particular case or problem, newly encountered, is very much like a particular case decided in the past. Arguing by analogy is normally employed where there is no pertinent case precedent available which precisely fits the facts of the case at bar. Such situations occur when changes in society and technology move faster than the development of the law, and they commonly arise in connection with the interpretation of new statutes, lightly rooted or with no roots at all in common law. To design an argument by analogy, the arbitrator must accomplish two goals: (1) he or she must find a decided case that reached a result consistent with the desired result; and (2) he or she must demonstrate that the facts of that case, although appearing to be different from the facts of the case at bar, are not really different at all. It is this second goal which normally provides the greater challenge to the arbitrator, because it requires the arbitrator to reframe the readers' perceptions of the two sets of facts. You should also realize that when constructing an argument by analogy, you are not limited to one analogous case. In your particular situation, several arguments by analogy might have to be made to support a conclusion that your desired result is the appropriate one.

• **Blending facts and authorities in argument.** It is important to keep in mind that the legal argument in your *ratio decidendi* must have an overall logical flow. The format described in Subsection 4.10.3 *supra*, suggests that the first few sentences of a legal argument should present a summary of the claims and defenses of the parties. This gives readers an overview of where you are headed (i.e. you tell 'em what you're gonna tell 'em). The step involving analysis of facts and authorities contains the reasoning supporting your (usually multiple) major and minor premises. In that step, you marshal all your facts and authorities and blend them in support of your proposition(s) (i.e. you tell 'em). Finally in, a closing sentence or two you tell the reader where you have taken him and draw a conclusion (i.e. tell 'em what you told 'em). Blending facts and authorities is truly the art of the process, and it may vary from case to case. In general, the blend as to each legal argument has these core configurations between the opening summary sentences and the concluding sentences.

---

1. Factual set-up for argument

2. Exposition of Mandatory Primary Authority (controlling cases, statutory authority, complementary cases)
    —   use of mirroring
    —   arguing or analogy

3. Exposition of secondary authority, as appropriate

4. Addressing authority advanced by losing party
    —   distinguishing cases
    —   reconciling apparent contradictions

5. Policy arguments

Beyond this core configuration, the art of blending facts and authorities is in how one uses portions of cases, quotations, and footnotes in inter-relating facts and authorities. No one arbitrator will perform his or her artistry exactly like another. Every design will be different and distinct, and as in all art, no design can be labeled "best." Its beauty and expressive quality will lie only in the eye of the beholder.

• **Relying on public policy.** In discussing reconciling apparent contradictions, *supra*, we discussed the concept of distilling a policy statement from precedent. That process of identifying policy is different from and much narrower than the concept of arguing public policy. Public policy is larger than specific issues, specific areas of the law. It is truly something beyond the province of lawyers. It is as much concern to lay people as it is to lawyers. Public policy may be as broad as the statement that "government favors the preservation of human life" or as narrow as "companies are morally obligated to provide their workers with safe working conditions." Support for public policy arguments can be found in both mandatory primary authorities and secondary authorities. However, you should be cautioned to use them only in very special circumstances. Using a public policy argument in an otherwise well-constructed arbitration opinion can weaken the overall effect of the brief. Public policy arguments are often considered to be arguments of last resort.

4.10.5 Avoiding certain types of arguments.

To enhance the overall persuasive effect of your opinion, there are at least four types of arguments you should avoid including or, at minimum, carefully consider the consequences before employing. The four argument types are: (1) fallacious arguments; (2) weak alternative arguments; (3) arguments based on hyperbole or on matters outside the record; and (4) arguments directed to personality or character of counsel. Each of these argument types is discussed separately, *infra*.

Fallacious arguments. You must avoid making fallacious arguments or using fallacious reasoning in communicating the ratio decidendi. Several examples of such arguments are presented below.

- **Extension:** carrying an argument beyond its reasonable limits.
- **Arguing in a circle:** using two unsupported assertions to "prove" each other.
- **Repeated assertion:** repeating an argument and treating the repetition as truth.
- **Straw man:** setting up a proposition just so it can be disproved; refuting an argument not advanced by a party and contending that the party's argument has been refuted.
- **Pseudo questions:** asking a question based on a false assumption and then answering it.
- **Non sequitur:** stating a conclusion that does not follow from the premises or evidence on which it is based.
- **Post hoc:** "after the fact, therefore because of the fact"—assuming a causal relationship where none is proven.
- **Combination/division:** connecting facts or arguments, and then drawing an inference without basis in fact; or dividing facts or arguments to make things seem what they are not.

- **Accidental result:** drawing a conclusion based on seeming circumstances and not on the facts or reason.
- **Confusing general and particular:** arguing that the improbable will be probable because some things happen contrary to probability; arguing a qualified (rather than a general) probability without clearly saying so.

Weak alternative arguments. In certain situations you may be tempted to add an alternative contention here and there for "security" purposes. Sometimes, when alternative arguments are of the same strength as the principal argument, they can be persuasive. However, it is more often the case that the alternative arguments are weaker, or in some respect less meritorious, than the principal argument to which they relate. Thus, their weakness may diminish the cogency of the principal argument. Your attempt to reinforce your central argument with wobbly satellite contentions may represent a sign of your own lack of confidence in that argument. The best tack normally is to proceed with a strong, polished central argument on a particular point, and forget about tying in weaker and less-convincing companion arguments.

Arguments based on hyperbole or on matters outside the record. Virtually every argument you make must be factually based in the record and not merely on hyperbole or what you *wished* the record contained. There are very limited exceptions which allow you to rely on information outside the record in connection with presenting arguments. These exceptions are principally embodied in the doctrine of judicial notice. Barring qualification under such exceptions, your arguments must be record-based.

Arguments directed at counsel, personally. Arguments containing insulting or deprecating remarks about the parties' counsel or their arguments are usually unprofessional. By including disrespectful comments in your arbitration opinion, you will probably reduce the chances that you will be selected as an arbitrator in future cases.

4.10.6 Using footnotes.

Figuratively, footnotes are the opinion writer's fine brush. They fill in the details after a coarser brush has created the background and has produced the principal forms and objects. Properly used, footnotes can add tone and color to what otherwise might be drab and expressionless. Of course, footnotes, like any vehicle of communication, can be misused or overused.

There are three principles of tasteful footnoting. The first such principle is to decide, carefully, whether the information proposed to be footnoted is more appropriate for inclusion in the text of your opinion. If you have something very important to say in relation to your facts or argument, it normally should appear in the text of your brief, not in a footnote.

If you decide to communicate information by use of a footnote rather than in the body of the opinion, then the second principle of tasteful footnoting will become relevant. That principle instructs that before a footnote is actually included in a draft or final version of your opinion, you should carefully reassess its purpose, utility, and efficacy. Do not hesitate to eliminate footnotes that serve little or no useful purpose, that tend to clutter and distract, that take readers down a long and convoluted spur, and that compromise their ability to easily relocate your principal train of thought. There are actually many legitimate purposes of and uses for footnotes, both as to fact statements and argument. Some of these purposes and uses are set forth below.

Use of footnotes in fact statements. Some legitimate purposes of and uses for footnotes in fact statements are as follows: (1) explanation of abbreviations or references to the record, which will be used throughout the opinion; (2) qualifications of a statement of fact; (3) clarification of a statement of fact; (4) description of useful background information on persons or events; (5) description of events occurring "in the meantime"; (6) quotation of the text of pertinent statutes, contracts, etc. (that you may wish to refer to directly later in the opinion); and (7) directory to other parts of the opinion.

Use of footnotes in written arguments. Footnotes in written arguments may have legitimate purposes and uses as follows: (1) citation of principal case(s) on point; (2) citation of secondary, comparison, or analogous cases; (3) in-depth or parenthetical description of cited cases; (4) description of pertinent procedural information; (5) addressing secondary or frivolous arguments of a party; or (6) stating the legal test pertinent to a point collateral to your analysis.

4.10.7 Using quotations.

Whether to quote; what to quote; and how to quote are largely matters of common sense. Most arbitrators would agree that quotations from authorities "should be used sparingly" and "should be as short as circumstances permit." Depending on your point of view or proclivities, the breadth of this guidance presents practically unlimited opportunities for either creativity or mischief. Here are a few additional qualifying guidelines.

Whether to quote. In determining whether to quote particular printed matter, there are several questions you should ask yourself to incline your thinking toward the acceptable quotation practices. Those questions are: (1) Is the quotation relevant? (2) Does it communicate information more effectively or efficiently than what you could say in your own words or through paraphrase? (3) Does it tend to be more persuasive than your statements or paraphrase? (4) Is the quotation format more convenient for the reader?

What to quote. The types of material which may be quoted are limited and vary from case to case. Commonly, quotable material includes excerpts from: (1) the hearing record; (2) case authority; (3) state or federal regulations; (4) rules of procedure and applicable committee comments; (5) legislative history; and (6) learned treatises.

How to quote. In order to determine how to quote properly or whether your quotation is proper in form and content, you should ask yourself these questions: (1) Is the quotation accurate? (2) Is the interpretation of the quotation the same, both in and out of its context? (3) Can the persuasive effect of the quotation be enhanced through parallel argument? (4) Can italics enhance the communicative and persuasive effects of the quotation? (5) Can juxtaposition of quoted material enhance communicative and persuasive effects?

4.10.8 Editing and proofreading.

Editing is a form of critique of written work product. If performed by the author of the work-product, it is a type of self-critique. Proofreading occurs after editing and is one of the final functions performed by the arbitrator prior to issuing the award. Simply defined, its purpose is to ensure that the written work product is error-free. Although editing and proofreading go hand-in-hand, different considerations apply to each. If you are a member of a three-person arbitration panel, you will, of course, have assistance in performing these tasks.

Editing. Some commentators suggest that an arbitrator should go through several stages of revising and editing prior to arriving at a finished work product. Other commentators disagree. Both groups are correct, because different writers think differently. Some arbitrators write (or dictate) many thoughts without initial concern for precise organization or for surplusage. They prefer to get everything out on paper and then "play" with it—adding, subtracting, combining, juxtaposing, comparing, and evaluating ideas and their relationships. Then they select the optimal configuration of ideas (in terms of amount, content and organization of information). This is their preferred style of editing. They may do this several times before they are satisfied that they have achieved the optimal configuration. They have a tendency to drive their secretaries or clerical assistants "bonkers"—particularly if those assistants personally have an editorial style of the second type. Such assistants usually have difficulty understanding why the writer "can't get it right the first time." Computerized word processors have eased the problem of clashing editor-types, but certainly they have not eliminated it.

The behavior of the second type of editor is largely mental and is characterized by reasonably long periods of pre-writing thought. Instead of putting all the ideas on paper and "playing" with them, they have the ability to do most, if not, all of the "playing" in their minds. Some, on a separate sheet of paper, will make a list of phrase-like ideas before writing a sentence or passage. The important distinction between this type of writer and the first type is that when he or she writes sentences to communicate thoughts, the sentences rarely require change or modification. If they do, it might consist only of the addition or deletion of a word or phrase, here and there. These people tend to have highly organized, graphic minds which can perceive, select, and sequence words before perceiving the physical representation of them on paper.

One of these editing styles is not necessarily better than the other. It is highly important, however, for you to realize what style of editor (or thinker) you are. If you are an editor of the first type, you should take your revision time into account when you are scheduling yourself for opinion writing. You should allot additional time in scheduling, depending on the nature and complexity of the problem. You should also take into account the issue of the availability of clerical assistance necessary to handle multiple revisions. You should also be careful not to criticize a subordinate colleague simply because he does not perform multiple written revisions on paper. The truth may be that he performed many revisions in his mind prior to committing his words to paper. As a first-type editor, realize that if you fail to make multiple revisions, for whatever reason, you probably will not produce a product of optimal quality. Also, if you are an editor of the first type, know when to stop editing. You may overshoot your filing deadline for your opinion and award. Similarly, if you are an editor of the second type, learn to tolerate the editor of the first type. You are both doing the same thing; you just employ different strategies for accomplishing it.

Proofreading. If listening is hearing with the mind engaged, proofreading is seeing with the mind engaged in a very intense, forced way. It is a uni-functional task—that is, to perform it effectively you cannot do it while simultaneously performing another task. For example, if you proofread while watching television or listening to the radio, you will probably overlook or not consciously detect some or many errors in the text. Effective proofreading requires total focused attention and full mental absorption in the task. Otherwise, glaring errors may escape your momentarily drifting eye.

Another preliminary observation about proofreading is that some people are better at it than others. For whatever reason of biology or experience, some people are programmed or mentally set to see differences rather than sameness or similarities. Where an error exists in written text, those who are programmed to see differences will normally detect the error. Those who are inclined to see sameness, regardless of how focused they try to be, might perceive only the similar aspects and ignore the slightly different aspect, or even rationalize the existence of a similar aspect not actually present.

There are three distinct stages of proofreading. Each stage must be performed separately. The first stage of proofreading is performed by the author of the opinion. In that stage the author focuses primarily on content, but glaring errors can be corrected as he goes along. In that stage, the author must satisfy himself that the meaning of the printed matter is accurate, and that the words he uses conveys what he intends to the reader. Looked at another way, this stage of proofreading is a final check on editing and clerical errors, which may have been carried along and obscured in several drafts of the document. The second stage of proofreading involves checking your citations and references to the record. This check should be made using the original source volumes and the record, and this task can be performed by someone other than the author of the opinion. Sometimes this task is performed after the first draft, but it is a much more reliable check if performed at the time of final draft.

The third stage of proofreading is focused on accuracy of details. When proofreading for accuracy of details, you should proofread everything. It is a common mistake to skim over the brief's cover and certain collateral pages and focus primarily on the statement of facts and the legal analysis. Some proofreaders, much to their later chagrin, also brush hurriedly past headings and subheadings in the statement of facts and legal arguments, only to note obvious errors after the opinion has been issued.

Here are a few items to watch for when you are proofreading an arbitration opinion:

- **Citations and references to the record.** Apart from ensuring that the content of citations and references to the record is accurate (i.e. that the references direct the reader to the intended sources of information), the form of the representation of the citations and record references must be accurate.

- **References to other parts of the opinion.** Another trap awaiting the unwary proofreader is set up by assuming the accuracy of references to other parts of the opinion. If you are the type of writer who goes through several drafts before achieving satisfaction with your work, you may add, shift, or delete information in the opinion throughout the course of the writing process. You may also completely reorganize the presentation of information. Thus, references in one portion of the opinion, directing the reader to another, may be erroneous. The portion of the opinion to which you direct the reader might have been deleted, or the target portion might be so substantially modified by addition or alteration of information that the reference may be inappropriate. Worse yet, the target information may be contained in a part of the opinion totally different than that indicated in the reference. Thus, when proofreading, you should stop when you see a reference to another part of the opinion and physically inspect the target portion of the opinion to ensure that the reference is still accurate.

- **Correction between footnote numbers in text and content of footnotes.** Footnotes provide a fertile source of errors, and proofreaders should make special efforts to proofread them carefully. A common error involving footnotes is one of correlation. Sometimes when preparing a draft of an opinion, the author might omit a footnote number in the text of the opinion. A secretary, trying to be helpful might insert a footnote number in the text after the sentence which he or she believes to be intended by the author. It may well be the wrong sentence. A reader of the footnote corresponding to that number might find the footnote irrelevant, and become bewildered or confused. Thus, the author must take care to see that the relationship between the footnote numbers appearing in the text and the content of the actual footnote is correct. That is, she must see to it that they correlate as she intended. Similar problems can occur if footnote numbers are duplicated in text or if the actual footnote (the content of it) is omitted through secretarial oversight.

- **Omissions, insertions, and transpositions of words, phrases, sentences, and paragraphs.** Technological advancements in word processing in the recent past have undeniably been awesome, but they have brought with them some horrors previously inexperienced. Word processors, while marvelous inventions, have capabilities which deserve watching. They (with an operator's help) can delete whole passages of written work instantaneously with the striking of a key. They can shift whole paragraphs and pages of text. They can add paragraphs from other texts, and they can transpose words, phrases, sentences, and passages within a split-second. These capabilities can be of tremendous assistance to opinion writers, but when they are misused or applied thoughtlessly, they can cause the opinion writer much grief.

- **Missing pages.** Although the error of missing pages (usually a result of mis-paginating) does not occur all that often, it is a practical disaster if it does occur, and the opinion is issued before the error is caught. Careful, final checking by the author of the opinion can practically eliminate any possibility that the missing page(s) error will occur.

4.11 DRAFTING THE DISPOSITION

Your disposition of the case should be set forth under a separate subheading.[37] It should summarize the decisions reached on all of the claims and issues of the case, and it should clearly, concisely, and precisely set forth the damage and equitable relief awarded with respect to each claim on which a claimant (counter-claimant, cross-claimant) has prevailed. If you do not address each claim and claimant separately, it is likely that you will face a motion for clarification after

---

37. Aldisert, *supra* note 15 at 163..

your opinion issues. Be sure to double-check your math on any figures included in your disposition.

If you are sitting as an appellate arbitrator, you should also set forth your disposition of the case under a separate subheading.[38] If you decide to affirm the hearing arbitrator or panel, this task is quite simple. However, if you decide to reverse, vacate and remand, or modify in some manner, the task becomes much more complex. If you decide to send the case back to the hearing panel for further consideration, be sure to be very precise in your directions as to what you want the panel members to review, factually and/or legally, and as to how you expect them to go about it. Your directions will be limited by what the pertinent rules or the parties' arbitration argument permits. Some appellate arbitrations permit the appellate arbitration panel to take evidence and finally decide the matter.

It is highly unusual for arbitrators to issue concurring or even dissenting opinions at the hearing level. However, with the increased use of appellate arbitration panels, it may become more prevalent for arbitrators to issue such opinions at both the hearing and appellate levels.[39]

4.12 DRAFTING FINDINGS OF FACT AND CONCLUSIONS OF LAW

You may wish to draft your opinion in the form of Findings of Fact and Conclusions of Law ("Findings and Conclusions").[40] If you opt to draft Findings and Conclusions you may use either a narrative format, which corresponds to the opinion format described above, or a numbered paragraph format. The latter format is sometimes beneficial if there will likely be an appeal or some type of review of the hearing panel's decision.

Regardless of which format you choose, you should be hesitant to adopt the proposed findings of fact submitted by counsel for the parties. It is possible that counsel has presented biased impressions of the evidence, inaccurately recited the evidence, or has omitted evidence material to the ultimate decision in the case. Your "Conclusions of Law" section should, in an organized way, identify and discuss all of the claims and issues presented in relation to the applicable law. Where appropriate, it should also give reasons why you deemed certain evidence credible, and other evidence not credible. Where possible, your legal conclusions should build on one another, incorporating logical inferences from the facts as presented in the preceding Findings of Fact. In some situations where the analysis of the applicable law is complicated, you may find it necessary to incorporate a separate section entitled "Discussion of the Law" between the "Findings of Fact" and "Conclusions of Law" sections.

---

38. *See* Aldisert, *supra* note 15 at 135 36
39. For guidance on how to draft concurring and dissenting opinions, *see* Aldisert, *supra* note 39 at 165–75.
40. *See* Aldisert, *supra* note 15 at 159–61.

4.13   SIGNING AND ISSUING THE AWARD

Your signature on an award is a prerequisite to its enforcement in court. If you are a member of a three-person arbitration panel whose members mutually agree with the result, it is best that each member sign the award. When more than one arbitrator has heard and decided a case, a majority is normally required to produce a valid, enforceable award, and each member of the majority must sign the award. If the arbitration agreement requires unanimity for a valid, enforceable award, then each member of the panel must sign the award if they can agree on the merits. If no unanimous decision can be reached, the arbitrators may issue an award reflecting the less-than-unanimous conclusions of the arbitrators, and the parties can then decide whether they wish to settle the case, select a new arbitration panel, or take the matter to court.[41]

If an arbitrator disagrees with the award signed by two other panel members, he or she may explicitly state their disagreement. The dissenting arbitrator is not obliged to give reasons for his or her disagreement.[42] Delivery of the award is normally accomplished pursuant to the rules of the dispute resolution organization, or in the absence of such rules, by registered or certified mail or other traceable method of delivery.[43]

4.14   RETAINING JURISDICTION TO ENFORCE OR MONITOR AWARD

There may be occasions, though rare, when you are asked by the parties to retain jurisdiction for a limited time after issuance of the award for the purpose of enforcing or monitoring the award. This might occur, for instance, in an arbitration of an employment class action where individual damage claims may be subject to calculation and thus objection, or where injunctive aspects of an award need to be at least initially monitored for compliance. If you become involved in such a complex arbitration, you should make it clear that the award is interim, and that the parties have stipulated that your jurisdiction will continue until final damage computations and monitoring are complete. It would be a good idea to attach the parties' stipulation to that effect to your award, so that if the matter is brought before a court prematurely by counsel or a class member, the court will be advised that the arbitration is still ongoing.

4.15   ENFORCEMENT, CHALLENGE, AND APPEAL OF AWARD

Once you have rendered a monetary award in an arbitration, it is rare that you will ever have contact with the parties or their dispute again. However, you should be aware of the grounds which parties may assert in court to have your

---

41. *See generally*, Domke, *supra* note 4 at §29:02.

42. *See generally*, DeSeife, *supra* note 11 at §§ 8:01 and 8:08.

43. Id. at § 8:01.

award vacated or, though rare, to have the matter remanded to you for further proceedings. Also, if your award involves equitable or injunctive relief, you may have a post-award monitoring or enforcement role, as discussed in Section 4.14, above. Therefore, it is important for you to have a working knowledge of the procedures and proceedings which may occur afterward in court concerning the enforcement, challenge, and appeal of an award.

4.15.1 Enforcement of the award.

The procedure for enforcing arbitration awards is summary in nature. The filing in court of a petition to confirm an award and enter judgment (with a proposed order and judgment) is the usual method of enforcement provided by most state statutes. Typically, the state court statutory period for filing the petition is one year from the date of the award. The Uniform Arbitration Act permits objections or a counter-claim to vacate the award within 90 days of filing the petition to confirm.[44]

The procedure is similar in the federal court system under the Federal Arbitration Act (9 U.S.C. §9). One party petitions to confirm an award; and a disagreeing opponent may cross-move to vacate it. Where there are no genuine issues of material fact, the confirmation order is granted, and summary judgment is entered. To enter summary judgment, the court normally requires the following documents to be on file:[45]

- the arbitration agreement
- papers dealing with the selection or appointment, if any, of an additional umpire
- any written extension of time within which to make the award
- the award
- each notice, affidavit, or other paper used upon an application to confirm the award, and a copy of each court order upon such application

A judgment confirming an arbitration award is docketed as in any other action and has the same force and effect as any other judgment.

4.15.2 Challenge of the award.

There are only a few grounds for challenging arbitration awards in court, and even those are very narrowly construed. Usually only statutory exceptions apply. These exceptions do not normally include mistakes of fact, errors of law, poor reasoning on the part of the arbitrator, or arbitrary and unjustified determinations. In fact, to secure judicial inquiry, a challenging party must demonstrate

---

44. Thomas Oehmke, *Commercial Arbitration*, Chapter 21, (The Lawyers Cooperative Publishing Co., 1987).

45. Oehmke, *supra* note 1 at §137:05.

extraordinary circumstances which indicate an arbitrator's abuse of power or use of power beyond his or her jurisdiction. The challenging party also carries the burden of proof.

In almost every instance, when a court is considering statutory exceptions to enforcement, it does so with a strong pro-enforcement bias. There are, however, several grounds upon which an arbitration award might be vacated.[46] These include:

Contract

- No written agreement to arbitrate
- Party breached part of agreement to arbitrate
- Arbitration agreement is invalid
- Arbitration was demanded after contract or statutory limitation

Hearing

- Arbitrator conducted hearing contrary to the arbitration statute or rules
- Party committed fraud in the arbitration
- Arbitrator refused to consider material facts
- Parties agreed to reopen the hearing because of the discovery of new evidence, but the arbitrator refused

Arbitrator

- Arbitrator displayed bias and partiality
- Arbitrator failed to disclose a serious conflict of interest
- Arbitrator was corrupt
- Arbitrator refused to postpone hearing when good cause was shown
- Arbitrator exceeded authority

Award

- Arbitrator decided non-arbitrable matters
- Arbitrators failed to make a mutual, final, and definite award
- Award was procured by corruption, fraud, or undue means
- Award was not rendered in a timely fashion, despite party's protest
- Evident material miscalculation of figures in the award
- Evident material mistake in the description of a person, thing, or property referred to in the award
- Award is contrary to public policy

Non-arbitrability of a dispute is a threshold matter of enforceability which can generally be resolved at the outset of the arbitration hearing and, if necessary,

---

46. See Oehmke, *supra* note 1 at §142:04.

ruled upon by a court at that time. Some courts will hold that this issue is waived if it is not brought up at the appropriate time. Arbitrability may also be challenged on the ground that the arbitration clause is invalid under the laws governing the original contract entered into by the parties. This type of challenge is rare, because the mere existence of an arbitration clause in a valid contract is difficult to rebut.

If an arbitrator makes a decision regarding a matter not included within the scope of the arbitration, a party may challenge the award. This challenge is construed as narrowly as any other challenge, however, and the burden of proof is just as high. Courts are normally unwilling to second-guess an arbitrator's interpretation of the parties' agreement. Courts often uphold provisions outside the scope of the arbitration agreement on the ground that the arbitrator simply interpreted the clause as ineffective to deny his own jurisdiction.

Evident partiality or corruption are also grounds upon which an award may be challenged. However, standards of conduct for arbitrators differ depending on who appointed them. An arbitrator appointed by a party, as opposed to one appointed as a neutral, often will not be held to the same requirement of impartiality. Courts have ruled that an arbitrator will not be held to the same standards of impartiality as a judge. There are also circumstances under which parties may not have the defense of bias available to them. These include prior knowledge of facts suggesting the arbitrator's partiality, and waiver based on lack of objections to partiality at the time that knowledge was gained.

Improperly refusing a postponement or refusing to hear evidence may constitute a procedural due process ground upon which an award may be challenged. However, as in all other cases of award challenges, the threshold of proof is very high. The challenger must demonstrate, not only disregard of due process, but actual harm as a result of such disregard. Inability to fully cross-examine a witness or reschedule a hearing because of a witness' prior speaking engagement have both been found not to be violations of a party's procedural due process rights.

Rulings contrary to law are also difficult to establish as a basis for challenging an arbitrator's award. The challenging party must demonstrate that an arbitrator appreciated the existence of a clearly governing standard, but decided to ignore it. In some jurisdictions, in order to be judicially vacated, the arbitrator's finding must be completely irrational. Courts will find a foundation for any award so long as in some logical way the award is derivable from the wording of the original contract.

Challenges based on awards being contrary to public policy have rarely been successful. This is generally because courts view the pubic policy favoring arbitration to override any dissatisfaction with an award based on its violation of some lesser public policy consideration.

The standard of proof required to establish corruption, fraud, or undue means is clear and convincing evidence. A party must demonstrate that it could not have discovered the fraud with the exercise of due diligence prior to the arbitration. The challenger must also demonstrate that the fraud was materially related to an issue in contest in the arbitration. Proof of perjury can be a successful challenge, if it meets the clear and convincing standard; so might a failure to disclose fees paid by one party to the arbitrator. In any case, in order for a challenge based on fraud, corruption, or undue means to be successful, the fraud, corruption, or undue means must stem from the behavior of the arbitrator.

Because the grounds for challenging an arbitration award are very narrow, agreed-to challenges may be a subject that parties might wish to explore, negotiate, and specify in an arbitration agreement. In appropriate situations, counsel may wish to design the arbitration process to provide for a pre-designated appellate tribunal, should the losing party in the arbitration wish to appeal, as described in Section 4.16 *infra*.

4.15.3 Appealing the award.

If an arbitration award is challenged in court and a final judgment entered, the judgment, as in any other case, is appealable to the appellate court. On appeal, the appellate court can confirm, vacate, recommit, modify, clarify, or correct an award. Rarely, if ever, would an appellate court reverse an award on the merits, even if there were a transcript of the arbitration proceedings. Instead, the appellate court might vacate an award, requiring the arbitration process to begin anew.[47]

Most appellate courts, in reviewing appeals from judgments entered on arbitration awards, abide by these presumptions:[48]

- the award is presumed to be valid
- there is no review for errors or misinterpretations of fact or law
- the arbitration proceedings will not be invalidated for failure to meet rules of evidence or other procedural requirements applicable to trials
- the arbitrator does not have to give reasons for the award

The Federal Arbitration Act (9 U.S.C. §16 et seq.) specifies district court orders related to arbitration proceedings which are appealable and which are not.[49] The appealable orders and decisions are as follows:

- order refusing to stay litigation
- order refusing to compel arbitration

---

47. *See* Oehmke, *supra* note 44 at §22:4.
48. Oehmke *supra* note 1 at §141:09.
49. *See* Oehmke, *supra* note 1 at §§ 156:07 and 156:08.

- order confirming an arbitrator's award or partial award
- order denying confirmation of an arbitrator's award or partial award
- order modifying an arbitrator's award
- order correcting an arbitrator's award
- order vacating an arbitrator's award
- interlocutory order granting, continuing, or modifying an injunction against an arbitration
- a final decision with respect to an arbitration

Orders and decisions declared unappealable by the Act are:

- order staying litigation, which allows arbitration to proceed
- order compelling or directing arbitration to proceed
- order refusing to modify or correct an award
- order refusing to grant, continue, or modify an injunction against an arbitration subject to the Act
- order which is interim and non-final

From the above listings, it is evident that the Federal Arbitration Act contains an intended legislative bias in favor of honoring parties' agreements to arbitrate their disputes to conclusion without judicial interference. Note especially that where a district court rejects a party's request to modify or correct an award, the decision is non-appealable.

4.16   THE ROLE OF THE APPELLATE ARBITRATOR

In the last decade of the twentieth century, the concept of an appellate arbitration tribunal came into existence through dispute resolution organizations' incorporation of procedures relating to appeals from arbitration awards. Thus, it is possible that on some occasions, you may be selected to serve as an arbitrator on an appellate arbitration panel. Consequently, you should be aware of the basic appellate arbitration procedures and the differences between the role of the hearing arbitrator and the appellate arbitrator.

The appellate arbitration procedures closely compare to appellate court procedures.[50] Typically, the parties agree to an optional appeal procedure prior to commencing the arbitration hearing. In such a situation, the appeal panel consists of three neutral members, unless the parties agree that there will be only one. A written notice of appeal identifying the elements of the challenged award and including a brief statement of the reasons for the appeal must be filed with the case administrator within 14 days after the award is final. Once a notice of appeal has been timely filed, the hearing award is no longer considered final for purposes of seeking judicial enforcement, modification, or vacation. Within seven days of

---

50. *See generally* Comprehensive Arbitration Rules and Procedures of JAMS/ENDISPUTE, paragraph 23.

the service of that notice, any opposing party may file a cross-appeal, specifying the elements of the award being appealed and including a brief statement of the basis of the cross-appeal.

If a party refuses to participate in the appeal procedure after having agreed to do so, the appellate panel will maintain jurisdiction over the appeal and will consider it as if all parties were participating. In such a situation, the appellate panel has the discretion to modify any award or element of award previously entered in favor of the non-participating party, if the record justifies such action.

The record on appeal normally consists of the stenographic or other record of the arbitration hearing, as well as all exhibits, deposition transcripts, and affidavits received into the record of the arbitration hearing by the hearing arbitrators. If they so elect, the parties, as a substitute for filing appeal briefs, may rely on memoranda or briefs previously submitted to the hearing arbitrators. Otherwise, the parties may agree to a briefing schedule on appeal. If they cannot agree, the case administrator sets the briefing schedule. Typically, the opening briefs are limited to twenty-five double-spaced pages; the response briefs, fifteen pages.

The parties may request oral argument, or the appellate arbitrators may schedule arguments on their own motion. The appellate panel will apply the same standard of review that the first-level appellate court in the pertinent jurisdiction would apply. The panel customarily has authority under relevant rules to affirm, reverse, or modify the award.

Rules allowing remand to the original arbitration hearing panel are unusual, but the parties could agree to such procedure in advance. Typically, the applicable rules permit the appellate panel to reopen the record at the appeal level in order to review evidence deemed improperly excluded by the arbitrator or deemed necessary in light of the appellate panel's interpretation of the relevant substantive law. The appellate panel must render its decision by majority vote within a time period specified by the rules—typically, 21 days from the date of oral argument, the receipt of new evidence, or receipt of the record and all briefs, whichever is applicable or later. Normally, the appellate panel's decision consists of a concise, written explanation, unless all the parties agree otherwise. The issued decision becomes the award in the arbitration, which is then final for purposes of judicial review.

An important distinction between the role of the hearing arbitrator and the appellate arbitrator can be seen in the different functions which the hearing and appellate opinions serve.[51] As with trial court opinions, arbitration hearing opinions are justificatory, designed to explain the tribunal's decision. In contrast, as with appellate court opinions, the appellate arbitration opinion's purpose is to identify and correct hearing panel errors (along with supporting reasons) and, if appropriate in the particular industry, to set precedents.

---

51. *See* Aldisert, *supra* note 15 at 151.

Chapter Five

Conducting the Cyberarbitration

> *The same way that e-commerce is the road ahead for conventional trade, e-arbitration and e-mediation are the beacons for solving disputes in the twenty-first century.*
> —*Dr. Petronio R. G. Muniz*
> *President, Instituto Arbiter*
> *Recife, Brazil*

❋ ❋ ❋ ❋

Not since the invention of the printing press has there been such great progress in the technology of communication as the development of the Internet.[1] In less than a decade, the Internet rapidly developed from a simple network of government, military, and research computer networks to a global medium for the instantaneous exchange of ideas and information. Today, the Internet renders anyone with a computer and a connecting device the ability to communicate with and transfer documents to anyone else globally who is similarly equipped. It has been said that this Electronic Revolution, or "E-Revolution," may have an even greater impact on the world of commerce than the Industrial Revolution.[2] It most definitely has had a faster impact. The time it took for other new technologies to be used by at least 50 million people in the twentieth century much exceeded the time the public has needed to adapt to the Internet. For example, radio required a 38-year user-acclimation period; television, 13 years; and cable television, 10 years. In contrast, it has been estimated that in the first five years of commercial Internet use, 200 million connected to the Internet in more than 100 countries worldwide. The U.S. Commerce Department has estimated by the year 2005, there will be more than one billion commercial users worldwide, generating more than $3.2 trillion in revenue. Indeed, the growth of Internet use is unparalleled by the usage of any other communication technology or commercial innovation in recorded history.

What does all of this mean for twenty-first century arbitrators? It means, quite simply, that arbitrators have to quickly learn and adapt to new methods of communication and related technology so that they can best perform their

---

1. Frank A. Cona, *Focus on Cyberlaw: Application of Online Systems in Alternative Dispute Resolution*, 45 Buffalo L. Rev. 975 (1997).

2. John W. Cooley, *New Challenges for Consumers and Businesses in the Cyber Frontier: E-Contracts, E-Torts, and E-Dispute Resolution*, 13 Loyola Consumer L. Rev. 102 (2001); *see generally* Robert Hemmesfaur (Ed.), *@ Risk: Internet and E-Commerce Insurance and Reinsurance Legal Issues* (Reactions Publishing Group, Ltd., London, 2000).

arbitral function in a dynamic and ever-expanding world of high-velocity information exchange, resulting in both durable deals and derisive disputes. The enormous quantity of personal interactions and commercial transactions occurring on the Internet is bound, unquestionably, to generate millions of disagreements over time and much thinking, on lawyers' parts, about how to resolve the resulting disagreements efficiently. Advocates may have to discard some traditional legal concepts and old ways of doing things in favor of more cyber-apropos methods. Newer and faster ways of conducting commerce via the Internet will continue to present a wide variety of risks and exposures for companies and consumers alike. Advocates and their clients will need to focus on some of the new legal issues that are certain to arise in electronic contract (e-contract) and electronic tort (e-tort) disputes. They will also need to consider new ways of incorporating the use of the Internet in resolving disputes which arise both in "real world" traditional ways and in cyberspace itself.[3] It is predictable that advocates, more and more, will be representing clients involved in disputes, commercial and otherwise, of an international character.[4] In doing so, advocates will need to become proficient in Electronic Dispute Resolution, which includes cyberarbitration (e-arbitration) and cybermediation (e-mediation). Neutrals who are to serve these parties and their advocates will have to be similarly proficient. It is the purpose of this chapter to prepare you to perform your neutral function efficiently and effectively, as the opening quote suggests, in one of the twenty-first century "beacons for solving disputes"—the process of cyberarbitration.

5.1 BASIC DEFINITIONS

Vocabulary is a basic ingredient to effective communication and learning. As a neutral performing the arbitrator function in a new forum for dispute resolution—cyberspace—you cannot afford to misuse vocabulary. You must know the commonly accepted meaning of new terms and how to use the terms appropriately. Once you know and understand the vocabulary of cyberarbitration, you will feel much more comfortable engaging in this new dispute resolution process. Appropriate word selection and usage are especially important first steps in your development of new cyberadvocacy skills. The purposes of including definitions of Internet terms here are to shorten your learning curve and to decrease your anxiety about being a cyberarbitrator.[5] The definitions presented here are not in

---

3. *See generally,* Ethan Katsh and Janet Rifkin, *Online Dispute Resolution* (Jossey-Bass, 2001); Ethan Katsh, *Online Dispute Resolution: Some Lessons from the E-Commerce Revolution,* 28 N. Ky. L. Rev. 810 (2001).

4. *See generally,* Robert C. Bordone, *Electronic Dispute Resolution: A Systems Approach— Potential, Problems, and a Proposal,* 3 Harv. Negotiation L. Rev. 175 (1998); Alan Wiener, *Regulations and Standards for Online Dispute Resolution: A Primer for Policymakers and Stakeholders* (Part 1) (Feb. 15, 2001), (http://www.mediate.com/articles/awiener2.cfm).

5. The definitions contained in this section are, in part, adapted from Bryan Pfaffenberger, *Webster's New World Computer Dictionary* (9th Ed.)(Hungry Minds, Inc. 2001) and Philip E. Margolis, *Random House Webster's Computer & Internet Dictionary* (3d Ed.) (Random House, 2000).

alphabetical order, but rather are listed in an order that promotes and facilitates understanding of terms, beginning, where possible, with the broadest definitions and continuing with related or included definitions of terms.

5.1.1 Cyberspace

Cyberspace is a metaphor used to describe the nonphysical, virtual terrain created by computer systems. (The prefix "cyber" means anything related to computers or to the Internet.) Like physical space, cyberspace contains objects (files, mail messages, graphics, etc.) and different modes of transportation and delivery. Unlike real space, exploring cyberspace does not require any physical movement other than pressing keys on a keyboard or moving a computer mouse. The following definitions are general terms related to cyberspace.

- **Internet.** An enormous and rapidly growing system of linked computer networks, connecting millions of computers worldwide, that facilitate data communication services such as remote login, file transfer, electronic mail (e-mail), the World Wide Web, and newsgroups. Using TCP/IP, also called the Internet protocol suite, the Internet assigns every online computer a unique Internet address, also called an IP address, so that any two connected computers can locate each other on the network and exchange data. "Online" means connected to a network or, more commonly, the Internet. "Protocol" is a standard in data communications and networking that specifies the format of data as well as the rules to be followed.

- **World Wide Web.** A global hypertext system or "Web" that uses the Internet as its transport mechanism. Communication between Web clients (browsers) and Web servers is defined by the Hypertext Transport Protocol (HTTP). In a hypertext system, users navigate by clicking a hyperlink embedded in the current document; this action displays a second document in the same or a separate browser window. Web documents are created using HTML or XHTML, a declarative markup language. Incorporating hypermedia (graphics, sounds, animations, and video), the Web has become the ideal medium for publishing information on the Internet and serves as a platform for the emerging electronic economy.

- **Domain.** In a computer network, a group of computers that are administered as a unit. On the Internet, this term refers to all the computers that are collectively addressable within one of the four parts of an Internet Protocol (IP) address. For example, the first part of an IP address specifies the number of a computer network. All the computers within this network are part of the same domain.

- **Domain name.** In the system of domain names used to identify individual Internet computers, a single word or abbreviation that makes up part of a computer's unique name. Consider this unique, fictitious name: (cool.law. nwu.edu). "Cool" is a specific computer in the "law" school at Northwestern University (nwu). At the end of the series of domain names is the top-level domain (here, edu), which includes hundreds of colleges and universities throughout the United States.

• **Domain name system (DNS).** In the Internet, the conceptual system, standards, and names that make up the hierarchical organization of the Internet into named domains.

• **IP.** Abbreviation for Internet Protocol. It is the standard that describes how an Internet-connected computer should break data down into packets for transmission across the network, and how those packets should be addressed so that they arrive at their destination. IP is the connectionless part of the TCP/IP protocols. The Transmission Control Protocol (TCP) specifies how two Internet computers can establish a reliable data link.

• **URI.** Abbreviation for uniform resource identifier. In the Hypertext Transfer Protocol (HTTP), a string of characters that identifies an Internet resource, including the type of resource and its location. There are two types of URIs: uniform resource locators (URLs) and relative URLs (RELURLs).

• **URL.** An acronym for uniform resource locator. On the World Wide Web, it is one of two basic kinds of URIs. It is the string of characters that precisely identifies an Internet resource's type and location. For example, consider the following fictitious URL:

http://www.wildcats.northwestern.edu/toros/refs/parking.html

This URL identifies a World Wide Web document (http://), indicates the domain name of the computer on which it is stored (www.wildcats.northwestern.edu), fully describes the document's location within the directory structure (toros/refs), and includes the document's name and extension (parking. html).

• **RELURL.** One of two basic kinds of uniform resource identifiers (URIs). It is a string of characters that gives a resource's file name (such as parking. html) but does not specify its type or exact location.

• **Hot link.** A method of copying information from one document (the source document) to another (the destination document) so that the destination document's information is updated automatically when the source document's information changes.

• **Cold link.** A method of copying information from one document (the source document) to another (the target document) so that a link is created.

Cold links are distinguished from hot links in that cold links are not automatically updated; one must update them manually with a command that opens the source document, reads the information, and recopies the information if it has changed.

- **Hyperlink.** In a hypertext system, an underlined or otherwise emphasized word or phrase that displays another document when clicked with the mouse.

- **Hypertext.** A method of preparing and publishing text, ideally suited to the computer, in which readers can choose their own paths through the material. In preparing hypertext, information is first "chunked" into small, manageable units, such as single pages of text. These units are called nodes. Then the hyperlinks (also called anchors) are embedded in the text. When a reader clicks on a hyperlink, the hypertext software displays a different node. The process of navigating among the nodes linked in this way is called browsing. A collection of nodes that are interconnected by hyperlinks is called a Web.

- **HTML.** Acronym for Hypertext Markup Language. It is a markup language for identifying the portions of a document (called elements) so that, when accessed by a program called a Web browser, each portion appears with a distinctive format. The agency responsible for standardizing HTML is the World Wide Web Consortium (W3C).

- **HTTP.** The Internet standard that supports the exchange of information on the World Wide Web. HTTP enables Web authors to embed hyperlinks in Web documents. HTTP defines the process by which a Web client, called a browser, originates a request for information and sends it to a Web server, a program designed to respond to HTTP requests and provide the desired information.

- **Web site.** A site (location) on the World Wide Web. Each Web site contains a home page, which is the first document users see when they enter the site. The site might also contain additional documents and files. Each site is owned and managed by an individual, company, or organization.

- **Web browser.** A software application used to locate and display Web pages. Most modern browsers can present multimedia information, including sound and video.

- **Web server.** A computer that delivers (serves up) Web pages. Every Web server has an IP address and possibly a domain name. For example, if you enter the URL http://www.advocacy.com/index.html this sends a request to the server whose domain name is advocacy.com. The server then fetches the page named index.html and sends it to your browser. Any computer can be turned into a Web server by installing server software and connecting the machine to the Internet.

- **Webmaster.** An individual who manages a Web site. Depending on the size of the site, the Webmaster might be responsible for any of the following: (1) making sure that the Web server hardware and software are running properly; (2) designing the Web site; (3) creating and updating Web pages; (4) replying to user feedback; (5) creating CGI scripts; (6) monitoring traffic through the site.

5.1.2   Electronic Dispute Resolution (EDR)

Electronic Dispute Resolution (EDR) is an umbrella term encompassing all forms of electronic-based methods of dispute resolution (e.g., cyberarbitration, cybermediation) and their related electronic support and information-delivery technology, such as telephone conferencing and voice mail, the Internet, videoconferencing technology, fax machines and fax software. EDR should not be confused with E-dispute Resolution. An "e-dispute" means a dispute arising out of online business transactions or online usage. Typical e-disputes stem from electronic contracts (e-contracts) in electronic commerce (e-commerce), or they are based on electronic torts (e-torts) which result in harm to a person or property in connection with Internet use.[6]

5.1.3   Videoconferencing

Videoconferencing means conducting a conference between two or more participants at different sites by using computer networks to transmit audio and video data. For example, a point-to-point (two person) video conferencing system works much like a video telephone. Each participant has a video camera, microphone, and speakers mounted on his or her computer. As the two participants speak to each other, their voices are carried over the network and delivered to the other's speakers, and whatever images appear in front of the video camera appear in a window on the other participant's monitor. Multipoint videoconferencing allows three or more participants to sit in a virtual conference room and communicate as if they were sitting right next to one another.

5.1.4   Telephonic Dispute Resolution (TDR)

Telephonic Dispute Resolution (TDR) is a term that encompasses telephone-based methods of dispute resolution, including telephone negotiation, telephone mediation, telephone arbitration, or telephone depositions. TDR can be used in conjunction with face-to-face and online dispute resolution processes.

---

6. John W. Cooley, *New Challenges for Consumers and Businesses in the Cyber-Frontier: E-Contracts, E-Torts, and E-Dispute Resolution*, 13 Loyola Consumer Law Review 102 (2001).

5.1.5 EDR information acquisition and delivery technology

The definitions in this Subsection provide meanings for Electronic Dispute Resolution information acquisition and delivery technology. These are also called EDR "tools".

- **Fax machine.** Abbreviation of facs(imile) machine, a fax machine is an electronic device that can send or receive text and pictures over a telephone line. It consists of an optical scanner for digitizing (dividing into a grid of dots) images on paper, a printer for printing incoming fax messages, and a telephone for making the connection. A related device is the fax modem. That device you can attach to a personal computer in order for you to transmit and receive electronic documents as faxes. Documents sent through a fax modem must already be in an electronic form (that is, in a disk file). Documents you receive are stored in files on your disk or received as hard copy on a fax machine. To create fax documents from images on paper, you need an optical scanner.

- **Voice mail.** A communications system in which telephone voice messages are transformed into digital form and are stored in a network. When the person to whom the message is directed logs on to the system and discovers that a message is waiting, the system plays the message. Voice mail also refers to e-mail systems that support audio. Users can leave spoken messages for one another and listen to the messages by executing the appropriate command in the e-mail system.

- **E-mail.** Short for e(lectronic) mail, it refers to the transmission of messages over communications networks. The messages can be notes entered from the keyboard or electronic files stored on disk. Most e-mail systems include a rudimentary text editor for composing messages, but many allow you to edit your messages using any editor you want. You then send the message to the recipient by specifying the recipient's e-mail address. You can also send the same message to several users at once. This is called broadcasting. Sent messages are stored in electronic mailboxes until the recipient accesses and displays them. Many systems visually and audibly alert the recipient when mail is received. After reading your mail, you can store it in a text file, forward it to others, or delete it. Copies of memos and attachments can be printed out on a printer if you want a hard copy. Emerging standards are making it possible for users of all types of different e-mail systems to exchange messages.

- **WebTV.** A general term for a whole category of products and technologies that enable one to surf the Web on your TV. Most WebTV products today consist of a small box that connects to a telephone line and a television. It makes a connection to the Internet via one's telephone service and then converts the downloaded Web pages to a format that can be displayed on the TV. These products also come with a remote control device so that one can navigate through the Web. In the future, WebTV products will not require telephone connections, but will instead access the Internet directly through the cable TV lines.

- **Chat Room.** Chat is real-time online communication between two or more computer users. Once an online chat has been initiated, either user can enter text in the conversation by typing on the keyboard and the entered text will appear on the other user's monitor. A chat room is a virtual space where a chat session takes place. Technically, a chat room is really a channel, but the term "room" is used to promote the chat metaphor. Web sites can be equipped with a chat room feature.

- **Threaded Discussions.** In online discussions, a thread is a series of messages that have been posted as replies to one another. A single forum or conference may contain a single topic or it may consist of many threads covering different subjects. Replies to messages are normally nested directly under the related message instead of messages being arranged in some other order, such as chronological or alphabetical order. Web sites can be equipped with a threaded discussion feature.

- **Instant Messaging.** A type of online service that enables you to create a private chat room with another individual. Typically, the instant messaging system alerts you whenever somebody on your private list is online. You can then initiate a chat session with that individual.

5.1.6   Online Dispute Resolution (ODR)

Online Dispute Resolution (ODR), also referred to as Cyber/Dispute Resolution and electronic Alternative Dispute Resolution and by their more aesthetic acronyms (C/DR) and eADR respectively,[7] encompasses processes for resolving disputes predominantly by online means. The term includes both disputes that arise off-line—in the real world—but are handled online and those disputes that arise in cyberspace (e.g., in electronic commerce).[8] It includes recognized forms of ADR, such as arbitration, mediation, and negotiation, which, in a cyberspace context are called cyberarbitration, cybermediation, and cybernegotiation. These cyberprocesses are also referred to respectively as e-arbitration, e-mediation, and e-negotiation. Cybernegotiation consists of two types: automated negotiation and

---

7. *See* T. Schultz, G. Kaufmann-Kohler, D. Langer, V. Bonnet, *Online Dispute Resolution: The State of the Art and the Issues*, E-Com Research Project of the University of Geneva, Geneva, 2001, http://www.online-adr. org, 3.

8. *See* generally Louise Ellen Teitz, *Symposium: Providing Legal Services for the Middle Class in Cyberspace: The Promise and Challenge of On-line Dispute Resolution*, 70 Fordham L. Rev. 985, 991 (2001).

assisted negotiation. Offline dispute resolution refers to traditional face-to-face negotiation, mediation, and arbitration.

5.1.7 Cyberarbitration

Arbitration that is conducted predominantly in cyberspace is referred to as cyberarbitration.

Cyberarbitrator. A cyberarbitrator who is experienced and/or trained in conducting cyberarbitration.

Cyberparty. A disputant in an ODR process, including cyberarbitration.

Cyberadvocate. A lawyer who represents a cyberparty in an ODR process, including cyberarbitration.

5.1.8 Cybermediation

Mediation that is conducted predominantly in cyberspace is referred to as cybermediation.

Cybermediator. A mediator who is experienced and/or trained in conducting cybermediation.

Cyberparty. A disputant in an ODR process, including cybermediation.

Cyberadvocate. A lawyer who represents a cyberparty in an ODR process, including cybermediation.

5.1.9 Cybernegotiation

Negotiation that is conducted predominantly in cyberspace is referred to as cybernegotiation. There are two types of cybernegotiation: automated negotiation and assisted negotiation.

Cybernegotiator. A person who negotiates in cyberspace.

Cyberparty. A disputant in an ODR process, including cybernegotiation.

Cyberadvocate. A lawyer who represents a cyberparty in an ODR process, including cybernegotiation.

Automated negotiation. Negotiation (bidding) by means of high automation programs. These are programs that basically consist of software that match demand/settlement responses without human intervention.[9]

Assisted negotiation. This process should not be confused with cybermediation. Assisted negotiation is a C/DR process in which the ODR

---

9. T. Schultz, G. Kaufmann-Kohler, D. Langer, V. Bonnet, *Online Dispute Resolution: The State of the Art and the Issues*, E-Com Research Project of the University of Geneva, Geneva, 2001, http://www.online-adr. org, 4-5.

organization provides only a secure site and possibly a storage means and other features, such as a threaded message board. No actual negotiation service (neutral third-party assistance) is provided. In this process, the parties have to reach an agreement without any external entity having the capacity to decide for them, not even a computer, as in automated negotiation.[10]

5.1.10 Internet regulatory organizations and related terms[11]

ICANN. Abbreviation for Internet Corporation for Assigned Names and Numbers. It is a private, California-based, nonprofit corporation managing Internet domain names and Internet Protocol (IP) addresses. It administers a dispute resolution system for resolving domain name disputes.

UDRP. Abbreviation for Uniform Dispute Resolution Policy. This policy establishes a procedure for the online resolution of disputes that concern domain names. This policy has been established by ICANN. The UDRP is a non-national authority for the resolution of domain name disputes. Its purpose is to avoid the competition and conflicts that arise from a variety of national courts and rules. The UDRP is intended to be applied only to very flagrant types of cybersquatting. The four institutions designated by ICANN to resolve domain name disputes are: WIPO, eResolution, the National Arbitration Forum, and the CPR Institute for Dispute Resolution.

ICC. Abbreviation for the International Chamber of Commerce. This organization advocates for minimal government regulation of e-commerce and asserts that self-regulation by the industry is the most effective way to build confidence in e-commerce.

GBDe. Abbreviation for Global Business Dialogue on Electronic Commerce. This initiative involves 72 companies around the world. Its objective is to endeavor to make e-commerce reach its full economic and social potential. It makes recommendations on ADR to Internet merchants, to ADD service providers, and to governments.

E-Commerce Group. Abbreviation for Electronic Commerce and Consumer Protection Group. It is a coalition of large companies that are involved in business-to-consumer e-commerce. The group seeks to foster consumer confidence and consumer protection by creating industry best practices and a predictable legal framework. It further promotes fair, timely, and affordable means to settle

---

10. T. Schultz, G. Kaufmann-Kohler, D. Langer, V. Bonnet, *Online Dispute Resolution: The State of the Art and the Issues*, E-Com Research Project of the University of Geneva, Geneva, 2001, http://www.online-adr.org, 5-6.
11. Adapted, in part, from T. Schultz, G. Kaufmann-Kohler, D. Langer, V. Bonnet, *Online Dispute Resolution: The State of the Art and the Issues*, E-Com Research Project of the University of Geneva, Geneva, 2001, http://www.online-adr.org, 84-86.

disputes and obtain redress concerning online transactions, and it encourage merchants to provide in-house procedures to resolve complaints and to provide third party dispute resolution programs, including online dispute resolution processes.

EuroCommerce. This is a lobby group that acts as the trade representation to the European Union institutions. It has published a European Code of Conduct for online commercial relations. It encourages online merchants to provide an in-house procedure for handling complaints.

FEDMA. Abbreviation for Federation of European Direct Marketing. It has 12 partners in national Direct Marketing Associations in the European Union and all those of Switzerland, Hungary, Poland, and the Czech and Slovak Republics. It has published a code on e-commerce and interactive marketing.

DSA. Abbreviation for the Direct Selling Association. This is a national trade association in the United States which represents companies that market products through personal explanation and demonstration. It has established Guidelines for Internet Use and a Code of Ethics for its members. Through its educational arm, the Direct Selling Education Foundation (DSEF), it conducts international seminars and other training on online transactions and dispute resolution.

5.2 COMPARISON OF FACE TO FACE, TELEPHONE, AND WRITTEN COMMUNICATION IN ARBITRATION

The twenty-first century arbitrator is constantly confronted with the question of what mode of communication he or she should be using at various stages of the arbitration process. The reason for this is that the arbitrator has many modes of communication from which to choose including face to face, videoconferencing, telephone, letter, e-mail, fax, or combinations of these modes. In this section we will review the relative advantages and disadvantages of the three primary modes of communication: face to face, telephonic, and written. It is hoped that the information here will assist you in choosing the appropriate mode of communication as the arbitration progresses.[12]

5.2.1 Face-to-face communication in arbitration

When people communicate with one another, 93 percent of the meaning of their messages is contained in their facial and vocal cues, rather than in the

---

12. *See generally,* Charles B. Craver, *Effective Legal Negotiation and Settlement* (4th Ed.) 310-16 (LEXIS Publishing, 2001); Edward Brunet and Charles B. Craver, *Alternative Dispute Resolution: The Advocate's Perspective (2d Ed.)* 159-62 (LexisNexis, 2001); Ethan Katsh, Janet Rifkin, and Alan Gaitenby, *E-Commerce, E-Disputes, and E-Dispute Resolution: In the Shadow of ebay Law,* 15 Ohio St. J. on Disp. Resol. 705 (2000); Janice Nadler, *Electronically-Mediated Dispute Resolution and E-Commerce* 17 Negotiation Journal No. 4 (2001); Michael Morris, Janice Nadler, Terri Kurtzberg, and Leigh Thompson, *Schmooze or Lose: Social Friction and Lubrication in E-mail Negotiations Group Dynamics: Theory Research and Practice* Vol. 6, No. 1 (March 2002).

content of the messages. Thus, generally speaking, the most communicatively efficient mode of arbitration is face to face. However, there may be situations where the disputing parties are so emotionally hostile toward one another that a face-to-face arbitration would do more harm than good. In such situations, a face-to-face meeting might also be counterindicated because there is no continuing relationship to be preserved. In some situations, face-to-face arbitration may be simply impossible because of geographical distance between or among the parties and their counsel. In some such situations, videotelephones or videoconferencing may serve as a near-equivalent substitute for a face-to-face meeting. In other arbitration situations, while a face-to-face meeting may be helpful during a portion of the process, the arbitrator and the advocates might conclude for strategic, tactical, or other reasons, that another mode of communication might be more appropriately used in other phases of the process.

5.2.2   Telephonic communication in arbitration

For some people, the telephone offers a more effective and efficient way to arbitrate than arbitrating in person. Some advocates and arbitrators, for example, are better skilled at sensing audible cues suggesting true meaning of a participant's telephone statement than they are at discerning nonverbal aspects of messages in a face-to-face meeting. These audible cues consist of, among others, pitch, pace, tone, volume, inflection, sighs, and pauses. Actually, nonverbal visual cues to meaning can be distracting and overwhelming to some people in an in-person situation.

There are some major disadvantages to arbitrating over the telephone. For example, it is often difficult to discern the identity of the speakers if a number of participants, including the arbitrator and several disputing parties, are engaged in the teleconference. Furthermore, in a document-rich case, discussing documents over the telephone can often be a cumbersome task if the documents are not quickly identifiable by volume and page number. Also, teleconferences can also become rambling, directionless conversations without strong supervision by the arbitrator. Teleconferences are usually less personal than face-to-face conversations. Such faceless verbal exchanges sometimes facilitate competitive or even deliberately deceptive tactics.

5.2.3   Written communication in arbitration

Letter and fax communication. Written communication in arbitration permits the transmission of detailed information to the arbitrator and/or the other parties. The writer has the luxury of not being interrupted during the course of his or her written communication. Written communication also serves as a permanent record of parties' and attorneys' stipulations or agreements.

Furthermore, advocates can avoid misunderstandings by taking the time to be careful and accurate in drafting communications to the arbitrator, opposing parties, and co-counsel. Letters or faxes received by advocates in an arbitration normally allow them to take as much time as necessary to review proposals and obtain input from their client, their partners, or co-counsel.

E-mail communication. There are many advantages to e-mail communication in arbitration. First, advocates can instantaneously communicate pleadings to the arbitrator and opposing counsel simultaneously. Amending and correcting pleadings is also facilitated by use of e-mail. Advocates can prepare and transmit their pleadings from any place in the world; likewise, arbitrators can issue their rulings from any location. Another advantage of e-mail arbitration is that split-second tactical decisions do not have to be made. Advocates and their clients can take time to consider and respond to positions or pleadings. Also, studies have shown that the absence of social status cues can influence people to respond openly and less hesitatingly than in a face-to-face setting.

E-mail communication in arbitration, however, is not without its shortcomings. The informality of e-mail communication is its strength as well as its weakness. People using e-mail can easily lapse into a mode where they are totally unconcerned about making a good appearance. In such state, they can be inappropriately informal and even offensive. One study showed that people are eight times more likely to "flame" in electronic discussion than in face-to-face discussion. Recipients of participants' messages can easily misunderstand or misinterpret them. The reason for this is that the recipient cannot always discern the emotive aspect accompanying the content of the message. Consider the e-mail statement, "You consistently have all the right answers." It is not clear whether the writer is exhibiting deference or sarcasm. Emoticons (typographical symbols indicating emotional cues) can help solve this problem, if used tastefully. Also, and more problematically, insults take on permanence. Hostile exchanges can escalate rapidly. Even intended innocuous language can be perceived as deliberately inflammatory and reinforce prior preliminary impressions of recipients, causing misinterpretations to be compounded to a crisis point. In addition, behavioral research has demonstrated that it can take four times as long for a three-person group to make a decision in a real-time (chat room type) computer conference as in a face-to-face conference. It can take 10 times as long for a four-person group, having no time restrictions, to come to a joint decision. These research results have implications for arbitrators in decision making as well as for advocates who try to jointly decide how to plan a discovery schedule. Unless you exercise special care, you can also easily compromise the confidentiality of the arbitration process. The split-second sending of an e-mail to an unintended addressee can be disastrous. Finally, research has shown that people are more intolerant about changing their decision on an issue when they commit their decision to writing, and especially when they publish that written decision to other persons. Written positions or hard-line proposals in e-mail can be more intractable than when they are expressed in person or over the telephone.

Using letters and faxes in arbitration may have its downside. It may cause an unwanted slowdown of the arbitration process. With regard to faxes, if time is of the essence, realize that there is a chance that faxes might get backlogged for transmission in your own mail room, and even if sent, they may get lost in opposing counsel's mail room or they may be misrouted.

These and other advantages and disadvantages of using letter, fax, and e-mail communication in arbitration are outlined in the charts below.

Arbitrating Using Traditional Means of Writing Letter and Fax

Advantages	Disadvantages
Transmit detailed information	May cause unwanted slowdown of arbitration
No interruptions	Inflexible; advocates may have to take a position too early in the arbitration process
Permanent record of advocates' positions, pleadings, and correspondence	Lawyer time involved may be more extensive
Misunderstandings more easily avoided	May spawn antagonistic responses
You have time to review documents and get input from other arbitrators	Faxes may be backlogged for transmission
	Faxes may get lost in the mailroom

E-mail

Advantages	Disadvantages
Messages instantneously communicated	Messages can be misunderstood and/or misinterpreted
Advocates can prepare and transmit pleadings and arbitrators can issue rulings from anywhere in the world	Insults take on permanence; hostile exchanges can escalate rapidly
Amendments or corrections to pleadings can be distributed immediately and simultaneously	Frustrating delays; takes up to four times longer for a group to reach consensus or a joint decision
Messages can be broadcasted to any number of people simultaneously	Unless caere is exercised, confidentiality can be easily compromised
Absence of social status cues can influence people to repond openly and less hesitatingly than in a face-to-face setting	Positions or hard-line proposals can be more intractable than when they are expressed in person or over the telephone
Advocates need not make split-second tactical decisions	

5.3 BENEFITS AND LIMITATIONS OF CYBERARBITRATION

There are both benefits and limitations associated with the use of cyberarbitration.[13] These are discussed generally in Sections 5.3.1 and 5.3.2. Two topics that deserve special analysis under this heading are confidentiality and cost of service. These topics are discussed in Sections 5.3.3 and 5.3.4, respectively.

5.3.1 Benefits

Cost. Some of the benefits of cyberarbitration are as follows. One of the obvious advantages of cyberarbitration over face-to-face arbitration is reduced cost. Expense of travel and accommodations is often prohibitive in small-dispute situations.

Also sending multiple faxes to several parties or telephoning many parties is also time consuming and expensive. In contrast, sending documents via e-mail or posting them on a Web site is virtually effortless. Other cost considerations are discussed, *infra*, Section 8.4.4.

Speed. Instantaneous transmission of information by electronic means in most cases accelerates the resolution process. Often, after the arbitrators reach consensus, using their generated written discussions and the digital findings and conclusions submitted by the advocates, they can quickly formalize, draft, and issue their award and supporting opinion, as appropriate.

Availability. Participants can be located anywhere in the world. Participants may communicate asynchronously—they choose when they want to respond, day or night.

Arbitrator expertise. A worldwide pool of arbitrators with special expertise can enhance the quality of the arbitration process.

Less confrontational. The parties are able to choose when they want to respond or participate in the process as it proceeds through its various stages. This allows time for parties to reflect on the materials they receive from opposing parties and co-parties, get initial legal advice, strategize with counsel or co-parties, carefully craft what they want to say, and even get final input from counsel or

---

13. *See generally*, Paul Schiff Berman, *The Globalization of Jurisdiction*, 151 U. Pa. L. Rev. 311 (2002); Karen Stewart and Joseph Matthews, *Online Arbitration of Cross-Border, Business to Consumer Disputes*, 56 U. Miami L. Rev. 1111 (2002); Lucille M. Ponte, *Throwing Bad Money after Bad: Can Online Resolution (ODR) Really Deliver the Goods for the Unhappy Internet Shopper?* 3 Tul. J. Tech. & Intell. Prop. 55 (2001); William Krause, *Do You Want to Step Outside? An Overview of Online Alternative Dispute Resolution* 19 J. Marshall J. Computer & Info. L. 457 (2001); Richard Michael Victorio, *Internet Dispute Resolution (IDR): Bringing ADR into the 21st Century*, 1 Pepp. Disp. Resol. L. J. 279 (2001); Elizabeth G. Thornburg, *Going Private: Technology, Due Process, and Internet Dispute Resolution*, 34 U.C. Davis L. Rev. 151 (2000); Paul D. Carrington, *Virtual Arbitration*, 15 Ohio St. J. on Disp. Resol. 669 (2000); Tiffany J. Lanier, *Where on Earth Does Cyber-Arbitration Occur? International Review of Arbitral Awards Rendered Online*, 7 ILSA J Int'l & Comp L. 1 (2000); Frank A. Cona, *Application of Online Systems in Alternative Dispute Resolution*, 45 Buffalo L. Rev. 975 (1997).

co-parties before they finally commit to a response or argument that their counsel will communicate to the arbitrator and to the other side. The online nature of the process eliminates the pressure to respond immediately to a received communication. Moreover, advocates can quickly consult legal and expert sources online and help their clients realistically assess the predictable outcome of a phase of the cyberarbitration proceedings. Cyberarbitration minimizes the effects of confrontational dynamics.

Cyberspace ensures a neutral forum. Cyberspace itself provides a neutral forum in the nature of an arbitrator's office or conference room. A dominant party is not able to exploit "home court advantage."

5.3.2   Limitations

Enforcement of arbitral awards. Determining what law governs the initial commercial contract and the terms of any award may be challenging. The parties can circumvent these problem areas by carefully crafting an arbitration agreement to include terms defining jurisdiction, applicable laws, and enforcement and review procedures. Self-executing award mechanisms, trustmark withdrawal, and escrow accounts are a few of the measures that can be used to ensure the enforcement of arbitral awards.

Uncertainty regarding confidentiality, privacy, anonymity, and authenticity. As discussed more thoroughly in Section 5.3.3, *infra*, maintaining confidentiality of communications in cyberspace can be a difficult task. The parties' fear of information leaks and invasion of privacy can create barriers to unfettered communication. Also, because of the faceless interaction in cyberspace, the identity of communicators and the authenticity of communications can sometimes be difficult to guarantee.

Absence of human factors. Online communication often lacks the spontaneity and vigor of face-to-face interaction and oral discussion. Also studies have shown that parties proceeding online are more likely to distrust and suspect lying or deceit on the part of other participants, and they are more likely to "flame" and reach impasse in negotiation of fact stipulations or resolution of discovery matters.

Computer accessibility and literacy. Varying degrees of computer accessibility and literacy may affect the quality of online communication between counsel and client. Occasionally, use of online technology can create a power imbalance among the parties or counsel. This imbalance may result from varying quality of computer equipment or software, the relative competence of the cyberarbitration participants to use the Internet or online information resources, or the unequal experience with using the services of a cyberarbitrator.

Unsuitability of disputes for cyberarbitration. Some disputes are comfortably amenable to resolution by cyberarbitration. These include disputes originating in cyberspace—intellectual property disputes and e-commerce disputes;

disputes that are fundamentally economic (insurance claims and construction defects); and disputes that concern undeveloped areas of the law—for example, a body of cyberspace customary law. Certain types of disputes may not be as appropriate for cyberarbitration. For example, a situation where the credibility of the parties is a crucial issue in a dispute might be more appropriate for a face-to-face (or a videoconference) arbitration so that the arbitrator could assess the parties' relative truthfulness. Moreover, personal injury cases where plaintiffs need to demonstrate the nature of their injuries, scars, etc. may be more appropriate for traditional arbitration or videoconferenced arbitration. Similarly, a patent or product liability case, where it is helpful to a resolution for the arbitration participants to see the configuration or operation of a particular piece of equipment, may be a candidate for a traditional arbitration.

The above described benefits and limitations of cyberarbitration and others are outlined in the chart below.

Benefits and Limitations of Cyberarbitration

Benefits	Limitations
Reduced cost in comparison with face-to-face arbitration	Enforcement of arbitral awards may be a problem
Accelerated proceedings	Determining what law governs the initial commercial contact and the terms of any award may be challenging
Participants can be located anywhere in the world	Varying degrees of computer accessibility and literacy may exist among counsel and their clients
Participants may communicate asynchronously—they choose when they want to respond, day or night	Power imbalance may be created by unequal online expertise / experience / equipment of parties or counsel
Arbitrators with special expertise may be hired worldwide	Online communication lacks the spontaneity and vigor of face-to-face interaction and oral discussion
Cyberarbitration minimizes the effects of confrontational dynamics	Parites are more likely to distrust or suspect lying or deceit on the part of other participants
Cyberspace itself provides a neutral forum in the nature of an arbitrator's office or conference room	Parties are more likely to "flame" and reach impasse
Parties can craft communications in an emotion-free setting	Parties may have uncertainty regarding confidentiality, privacy, anonymity, and authenticity
Advocates have easy access to legal and expert sources to help them give realistic advice to clients at particular points in the arbitration proceedings	Some disputes may not be suitable for resolution by means of cyberarbitration
Often, after the arbitrators reach consensus, using their generated written discussions they can quickly formalize, draft, and issue their award and supporting opinion, as appropriate	When the parties' credibility is in issue, traditional arbitration may be more effective than cyberarbitration

5.3.3   Confidentiality

Confidentiality has always been an important aspect of the arbitration process. The participants' agreement to maintain the confidentiality of the arbitration proceedings is usually sufficient in face-to-face arbitrations to guarantee non-disclosure of sensitive information. It is the responsibility of each participant in offline (or online) arbitrations not to mistakenly disclose information by e-mail or other means. ODR, however, has created a new threat to arbitration confidentiality.[14] Regardless of the participants' agreement to maintain confidentiality of online arbitration proceedings, breaches of security can originate externally from nonparticipants who intentionally invade, acquire, and perhaps even alter information the participants want to preserve as confidential and unchanged. It is generally accepted among the ODR provider community that electronic messages need to be protected by electronic means and that electronic arbitration communications and access to the data must be secured, before, during, and after the cyberarbitration. Thus, protection is needed with respect to both the transmission and the storage of confidential arbitration information. These two aspects require different means of protection. The risks to be protected against are: (1) the risk that unauthorized third parties will gain access to the information (*i.e.*, risk of compromising the *confidentiality* of the message); and (2) the risk that such third parties will alter it (*i.e.*, the risk of compromising the *integrity* of the message). A current serious limitation of cyberarbitration is that ODR providers cannot always guarantee that arbitration communications and documentation will not be disclosed.

Transmission of information. Unencrypted e-mail is considered to be about as secure as postcards. E-mail is capable, however, of being secured by several means. One means is through a software called Secure Multipurpose Internet Mail Exchange Protocol (S/MIME). If correctly used, the software provides the recipient with strong evidence of the origin of the contents of the message. It also has a feature that confirms to the sender that his or her message was delivered to a specific recipient. Another product that is free of charge but difficult to employ by non-specialists is Pretty Good Privacy (PGP). It is a message protection software with the same quality of service as S/MIME and is available from the Massachusetts Institute of Technology.

Alteration of a transmitted message can be reduced by digital signatures. These are cryptographic instruments trusted to third parties called signature- or key-holders. If a sender uses such a private key to electronically sign a message, the receiver can verify both the origin and the integrity of the message.

---

14. *See generally,* T. Schultz, G. Kaufmann-Kohler, D. Langer, V. Bonnet, Online *Dispute Resolution: The State of the Art and the Issues,* E-Com Research Project of the University of Geneva, Geneva, 2001, http://www.online-adr.org, 44-50.

Other means of protection must be used to secure information that is posted on a Web site, as opposed to being sent by e-mail.

The Hypertext Transfer Protocol (HTTP) is the generally accepted protocol for online transactions. In addition to this Web-based security feature, Secure Sockets Layer (SSL) provides protection of the confidentiality and integrity of Web-based communications.

Web site storage of confidential information is also a risk area. Site storage systems consist of a database and Web server. ODR providers must protect these against such risks as intrusions, viruses, and disk crashes. These storage systems can be protected by firewalls, but it is more effective to implement protection for each document instead of the system as a whole.

Because security systems are not yet widely available to satisfy high expectations of security in the ODR provider field, advocates and arbitrators may do well to carefully weigh the risks of using ODR for disputes in which the financial stakes are very high.

5.3.4   Cost or financing of service

Fees for use of ODR services are generally of three types: bilateral (or multilateral), unilateral, or external source.[15] In the bilateral (or multilateral) model, each party pays its proportional share of the user fee. This seems fair on its face, but one problem with this model is that the cost for the consumer may be disproportionate compared to the amount at stake. A very large majority of ODR providers charge users under this model.

In the unilateral user fee model, the business (merchant or insurance company) pays the entire fee for the ODR service. The payment can be in the form of an annual membership fee (*e.g.*, a trustmark fee) or a fee per case. The problem with this model is the inevitable appearance of bias. It might appear to the non-business user, for example, that the business payor of the user fee is being favored in the process. The appearance of bias can be lessened by the ODR provider's implementation of strict procedural rules, ensuring the availability of an adequate selection of independent neutrals, publishing clear policies of neutrality and impartiality, and establishing an independent supervisory or auditing body.

Approximately 10 percent of ODR service providers operate under the external source fee model. In this model, a third party—university or a governmental or non-governmental organization (*e.g.*, a consumer association) pays the entire fee for the ODR service. In general, this model provides the highest guarantee of independence and impartiality.

---

15. *See generally,* T. Schultz, G. Kaufmann-Kohler, D. Langer, V. Bonnet, *Online Dispute Resolution: The State of the Art and the Issues*, E-Com Research Project of the University of Geneva, Geneva, 2001, http://www.online-adr.org, 74-77.

5.4   ETHICS OF CYBERARBITRATION

The State codes of professional conduct for lawyers, most of which incorporate the American Bar Association's Model Rules of Professional Conduct, guide an advocate's conduct in representing clients in cyberarbitration.[16] (See Appendix L.) The ABA maintains a Web site (http://www.elawyering.org) that provides guidance for lawyers who practice online. The site also provides ethical guidance at http://www.elawyering.org/ethics/advice.asp. The Elawyering Task Force, ABA, Legal Websites Best Practice Guidelines (2001) can be accessed at http://www.elawyering.org/tools/practices/asp.

Arbitrators' conduct is generally governed by the Code of Ethics for Arbitrators in Commercial Disputes—Revised 2004. (See Section 1.3 and Appendix K).

One critical ethical duty of arbitrators and advocates in cyberarbitration is maintaining confidentiality in cyberspace. Online communication presents a minefield of opportunities for inadvertent and harmful disclosures of confidential information by incautious and unwary advocates and arbitrators.[17] Following the guidance presented below will help you avoid making those instant, and unintentional, harmful disclosures.

Carefully manage the power of the "cc." Anyone who is or who has been a subscriber to a listserv knows how useful some of the received information is and how annoying some of it can be. Thus, when communicating by e-mail or by e-mail list, make a quick check to see if all the addressees actually need to receive or would even want to receive the information you are sending. There are times when, as an arbitrator, you will want to communicate with all participants in the arbitration, but there will be other times when the information sent will be merely ministerial and applicable only to your co-arbitrators. Also, while the "cc" option is a powerful e-mail tool, it is a horrible "accident waiting to happen." Critical, highly confidential decisional information can be disclosed in a split, unthinking, second and can doom an arbitration and perhaps put an arbitrator's neutrality in serious jeopardy. Before commencing an online arbitration, arbitrators normally take great pains to advise parties and counsel about the dangers of unintentional disclosures of confidentiality and to discuss procedures for preventing it from happening.

Take security precautions vis-à-vis other Web users. If you are engaged in the arbitration of a high-profile case online, do not be too surprised if you have interlopers—related to the dispute or not—trying to acquire information on the arbitration progress. If you use chat rooms, make sure they are secure and keep an eye out for new entrants whose identity you do not know.

---

16. *See generally,* Louise Ellen Teitz, *Providing Legal Services for the Middle Class in Cyberspace: The Promise and Challenge of On-Line Dispute Resolution,* 70 Fordham L. Rev. 985, 987-91 (2001).

17. M. Ethan Katsh, *Dispute Resolution in Cyberspace,* 28 Conn. L. Rev. 953, 971-74 (1996).

Maintain appropriate confidentiality within your groups. It was pointed out above that the "cc" feature of e-mail is a powerful and useful tool, but that it can cause disastrous disclosures of information. Before you send any e-mail messages, you should ensure that the principal addressees and the "cc" addressees are appropriate. You may be involved in several online arbitrations at once. If you are simultaneously involved in several cyberarbitrations and cybermediations, it is important for you to keep the e-mail addresses of participants in the various cases segregated from each other so that you do not inadvertently dispatch an e-mail to a participant in a separate ADR case.

5.5 COMPARISON OF VARIOUS COMMUNICATION MODES IN CYBERARBITRATION

Below is a chart which shows, in order of increasing expense, the available communication modes, the best situation(s) for use, and some of their respective advantages and disadvantages. The face-to-face communication mode, which is normally the optimal, but most expensive mode, does not appear in the chart.

Communication Modes

Communication Mode	Best Use	Advantages	Disadvantages
E-mail	For sequential, leisurely written communication where quick reply is not normally needed or expected.	Messages can be broadcast to any number of people simultaneously. See also the chart in Section 5.2.	Confidentiality can be easily compromised. See also the chart in Section 5.2.
Threaded Discussions	For sequential, leisurely communication in which all the written dialogue of a number of participants remains on the screen.	By scrolling up, participants can view all dialogue occurring previously on a particular topic. It produces a "record" of the conversation.	A couple of participants may dominate dialogue on minor points while other participants are trying to get them involved in discussing topics more important to the group as a whole.
Instant Messaging	Provides a private space for real-time written conversation with another individual.	System can alert the two users that they are simultaneously online so they can engage in conversation.	Normally, the two participants must have the same Internet provider.
Chat Rooms	Provides a private space where several persons may engage in real-time written conversation.	Persons can schedule a chat room meeting at mutually convenient times, accommodating time zones and locations of participants.	Conversations can become sarcastic and hostile, depending on the topic being discussed.

Conducting the Cyberarbitration

Communication Mode	Best Use	Advantages	Disadvantages
Regular Mail or Traceable Carrier	Provides an alternative to digitally sent written materials, where addresses do not have the necessary or adequate equipment to send or receive the material by Internet means.	Addresses are more likely to receive accurate duplicates of original hard copy pages. Objects may be sent by mail, which is not possible using the Internet.	Mail sent internationally may be delayed in arriving at its destination, or it may get lost. There may be customs problems, also. Cost of mailing may be prohibitive.
Voice Mail	For use when called person is unavailable, but can return the call later; also useful to record a message containing information that needs no response by called person.	Minimizes or eliminates "phone tag" and can facilitate the transfer of extensive information to the called person.	Voice mail messages in which the caller does not leave a telephone number or e-mail address where he/she can be reached can be annoying.
Fax	For use when transmitting a reasonably small number of pages of information.	Faxing is a very useful alternative to Internet transmission of information where time is of the essence and digital copy of a document is available.	Sometimes faxed copies are illegible or incomplete; sometimes it is impossible to tell who the sender is.
Teleconference	For use when it is more efficient for people to talk orally with one another.	It allows full exploration of topics by a limited number of participants in a relatively short period of time when they are prepared by reading pre-conference material. It facilitates and accelerates decision making.	It is often difficult to know who the speaker is during the course of the conversation. The number of participants in a teleconference is limited by practical considerations of complexity of interactions, time, and expense.
Webcam	For use by two persons when seeing images of each other is important while communicating.	Webcam imitates face-to-face communication between two people.	Special cameras and software need to be purchased by each participant.
Netcam	For use when it is important that several known recipients on a network see images of each other while communicating.	Netcam imitates face-to-face communication between several persons in a network.	Special equipment needs to be purchased by the participants in netcam communication.

Videoconference	For use when it is important that several participants at different sites interact electronically with each other visually and auditorily; useful for meetings and for depositions where seeing and hearing the testifying witness is important.	The videoconference most closely imitates face-to-face communication between any number of participants.	Cost of extensive use of this medium of communication can be prohibitive.

5.6   CYBERSPACE NETIQUETTE

Communication on the Internet involves different dynamics and rules than does communication through other media.[18] Thus, when you are communicating messages or conducting an arbitration online, you will have to take into account the benefits and limitations of this medium in order to capitalize on the experience. One principal difference between online communication and ordinary verbal communication is that in e-mail or threaded discussions you have the opportunity to compose, read, reflect, and modify the content of your message before you send or convey it. Thus, you can catch errors or unintentional misstatements of facts before you actually communicate them. In a chat-room mode, this advantage is not present and you must take care to carefully and tactfully craft your message as your fingers fly.

When you are conducting an arbitration online, you may find this set of communication guidelines—or "netiquette"—helpful.[19] In the discussion that follows, it should be understood that no communications are ex parte; that is, no counsel or party is communicating with the arbitrator without simultaneously copying the opposing party and that the arbitrator is sending e-mails to the parties simultaneously.

Communicate only with permission. You must take special precautions to ensure that you know who is "in the loop" for communicating online. You should clarify with counsel whether they prefer to have all of your e-mail sent solely to them, or whether they want copies sent to their clients also. You should also, of course, specify whether or not you want your client to be a recipient of participants' e-mail. In some situations you may want your client to receive the arbitrator's e-mail, but not the e-mail of other lawyers. There may be other people

---

18. *See generally,* Jeffrey G. Kichaven, *Virtual Mediation* 7-8 (Business Law Today, ABA, May/June 1996).

19. *See generally,* Jeffrey Krivis, *Mediating in Cyberspace* 128-31 (CPR Institute for Dispute Resolution, Alternatives to the High Cost of Litigation, Vol. 14, No. 10, November 1996); John R. Helie and James C. Melamed, *Email Management and Etiquette,* (http://www.mediate.com/articles/email.cfm).

outside of the circle of actual participants in the cyberarbitration who need to be kept abreast of various happenings during the course of the arbitration. Make sure you know whom you are authorized to contact and whom you are not to contact. Sending an e-mail message to a person not authorized to receive it could doom an arbitration in some situations.

Don't take time for granted. When you are communicating sequentially in cyberspace, you may find that people behave as though there are no time constraints—as if they have "all the time in the world." Because this phenomenon is widespread, accomplishing simple tasks, such as receiving a ruling from the arbitrator or receiving co-parties' views on certain issues by e-mail, may seem to take forever. To minimize this problem, at the outset of the arbitration, you may want to establish a protocol covering time periods within which counsel are expected to respond by e-mail.

Be conscious of time zones. While you may need to set time limits for replies, be conscious that a co-arbitrator's or a party's ability to reply may be hampered by the timing of your request. On the Web, you may be communicating with people who live and work in various parts of the United States and even in various countries in the world who are in different time zones. Some of these people may even be traveling through various time zones during the course of an extended cyberarbitration. Thus, if you send an e-mail to someone in the early morning from New York to San Francisco, do not expect even the earliest response to be before mid-afternoon. You must factor in not only the time zone differential, but also the time it will take the party to communicate with others—perhaps even by e-mail—before the party will be able to respond to you. Also, if an attorney, for example, had to be in court early in the morning, he or she may not even have a chance to check e-mail until later in the day, which will additionally delay the response. Thus, be mindful of these delaying factors and take care to avoid setting unrealistic reply deadlines for your cyberarbitration participants.

Respect people's space. Avoid overwhelming the arbitrator, the parties, and their counsel with e-mail messages. It is disconcerting for someone to open his or her mailbox to find a whole list of e-mails from the same person. People have lives; and counsel not only have personal lives, but they also have other clients to represent. Neutrals may have several separate cases they are cyberarbitrating or cybermediating simultaneously. While the cyberarbitration you are engaged in may be the only one you are currently working on, do not convey that impression to the participants, and do not let the arbitration overtake your life. Sometimes people arbitrate online because they like the often leisurely pace and opportunity for considered attorney-client decision making. Be cognizant of that possibility and avoid being obsessive. Also, realize that your unrelenting e-mail involvement may unnecessarily increase the costs for all parties in the case, including your own client. Realize that every e-mail you send not only documents time you've spent on the case, but also the takes up the time of co-arbitrators and of other counsel who must communicate with their clients and get back to you and the arbitrator. High aggregate fees can mount quickly.

Request and provide confirmations. Breakdown in communication may occur simply because a co-arbitrator and other counsel never received your e-mail communication. This may occur because of an address error, misdirection, or even an inadvertent failure to "send" the prepared message. Thus, if you are dispatching an important e-mail message, it is a good idea to request the addressees to acknowledge receipt of the message even before they review and consider its content. If you do not receive confirmation from each addressee, then you will be able to investigate right away whether you will need to resend the message or relay it to him or her via another mode of communication. Similarly, if a co-arbitrator or other counsel request that you acknowledge receipt of an e-mail, you should confirm receipt immediately and respond to the substance of the message later.

Check and answer e-mail regularly. As an arbitrator in a cyberarbitration, you will need to develop the discipline of checking and answering e-mail periodically during each day. Because e-mail is not as intrusive as telephone contact, you will find that some counsel, or parties, or a co-arbitrator, as the case may be, may send you e-mail on the weekend. The policy you adopt for handling e-mail communication on the weekends will conform to your individual preferences or lifestyle. Some cyberarbitration participants prefer not to respond to such communications until the next business day; others prefer to respond in order to sustain the momentum of dialogue or to keep their mailboxes cleared out.

Give notice of extended absences. If you are involved in a cyberarbitration, it is important that you let your participants know when you are going to be unavailable for e-mail communication for a day or more. They will appreciate your courtesy, and by mutual agreement you and they might be able to arrange some alternate mode of communication to substitute for e-mail, in case of an emergency for example.

Forward e-mails with an explanation. You have probably received forwarded e-mails from senders who provide no accompanying explanation. This can be disconcerting and annoying. Often, when you receive such an unadorned forwarded message, you are not sure why you have received it and what you are expected to do with it now that you have it. Thus, when you are forwarding messages, you should get into the habit of inserting a short explanatory note prior to any message you forward so that the receiving party will understand why you are sending it and whether he or she needs to respond to you in some way.

Attach only necessary documents. Be respectful of people's time. If you attach a document to an e-mail, make sure that each addressee needs to review it. Before you attach a document, review your list of addressees and segregate those out who do not need to receive it. Then send a separate e-mail to those people without the document attached.

Police hostile or hurtful language. E-mail is a type of communication that can quickly degenerate into an abusive exchange. It can create a faceless "bunker" mentality among opposing counsel that is regrettably conducive to sniping and taking "pot shots" at others in an insulting way. Insults can be exchanged privately— one on one—or in the open for all to see. Such exchanges can quickly escalate into situations that are difficult to bring back into balance. As a professional matter, you must be vigilant to halt even the slightest signs of hostile or hurtful language. Left unattended, such offensive remarks can disrupt the cyberarbitration at the very least, and at worst they can cause the process to disintegrate.

Be polite and diplomatic in your own language. As a cyberarbitrator, you can provide a model for the type of written communication that you expect the others to use in an online arbitration. You will find, generally speaking, that if you make an effort to use polite, respectful, and diplomatic language, the other participants will do likewise.

Keep communications crisp, pithy, and relevant. Most of us have experienced online communication where a participant goes well outside the relevant topic and writes interminably about matters that fail to move the discussion to a common goal. In an online arbitration, counsel may engage in this type of communication to divert the process from an issue where his or her position is weak to issues where he or she can speak from a position of strength. This kind of communication may also indicate a desire on counsel's part to control the agenda. Normally arbitrators will nip this kind of communication in the bud and encourage the participants to keep communications crisp, pithy, and relevant. You may want to consider setting length limits on e-mail communication.

Mind your grammar, spelling, and punctuation. Your e-mail communications need not be perfect, but you should pay respect to common rules of grammar, spelling, and punctuation. Consider this sentence from a hypothetical e-mail message between co-counsel in a cyberarbitration:

> "i think your principle goal here, mary, is far out. don't go there. you'll be disappointed and hack-off the our oponents."

This sentence communicates much about its writer. Failure to use capital letters and to spell properly says that the writer is in a hurry and may be invested only superficially in the communication process. Use of slang and failure to capitalize names can be degrading to receivers of e-mail. A good rule of thumb is to take the type of drafting care with your e-mail communications that you expect others to take when they are sending e-mails to you.

Use emoticons and abbreviations minimally. Emoticons are groups of punctuation and other symbols used to convey emotions. Do not assume that everyone knows what emoticons mean. You may do harm in an e-mail communication if you intend one meaning by your use of an emoticon and your addressee infers another meaning. Here is a list of common emoticons so that you will be able to understand them if you receive them in online communication:

|-) happy, humorous

|-(unhappy

|-0 shocked

|-} wry, ironic

<g> grin

<s> sigh

<VBG> very big grin

Abbreviations can save time and space, but if your addressees do not understand what they mean, they can be aggravating to them. It is a wise practice to use abbreviations minimally or not at all, or when you first use them, to put their meanings in parentheses. Here are a few common abbreviations that you may receive or even use in your online communications:

BTW by the way

F2F face to face

FYI for your information

imo in my opinion

imho in my humble opinion

LOL laughing out loud

TIA thanks in advance

BR best regards

BPR best personal regards

Use telephone backup. When arbitrating online, sometimes there is no equal substitute for picking up the telephone and talking directly to someone, such as your co-arbitrators. Some people communicate better verbally than in writing. Also, people can often relay communications more effectively and meaningfully by voice. For example, in a speaking context, you can give support, provide detailed explanations, and answer questions more quickly and sensitively. Thus, while written online communication can be very effective in arbitration, telephone backup will also be quite useful from time to time.

Save your e-mail correspondence. It is a wise practice to save (and digitally back up) all your e-mail correspondence relating to a particular arbitration, at least until the arbitration has concluded, and sometimes well beyond the conclusion. You will find it helpful to refer back to certain e-mail communications from time to time—especially near the end of the arbitration when you are drafting the award and supporting opinion, if applicable. You may also find it useful during the course of the arbitration to print out hard copies of critical communications for your reference. The e-mail correspondence may also be helpful to you long after the arbitration if an issue arises as to whether a party is in compliance with the your award. Exactly how long you retain your e-mail correspondence after the conclusion of the arbitration will be dictated by your personal or your ADR firm's document retention policies or, perhaps, the rules of your particular jurisdiction.

5.7 GATHERING RELEVANT INTERNET INFORMATION

5.7.1 General

In your preparation for a cyberarbitration, apart from reviewing documents relevant to the case, you should realize that the advocates have at their fingertips a virtual wealth of Internet information useful to their arbitration presentations. Remember that, in cyberarbitration, oftentimes you will be asked to take judicial notice of certain facts. Through Web research in advance of the cyberarbitration, advocates can also gather information highly relevant to the matters at issue in the arbitration, other than the information disclosed to them by opposing counsel. This information may be used by them as part of their direct case or on cross-examination. Of course, if they intended to use information discovered by use of the Internet, they would have to disclose to opposing counsel the nature of this information and their intent to use it at the cyberarbitration hearing. Such research might yield these types of information, to name only a few: (1) applicable cases decided by relevant courts in the last few days (or hours) (LEXIS, WestLaw, etc.); (2) newspaper articles concerning statements made by various arbitration parties publicly (NEXIS); (3) background information on the parties and their counsel contained in Web professional directories or on corporate Web sites; (4) prospecti or annual reports of corporate parties; (5) information showing structures of corporations, identifying subsidiaries, interlocking directorates, or other linkages; (6) articles or book synopses written by various parties, and/or their counsel or other experts, taking positions opposite those being taken in the cyberarbitration; (7) items of information in the judicial notice category: day of week on a particular date, weather conditions on a particular date in a particular city, date and time of day that a particular historical or catastrophic event occurred, etc.; (8) state government information; and (9) federal government information.[20] To gather this information and/or review it, the arbitrator(s) and advocates must be able to use not only computer-aided legal research techniques (in which lawyers are by now reasonably skilled) but also general Web research techniques. Some tips on using the latter techniques follow.

5.7.2 Search engines

A search engine is a program that searches one or more documents for specified key words and returns a list of locations where those keywords were found. Some search engines are capable of doing Boolean searches; others are not. A Boolean search involves using Boolean operators (i.e., AND, OR, and NOT) that are used to refine or broaden a search. (See below in this Subsection). You may find the following legal search engines useful in preparing for cyberarbitration: (type first http://www.)

> abanet.org
>
> American Law Sources Online
>
> Catalaw (meta search engine)
>
> CyberAttorney
>
> Findlaw
>
> GSU Law (meta search engine)
>
> Hieros Gamos
>
> InternetLegalResourceGuide
>
> Law.com
>
> LawCrawler
>
> LawGuru

The chart below identifies the leading general search engines and describes relevant attributes.

---

20. For a comprehensive collection of Internet reference tools covering topics of arbitration institutions and rules, link collections and bookmarks, foreign laws, arbitration journals and newsletters, national arbitration laws, international treaties and model laws, currency converters, public company information, online newspapers, travel and weather information, see Bernhard F. Meyer-Hauser, *Online Aid for Arbitrators and Arbitration Counsel*, 8 Croat.Arbit. Yearb. 9 (2001)

Search Engines	Relevant Attributes
Alta Vista	Searches in any language using Boolean operators and date limitation
Excite	Uses Boolean operators and offers extensive retrieval options
Fast/All the Web	Allows Boolean queries and content limitors
Go	Good coverage of Web, newsgroup information, and news and company sites
Google.com	No Boolean operators: very accurate searching
Google/Uncle Sam	Specialized search engine for searching government information.
Hot Bot	"Super Search" feature offers the user word filters, page, location, and media type limitation; drop-down menus give use straightforward limiting options
Lycos	Full Boolean search engine available; indexing of fifty million Web pages
Northern Light	Great degree of precision searching; limits include dates, subjects, sources, and document types
Yahoo!	Considered more of a search directory than a traditional search engine.

Other search engines and meta search engines include: (type first http://www.)

About.com

Ask Jeeves

Looksmart

Search.com

Cyber 411

Inference

Metacrawler

ProFusion

SavvySearch

5.7.3 Other Internet reference tools

Other reference tools that advocates may use to find information to aid their cyberarbitration presentations are listed in the chart below, with comments as appropriate: (type first http://www.)

Reference Tool	Comments
clearinghouse.net	Argus Clearninghouse reviews and rates top Web sites
ipl.org	Internet Public Library
lli.org	Librarian's Index to the Internet
vlib.stanford.edu/overview.html	The WWW Virtual Library
anywho.com	Phone and address lookup site from AT&T locates people when you have only partial information; includes a reverse telephone number lookup feature
switchboard.com	Phone and address lookup site
whowhere.com	Phone and address lookup site
infospace.com	E-mail, business, and residential address lookup site
zip2.com	Business address and phone number lookup site
companysleuth.com	Background on businesses, including information on litigation and patent applications
mapquest.com	Detailed street maps for any place in the U.S.
Nyp.org/branch/eresources.html	New York Public Library. A library card is required; library barcode number is used as a password; has several excellent electronic databases available to the public including Proquest, which provides full-text articles from many newspapers and periodicals
iTools.com/research-it	All-in-one reference desk: dictionary, quotes, translators, and more
onelook.com	Four hundred dictionaries; specialized and general
britannica.com	Encyclopedia Brittanica; free of charge
thesaurus.com	Roget's Internet Thesaurus
infoplease.com	Information Please Almanac; dictionary and full Columbia Encyclopedia
biography.com/find/find.html	Cambridge Biographical Encyclopedia; brief cross-referenced biographies of more than 15,000 notable people
dictionaries.travlang.com	Provides word translation from English into many other languages
nolo.com/dictionary/wordindex.cfm	Nolo's legal dictionary
odci.gov/cia/publications/pubs.html	C.I.A. World Factbook; brief profiles of countries around the world
usps.gov	U.S. Postal Service's Zip Code finder and express mail tracker
ups.com	Track UPS packages
fedex.com	Track FedEx packages

5.7.4   Tips for using search engines

When conducting a search, break down the topic into key concepts. For example, to find out what the Federal Aviation Administration ("FAA") has said about making handicapped seating available on commercial airliners, the keywords might be:

FAA handicapped seating

• **Boolean AND.** If you connect search terms with AND, you tell the search engine to retrieve Web pages containing all the keywords. Consider the following search command:

FAA and handicapped and seating

In this example, the search engine will not return pages with just the word FAA; nor will it return pages with the word FAA and the word handicapped. Rather the search engine will only return pages where the words FAA, handicapped, and seating all appear somewhere on the page. Thus, the word AND helps to narrow your search results to pages where all keywords appear.

• **Boolean OR.** If you connect search terms with OR, you tell the search engine to return pages with a single keyword, several keywords, and all keywords. Thus, OR expands your search results. Use OR when you have synonyms for a keyword. It is best to surround OR statements with parentheses. Combine OR statements with AND statements if you wish to narrow your results as much as possible. For example, the following search statement locates information on buying an insolvent company:

(company or corporation or business) and (buy or purchase) and insolvent

• **Boolean AND NOT.** If you connect search terms with AND NOT, you tell the search engine to retrieve Web pages containing one keyword but not the other. Consider this example:

insurance and not life

This search statement tells the search engine to return Web pages about insurance, but not Web pages concerning life insurance. Essentially, you should use AND NOT when you have a keyword that has multiple meanings.

• **Implied Boolean.** Plus and Minus In some search engines, plus and minus symbols can be used as alternatives to full Boolean AND and AND NOT. The plus sign is the equivalent of AND, and the minus sign is the equivalent of AND NOT. No space is placed between the plus or minus sign and the keyword.

• **Phrase searching.** Placing a group of words in double quotes tells the search engine to only retrieve documents in which those words appear side by side.

Phrase searching is a powerful tool for narrowing searches. Examples are: "mediation advocacy training"; "evaluative mediator"; "online dispute resolution service."

• Combining phrase searching with implied Boolean or full Boolean Consider the following examples:

+ "deep vein thrombosis" +cause

"deep vein thrombosis" and cause

These search statements tell the search engine to retrieve pages where the words "deep vein thrombosis" appear side by side and the word "cause" appears somewhere on the page.

• **Plural forms, capital letters, and alternate spellings.** Most search engines interpret singular keywords as singular or plural. If you desire plural forms only, type your keywords that way. If you want both upper and lowercase occurrences returned, type your keywords in all lowercase letters. On the other hand, if you want to limit your results to initial capital letters (e.g., Abraham Lincoln) or all upper case letters (TOP SECRET), you should type your keywords accordingly. A few search engines allow variations in spelling or word forms by use of the asterisk (*) symbol. For example, capital* returns Web pages with capital, capitals, capitalize, and capitalization.

• **Title search.** A Web page is composed of a number of fields, such as title, domain, host, URL, and link. If you combine field searches with phrase searches and Boolean logic, you increase your search effectiveness. Consider these examples:

+title: "Abraham Lincoln" +President +"Mary Todd"

title: "Abraham Lincoln" and President and "Mary Todd"

The above title search tells the search engine to return Web pages where the phrase Abraham Lincoln appears in the title and the words President and Mary Todd appear somewhere on the page. Like plus and minus, there is no space between the colon after title and the keyword.

• **Domain search.** The domain search allows you to limit your results to certain domains such as Web sites from educational institutions, other countries, or the government. The current U.S. domains include the following:

.com = commercial business

.edu = educational institution

.gov = governmental institution

.org = a nonprofit organization

.mil = a military site

.net = a network site

Consider these examples:

domain:edu and "cloning" and animal*

domain:uk and title: "Winston Churchill"

domain:gov and "freedom of information" and bribe*

• **Host search.** This type of search allows to search all the pages at a Web site for keywords or phrases of interest. An example is shown below.

+host:www.abanet.org +cyber*

host:www.abanet.org and cyber*

• **URL search.** If you do a URL search, you tell the search engine to return the Web pages where the keyword appears in the URL or Web site address. A URL search narrows results to Web pages devoted to the keyword topic. Consider these examples:

+url:mediation +title:articles

url:mediation and title:articles

• **Link search.** If you want to know what Web sites are linked to a particular site of interest, use a link search. For example, you would use this type of search if you have a home page and you want to know if anyone has put a link to your page on their Web site. Typically, researchers use link searches for conducting backward citations. Consider these examples:

link:www.nita.org

ink:www.mediate.com

link:www.onlineresolution.com

EPILOGUE

Truth Never Dies

Truth never dies. The ages come and go.
The mountains wear away, the stars retire.
Destruction lays earth's mighty cities low;
And empires, states, and dynasties expire;
But caught and handed onward by the wise,
Truth never dies.

Though unreceived and scoffed at through the years;
Though made the butt of ridicule and jest;
Though held aloft for mockery and jeers,
Denied by those of transient power possessed,
Insulted by the insolence of lies,
Truth never dies.

It answers not. It does not take offense,
But with almighty silence bides its time;
As some great cliff that braves the elements
And lifts through all the storms its head sublime,
It ever stands, uplifted by the wise;
And never dies.

As rests the Sphinx amid Egyptian sands;
As looms on high the snowy peak and crest;
As firm and patient as Gibraltar stands,
So truth, unwearied, waits the era blessed
When men shall turn to it with great surprise.
Truth never dies.

—Author unknown

CONTENTS OF THE APPENDICES

A. Grounds for Various Arbitration Rulings........................279

B. Arbitrator's Prehearing Functions and Duties Checklist 307

C. Arbitrator's Hearing Functions and Duties Checklist 313

D. Arbitrator's Post-hearing Functions and Duties Checklist.............327

E. Sample Arbitration Clauses for a Commercial Contract...............335

F. AAA Commercial Arbitration Rules.............................339

G. JAMS Comprehensive Arbitration Rules and Procedures 361

H. AAA International Arbitration Rules............................373

I. 1958 New York Convention on the Recognition and
    Enforcement of Foreign Arbitral Awards 387

J. AAA Supplementary Procedures for Online Arbitration...............393

K. The Code of Ethics for Arbitrators in Commercial Disputes—
    Revised 2004..399

L. Selected ABA Model Rules of Professional Conduct.....................415

M. American Bar Association Litigation Section's
    Civility Guidelines 427

N. Uniform Arbitration Act 431

O. Federal Arbitration Act...455

P. Organizations Offering ADR Services.............................465

APPENDIX A

Grounds for Various Arbitration Rulings

A.   INTRODUCTION.

Appendix A is an idea generator. Its principal purpose is to provide the arbitrator with a kaleidoscope of ideas for providing support or reasons for various oral rulings on motions or objections arising during the course of an arbitration. It can also be used by the arbitrator as a resource to focus legal research when with preparing written rulings on motions and objections during the course of or after an arbitration hearing. In some situations, a single ground will be sufficient independently to provide support for a particular ruling; in others, several grounds may be combined to provide such support.

Index of Motions and Objections

1. Motion to Dismiss Based on Failure of Party to Initiate Timely Arbitration.
2. Motion to Dismiss Claim Because of Lack of Arbitrability.
3. Motion to Dismiss for Failure to State a Claim.
4. Motion to Dismiss Based on Res Judicata, Collateral Estoppel, or Waiver.
5. Motion to Dismiss for Failure to Prosecute Claim.
6. Motion for Entry of Default Award for Failure to Defend.
7. Motion to Dismiss or to Join a Party.
8. Motion to Sever Claim or Cause of Action.
9. Motion for More Definite Statement.
10. Motion for Entry of an Award on the Pleadings.
11. Motion to Strike Pleadings.
12. Motion for Summary Judgment.
13. Motion to Compel Discovery.
14. Motions for Restraining Orders or Injunctions.
15. Motion for Continuance.
16. Motion for Bifurcated Discovery and/or Arbitration Hearing.
17. Motion for Disqualification of Attorney.
18. Objection to Opening Statement.
19. Motion for Arbitrator to Take Judicial Notice.
20. Motion to Exclude Evidence on Relevance Grounds.
21. Objection to Character Evidence.
22. Objection to Evidence of Habit, Custom, or Common Practice.

23. Objection to Evidence of Subsequent Remedial Measures.
24. Objection to Evidence Based on Assertion of Privilege.
25. Objection to Scope of Direct Examination.
26. Objection to Scope of Cross-Examination.
27. Objection to Scope of Redirect Examination.
28. Objection to Scope of Recross-Examination.
29. Objection to Questioning Procedure or to Substance of Testimony on Direct Examination.
30. Objection to Questioning Procedure or to Substance of Testimony on Cross-Examination.
31. Objection to Expert Testimony.
32. Objection to Hearsay Evidence.
33. Assertion of Exception to Hearsay Rule–Admission of Party.
34. Assertion of Exception to Hearsay Rule–Prior Statement of Witness.
35. Assertion of Exception to Hearsay Rule–Excited Utterance.
36. Assertion of Exception to Hearsay Rule–State of Mind: Emotional or Mental State.
37. Assertion of Exception to Hearsay Rule–Statement of Physical Condition.
38. Assertion of Exception to Hearsay Rule: Private, Published, and Institutional Records.
39. Assertion of Exception to Hearsay Rule–Public Records.
39. Assertion of Exception to Hearsay Rule–Declarant Unavailable.
40. Objection to Evidence Based on Lack of Foundation.
41. Objection to Evidence Based on Best Evidence Rule.
42. Objection Relating to Closing Argument.
43. Motion for Reconsideration or for Order for Additional or Amended Findings.
44. Objection Relating to Interest on Award.
45. Objection Relating to Award of Costs.
46. Objection Relating to an Award of Attorney's Fees.
47. Motion to Reopen Arbitration Hearing.

B.   ORDERS AND RULINGS ENTERED PRIOR TO HEARING.

1. Motion to Dismiss Based on Failure of Party to Initiate Timely Arbitration.

Order Denying Dismissal of Arbitration Proceedings	Order Granting Dismissal of Arbitration Proceedings
Possible Grounds:	Possible Grounds:
1. Tolling of time limits	1. Tolling inapplicable
2. Moving party waived right to object	2. Moving party's waiver of right to object was ineffective
3. Moving party fraudulently concealed evidence of breach of agreement	3. Non-moving party lacked diligence in complying with initiation clause
4. Moving party is estopped to complain because of its prior statements or conduct	4. Moving party's silence did not constitute acquiescence in untimely initiation
5. Moving party relied on wrong clause/statute/rule	5. Non-moving party relied on wrong clause/statute/rule
6. Sufficient evidence of prior acknowledgment by moving party that initiation was timely	6. Insufficient evidence of moving party's prior acknowledgment of timeliness

2. Motion to Dismiss Claim Because of Lack of Arbitrability.

Order Denying Dismissal	Order Granting Dismissal
Possible Grounds:	Possible Grounds:
1. Arbitrability founded in case law	1. Non-moving party waived right to arbitrate claim
2. Statute/rule permits or requires arbitration of claim	2. Non-moving party is estopped from arbitrating claim
3. Parties agreed to arbitrate claim	3. Parties did not agree to arbitrate claim

3. Motion to Dismiss for Failure to State a Claim.

Order Denying Dismissal	Order Granting Dismissal
Possible Grounds:	Possible Grounds:
1. Allegations sufficient	1. Allegations insufficient and not remediable
2. Errors in statement of claim correctable	2. Allegations consist of legal conclusions
3. Statement of claim is amendable	3. Uncontradicted evidence of affirmative defense obviates non-moving party's ability to state claim
4. Motion to dismiss is insufficiently specific	4. Statement of claim fails to comply with provisions of the arbitration rules

4. Motion to Dismiss Based on Res Judicata, Collateral Estoppel, or Waiver.

Order Denying Res Judicata or Collateral Estoppel Effect	Order Barring Action or Relitigation of an Issue
Possible Grounds:	Possible Grounds:
1. Lack of final judgment on merits	1. Prerequisites for res judicata met
2. Prior judgment is null and void	2. Prior judgment is valid
3. Lack of identity of parties or privity	3. Matters that could have been litigated are barred by res judicata (not collateral estoppel)
4. Different cause of action	4. Failure to plead compulsory counterclaim constitutes waiver, and res judicata doctrine bars later suit on such claim
5. Waiver	5. Collateral estoppel bars claim where party had full and fair opportunity to litigate it in prior action
6. Lack of mutuality as required by collateral estoppel doctrine	6. Negligence in litigating prior action is not a defense to the application of collateral estoppel
7. Lack of full and fair opportunity to litigate as required by collateral estoppel doctrine	7. Statute or rule provision specifically bars relitigation of cause of action or claim

5. Motion to Dismiss for Failure to Prosecute Claim.

Order Denying Dismissal	Order Granting Dismissal
Possible Grounds:	Possible Grounds:
1. No abandonment	1. Prejudice to defendant
2. Complicated nature of case	2. Abuse of process
3. Illness	3. Negligence of complainant or counsel
4. Attorney error	4. Non-compliance with arbitrator's orders
5. Delay due to defendant	5. Complainant's specific intent to delay proceedings

6. Motion for Entry of Default Award for Failure to Defend.

Order Refusing Default Award	Order Granting Default Award
Possible Grounds:	Possible Grounds:
1. Compliance with statutes and rules	1. Mandatory statutory provision
2. Non-arbitrability	2. Mandatory rule provision
3. Sufficient appearance	3. Arbitration clause provision
4. Waiver by moving party	4. Non-moving party waived right to object to entry of default award
5. Moving party's defective pleadings	5. Non-moving party estopped from objecting to entry of default award
6. Improper or inadequate notice	6. Proper notice served on non-moving party
7. Inadequate proof of liability (if jurisdiction requires proof of all elements of claims)	7. Moving party presents adequate proof of liability (if required) and damages
8. Inadequate proof of damages	8. Non-moving party's failure to comply with arbitrator's orders or rulings

7. Motion to Dismiss or to Join a Party.

Order Denying Dismissal of Party (Or Granting Motion to Join Party)	Order Granting Dismissal of Party (Or Denying Motion to Join Party)
Possible Grounds:	Possible Grounds:
1. Statutory, rule, or contract provision	1. Statutory or rule provision
2. Untimely motion	2. Not a party to arbitration agreement
3. Other waiver	3. Party has no interest or involvement in subject matter of arbitration

8. Motion to Sever Claim or Cause of Action.

Order Denying Severance of Cause of Action	Order Granting Severance of Cause of Action
Possible Grounds:	Possible Grounds:
1. Complete relief otherwise unattainable	1. Fairness, convenience, or certain prejudice to moving party if there is a single hearing
2. Causes of action/claims interwoven and covered by arbitration clause	2. Avoidance of confusion
3. Prejudice to defendant who would be required to defend in two separate arbitrations	3. Cause of action or claim not covered by arbitration clause, or non-moving party waived right to object to severance

9. Motion for More Definite Statement.

Order Denying Motion for More Definite Statement	Order Granting Motion for More Definite Statement
Possible Grounds:	Possible Grounds:
1. Pleading is acceptable	1. Ambiguous and/or vague pleadings
2. Moving party is seeking opponent's contentions, rather than factual allegations	2. Moving party is unable to formulate a response on the basis of the information provided and will be prejudiced
3. Motion is inadequate, unclear, or incomplete	3. Pleading fails to state a claim for relief

10. Motion for Entry of an Award on the Pleadings.

Order Denying Motion for Award on the Pleadings	Order Granting Motion for Award on the Pleadings
Possible Grounds:	Possible Grounds:
1. Pleading attacked is not fatally defective and can be amended	1. Pleading is fatally defective, and defect cannot be cured
2. Resolving all doubts in favor of the non-movant, there is an issue of fact which requires determination	2. No issues of fact are in dispute, and only an issue or issues of law need to be resolved
3. Movant waived right to move for judgment on the pleadings by its conduct	3. Non-moving party elects not to respond to motion, thereby waiving right to object to an award on the pleadings
4. Motion is premature	4. Non-movant admitted allegations of pleadings in answers to requests to admit or in answers to interrogatories

11. Motion to Strike Pleadings.

Order Denying Motion to Strike Pleadings	Order Granting Motion to Strike Pleadings
Possible Grounds:	Possible Grounds:
1. Pleadings are sufficient	1. Pleadings are insufficient and vague
2. Granting motion to strike would leave pleadings ambiguous	2. Pleadings are irrelevant, frivolous, or redundant
3. No prejudice to moving party if motion is denied	3. Pleadings are scandalous, impertinent, or a sham
4. Movant waived right to move to strike by prior conduct	4. Denying motion to strike would materially prejudice movant in presenting case

12. **Motion for Summary Judgment.**

Order Denying Motion for Summary Judgment	Order Granting Motion for Summary Judgment
Possible Grounds:	Possible Grounds:
1. Fact in issue is genuine	1. No genuine issue of material fact
2. Fact in issue is material	2. Lack of counter-affidavits or other responding materials
3. Movant failed to comply with statute or rule regarding inclusion of affidavits, transcripts, or other supporting materials	3. Movant prevails on the issues of law raised

13. **Motion to Compel Discovery.**

Order Denying Motion to Compel Discovery	Order Granting Motion to Compel Discovery
Possible Grounds:	Possible Grounds:
1. Information sought is privileged or otherwise immune from production	1. Information sought is reasonably calculated to lead to the discovery of admissible evidence
2. Motion is made to embarrass or harass a party, or for purposes of delay	2. Asserted privilege is nonexistent or inapplicable
3. Discovery request is overbroad or burdensome	3. Scope of discovery request is reasonable, and procedures can be prescribed, which facilitates production and lessens its cost

14. **Motions for Restraining Orders or Injunctions.**

Order Denying Motion for TRO, Injunction, or Other Interim Relief	Order Granting Motion for TRO, Injunction, or Other Interim Relief
Possible Grounds:	Possible Grounds:
1. Movant has adequate legal remedy	1. Irreparable injury will occur if interim relief is denied
2. Order granting interim relief would restrain non-movant from exercising legal or Constitutional rights	2. Movant has no adequate remedy at law
3. Movant lacks clean hands in connection with the matter for which he or she seeks relief	3. Movant is likely to succeed on the merits of his or her claims in the arbitration hearing
4. Movant is guilty of laches or has acquiesced in non-movant's acts	4. Statute or rule authorizes interim relief to be granted on the specific facts presented
5. Any order entered would be overly broad or vague and incapable of compliance	5. Public will not suffer substantial harm if interim relief is granted
6. Movant will not likely succeed on the merits of his or her claims in the arbitration proceeding	6. Substantial public harm will occur if interim relief is not granted

15. Motion for Continuance.

Order Denying Motion for Continuance	Order Granting Motion for Continuance
Possible Grounds:	Possible Grounds:
1. Reasons for continuance are inconsequential, frivolous, or not convincing	1. Movant would suffer significant prejudice in presenting case if motion were denied
2. Movant has shown lack of due diligence	2. Movant has shown due diligence
3. Movant has failed to show that evidence, which would be unavailable if continuance is denied, is material and not merely cumulative	3. Statute or rule specifically requires a continuance be granted in circumstances presented

16. Motion for Bifurcated Discovery and/or Arbitration Hearing.

Order Denying Bifurcated Discovery and/or Trial	Order Granting Bifurcated Discovery and/or Trial
Possible Grounds:	Possible Grounds:
1. Issues of liability and damages are intertwined	1. Evidence on liability and damages is significantly different
2. Multiple hearings would be overly duplicative and would require recalling of several witnesses	2. Bifurcation would expedite arbitration proceedings and lessen their overall cost
3. Bifurcation would add time and expense with no counter-balancing advantages	3. Bifurcation would be more convenient for the parties, the arbitrators, and the witnesses
4. Issues in case are relatively simple and straightforward	4. Parties consent to bifurcation

17. Motion for Disqualification of Attorney.

Order Denying Disqualification of Attorney	Order Granting Disqualification of Attorney
Possible Grounds:	Possible Grounds:
1. Attorney's client consents to representation after full disclosure of apparent or actual conflict of interest	1. Attorney's conflict of interest which client has not or cannot waive
2. Disqualification would work a substantial hardship to the attorney's client	2. Attorney's representation of a party in a present matter adverse to the interests of a former client, if there is a substantial relationship between the subject matters of the present and former representations
3. Moving party failed to promptly object	3. Attorney, or another attorney in his/her law firm will be called as a witness on behalf of the attorney's client
4. Moving party would not be prejudiced if disqualification is denied	4. Attorney is senile, mentally incompetent, or under the influence of drugs or alcohol

C. ORDERS AND RULINGS ENTERED DURING THE COURSE OF ARBITRATION HEARING.

18. Objection to Opening Statement.

Order Sustaining Objection to Opening Statement	Order Overruling Objection to Opening Statement
Possible Grounds:	Possible Grounds:
1. Attorney is presenting legal arguments	1. Attorney may refer briefly to applicable statute or rule in opening statement
2. Attorney is presenting personal opinion, touting own credibility, or asserting personal knowledge of facts	2. Attorney is not presenting personal opinion, touting own credibility, or asserting personal knowledge of facts
3. Attorney is raising matters outside scope of pleadings	3. Attorney is referring to matters within scope of pleadings
4. Attorney is discussing excluded or inadmissible evidence	4. No ruling has been made with regard to the challenged evidence
5. Attorney's comments are demeaning to opponent's client or witnesses	5. Attorney's references to opposing party's behavior is within the bounds of permissible comment
6. Attorney is exceeding time limits for opening statement	6. Objecting party may have additional time to respond if it desires

19. Motion for Arbitrator to Take Judicial Notice.

Judicial Notice Refused	Judicial Notice Taken
Possible Grounds:	Possible Grounds:
1. Facts sought to be judicially noticed are uncertain or doubtful	1. Facts sought to be judicially noticed
2. Facts are known to judge personally, but are not common knowledge	2. Judicial notice of certain facts is required by statute or rule

20. Motion to Exclude Evidence on Relevance Grounds.

Order Sustaining Objection to Relevance (Evidence Admitted)	Order Overruling Objection to Relevance (Evidence Admitted)
Possible Grounds:	Possible Grounds:
1. Evidence does not tend to prove or disprove issues in case	1. Evidence tends to prove or disprove issues in case
2. Evidence does not render a fact more or less probable	2. Objection is untimely, and right to object is therefore waived
3. Evidence is not logically linked to other evidence to aid arbitrator in determining a fact in issue	3. Evidence that is weak, incomplete, or slightly prejudicial does not require exclusion on ground of irrelevance

21. Objection to Character Evidence.

Order Sustaining Objection to Evidence of Character (Evidence Excluded)	Order Overruling Objection to Evidence of Character (Evidence Admitted)
Possible Grounds:	Possible Grounds:
1. Character of party is not at issue	1. Character of party is at issue
2. Unless witness's character has been attacked, character evidence is inadmissible to enhance witness's credibility	2. Evidence of witness's bad reputation for truthfulness or veracity is admissible for impeachment purposes
3. Improper evidence of character is offered (specific acts or personal opinion of witness instead of general reputation of witness in the community)	3. Evidence of a witness's good character or reputation for truthfulness or honesty is admissible to rebut impeaching evidence

22. Objection to Evidence of Habit, Custom, or Common Practice.

Order Sustaining Objection to Admissibility (Evidence Excluded)	Order Overruling Objection to Admissibility (Evidence Admitted)
Possible Grounds:	Possible Grounds:
1. In some jurisdictions, evidence of habit is not admissible to show that a person acted in a particular way at a particular time	1. Federal Rules of Evidence and some jurisdictions allow evidence of habit to be used to prove an act or a specific occasion, if the habit is sufficiently regular and uniform, particularly if there are no eyewitnesses available to testify
2. Evidence of habit is not sufficiently regular or uniform	2. Evidence of habit or customary practices of business organizations (as opposed to individuals) is routinely admissible
3. Evidence of habit is not sufficiently routine	3. Except in cases of negligence per se, or inherently dangerous activities, or dissimilar circumstances, evidence of habit of normally prudent people in performing an act or using a instrument is admissible to permit the arbitrator to decide if the particular use which caused an injury was or was not negligent under the circumstances of its use.

23. Objection to Evidence of Subsequent Remedial Measures.

Order Sustaining Objection to Evidence of Subsequent Remedial Measures (Evidence Excluded)	Order Overruling Objection to Evidence of Subsequent Remedial Measures (Evidence Admitted)
Possible Grounds:	Possible Grounds:
1. Evidence of subsequent remedial measures is inadmissible to prove negligence	1. Evidence of subsequent remedial measures is admissible to show that such measures are feasible, if feasibility of remedial measures is an issue in case
2. Control of premises is not an issue in the case	2. Evidence is admissible to show control of premises or object, if control is a matter in dispute
3. Physical condition at time of accident is not an issue in the case	3. Evidence is admissible to establish physical conditions existing at time of accident
4. Evidence is not being offered to impeach credibility of witness	4. Evidence may be admitted to impeach credibility of a witness
5. This is not a strict product liability case	5. Evidence is admissible in strict product liability case

24. Objection to Evidence Based on Assertion of Privilege.

Order Sustaining Objection Based on Assertion of Privilege (Evidence Excluded)	Order Overruling Objection Based on Assertion of Privilege (Evidence Admitted)
Possible Grounds:	Possible Grounds:
1. Communication is privileged on basis of common law	1. No common law privilege exists in jurisdiction
2. Communication is privileged on basis of statute	2. No statutory privilege exists in jurisdiction
3. Communication is privileged by prior agreement of the parties	3. Objector has no right to claim privilege, because no requisite privileged relationship existed, or because of some other technical noncompliance with case law or statute
4. Privilege was not waived, or if waived, waiver was timely withdrawn	4. Objector waived privilege by word or action, such as failure to timely object, or by voluntary disclosure of privileged matter in discovery or privately to third persons

25. Objection to Scope of Direct Examination.

Ruling Excluding Testimony	Ruling Allowing Testimony
Possible Grounds:	Possible Grounds:
1. Evidence is irrelevant	1. Evidence is relevant and material
2. Evidence is immaterial	2. Evidence relates to background of witness

26. Objection to Scope of Cross-Examination.

Ruling Excluding Testimony	Ruling Allowing Testimony
Possible Grounds:	Possible Grounds:
1. Questions seek evidence beyond scope of direct examination	1. Questions seek evidence within scope of direct examination
2. Cross-examiner is attempting to impeach witness on a collateral matter	2. Questions seek evidence relating to credibility of witness

27. Objection to Scope of Redirect Examination.

Ruling Excluding Testimony	Ruling Allowing Testimony
Possible Grounds:	Possible Grounds:
1. Questions seek to elicit information unrelated to any issue yet raised by either party	1. Questions seek to elicit testimony clarifying the subject matter of the direct examination or any new matters brought out by cross-examination
2. Questions do not seek information designed to rehabilitate witness	2. Questions seek information designed to rehabilitate witness, by bringing forth matters rebutting or explaining unfavorable inferences raised on cross-examination

28. Objection to Scope of Recross-Examination.

Ruling Excluding Testimony	Ruling Allowing Testimony
Possible Grounds:	Possible Grounds:
1. Questions seek information that is cumulative or not within scope of redirect examination	1. Questions seek information responsive to new matters arising on recross-examination

29. Objection to Questioning Procedure or to Substance of Testimony on Direct Examination.

Order Sustaining Objection (Evidence Excluded)	Order Overruling Objection (Evidence Admitted)
Possible Grounds:	Possible Grounds:
1. Examiner has asked a leading question, not satisfying a permitted exception to the rule against leading questions on direct examination	1. Leading question on direct examination is appropriate where witness is hostile or where answers of the witness have surprised direct examiner
2. Questions seek cumulative information or are repetitious	2. Leading questions are addressed to preliminary or background matters not in dispute, or they seek to direct witness to a particular subject
3. Questions seek information not based on witness's firsthand knowledge or opportunity to observe	3. Leading questions are permissible where direct examiner has difficulty obtaining intelligible answers because the witness is a child, is timid or ignorant, or has difficulty understanding English
4. In some jurisdictions, it is improper to allow witness to use a memorandum to refresh past recollection, where no past recollection is revived, if the memorandum is not made at or about the time the events were fresh in the witness's mind	4. Cumulative questioning is permissible where a witness does not understand the question, or gives unclear testimony, or where the witness's answer is incomplete
5. In some jurisdictions, it is improper for witness to use a writing to refresh recollection if no proper foundation is laid for the use of the writing or if adversary is denied opportunity to inspect the writing	5. Witness must testify from personal knowledge or observation, but the opportunity to observe may be limited, attention may be imprecise, and the recall of witness need not be absolutely certain
6. Traditionally, lay witness may not give opinion testimony, particularly when the opinion will prejudice, confuse, or mislead the fact finder	6. Most jurisdictions allow witness to refresh memory by use of a written memorandum, whether written by witness or someone else, and whether the document is an original or a copy
7. Lay witness may not express an opinion about an ultimate fact or issue or to state how he/she thinks a case ought to be decided	7. Most jurisdictions allow a witness's recollection to be refreshed by a photograph, report, record, object, document, or even a leading question
8. Lay witness may not give an opinion on conclusions of law	8. Lay witness may give opinion evidence as a matter of convenience, if it would be difficult or impossible for the witness to recall actual and accurate details, or if the witness is more knowledgeable about the particular subject than the average fact finder

30. Objection to Questioning Procedure or to Substance of Testimony on Cross-Examination.

Order Sustaining Objection to Testimony on Cross-examination (Evidence Excluded)	Order Overruling Objection to Testimony on Cross-examination (Evidence Admitted)
Possible Grounds:	Possible Grounds:
1. Question asked by cross-examiner is improper in that it is insulting, harassing, repetitive, argumentative, or causes undue embarrassment	1. Question seeks information showing that witness made a prior inconsistent statement (or made a prior statement with an omission) that is materially inconsistent with witness's current testimony
2. Question seeks information that is not impeaching in that witness's prior statement is not in fact inconsistent with witness's present testimony	2. Question seeks information showing that witness's credibility is impeached because his or her mind or memory is impaired in such a way that the witness's capacity to perceive, remember, or describe correctly is affected
3. Question seeks to impeach witness by eliciting a witness's prior statement without laying a proper foundation for the prior statement	3. Question seeks information showing that the witness's credibility is impeached because the witness is biased, prejudiced, or has an interest in the outcome of the arbitration
4. In some jurisdictions, questions seeking information that would impeach a witness's testimony only on a collateral matter are improper	4. Question seeks information showing that the witness's credibility is impeached because he or she has been convicted of a crime (In some jurisdictions, the crime must be punishable by imprisonment of more than one year, involve dishonesty, involve moral turpitude, and the conviction must predate the current testimony by a certain limited time period)
5. Question seeks information regarding an arrest, accusation, or prosecution of witness, where no conviction can be proved	5. Question seeks information that witness's credibility is impeached because of the witness's character or reputation for lack of truthfulness
6. Question seeks information regarding witness's drug use solely for the purpose of showing witness is generally unreliable or lacks truthfulness	6. Question seeks information to show that witness is under the influence of drugs while testifying or that the witness was under the influence of drugs at the time of the occurrence at issue

31. Objection to Expert Testimony.

Order Sustaining Objection to Expert Testimony (Evidence Excluded)	Order Overruling Objection to Expert Testimony (Evidence Omitted)
Possible Grounds:	Possible Grounds:
1. Expert's testimony is not limited to matters within his/her expertise	1. Expert is testifying within area of expertise
2. Witness was not properly qualified as expert	2. Expert opinion may be based, in part, on hearsay evidence
3. In some jurisdictions, expert may not give an opinion on an improper hypothetical question	3. Expert witness is properly qualified to testify on the basis of experience, education, and training
4. In some jurisdictions, an expert may not state an opinion based on facts and data not in evidence	4. Some jurisdictions allow expert to give opinion on an ultimate issue in the case
5. In some jurisdictions, expert may not give opinion testimony when the subject matter of the testimony is within the understanding of the average fact finder	5. Expert may testify as to the particular hypothetical question asked
6. Ordinarily, an expert may not testify to a conclusion of law	6. Expert's prior relationship with party or counsel is insufficient to render testimony non-probative
7. Expert failed to disclose report prior to hearing	7. Error in expert's list of credentials is insufficient to bar his/her testimony

32. Objection to Hearsay Evidence.

Order Sustaining Objection to Hearsay Generally (Evidence Excluded)	Order Overruling Objection to Hearsay Generally (Evidence Admitted)
Possible Grounds:	Possible Grounds:
1. The statement is other than one made by the declarant while testifying at a trial or hearing, and it is being offered in evidence to prove the truth of the matter asserted	1. Objection is untimely
2. The witness's own previous out-of-arbitration statement may constitute hearsay	2. Statement is not offered to prove the truth of the matter asserted, but rather the effect of the statement on the hearer
3. Conduct, which was intended as an assertion, may be considered as a "statement" excluded by the rule against hearsay	3. The witness's own prior statement is not hearsay because: it was given under oath, and it is inconsistent with the witness's current testimony; or, it is consistent with current testimony, and it is offered to rebut a charge of recent fabrication; or, it is a statement of past identification; or, it is an admission against interest and offered against that party as such
4. The statement does not satisfy any exception to the rule against hearsay (see below)	4. The statement satisfies one of the exceptions to the rule against hearsay (see next)

33. Assertion of Exception to Hearsay Rule–Admission of Party.

Ruling Excluding Evidence (Exception Does Not Apply)	Ruling Admitting Evidence (Exception Applies)
Possible Grounds:	Possible Grounds:
1. Person making admission lacks capacity to make an admission	1. A written or oral admission of a party or his/her representative is admissible as substantive evidence of the fact admitted even if it is not against interest when made and even if it is opinion or legal conclusion
2. Inconsistent statements in pleadings or pleadings in the alternative are not considered to be admissions	2. An admission in a pleading can be considered a judicial admission which waives production of evidence and removes the admitted fact from controversy
3. An admission by an agent or employee should not be received into evidence if the employment or agency relationship was terminated before the statement was made; or if the statement was not made within the scope of agency or employment	3. An admission by an agent or employee of a party may constitute the party's admission if the statement was made within the scope of the agent's or employee's duties and if it was made while the agency or employment was still in effect
4. Declarant was not in privity with the party to whom admission is to be attributed	4. An admission can be by conduct or by express adoption of another's statement
5. Silence in the face of an oral statement may not be considered an admission if the silent person did not hear or understand it; had physical or emotional impediments to responding; had a relationship with speaker such that a denial was difficult or unlikely; reasonably thought the oral statement did not call for a response	5. Silence can constitute an admission where there is a failure to deny or object to an oral or written statement calling for a response or denial
6. Subsequent remedial measures, offers to compromise a claim, or offers to pay medical expenses ordinarily do not constitute admissions	6. An admission may be received into evidence if made by someone in privity with the party against whom the declaration is offered as long as the declaration relates to the interest in property and is made when the declarant has an interest in the property

34. Assertion of Exception to Hearsay Rule–Prior Statement of Witness.

Ruling Excluding Evidence (Exception Does Not Apply)	Ruling Admitting Evidence (Exception Applies)
Possible Grounds:	Possible Grounds:
1. In some jurisdictions, prior statements are only admissible for the limited purpose of impeachment and may not be used as substantive evidence unless they fall within another recognized exception to the hearsay rule	1. The witness admits in present testimony that the prior inconsistent statement is true
2. In some jurisdictions, no inconsistency can exist where the witness's present testimony is strictly "I don't remember"	2. "Inconsistent" means any material variation between the prior statement and the present testimony of the witness, including omission from the prior statement of a material fact that the witness includes in present testimony
3. A consistent statement made after the source of bias, interest, influence, or incapacity arose is irrelevant and inadmissible	3. A consistent statement made soon after the event testified to transpired is admissible to counter allegation that the witness's memory at trial is impaired or that the present testimony is a recent fabrication
4. Consistent statements cannot be used to counter impeachment by prior inconsistent statements since the inconsistency remains despite any statement to the contrary	4. Some jurisdictions admit prior consistent statements to rebut any form of impeachment, including prior inconsistent statements
5. Assertion of exception to hearsay rule is untimely or was waived	5. Assertion of exception to hearsay rule has not been waived

35. Assertion of Exception to Hearsay Rule–Excited Utterance.

Ruling Excluding Evidence (Exception Does Not Apply)	Ruling Admitting Evidence (Exception Applies)
Possible Grounds:	Possible Grounds:
1. Proponent of evidence failed to put forward sufficient independent evidence to support a finding that a startling event occurred and that the declarant actually witnessed it	1. An excited utterance is admissible regardless of whether the statement explains or illuminates the event which provoked it
2. The utterance was not reasonably contemporaneous with the event to which it relates	2. The only tests of competency applying to a declarant of an excited utterance is the ability to observe and communicate
3. Present sense impression was not contemporaneous with event it describes	3. Declarant's emotional condition compensated for and explained the considerable length of time between the excited utterance and the preceding event to which it related
4. Declarant's statement was self-serving, and he/she had time to reflect and fabricate before speaking	4. Even though declarant's statement was not an excited utterance, it qualifies for admission as a present sense impression
5. Assertion of exception to the hearsay rule is untimely or was waived	5. Even though there was a substantial time lapse between the event and the declarant's present sense impression, there is substantial circumstantial evidence corroborating the accuracy of the statement

36. Assertion of Exception to Hearsay Rule–State of Mind: Emotional or Mental State.

Ruling Excluding Evidence (Exception Does Not Apply)	Ruling Admitting Evidence (Exception Applies)
Possible Grounds:	Possible Grounds:
1. Statement of witness's belief is inadmissible to prove a fact	1. Statement of intent to perform a certain act is admissible as circumstantial evidence that the declarant acted according to his/her stated intent
2. Declarant's mental or emotional condition did not exist at the time statement was made	2. In some jurisdictions, a declaration of intent by one person to prove that another person acted accordingly is admissible
3. Statement by one person as to the mental or emotional condition of another is inadmissible under the state of mind exception	3. In some jurisdictions, all statements of a deceased declarant, made in good faith with personal knowledge before the litigation commenced, are admissible
4. A declaration of mental or emotional condition is inadmissible because the declarant's state of mind is not an issue in the case	4. Mental or emotional condition of the declarant is the key fact on which an element of the case depends

37. Assertion of Exception to Hearsay Rule–Statement of Physical Condition.

Ruling Excluding Evidence (Exception Does Not Apply)	Ruling Admitting Evidence (Exception Applies)
Possible Grounds:	Possible Grounds:
1. Statements of medical history, past pain, symptoms, or causation do not fall within hearsay exception for physical condition	1. In some jurisdictions, a spontaneous statement of physical condition is admissible even though it was made to a non-physician, and Federal Rules of Evidence extend rule to statements of medical history, past or present symptoms, pain sensations, or general causation made for the purpose of medical diagnosis or treatment
2. Statements were made for the purpose of preparing a physician to testify on declarant's behalf	2. Non-spontaneous statement regarding physical condition was made to a physician for the purpose of obtaining his testimony, but the declarant had a significant treatment motive in consulting the physician, and evidence that the declarant followed the physician's advice is highly probative of a treatment motive
3. Statements made to physician related to fault and are not admissible under the physical condition exception	3. Under the Federal Rules of Evidence, all statements on which a non-treating physician relied in forming his/her opinion are admissible as substantive evidence
4. Assertion of the exception is untimely or was waived	4. Declaration of someone other than patient is admissible, because it was made for the purpose of obtaining medical treatment

38. Assertion of Exception to Hearsay Rule: Private, Published, and Institutional Records.

Ruling Excluding Evidence (Exception Does Not Apply)	Ruling Admitting Evidence (Exception Applies)
Possible Grounds:	Possible Grounds:
1. Proponent of evidence has not shown that the private record was made when the facts were still fresh in the declarant's mind, and that the information in the private record was true and accurate when the private record was made	1. Under Federal Rules of Evidence, total loss of memory is not required as a prerequisite to admission of past recollection recorded
2. Business record is inadmissible were the informant had no business duty to report the information to the author	2. "Business record" is liberally construed and "business" consists of almost any regularly conducted, organized activity for purposes of the exception
3. Record was prepared with a view toward litigation and not in the regular course of business	3. Computer printouts, results of psychological tests, desk calendars, notes of conversations, photographs, and short-hand notes have qualified for admissibility under the business records exception
4. Too much time lapsed between the event and the recording to allow record to be admitted under the business records exception	4. Party has not waived right to assert the exception

39. Assertion of Exception to Hearsay Rule–Public Records.

Ruling Excluding Evidence (Exception Does Not Apply)	Ruling Admitting Evidence (Exception Applies)
Possible Grounds:	Possible Grounds:
1. Record contains information given to the author by another person, and the informant's statements do not fall within an exception to the hearsay rule	1. Investigatory records of public agencies are admissible if they involve "factual findings," findings of law, and conclusions based on disputed factual information supplied to the author by other persons
2. The broader business records exception cannot be used to justify admissibility of investigatory records of public agencies	2. The public records exception does not exclude investigatory records of a public agency on the ground that they were primarily prepared with a view to litigation
3. Source of information contained in public record lacks trustworthiness	3. A report made to a public agency by one with a professional duty is admissible under the public records exception
4. Declarations of remote cause in death certificates, as opposed to immediate cause, are inadmissible because such statements were made to the examining physician by another person	4. Judgment of a foreign court in a criminal matter qualifies for admission under the public records exception if the foreign proceedings were conducted according to standards of civilized jurisprudence
5. Mere fact that report is required by law does not satisfy admissibility requirement that declarant has an official or professional duty to report	5. Evidence of prior conviction is admissible in the present proceeding to prove a fact that was a necessary element of the criminal offense
6. Evidence of a prior conviction is inadmissible to prove facts that were not essential to sustain the judgment	6. Party did not waive right to assert exception to hearsay rule

40. Assertion of Exception to Hearsay Rule—Declarant Unavailable.

Ruling Excluding Evidence (Exception Does Not Apply)	Ruling Admitting Evidence (Exception Applies)
Possible Grounds:	Possible Grounds:
1. Advantages of proceeding with hearing without declarant's live testimony do not outweigh need for granting a postponement	1. Declarant's testimony is unavailable when declarant is dead, sick, insane, beyond reach of process, invokes a privilege against testifying, or refuses to testify
2. Proponent of evidence failed to show that he/she exhausted all reasonable means to obtain the testimony by making a good faith effort to locate missing declarant and by taking all reasonable steps necessary to subpoena declarant to ensure presence at hearing	2. In some jurisdictions, when the declarant is beyond reach of process, proponent need not make an effort to secure declarant's voluntary testimony
3. Prior testimony of unavailable declarant is inadmissible, because party against whom the testimony is offered did not have an adequate opportunity and similar motive to examine the declarant when the testimony was taken	3. Prior testimony is admissible because party against whom it is being offered (or predecessor in interest) had an opportunity and similar motive to develop the testimony during the former proceedings
4. Declaration against interest was not against declarant's interest at the time the statement was made	4. Declarations against interest includes statements against proprietary, pecuniary, penal, and social interests.
5. Declaration against interest is inadmissible because, at the time the statement was made, the declarant would not have been competent to testify	5. Unlike an admission, which may only be used against the party who made it or his/her privies in interest, a declaration against interest may be introduced in evidence by or against anyone
6. Assertion of exception to hearsay rule is untimely or was waived	6. Many of the traditional restrictions on use of a dying declaration have been abandoned; it is now usually admissible in civil cases; where declarant believed death was imminent though he/she later recovered, and statements are not necessarily restricted to the cause or circumstances of death

41. Objection to Evidence Based on Lack of Foundation.

Ruling Excluding Evidence (Foundation Inadequate)	Ruling Admitting Evidence (Foundation Adequate)
Possible Grounds:	Possible Grounds:
1. Proponent of evidence has not advanced sufficient admissible evidence to support a finding of authenticity	1. Question of whether the proponent of evidence has proved an adequate chain of custody goes to weight rather than to the admissibility of the evidence
2. Lay witness may not authenticate genuineness of handwriting by making only a single comparison with another sample for purposes of adversary proceedings	2. Methods of authentication may be used alone or in combination to build a prima facie case of authenticity
3. Fact that telephone caller identified himself is insufficient in itself to authenticate the identity of the caller	3. A privately maintained document is properly authenticated by the testimony of a witness with knowledge of either a direct or circumstantial nature, and answers to interrogatories are properly considered as testimony for purposes of authentication
4. Proponent of evidence failed to authenticate specimen	4. Authenticity may be proven by showing that the document contains information only the purported author was likely to know, that the appearance of the document suggests a single source, that the document was a reply to another authenticated communication, or that the document reflects the special linguistic characteristics of its author
5. Proponent of computer-generated evidence failed to authenticate it by testimony that describes the process or system and proves that it produces accurate results	5. In some jurisdictions, certain documents are presumed authentic—i.e. are self-authenticating: newspapers, periodicals, trade inscriptions, commercial paper, and certified copies of public documents, including judgments of conviction

42. Objection to Evidence Based on Best Evidence Rule.

Ruling Excluding Secondary Evidence	Ruling Admitting Secondary Evidence
Possible Grounds:	Possible Grounds:
1. Secondary evidence is inadmissible where there is an insufficient showing that the original could not be produced	1. Best evidence rule does not apply where a writing is not offered to prove its contents, such as instances: where witness testifies about an event that was only incidentally memorialized in writing; where a writing is used to refresh a witness's recollection or to illustrate his/her testimony; or where a witness testifies that records do not contain a particular entry
2. Best evidence rule may be applied to exclude the testimony of a witness concerning the identity, rather than the contents, of a writing, if the witness had to take note of the contents in order to make the identification	2. A duplicate is admissible to the same extent as an original, unless a genuine question is raised concerning the authenticity of the original or it would be unfair to admit the duplicate in lieu of the original
3. Original of a photograph or recording must be produced to prove its contents	3. Secondary evidence is admissible to prove contents of original if: there is proof that the original was lost or destroyed but not in bad faith; the original is outside the reach of the process; or the writing is collateral to a material issue
4. Photocopies are secondary evidence and inadmissible unless production of the original is excused	4. Secondary evidence is admissible where original was destroyed by accident, mistake, or in the ordinary course of business
5. Duplicate document is inadmissible because it is incomplete or illegible, or evidence shows that the original document may have been intentionally destroyed thereby producing an inference of fraud	5. Contents of a public record may be proven by a certified copy
6. Proponent's request to offer secondary evidence is untimely	6. Objector waived right to require best evidence

43. Objection Relating to Closing Argument.

Order Overruling Objection to Scope and Content of Closing Argument	Order Sustaining Objection to Scope and Content of Closing Argument
Possible Grounds:	Possible Grounds:
1. Comment on discrepancy between pleading and proof is proper in closing argument	1. Scope of closing argument is properly confined to the record
2. Counsel may argue law in closing argument	2. Counsel refers to facts not in evidence or misstates the evidence in the record
3. Counsel is allowed wide latitude to make emotional argument in closing	3. Counsel's overly emotional appeals are improper
4. Counsel may legitimately comment on failure of opponent to call an available witness	4. Counsel may not express his/her personal belief in the justness of the client's cause or the credibility of the witnesses, nor assert his/her personal knowledge of the facts in issue

D.   ORDERS AND RULINGS ENTERED AFTER TRIAL.

44. Motion for Reconsideration or for Order for Additional or Amended Findings.

Order Denying Reconsideration or Additional or Amended Findings	Order Granting Reconsideration or Additional or Amended Findings
Possible Grounds:	Possible Grounds:
1. Movant's request is untimely	1. Judicial opinion issued after the close of the evidence but before ruling should be considered by the arbitration panel
2. Movant's request for reconsideration is without merit	2. Reconsideration of quality or quantity of evidence pertaining to a critical aspect of claim or defense is proper
3. Movant had access to evidence he/she now wishes to present to the arbitration panel as "newly discovered evidence"	3. Additional findings are necessary to effectuate the arbitration award

45. Objection Relating to Interest on Award.

Order Refusing to Award Interest or Reducing the Amount of Interest Awarded	Order Awarding Interest
Possible Grounds:	Possible Grounds:
1. Party was not deprived of use of money for the period during which interest was awarded	1. Statute requires award of interest
2. No interest may be imposed where money is not part of award, such as an award in rem	2. Rule requires award of interest
3. Statute does not allow an award of interest	3. Agreement requires award of interest
4. By statute, interest is not due on a lump sum payable in installments	4. Case law requires award of interest
5. Wrong date used to begin interest computation	5. Law permits pre-award interest
6. Improper method used to compute interest	6. Additional interest is awardable because of error in computation

46. Objection Relating to Award of Costs.

Order Refusing to Allow Costs	Order Allowing Costs
Possible Grounds:	Possible Grounds:
1. No statute or rule expressly provides for the awarding of costs	1. Statute or rule makes the award of costs mandatory
2. Party requesting costs is not a "prevailing party" within the meaning of the statute or rule	2. Costs may be assessed against a party for misconduct of its attorney, such as for filing untrue pleadings, or for unduly delaying proceedings
3. Prevailing plaintiff is not entitled to costs because defendant offered a sum to settle before hearing pursuant to rule, and plaintiff is being awarded an amount less than that sum	3. Defendant offered an amount in judgment prior to arbitration, and plaintiff proceeded to trial and recovered less than the amount offered
4. Entity requesting costs is not technically a party to the arbitration	4. Party requesting costs was prevailing party
5. Party failed to submit a bill of costs in accordance with the pertinent statute or rule	5. Party requesting costs is a bonafide party to the arbitration
6. Party's request for costs is premature; it must await outcome of arbitration of consolidated case	6. Party's request for costs is timely
7. Party waived its right to request costs prior to the hearing	7. Party has not waived its right to request costs

47. Objection Relating to An Award of Attorney's Fees.

Order Refusing Attorney's Fees	Order Allowing Attorney's Fees
Possible Grounds:	Possible Grounds:
1. No statute, rule, or contract provision provides for an award of attorney's fees	1. Statute or rule specifically provides for an award of attorney's fees
2. Party requesting fees is not a prevailing party	2. Successful litigant sued on behalf of a class and provided a common benefit
3. Party requesting fees did not actually incur the expenses of an attorney	3. Party seeks attorney's fees because opposing party acted in bad faith
4. Prevailing party acted for himself, and there is no common benefit	4. Party seeks attorney's fees because opposing party conducted the arbitration vexatiously, oppressively, or unreasonably
5. Prevailing party is not entitled to attorney's fees under the bad faith exception to the rule precluding them when the opposing attorney merely litigates a claim in an unsettled area of the law and loses	5. Party seeks attorney's fees because opposing party willfully abused the judicial process
6. Attorney's fees may be reduced if the award is based on an improper method of calculation	6. Party seeks attorney's fees because opposing party perpetrated a fraud on the court
7. Party waived right to request attorney's fees	7. Party did not waive right to request attorney's fees

48. Motion to Reopen Arbitration Hearing.

Order Refusing to Reopen Arbitration Hearing	Order Allowing Reopening of Arbitration Hearing
Possible Grounds:	Possible Grounds:
1. Motion to reopen hearing is untimely	1. Motion to reopen hearing is timely made
2. Movant failed to comply with requirements of statute or rule	2. Newly discovered evidence came to light after the arbitration hearing; the party discovering the evidence was not negligent in failing to discover it prior to the hearing; the evidence is material and not merely cumulative, the evidence is such that it is reasonably probable that it would change the result of the arbitration
3. Movant failed to specify grounds for reopening hearing	3. Movant would be greatly prejudiced if hearing were not reopened
4. Offer of proof, if admitted as evidence, would not change arbitrators' decision	4. Arbitrators reopen hearing on their own motion to take additional evidence
5. No just cause exists for reopening hearing	5. Hearing is reopened to permit counsel to argue applicability of recent Supreme Court decision to the facts of this case
6. Movant waived his right to request reopening of hearing	6. Movant did not waive his right to request reopening of hearing

APPENDIX B

Arbitrator's Pre-hearing Functions and Duties Checklist

1. Reviewing the Arbitration Clause
__ Intent to arbitrate

__ Disputes arbitrable

__ Joinder of claims or parties

__ Location of arbitration

__ Time limits

__ Third-arbitrator selection procedure

__ Scope of arbitrator's authority and jurisdiction

__ Pleadings and discovery

__ Confidentiality

__ Evidence

__ Designation of law governing arbitration agreement

__ Court to have jurisdiction to enforce agreement and award

__ Payment of arbitration fees and expenses

2. Reviewing the Arbitration Demand and Response
__ Demand

   __ Names of parties and counsel

   __ Review of claimant's version of facts

   __ Review of claims

   __ Requested relief

__ Response

   __ Names of parties and counsel

   __ Review of respondent's version of facts

   __ Review of denials

   __ Note any affirmative defenses

   __ Note any counterclaims

3. Reviewing the Pertinent Rules
__ More than one set of rules applicable?

__ Testimony under oath?

__ Evidence by affidavit?

__ Authorized representatives?

__ Decision and award—requirements?

4. Conflict Check (Consider members of law firm also)

__ Do I presently represent any person in a proceeding adverse to any party to the arbitration?

__ Have I represented any other person against any party to the arbitration?

__ Have I had any professional or social relationship with any party or witness identified to date in this proceeding or the entities for which they work?

__ Have I had any social or professional relationship of which I am aware with any relative of any of the parties to this proceeding, any relative of counsel to this proceeding, or any of the witnesses identified to date in this proceeding?

__ Have I ever served as an arbitrator in a proceeding in which any of the identified witnesses or named individual parties gave testimony?

__ Have I, any member of my immediate family, or any close social or business associate been involved in the last five years in a dispute involving the subject matter contained in the case to which I am assigned?

__ Have I had any social or professional relationship with any other arbitrator assigned to this case?

__ Have I served as an expert witness or consultant to any party, attorney, witness, or other arbitrator identified in this case?

__ Have any of the party representatives appeared before me in past arbitration cases?

__ Am I a member of any organization that is not listed on my biographical sheet?

__ Have I ever sued or been sued by either party or its representative?

5. Arbitrator's Oath

__ Is an arbitrator's oath required?

__ Orally or in writing?

__ Have parties waived the arbitrator's oath?

6. Choosing the Third Arbitrator

__ Review code of ethics to be refreshed on ethical obligations of "non-neutral" arbitrators

__ Determine whether the third arbitrator should be lawyer or other type of professional expert

__ Develop list of potential arbitrators

__ Contact and collaborate with other party-appointed arbitrator

__ Be mindful of candidate's potential conflicts of interest

7. Selecting Chair of Arbitration Panel

__ In party-appointed situation, chair is usually the third arbitrator or "umpire"

__ Usual role of chair of arbitration panel:

    __ Assignment of duties to the other panel members

    __ In administered proceedings, interacting with the case administrator on procedural matters, including payment of the arbitrators' fees and expenses

    __ In non-administered proceedings, the chair is usually responsible for sending out notices and scheduling orders

    __ Entering rulings on routine or uncontested motions

    __ Setting the agenda for arbitrator meetings and preliminary or mid-hearing meetings with the parties pre-hearing and their counsel

    __ Making the opening statement on behalf of the arbitration panel at the beginning of the hearing on the merits

    __ Ruling on uncomplicated evidentiary objections or motions during the course of the hearing on the merits

    __ Entering an order closing the evidence

    __ Ensuring that the award is timely prepared and issued

__ Selection criteria for chair of panel:

    __ Can the arbitrator effectively assume the role of the chair of the panel?

    __ Does the panel member desire to be the panel chair?

    __ What are the predictable demands on the selected arbitrator considering the nature of the case and the parties?

    __ Does the chair need to be a lawyer?

    __ Is the relative celebrity, prestige, or peer status of the arbitrators a consideration?

    __ Should preference be given to the most senior member of the panel?

    __ Should preference be given on the basis of an arbitrator's prior arbitration experience?

    __ What is the relative availability of the arbitrators to respond to situations involving emergency motions or other requests of the parties?

___ In a non-administered arbitration, what is the availability of the arbitrator's support staff to coordinate the rescheduling of hearing dates, type and issue the panel's notices and pre-hearing rulings?

___ In a non-administered arbitration, what is the relative geographic location of the arbitrators in comparison to the locations of the parties, and should preference be given to the arbitrator most centrally or most proximately located?

8. The Arbitrators' Initial Conference

___ Discussion of any preliminary motions

___ Planning of preliminary hearing

9. Conducting the Preliminary Hearing

___ Cover all pertinent topics with parties and counsel

    ___ Expectation of civility and professionalism

    ___ Applicable rules and governing law

    ___ Arbitrability of all issues

    ___ Discovery

    ___ Pre-hearing motions and briefing schedules

    ___ Amended pleadings

    ___ Addition or joinder of parties

    ___ Witness lists

    ___ Observers and other attendees

    ___ Hearing exhibits

    ___ Fact stipulations

    ___ Order of evidence

    ___ Sequestration of witnesses

    ___ Burden and standard of proof

    ___ Position statements or pre-hearing briefs

    ___ Stenographer

    ___ Interpreter

    ___ Special needs for physically impaired attendees

    ___ Hearing date

    ___ Place of hearing; arrangement of hearing room

    ___ Length of hearing

    ___ Subpoenas

__ Prohibition against ex parte communications

__ Site inspections

__ Audio-visual aids

__ Experts

__ Need for final oral arguments; post-hearing briefs

__ Nature and form of award

__ Any appeal procedures

__ Pre-arbitration mediation

__ Additional preliminary hearings

__ Considering procedural alternatives

__ Videotaped or telephone testimony

__ Bifurcation

__ Consolidation of claims

__ Phasing the arbitration

__ Class action procedure

__ Written order summarizing the results of the preliminary hearing

__ Date of the preliminary hearing

__ Identity of the arbitrators

__ Identity of the parties and their respective counsel

__ Dates by which parties must amend/specify claims and counter-claims or file any motions (e.g. to join additional parties)

__ Date by which parties should file stipulation of uncontested facts

__ Date by which parties must serve and file a disclosure of witnesses reasonably expected to be called at the hearing on the merits

__ A description of the information that must be provided regarding each proposed witness (e.g., full name, short summary of anticipated testimony, copies of expert reports, written curriculum vitae of experts)

__ A directive that each party must update its witness information as it becomes available

__ A directive to counsel that they must make arrangements to schedule the attendance of witnesses so that the hearing can proceed without any unnecessary delay

__ A directive that each party must notify the other party or parties of the sequence in which that party intends to call its witnesses

___ Date by which the parties must exchange copies of (or make available for inspection) all exhibits to be offered and all schedules, summaries, diagrams, and charts to be used at the hearing

___ A directive that each proposed exhibit must be premarked for identification with a prescribed designation

___ A directive urging the parties to attempt to agree upon and submit a jointly prepared, consolidated, and comprehensive set of joint exhibits

___ Date by which the exhibits must be filed with the arbitrators or the administering organization

___ Date on which the hearing on the merits will commence

___ A statement as to the parties' estimates, disclosed at the preliminary hearing, as to the expected length of their respective cases

___ (In an administered case) a directive that no direct oral or written communication between the parties and the arbitrators will be allowed, except at the oral hearings

___ Date by which pre-hearing briefs must be served and filed, and a directive as to their required form and content

___ A statement as to the type of form of award that the parties agreed to during the preliminary conference

___ A statement as to whether the parties agreed to arranging for a court reporter for the hearing on the merits

___ Date by which any preliminary motions must be filed or otherwise be waived

___ Date for subsequent preliminary hearing, if needed

10. Supervising Pre-hearing Discovery
___ Should discovery be permitted?

___ Kind of discovery?

___ How much discovery?

___ Subpoenas?

___ When should motions be filed?

11. Preparing for the Arbitration Hearing
___ Read pre-hearing briefs and materials

___ Anticipate procedural and evidentiary problems

___ Prepare lists of questions

APPENDIX C

Arbitrator's Hearing Functions and Duties Checklist

1. Arbitrators' Conference

__ How evidentiary objections will be handled

__ Changes in the schedules of the arbitrators

__ When breaks in the hearing will be taken

__ Which panel member will record the admission or exclusion of exhibits

__ Which panel member will complete the daily status form if required to be submitted by the dispute resolution organization

__ How the arbitrators plan to conduct any questioning of witnesses

__ Whether post-hearing briefs should be needed or anticipated

__ Whether the question of the desirability of a written opinion should be discussed with the advocates initially

__ Whether all or some of the witnesses should be sequestered

__ What form the witnesses' oaths or affirmation should take

__ Whether the arbitrators have specific instructions on how documentary evidence, including stipulations, should be introduced

__ Discussion of any pre-hearing motions and need for oral argument on them

__ Other matters as the particular situation requires

2. Sequence of Hearing

__ Arbitrator or panel chair makes opening statement

__ Arbitrator handles any preliminary matters

__ Parties make respective opening statements

__ Claimant presents evidence of direct case

__ Claimant rests direct case

__ Respondent presents evidence of direct case

__ Respondent rests direct case

__ Claimant presents optional rebuttal evidence

__ Respondent presents surrebuttal evidence as arbitrator permits

__ Parties rest their cases

__ Claimant presents final argument

__ Respondent presents final argument.

__ Claimant presents rebuttal argument

__ Respondent presents surrebuttal argument as permitted by arbitrator

3. Arbitrator's Opening Statement

__ Personal introductions

__ Disclaimer of bias and impartiality

__ Explanation of arbitration process and legal effect of award

__ Procedural ground rules

__ Arbitrator's instructions to testifying witnesses

__ Answer questions of parties or counsel

4. Handling Preliminary Matters

__ Rule on motions

__ Confirm witness schedule

__ Swear witnesses

Refer to appendix a for various possible grounds to support rulings on objections and motions relating to opening statements, examination, evidence, and final argument.

5. Parties' Opening Statements

__ Oral/written. Effective advocates' opening statement normally contain:

    __ Introduction and summary

    __ Presentation of facts. Effective advocates usually:

    __ Are brief

    __ Apply principles of primacy and recency

    __ Tie evidence to legal issues

    __ Put puzzle together

    __ Focus on operative facts

    __ Emphasize undisputed evidence

    __ Discard tangential facts

    __ Deal with bad facts minimally

__ Brief statement of law.

__ Comment on opposition's case. Effective advocates normally:

    __ Anticipate the respondent's opening

___ Avoid being personally derisive

___ Avoid addressing respondent's case in detail

___ Comment on claimant's opening

___ Summary and request for relief

___ Typical objections and responses during the opening statement

___ Improper argument

___ Personal knowledge of facts

___ Raising issues or matters outside the pleadings

___ Discussing excluded evidence

___ Comments that demean client or witnesses

6. Direct Examination

___ Typical goals

___ Introduce undisputed facts

___ Enhance likelihood of disputed facts

___ Lay foundations for introduction of exhibits

___ Reflect upon the credibility of witnesses

___ Hold attention of the arbitrator

___ Basic rules advocates must follow in conducting direct examination:

___ Witnesses must be legally competent

___ Use non-leading questions

___ Avoid questions eliciting narrative testimony

___ Avoid opinion testimony from lay witnesses, with narrow exceptions

___ Recollection may be refreshed by document or a leading question

___ Questioning technique. Effective advocates:

___ Use short, open questions

___ Use directive and transitional questions

___ Reinitiate primacy

7. Cross-Examination

___ Basic rules advocates must follow in conducting cross-examination

___ Leading questions permitted

___ Scope limited to scope of direct examination

___ Avoid argumentative questions

___ Avoid intimidating behavior

__ Avoid unfair characterizations

__ Do not assume facts not in evidence

__ Avoid propounding compound or other defective questions

__ Purposes of cross-examination

    __ Repair or minimize damage

    __ Enhance case

    __ Detract from their case

    __ Establish foundation

    __ Discredit direct testimony

    __ Discredit witness

    __ Reflect on credibility of another

__ Organization of cross-examination

    __ No need to start strong

    __ Use topical organization

    __ Give details first

    __ Scatter inferential or circumstantial evidence

    __ Save a zinger for the end

__ A classic format for cross-examination

    __ Friendly information

    __ Affirmative information

    __ Incontrovertible information

    __ Challenging information

    __ Hostile information

    __ Zinger

__ Typical questioning technique of advocates

    __ Use short, leading, propositional questions

    __ Use questions that achieve control

    __ Use incremental questions

    __ Use sequenced questions for impact

    __ Use sequenced questions for indirection

    __ Use sequenced questions for commitment

    __ Create a "conceptual corral"

    __ Avoid ultimate questions

    __ Listen to the witness and insist on an answer

__ Effective advocates avoid questions that lose control:

   __ Non-leading questions

   __ "Why" questions

   __ "Fishing" questions

   __ Long questions

   __ "Gap" questions

   __ "You testified" questions

   __ Characterization questions

8. Impeachment

__ Effective advocates' tactical considerations:

   __ Impeach witness only on significant matters

   __ Impeach only on true inconsistencies

   __ Impeach only when success is likely

   __ Do not impeach favorable information

   __ Consider "rule of completeness"

   __ Consider refreshing witness's recollection

__ Typical procedure for impeaching a witness with a prior inconsistent statement:

   __ Recommit witness

   __ Validate prior statement

   __ Confront witness with prior statement

__ Impeachment with other prior inconsistencies

   __ By omission or silence

   __ By prior inconsistent actions

__ Character impeachment

   __ Conviction of crime

   __ Past untruthfulness and other bad acts

   __ Impaired perception or recollection

__ "Case data" impeachment

   __ Personal interest

   __ Motive

   __ Bias or prejudice

9. Expert Testimony

___ Typical procedure used by advocates for conducting direct examination of expert witness:

    ___ Humanize the expert witness

    ___ Use plain language

    ___ Avoid narrative

    ___ Use examples and analogies

    ___ Use visual aids

    ___ Use internal summaries

    ___ Use concept of consensus

    ___ Use leading questions as necessary

    ___ Encourage powerful language

    ___ Use enumeration

    ___ Consider inoculation

    ___ Don't stretch witness's expertise

___ Typical procedure used by advocates for conducting cross-examination of expert witness:

    ___ Challenge the witness's credentials

    ___ Voir dire on credentials

    ___ Cross-examine on credentials

    ___ Limit scope of witness's expertise

    ___ Stress missing credentials

    ___ Contrast expert's credentials

___ Typical ways advocates obtain favorable information

    ___ Affirm own expert

    ___ Elicit areas of agreement

    ___ Criticize opposing party's conduct

___ Use learned treatises

___ Advocates challenge expert's impartiality on the basis of:

    ___ Fees

    ___ Relationship with party or counsel

    ___ Positional bias

___ Advocates point out omissions

__ Advocates substitute information:

    __ Change assumptions

    __ Vary the facts

    __ Challenge expert's degree of certainty

    __ Challenge factual underpinnings of opinion

    __ Challenge technique or theory

10. Foundations for Evidence

__ General requirements

    __ Relevance

    __ Authenticity

    __ Specific requirements depending on nature of evidence

__ Foundations for testimonial evidence

    __ Conversations:

        __ Date, time, and place of conversation

        __ Persons present

    __ Telephone conversations and voice identification:

        __ Same as for conversations, plus

        __ Voice identification

    __ Prior identification:

        __ Witness made prior identification

        __ After perceiving the person identified

    __ Habit and routine:

        __ Witness with personal knowledge of the regular conduct of the person or organization involved

        __ Asserted conduct was, in fact, of a consistently repeated nature

__ Foundations for oral hearsay statement exceptions:

    __ Foundation for oral party admissions (and also for written party admissions):

        __ Witness can authenticate the statement

        __ Statement was made by the party against whom it is offered

        __ Statement is adverse to the opposing party's claim or defense

    __ Foundation for oral (or written) admissions of an agent or employee of party

        __ Same as for party, above, plus

__ Declarant was an agent or employee of the opposing party at the time that the statement was made

__ Statement concerned a matter that was within the scope of the agency or employment

__ Foundation for present sense impression:

    __ Declarant perceived an event

    __ Declarant described the event

__ Description was given while the event occurred or immediately afterwards

__ Foundation for excited utterance:

    __ Declarant perceived a startling event or experienced a stressful condition

    __ Declarant made a statement concerning the event or condition

    __ Statement was made while the declarant was under the stress of the event or condition

__ Foundation for state of mind:

    __ Statement actually probative of declarant's mental, emotional, or physical condition

    __ Statement made during the existence of such condition

    __ Date and time statement was made

    __ Where it was made

    __ Who was present

    __ What was said

__ Foundation for medical treatment:

    __ Declarant made a statement for purpose of obtaining medical care or diagnosis

    __ Declarant made statement to physician or medical person

    __ Statement may include medical history or past symptoms, but it must relate to a then present bodily condition

__ Foundation for dying declaration:

    __ Declarant made a statement while believing that his or her death was imminent

    __ Statement concerned what he or she believed to be the cause of death

__ Foundations for documents

  __ General foundation requirements:

    __ Authentication

    __ Handwriting and signature

    __ Circumstantial evidence of authorship and origin

    __ Mailing or transmission

    __ Original writing (or "best evidence") rule

__ Foundations for documentary hearsay exceptions

  __ Foundation for business records and computer print-outs:

    __ Documents are records kept in the course of a regularly conducted business activity

      __ Made at or near the time of a transaction or event

      __ Made by, or based on information transmitted from, a person with knowledge

      __ Made as a part of the regular practice of that business activity

  __ Foundation for summaries:

    __ Original documents are so voluminous that they cannot be conveniently examined in the arbitration hearing

    __ Witness has examined the original data

    __ Witness is qualified to produce a summary of the information

    __ Exhibit is a fair and accurate summary of the underlying information

  __ Foundation for recorded recollection:

    __ Witness once had personal knowledge of the relevant facts or events

    __ Witness cannot currently recall the events fully and accurately

    __ Witness previously made an accurate memorandum or record of the facts

    __ At a time when the events were fresh in his or her memory

  __ Foundation for public records:

Note: most government records are self-authenticating, not requiring a government witness to testify.

    __ Document must be made by a public office or agency

    __ Set forth the activities of the office or agency, or

    __ Set forth matters observed pursuant to a duty imposed by law, or

    __ Set forth, in limited circumstances, certain investigative findings, or

    __ Set forth officially required records of vital statistics

__ Foundation for absence of public record:

Note: this evidence may be offered by certification from the appropriate official, in which case no witness needs to be called. The evidence may also be offered via testimony.

    __ Certain events, occurrences, or matters were regularly recorded in some form

    __ By a public office or agency

    __ A diligent search has failed to disclose a record of a particular fact or event

__ Foundation for previous testimony:

    __ Declarant is currently "unavailable" to testify

    __ Testimony was given under oath in court or at a deposition

    __ Party against whom the testimony is being offered had a fair opportunity to examine the witness when the testimony was originally given

__ Foundation for written admissions of a party:

    __ Same as for oral admissions, above

    __ Proof that writing was made or adopted by the party against whom it is being offered, or by an agent, servant, or employee of such party

__ Foundations for real and demonstrative evidence

  __ Foundation for real evidence/tangible objects:

    __ Recognition of exhibit

    __ Witness was familiar with the object at the time of the underlying events

    __ Witness is able to recognize the exhibit as that very same object

  __ Chain of custody

    __ Location, handling, and care of an object between the time of its recovery and the time of trial

    __ Needed where:

      __ Object is not uniquely recognizable and has not been marked, or

__ Object's physical properties are in issue

__ Foundations for photography and other recording devices

    __ Foundation for still photographs:

        __ Photograph "fairly and accurately" portrays the scene shown

        __ Witness may be photographer or any person who is familiar with the scene as it appeared at a relevant time

    __ Foundation for motion pictures and videotapes:

        __ Similar to requirements for photographs

        __ Operator of the camera needs to be called only if special features were employed, or if the date of the filming is in issue

    __ Foundation for audiotapes:

        __ Depends upon the purpose for which it is offered

        __ Voice exemplar: witness who is able to recognize the voices of the various speakers

        __ Recorded music: witness who is familiar with the material recorded

    __ Foundation for X-rays and similar images:

        __ Qualified witness testifies that X-ray, CAT scan, or MRI image is a fair representation of internal structure of the patient's body

        __ Witness testifies to identifying marks on film to demonstrate it is a business record of the hospital or clinic

__ Foundations for demonstrative evidence

    __ Foundation for map, charts, or other diagrams:

        __ Similar to photograph

        __ Witness must be familiar with the scene, location, or structure as it appeared at a relevant time, and

        __ Witness must testify that exhibit constitutes a fair representation

    __ Foundation for models and reproductions

        __ Similar to photograph

        __ Witness must be familiar with the real location or object, and must testify to the model's accuracy

    __ Foundation for illustrative aids:

        __ Exhibit is accurate

        __ Exhibit will assist witness in explaining his or her testimony

11. Common Objections

___ Form of question objections:

    ___ Leading question

    ___ Compound question

    ___ Vague question

    ___ Argumentative question

    ___ Narrative question

    ___ Asked and answered

    ___ Assuming facts not in evidence

    ___ Non-responsive answer to question

___ Substantive objections:

    ___ Hearsay objection

    ___ Irrelevant

    ___ Unfair prejudice

    ___ Improper character evidence

    ___ Lack of personal knowledge

    ___ Improper lay opinion

    ___ Speculation or conjecture

    ___ Authenticity

    ___ Lack of foundation

    ___ Best evidence

    ___ Privilege

    ___ Subsequent remedial measures

    ___ Settlement offers

12. Final Argument

___ Structure. Effective advocates' final argument has:

    ___ Topical organization

    ___ Chronological organization

    ___ Other organizing tools. Effective advocates:

        ___ Start and end strong

        ___ Claimant should advance affirmative case first

        ___ Cluster circumstantial evidence and accumulate details

        ___ Bury concessions

        ___ Weave in witness credibility

__ Carefully consider how to approach damages

__ Content. Effective advocates:

    __ Tell a persuasive story

    __ What happened?

    __ Why did it happen?

    __ How can we be sure?

    __ Is it plausible?

    __ Tie up cross-examinations

    __ Comment on promises

    __ Resolve problems and weaknesses

    __ Discuss damages

13. Concluding the Hearing

__ Determine when evidence will be "closed"

__ Determine whether parties should file post-hearing briefs

__ Set post-hearing briefing or oral argument schedule

    __ Make final remarks

APPENDIX D

Arbitrator's Post-hearing Functions and Duties Checklist

1. Ruling on Post-hearing Motions

___ If a party has filed a motion to reopen the hearing, has the party established "good cause", e.g.:

    ___ Is the party advancing "newly discovered" evidence that was not known or could not have been presented at the time of the hearing?

    ___ Can the party show that reopening of hearing will not seriously affect a substantial right of another party?

___ If a party has filed a motion to modify or correct the award, is the motion based on one or more of the following grounds:

    ___ an evident material mistake in the figures referred to in the award

    ___ an evident material mistake in the description of any person, thing, or property referred to in the award

    ___ the arbitrators have issued an award concerning a matter not submitted to them

    ___ the form of the award is incorrect

    ___ information needs to be added or deleted to effect the intent of the award

    ___ clarification is needed to promote justice between the parties

2. Deciding the Merits of the Claims and Defenses

___ The decision-making process—general:

    ___ Defining the problem

    ___ Establishing the boundary conditions

    ___ Finding a satisfactory and fair tentative solution

    ___ Ensuring self-implementation of the tentative solution

    ___ Trouble-shooting and finalizing into a decision

___ The decision-making procedure:

    ___ Read notes taken at hearing

    ___ Review transcript (if any)

    ___ Review hearing exhibits

    ___ Read pertinent case law

    ___ Analyze and decide various issues in case

__ Draft award and opinion (if appropriate)

__ Customary standards for interpreting contract language:

  __ Ambiguity

  __ Intent of parties

  __ Mutual mistake

  __ Legal validity

  __ Normal and technical word usage

  __ Construing agreement as a whole

  __ Avoiding absurd, harsh, or ludicrous results

  __ Expressing one matter precludes another

  __ General category determined by specific examples

  __ Specific versus general language

  __ Pre-contract negotiations

  __ Compromise offers not to be considered

  __ Experience or training of parties or agents

  __ Custom and past practice of the parties

  __ Industry practice

  __ Prior settlements

  __ Interpretation against drafter

  __ Handbooks and manuals

  __ Implication of insurance policy

__ Application of basic legal and equitable principles: (See § 4.3.5)

  __ Basic contract principles

  __ Basic tort principles

  __ Basic equitable principles

__ Determine Liability

  __ Claimant's theory of claim and related evidence:

    __ What were the elements of claimant's claim?

    __ Did the claimant satisfy its burden to prove each element of its claim?

    __ Did the parties stipulate to the existence of any element of claimant's claim?

    __ Did respondent admit to an element of claimant's claim, either in pleadings or during the arbitration hearing?

___ Was any item of evidence, critical to the proof of an element of claimant's claim, deemed inadmissible by the arbitrator?

___ Was the testimony of claimant's witnesses credible?

>___ What motivations were operating to influence witnesses to **exaggerate** material and relevant facts or events?

>___ What motivations were operating to influence witnesses to **misrepresent** material and relevant facts or events?

>___ What motivations were operating to influence witnesses to omit material and relevant facts or events?

___ Was the testimony of claimant's witnesses reliable?

>___ What portion of testimony consisted of direct evidence?

>___ What portion of testimony consisted of circumstantial evidence?

>___ What portion of testimony consisted of unreliable hearsay?

___ Was the claimant's documentary evidence credible?

___ Was the claimant's documentary evidence reliable?

___ What weight, if any, should be given to claimant's affidavits?

___ Was the respondent able to impeach the veracity of claimant's critical testimonial evidence?

___ Was the respondent able to impeach the veracity of claimant's critical documentary evidence?

___ Respondent's Theory of Defense and Related Evidence

___ What were the elements of respondent's defense?

___ Did the respondent satisfy its burden to prove each element of its defense?

___ Did the parties stipulate to the existence of any element of respondent's defense?

___ Did claimant admit to an element of respondent's defense either in pleadings or during the arbitration hearing?

___ Was any item of evidence, critical to the proof of an element of respondent's defense, deemed inadmissible by the arbitrator?

___ Was the testimony of respondent's witnesses credible?

    ___ What motivations were operating to influence witnesses to **exaggerate** material and relevant facts or events?

    ___ What motivations were operating to influence witnesses to **misrepresent** material and relevant facts or events?

    ___ What motivations were operating to influence witnesses to omit material and relevant facts or events?

    ___ Was the testimony of respondent's witnesses reliable?

    ___ What portion of testimony consisted of direct evidence?

    ___ What portion of testimony consisted of circumstantial evidence?

    ___ What portion of testimony consisted of unreliable hearsay?

___ Was the respondent's documentary evidence credible?

___ Was the respondent's documentary evidence reliable?

___ What weight, if any, should be given to respondent's affidavits?

___ Was the claimant able to impeach the veracity of respondent's critical testimonial evidence?

___ Was the claimant able to impeach the veracity of respondent's critical documentary evidence?

___ Determination of Liability on Claim

    ___ If the parties' lay testimonial evidence was in direct conflict, which testimony was more believable?

    ___ If the parties' expert testimonial evidence was in direct conflict, which testimony was more convincing?

    ___ If the parties' documentary evidence was conflicting, which documentary evidence was more believable?

    ___ Was the claimant's evidence sufficient overall?

    ___ Was the claimant's evidence sufficient as to a portion of its claim?

    ___ Has the claimant satisfied the overall standard of proof as to this claim or a portion of it–preponderance of the evidence; clear and convincing evidence, etc?

    ___ Was the respondent's theory of defense and related evidence sufficient to defeat claimant's claim?

___ Determine compensatory damages and other remedies

    ___ Reasonable damages

    ___ Liquidated damages

__ Consequential damages (check rules)

__ Any punitive damages (check agreement, rules, and law carefully)

__ Attorney's fees (check contract, rules law)

__ Costs

__ Interest

3. Drafting Award

__ Know jurisdictional requisites, such as, the award normally:

 __ should always be in writing, signed by you and the other arbitrators on the panel, and, if required by rules or the parties' agreement, notarized and witnessed

 __ should be clear and concise

 __ does not include a written opinion explaining the arbitrator's reasoning

 __ must contain a ruling on all claims (principal claims, counter-claims, cross-claims, third-party claims, etc.) and damage requests (compensatory, consequential, punitive, etc.) in issue

 __ must name the winning party on each claim, and the party against whom the award is rendered

 __ must specify the precise dollar amount of the award on each claim

 __ must apportion all administrative fees and expenses for the hearing and assess the arbitrator's fees and attorney's fees, if appropriate

 __ fix interest rate on award, as appropriate

 __ must be timely issued

4. Drafting Opinion Supporting Award

__ Five parts of an opinion

 __ Opening or orientation

 __ Summary of claims and defenses and other issues

 __ Statement of facts

 __ Discussion, analysis, and application of relevant law or equitable principles

 __ Disposition

__ Opening

 __ Identification of the parties

 __ Description of type and nature of case

 __ Description of relief sought

__ Principal issue(s) presented

__ Summary of claims and defenses

 __ Principal claims and defenses

 __ Cross-claims and counterclaims

__ Statement of facts

 __ Mechanics of drafting a statement of facts

  __ Rules or contract provisions

  __ Story development

   __ Organization

   __ Background

   __ Chronology

   __ Synthesis

   __ Direction

   __ Closure

 __ Headings and subheadings

 __ References to record

 __ Quotations and footnotes

__ Write with accuracy

 __ Ensure each fact is supported by record

 __ Take care not to modify content of record

 __ Be careful not to omit material facts

 __ Use correct words

__ Write objectively

__ Write to persuade

 __ Carefully select evidence

 __ Craft fact sentences

 __ Juxtapose fact sentences meaningfully

__ Discussing, analyzing, and applying relevant law or equitable principles —general

 __ Use simple, direct writing style

 __ Use headings and subheadings liberally

__ Drafting the reasoning of the opinion

 __ Think like a judge

 __ Use effective argument format

    __ Know and apply skills of legal analysis

        __ Apply correct burden and standard of proof

        __ Select and use appropriate case authority

    __ Select and use appropriate statutory authority

    __ Apply appropriate techniques for using and arguing facts

    __ Blend facts and authorities

    __ Argue public policy as appropriate

__ Use charts, diagrams, and graphic illustrations where appropriate

__ Avoid certain types of reasoning

    __ Fallacious arguments

    __ Weak alternative arguments

    __ Arguments based on hyperbole or arguments outside of record

    __ Arguments directed at counsel, personally

__ Edit and proofread

__ Draft disposition

__ Sign and issue award

Revised November 2004

JAMS Guide to Dispute Resolution Clauses for Commercial Contracts

Introduction

In today's competitive marketplace most companies either cannot afford or do not wish to incur the time, expense and adverse business consequences of traditional litigation. Unfortunately, in every business relationship there is the potential for conflict over contractual agreements or business operations. When such conflicts arise, there is no need to incur the onerous expense and delays involved in traditional litigation. There are readily available alternative dispute resolution ("ADR") procedures that will enable you to resolve your disputes relatively quickly, fairly and cost-effectively. The costs and risks of dispute resolution, as any other, can be controlled.

Planning is the key to avoiding the adverse effects of litigation. The optimal time for businesses to implement strategies for avoidance of those adverse effects is before any dispute arises. We at JAMS recommend, therefore, that whenever you negotiate or enter into a contract, you should carefully consider and decide on the procedures that will govern the resolution of any disputes that may arise in the course of the contractual relationship. This enables the company to create an enforceable dispute resolution strategy that incorporates its choice of dispute resolution forums, procedures and providers.

JAMS offers a selection of specialized Rules to govern arbitration or mediation proceedings. JAMS also offers sample dispute resolution clauses that may be inserted into a contract prior to any dispute ever arising. These sample dispute resolution clauses are set forth below.

For more information on using dispute resolution clauses, please contact your JAMS Case Manager or call 1-800-352-5267 to reach the JAMS office nearest you.

NOTICE: If you incorporate any of these clauses into a contract that applies to a number of contracting parties (such as, for example, in a standard employment agreement or in a consumer agreement), please advise JAMS at 949-224-1810 as special requirements may be applicable.

MEDIATION

MEDIATION is a process in which the parties are assisted by a neutral mediator who helps them to negotiate resolution of their dispute. Mediation is a non-binding procedure, but once an agreement has been reached and documented, that agreement is binding on the parties and can be enforced. Mediation has proven to be an effective procedure for resolving disputes that cannot be resolved through direct, unassisted negotiations. Intervention by a highly skilled JAMS mediator results in resolution of contractual disputes approximately 80-90% of the time.

Clause Providing for Compulsory Mediation Prior to Litigation:

Except as provided herein, no civil action with respect to any dispute, claim or controversy arising out of or relating to this Agreement may be commenced until the matter has been submitted to JAMS for mediation. Either party may commence mediation by providing to JAMS and the other party a written request for mediation, setting forth the subject of the dispute and the relief requested. The parties will cooperate with JAMS and with one another in selecting a mediator from JAMS panel of neutrals, and in scheduling the mediation proceedings. The parties covenant that they will participate in the mediation in good faith, and that they will share equally in its costs. All offers, promises, conduct and statements, whether oral or written, made in the course of the mediation by any of the parties, their agents, employees, experts and attorneys, and by the mediator and any JAMS employees, are confidential, privileged and inadmissible for any purpose, including impeachment, in any litigation or other proceeding involving the parties, provided that evidence that is otherwise admissible or discoverable shall not be rendered inadmissible or non-discoverable as a result of its use in the mediation. Either party may seek equitable relief prior to the mediation to preserve the status quo pending the completion of that process. Except for such an action to obtain equitable relief, neither party may commence a civil action with respect to the matters submitted to mediation until af-

ter the completion of the initial mediation session, or 45 days after the date of filing the written request for mediation, whichever occurs first. Mediation may continue after the commencement of a civil action, if the parties so desire. The provisions of this Clause may be enforced by any Court of competent jurisdiction, and the party seeking enforcement shall be entitled to an award of all costs, fees and expenses, including attorneys' fees, to be paid by the party against whom enforcement is ordered.

Due to a high demand for this service, JAMS will shortly publish International Mediation Rules that will govern international mediations.

Clauses Providing for Compulsory Mediation Followed by Arbitration (Step Clauses):

A "step clause" provides for a mediation or other ADR process to precede an arbitration proceeding. The first Step Clause below assures the parties that a preliminary remedy in aid of arbitration will be available during the pendency of any mediation proceeding. The second Step Clause below provides no such assurance (although a preliminary remedy might otherwise be available depending upon the facts and the jurisdiction in which the application is brought), and simply provides for mediation to precede an arbitration.

Step Clause 1 (this Clause follows the contract's arbitration clause):

Prior to the appointment of the arbitrator(s), and within 10 days from the date of commencement of the arbitration, the parties shall submit the dispute to JAMS for mediation. The parties will cooperate with JAMS and with one another in selecting a mediator from JAMS panel of neutrals, and in promptly scheduling the mediation proceedings. The parties covenant that they will participate in the mediation in good faith, and that they will share equally in its costs. All offers, promises, conduct and statements, whether oral or written, made in the course of the mediation by any of the parties, their agents, employees, experts and attorneys, and by the mediator or any

JAMS Guide to Dispute Resolution Clauses for Commercial Contracts

JAMS employees, are confidential, privileged and inadmissible for any purpose, including impeachment, in any arbitration or other proceeding involving the parties, provided that evidence that is otherwise admissible or discoverable shall not be rendered inadmissible or non-discoverable as a result of its use in the mediation. If the dispute is not resolved within 30 days from the date of the submission of the dispute to mediation (or such later date as the parties may mutually agree in writing), the administration of the arbitration shall proceed forthwith. The mediation may continue, if the parties so agree, after the appointment of the arbitrators. Unless otherwise agreed by the parties, the mediator shall be disqualified from serving as arbitrator in the case. The pendency of a mediation shall not preclude a party from seeking provisional remedies in aid of the arbitration from a court of appropriate jurisdiction, and the parties agree not to defend against any application for provisional relief on the ground that a mediation is pending.

Step Clause 2 (this Clause follows the contract's arbitration clause):

The parties agree that any and all disputes, claims or controversies arising out of or relating to this Agreement shall be submitted to JAMS, or its successor, for mediation, and if the matter is not resolved through mediation, then it shall be submitted to JAMS, or its successor, for final and binding arbitration pursuant to the arbitration clause set forth above. Either party may commence mediation by providing to JAMS and the other party a written request for mediation, setting forth the subject of the dispute and the relief requested. The parties will cooperate with JAMS and with one another in selecting a mediator from JAMS panel of neutrals, and in scheduling the mediation proceedings. The parties covenant that they will participate in the mediation in good faith, and that they will share equally in its costs. All offers, promises, conduct and statements, whether oral or written, made in the course of the mediation by any of the parties, their agents, employees, experts and attorneys, and by the mediator or any JAMS employees, are confidential, privileged and inadmissible for any purpose, including impeachment, in any arbitration or other proceeding

involving the parties, provided that evidence that is otherwise admissible or discoverable shall not be rendered inadmissible or non-discoverable as a result of its use in the mediation. Either party may initiate arbitration with respect to the matters submitted to mediation by filing a written demand for arbitration at any time following the initial mediation session or 45 days after the date of filing the written request for mediation, whichever occurs first. The mediation may continue after the commencement of arbitration if the parties so desire. Unless otherwise agreed by the parties, the mediator shall be disqualified from serving as arbitrator in the case. The provisions of this Clause may be enforced by any Court of competent jurisdiction, and the party seeking enforcement shall be entitled to an award of all costs, fees and expenses, including attorneys' fees, to be paid by the party against whom enforcement is ordered.

ARBITRATION

ARBITRATION provides a faster and more cost-effective method of obtaining a final and binding resolution of a dispute that cannot be resolved through direct or assisted negotiations. JAMS offers a distinguished panel of experienced neutrals from which you may choose your arbitrators. JAMS also provides you with a choice of arbitration rules and procedures that have been crafted to suit various types of commercial disputes. JAMS Streamlined Arbitration Rules and Procedures provide for an expedited process with minimal discovery and less formality. JAMS Comprehensive Arbitration Rules and Procedures provide for a more formal process, including more complete — yet still expedited — information exchange. We recommend that you use the Streamlined Arbitration Rules when the amount in controversy is likely to be less than $250,000, and that you use the Comprehensive Arbitration Rules when the amount in controversy is likely to exceed that figure. However, you may agree to use either set of Arbitration Rules, regardless of the amounts in dispute.

JAMS will shortly publish International Arbitration Rules that will govern international arbitrations. The Rules will provide for compre-

hensive arbitrator selection, and other procedures more common in the resolution of international disputes.

Standard Commercial Arbitration Clause*

*Any dispute, claim or controversy arising out
of or relating to this Agreement or the breach,
termination, enforcement, interpretation or
validity thereof, including the determination
of the scope or applicability of this agreement
to arbitrate, shall be determined by arbitration in (insert the desired place of arbitration),
before (one) (three) arbitrator(s). The arbitration shall be administered by JAMS pursuant
to its Comprehensive Arbitration Rules and
Procedures (Streamlined Arbitration Rules and
Procedures). Judgment on the Award may be
entered in any court having jurisdiction. This
clause shall not preclude parties from seeking
provisional remedies in aid of arbitration from
a court of appropriate jurisdiction.*

*(Optional) Allocation of Fees and Costs: The
arbitrator may, in the Award, allocate all or
part of the costs of the arbitration, including
the fees of the arbitrator and the reasonable
attorneys' fees of the prevailing party.*

Sometimes contracting parties may want their
agreement to allow a choice of provider organizations (JAMS being one) that can be used
if a dispute arises. The following clause permits a choice between JAMS or another provider organization at the option of the first
party to file the arbitration.

Standard Commercial Arbitration Clause Naming JAMS or Another Provider*

*Any dispute, claim or controversy arising out
of or relating to this Agreement or the breach,
termination, enforcement, interpretation or
validity thereof, including the determination
of the scope or applicability of this agreement
to arbitrate, shall be determined by arbitration in (insert the desired place of arbitration),
before (one) (three) arbitrator(s). At the option of the first to commence an arbitration,
the arbitration shall be administered either by
JAMS pursuant to its (Comprehensive Arbitration Rules and Procedures) (Streamlined Arbitration Rules), or by (name an alternate provider) pursuant to its (identify the rules that
will govern). Judgment on the Award may be
entered in any court having jurisdiction. This
clause shall not preclude parties from seeking
provisional remedies in aid of arbitration from
a court of appropriate jurisdiction.*

*(Optional) Allocation of Fees and Costs: The
arbitrator may, in the Award, allocate all or
part of the costs of the arbitration, including
the fees of the arbitrator and the reasonable
attorneys' fees of the prevailing party.*

* The drafter should select the desired option
from those provided in the parentheses.

JAMS Guide to Dispute Resolution Clauses for Commercial Contracts

APPENDIX F

AAA Commercial Arbitration Rules
Effective July 1, 2003

Reproduced with permission from the American Arbitration Association, ©2003

1. R-1. Agreement of Parties*+

(a) The parties shall be deemed to have made these rules a part of their arbitration agreement whenever they have provided for arbitration by the American Arbitration Association (hereinafter AAA) under its Commercial Arbitration Rules or for arbitration by the AAA of a domestic commercial dispute without specifying particular rules. These rules and any amendment of them shall apply in the form in effect at the time the administrative requirements are met for a demand for arbitration or submission agreement received by the AAA. The parties, by written agreement, may vary the procedures set forth in these rules. After appointment of the arbitrator, such modifications may be made only with the consent of the arbitrator.

(b) Unless the parties or the AAA determines otherwise, the Expedited Procedures shall apply in any case in which no disclosed claim or counterclaim exceeds $75,000, exclusive of interest and arbitration fees and costs. Parties may also agree to use these procedures in larger cases. Unless the parties agree otherwise, these procedures will not apply in cases involving more than two parties. The Expedited Procedures shall be applied as described in Sections E-1 through E-10 of these rules, in addition to any other portion of these rules that is not in conflict with the Expedited Procedures.

(c) Unless the parties agree otherwise, the Procedures for Large, Complex Commercial Disputes shall apply to all cases in which the disclosed claim or counterclaim of any party is at least $500,000, exclusive of claimed interest, arbitration fees and costs. Parties may also agree to use the Procedures in cases involving claims or counterclaims under $500,000, or in nonmonetary cases. The Procedures for Large, Complex Commercial Disputes shall be applied as described in Sections L-1 through L-4 of these rules, in addition to any other portion of these rules that is not in conflict with the Procedures for Large, Complex Commercial Disputes.

(d) All other cases shall be administered in accordance with Sections R-1 through R-54 of these rules.

* The AAA applies the *Supplementary Procedures for Consumer-Related Disputes* to arbitration clauses in agreements between individual consumers and businesses where the business has a standardized, systematic application of arbitration clauses with customers and where the terms and conditions of the purchase

339

of standardized, consumable goods or services are nonnegotiable or primarily non-negotiable in most or all of its terms, conditions, features, or choices. The product or service must be for personal or household use. The AAA will have the discretion to apply or not to apply the Supplementary Procedures and the parties will be able to bring any disputes concerning the application or non-application to the attention of the arbitrator. Consumers are not prohibited from seeking relief in a small claims court for disputes or claims within the scope of its jurisdiction, even in consumer arbitration cases filed by the business.

+A dispute arising out of an employer promulgated plan will be administered under the AAA's National Rules for the Resolution of Employment Disputes.

R-2. AAA and Delegation of Duties

When parties agree to arbitrate under these rules, or when they provide for arbitration by the AAA and an arbitration is initiated under these rules, they thereby authorize the AAA to administer the arbitration. The authority and duties of the AAA are prescribed in the agreement of the parties and in these rules, and may be carried out through such of the AAA's representatives as it may direct. The AAA may, in its discretion, assign the administration of an arbitration to any of its offices.

R-3. National Roster of Arbitrators

The AAA shall establish and maintain a National Roster of Commercial Arbitrators ("National Roster") and shall appoint arbitrators as provided in these rules. The term "arbitrator" in these rules refers to the arbitration panel, constituted for a particular case, whether composed of one or more arbitrators, or to an individual arbitrator, as the context requires.

R-4. Initiation under an Arbitration Provision in a Contract

(a) Arbitration under an arbitration provision in a contract shall be initiated in the following manner:

(i) The initiating party (the "claimant") shall, within the time period, if any, specified in the contract(s), give to the other party (the "respondent") written notice of its intention to arbitrate (the "demand"), which demand shall contain a statement setting forth the nature of the dispute, the names and addresses of all other parties, the amount involved, if any, the remedy sought, and the hearing locale requested.

(ii) The claimant shall file at any office of the AAA two copies of the demand and two copies of the arbitration provisions of the contract, together with the appropriate filing fee as provided in the schedule included with these rules.

(iii) The AAA shall confirm notice of such filing to the parties.

(b) A respondent may file an answering statement in duplicate with the AAA within 15 days after confirmation of notice of filing of the demand is sent by the AAA. The respondent shall, at the time of any such filing, send a copy of the answering statement to the claimant. If a counterclaim is asserted, it shall contain a statement setting forth the nature of the counterclaim, the amount involved, if any, and the remedy sought. If a counterclaim is made, the party making the counterclaim shall forward to the AAA with the answering statement the appropriate fee provided in the schedule included with these rules.

(c) If no answering statement is filed within the stated time, respondent will be deemed to deny the claim. Failure to file an answering statement shall not operate to delay the arbitration.

(d) When filing any statement pursuant to this section, the parties are encouraged to provide descriptions of their claims in sufficient detail to make the circumstances of the dispute clear to the arbitrator.

R-5. Initiation under a Submission

Parties to any existing dispute may commence an arbitration under these rules by filing at any office of the AAA two copies of a written submission to arbitrate under these rules, signed by the parties. It shall contain a statement of the nature of the dispute, the names and addresses of all parties, any claims and counterclaims, the amount involved, if any, the remedy sought, and the hearing locale requested, together with the appropriate filing fee as provided in the schedule included with these rules. Unless the parties state otherwise in the submission, all claims and counterclaims will be deemed to be denied by the other party.

R-6. Changes of Claim

After filing of a claim, if either party desires to make any new or different claim or counterclaim, it shall be made in writing and filed with the AAA. The party asserting such a claim or counterclaim shall provide a copy to the other party, who shall have 15 days from the date of such transmission within which to file an answering statement with the AAA. After the arbitrator is appointed, however, no new or different claim may be submitted except with the arbitrator's consent.

R-7. Jurisdiction

(a) The arbitrator shall have the power to rule on his or her own jurisdiction, including any objections with respect to the existence, scope or validity of the arbitration agreement.

(b) The arbitrator shall have the power to determine the existence or validity of a contract of which an arbitration clause forms a part. Such an arbitration clause shall be treated as an agreement independent of the other terms of the contract. A decision by the arbitrator that the contract is null and void shall not for that reason alone render invalid the arbitration clause.

(c) A party must object to the jurisdiction of the arbitrator or to the arbitrability of a claim or counterclaim no later than the filing of the answering statement to the claim or counterclaim that gives rise to the objection. The arbitrator may rule on such objections as a preliminary matter or as part of the final award.

R-8. Mediation

At any stage of the proceedings, the parties may agree to conduct a mediation conference under the Commercial Mediation Procedures in order to facilitate settlement. The mediator shall not be an arbitrator appointed to the case. Where the parties to a pending arbitration agree to mediate under the AAA's rules, no additional administrative fee is required to initiate the mediation.

R-9. Administrative Conference

At the request of any party or upon the AAA's own initiative, the AAA may conduct an administrative conference, in person or by telephone, with the parties and/or their representatives. The conference may address such issues as arbitrator selection, potential mediation of the dispute, potential exchange of information, a timetable for hearings and any other administrative matters.

R-10. Fixing of Locale

The parties may mutually agree on the locale where the arbitration is to be held. If any party requests that the hearing be held in a specific locale and the other party files no objection thereto within 15 days after notice of the request has been sent to it by the AAA, the locale shall be the one requested. If a party objects to the locale requested by the other party, the AAA shall have the power to determine the locale, and its decision shall be final and binding.

R-11. Appointment from National Roster

If the parties have not appointed an arbitrator and have not provided any other method of appointment, the arbitrator shall be appointed in the following manner:

(a) Immediately after the filing of the submission or the answering statement or the expiration of the time within which the answering statement is to be filed, the AAA shall send simultaneously to each party to the dispute an identical list of 10 (unless the AAA decides that a different number is appropriate) names of persons chosen from the National Roster. The parties are encouraged to agree to an arbitrator from the submitted list and to advise the AAA of their agreement.

(b) If the parties are unable to agree upon an arbitrator, each party to the dispute shall have 15 days from the transmittal date in which to strike names objected to, number the remaining names in order of preference, and return the list to the AAA. If a party does not return the list within the time specified, all persons named therein shall be deemed acceptable. From among the persons who have been approved on both lists, and in accordance with the designated order of mutual preference, the AAA shall invite the acceptance of an arbitrator to serve. If the parties fail to agree on any of the persons named, or if acceptable arbitrators are unable to act, or if for any other reason the appointment cannot be made from the submitted lists, the AAA shall have the power to make the appointment from among other members of the National Roster without the submission of additional lists.

(c) Unless the parties agree otherwise when there are two or more claimants or two or more respondents, the AAA may appoint all the arbitrators.

R-12. Direct Appointment by a Party

(a) If the agreement of the parties names an arbitrator or specifies a method of appointing an arbitrator, that designation or method shall be followed. The notice of appointment, with the name and address of the arbitrator, shall be filed with the AAA by the appointing party. Upon the request of any appointing party, the AAA shall submit a list of members of the National Roster from which the party may, if it so desires, make the appointment.

(b) Where the parties have agreed that each party is to name one arbitrator, the arbitrators so named must meet the standards of Section R-17 with respect to impartiality and independence unless the parties have specifically agreed pursuant to Section R-17(a) that the party-appointed arbitrators are to be non-neutral and need not meet those standards.

(c) If the agreement specifies a period of time within which an arbitrator shall be appointed and any party fails to make the appointment within that period, the AAA shall make the appointment.

(d) If no period of time is specified in the agreement, the AAA shall notify the party to make the appointment. If within 15 days after such notice has been sent, an arbitrator has not been appointed by a party, the AAA shall make the appointment.

R-13. Appointment of Chairperson by Party-Appointed Arbitrators or Parties

(a) If, pursuant to Section R-12, either the parties have directly appointed arbitrators, or the arbitrators have been appointed by the AAA, and the parties have authorized them to appoint a chairperson within a specified time and no appointment is made within that time or any agreed extension, the AAA may appoint the chairperson.

(b) If no period of time is specified for appointment of the chairperson and the party-appointed arbitrators or the parties do not make the appointment within 15 days from the date of the appointment of the last party-appointed arbitrator, the AAA may appoint the chairperson.

(c) If the parties have agreed that their party-appointed arbitrators shall appoint the chairperson from the National Roster, the AAA shall furnish to the party-appointed arbitrators, in the manner provided in Section R-11, a list selected from the National Roster, and the appointment of the chairperson shall be made as provided in that Section.

R-14. Nationality of Arbitrator

Where the parties are nationals of different countries, the AAA, at the request of any party or on its own initiative, may appoint as arbitrator a national of a country other than that of any of the parties. The request must be made before the time set for the appointment of the arbitrator as agreed by the parties or set by these rules.

R-15. Number of Arbitrators

If the arbitration agreement does not specify the number of arbitrators, the dispute shall be heard and determined by one arbitrator, unless the AAA, in its discretion, directs that three arbitrators be appointed. A party may request three arbitrators in the demand or answer, which request the AAA will consider in exercising its discretion regarding the number of arbitrators appointed to the dispute.

R-16. Disclosure

(a) Any person appointed or to be appointed as an arbitrator shall disclose to the AAA any circumstance likely to give rise to justifiable doubt as to the arbitrator's impartiality or independence, including any bias or any financial or personal interest in the result of the arbitration or any past or present relationship with the parties or their representatives. Such obligation shall remain in effect throughout the arbitration.

(b) Upon receipt of such information from the arbitrator or another source, the AAA shall communicate the information to the parties and, if it deems it appropriate to do so, to the arbitrator and others.

(c) In order to encourage disclosure by arbitrators, disclosure of information pursuant to this Section R-16 is not to be construed as an indication that the arbitrator considers that the disclosed circumstance is likely to affect impartiality or independence.

R-17. Disqualification of Arbitrator

(a) Any arbitrator shall be impartial and independent and shall perform his or her duties with diligence and in good faith, and shall be subject to disqualification for

(i) partiality or lack of independence,

(ii) inability or refusal to perform his or her duties with diligence and in good faith, and

(iii) any grounds for disqualification provided by applicable law. The parties may agree in writing, however, that arbitrators directly appointed by a party pursuant to Section R-12 shall be nonneutral, in which case such arbitrators need not be impartial or independent and shall not be subject to disqualification for partiality or lack of independence.

(b) Upon objection of a party to the continued service of an arbitrator, or on its own initiative, the AAA shall determine whether the arbitrator should be disqualified under the grounds set out above, and shall inform the parties of its decision, which decision shall be conclusive.

R-18. Communication with Arbitrator

(a) No party and no one acting on behalf of any party shall communicate ex parte with an arbitrator or a candidate for arbitrator concerning the arbitration, except that a party, or someone acting on behalf of a party, may communicate ex parte with a candidate for direct appointment pursuant to Section R-12 in order to advise the candidate of the general nature of the controversy and of the anticipated proceedings and to discuss the candidate's qualifications, availability, or independence in relation to the parties or to discuss the suitability of candidates for selection as a third arbitrator where the parties or party-designated arbitrators are to participate in that selection.

(b) Section R-18(a) does not apply to arbitrators directly appointed by the parties who, pursuant to Section R-17(a), the parties have agreed in writing are non-neutral. Where the parties have so agreed under Section R-17(a), the AAA shall as an administrative practice suggest to the parties that they agree further that Section R-18(a) should nonetheless apply prospectively.

R-19. Vacancies

(a) If for any reason an arbitrator is unable to perform the duties of the office, the AAA may, on proof satisfactory to it, declare the office vacant. Vacancies shall be filled in accordance with the applicable provisions of these rules.

(b) In the event of a vacancy in a panel of neutral arbitrators after the hearings have commenced, the remaining arbitrator or arbitrators may continue with the hearing and determination of the controversy, unless the parties agree otherwise.

(c) In the event of the appointment of a substitute arbitrator, the panel of arbitrators shall determine in its sole discretion whether it is necessary to repeat all or part of any prior hearings.

R-20. Preliminary Hearing

(a) At the request of any party or at the discretion of the arbitrator or the AAA, the arbitrator may schedule as soon as practicable a preliminary hearing with the parties and/or their representatives. The preliminary hearing may be conducted by telephone at the arbitrator's discretion.

(b) During the preliminary hearing, the parties and the arbitrator should discuss the future conduct of the case, including clarification of the issues and claims, a schedule for the hearings and any other preliminary matters.

R-21. Exchange of Information

(a) At the request of any party or at the discretion of the arbitrator, consistent with the expedited nature of arbitration, the arbitrator may direct

(i) the production of documents and other information, and

(ii) the identification of any witnesses to be called.

(b) At least five business days prior to the hearing, the parties shall exchange copies of all exhibits they intend to submit at the hearing.

(c) The arbitrator is authorized to resolve any disputes concerning the exchange of information.

R-22. Date, Time, and Place of Hearing

The arbitrator shall set the date, time, and place for each hearing. The parties shall respond to requests for hearing dates in a timely manner, be cooperative in scheduling the earliest practicable date, and adhere to the established hearing schedule. The AAA shall send a notice of hearing to the parties at least 10 days in advance of the hearing date, unless otherwise agreed by the parties.

R-23. Attendance at Hearings

The arbitrator and the AAA shall maintain the privacy of the hearings unless the law provides to the contrary. Any person having a direct interest in the arbitration is entitled to attend hearings. The arbitrator shall otherwise have the power to require the exclusion of any witness, other than a party or other essential person, during the testimony of any other witness. It shall be discretionary with the arbitrator to determine the propriety of the attendance of any other person other than a party and its representatives.

R-24. Representation

Any party may be represented by counsel or other authorized representative. A party intending to be so represented shall notify the other party and the AAA of the name and address of the representative at least three days prior to the date set for the hearing at which that person is first to appear. When such a representative initiates an arbitration or responds for a party, notice is deemed to have been given.

R-25. Oaths

Before proceeding with the first hearing, each arbitrator may take an oath of office and, if required by law, shall do so. The arbitrator may require witnesses to testify under oath administered by any duly qualified person and, if it is required by law or requested by any party, shall do so.

R-26. Stenographic Record

Any party desiring a stenographic record shall make arrangements directly with a stenographer and shall notify the other parties of these arrangements at least three days in advance of the hearing. The requesting party or parties shall pay the cost of the record. If the transcript is agreed by the parties, or determined by the arbitrator to be the official record of the proceeding, it must be provided to the arbitrator and made available to the other parties for inspection, at a date, time, and place determined by the arbitrator.

R-27. Interpreters

Any party wishing an interpreter shall make all arrangements directly with the interpreter and shall assume the costs of the service.

R-28. Postponements

The arbitrator may postpone any hearing upon agreement of the parties, upon request of a party for good cause shown, or upon the arbitrator's own initiative.

R-29. Arbitration in the Absence of a Party or Representative

Unless the law provides to the contrary, the arbitration may proceed in the absence of any party or representative who, after due notice, fails to be present or fails to obtain a postponement. An award shall not be made solely on the default of a party. The arbitrator shall require the party who is present to submit such evidence as the arbitrator may require for the making of an award.

R-30. Conduct of Proceedings

(a) The claimant shall present evidence to support its claim. The respondent shall then present evidence to support its defense. Witnesses for each party shall also submit to questions from the arbitrator and the adverse party. The arbitrator has the discretion to vary this procedure, provided that the parties are treated with equality and that each party has the right to be heard and is given a fair opportunity to present its case.

(b) The arbitrator, exercising his or her discretion, shall conduct the proceedings with a view to expediting the resolution of the dispute and may direct the order of proof, bifurcate proceedings and direct the parties to focus their presentations on issues the decision of which could dispose of all or part of the case.

(c) The parties may agree to waive oral hearings in any case.

R-31. Evidence

(a) The parties may offer such evidence as is relevant and material to the dispute and shall produce such evidence as the arbitrator may deem necessary to an understanding and determination of the dispute. Conformity to legal rules of evidence shall not be necessary. All evidence shall be taken in the presence of all of the arbitrators and all of the parties, except where any of the parties is absent, in default or has waived the right to be present.

(b) The arbitrator shall determine the admissibility, relevance, and materiality of the evidence offered and may exclude evidence deemed by the arbitrator to be cumulative or irrelevant.

(c) The arbitrator shall take into account applicable principles of legal privilege, such as those involving the confidentiality of communications between a lawyer and client.

(d) An arbitrator or other person authorized by law to subpoena witnesses or documents may do so upon the request of any party or independently.

R-32. Evidence by Affidavit and Post-hearing Filing of Documents or Other Evidence

(a) The arbitrator may receive and consider the evidence of witnesses by declaration or affidavit, but shall give it only such weight as the arbitrator deems it entitled to after consideration of any objection made to its admission.

(b) If the parties agree or the arbitrator directs that documents or other evidence be submitted to the arbitrator after the hearing, the documents or other evidence shall be filed with the AAA for transmission to the arbitrator. All parties shall be afforded an opportunity to examine and respond to such documents or other evidence.

R-33. Inspection or Investigation

An arbitrator finding it necessary to make an inspection or investigation in connection with the arbitration shall direct the AAA to so advise the parties. The arbitrator shall set the date and time and the AAA shall notify the parties. Any party who so desires may be present at such an inspection or investigation. In the event that one or all parties are not present at the inspection or investigation, the arbitrator shall make an oral or written report to the parties and afford them an opportunity to comment.

R-34. Interim Measures

(a) The arbitrator may take whatever interim measures he or she deems necessary, including injunctive relief and measures for the protection or conservation of property and disposition of perishable goods.

(b) Such interim measures may take the form of an interim award, and the arbitrator may require security for the costs of such measures.

(c) A request for interim measures addressed by a party to a judicial authority shall not be deemed incompatible with the agreement to arbitrate or a waiver of the right to arbitrate.

R-35. Closing of Hearing

The arbitrator shall specifically inquire of all parties whether they have any further proofs to offer or witnesses to be heard. Upon receiving negative replies or if satisfied that the record is complete, the arbitrator shall declare the hearing closed. If briefs are to be filed, the hearing shall b e declared closed as of the final date set by the arbitrator for the receipt of briefs. If documents are to be filed as provided in Section R-32 and the date set for their receipt is later than that set for the receipt of briefs, the later date shall be the closing date of the hearing. The time limit within which the arbitrator is required to make the award shall commence, in the absence of other agreements by the parties, upon the closing of the hearing.

R-36. Reopening of Hearing

The hearing may be reopened on the arbitrator's initiative, or upon application of a party, at any time before the award is made. If reopening the hearing would prevent the making of the award within the specific time agreed on by the parties in the contract(s) out of which the controversy has arisen, the matter may not be reopened unless the parties agree on an extension of time. When no specific date is fixed in the contract, the arbitrator may reopen the hearing and shall have 30 days from the closing of the reopened hearing within which to make an award.

R-37. Waiver of Rules

Any party who proceeds with the arbitration after knowledge that any provision or requirement of these rules has not been complied with and who fails to state an objection in writing shall be deemed to have waived the right to object.

R-38. Extensions of Time

The parties may modify any period of time by mutual agreement. The AAA or the arbitrator may for good cause extend any period of time established by these rules, except the time for making the award. The AAA shall notify the parties of any extension.

R-39. Serving of Notice

(a) Any papers, notices, or process necessary or proper for the initiation or continuation of an arbitration under these rules, for any court action in connection therewith, or for the entry of judgment on any award made under these rules may be served on a party by mail addressed to the party, or its representative at the last known address or by personal service, in or outside the state where the arbitration is to be held, provided that reasonable opportunity to be heard with regard to the dispute is or has been granted to the party.

(b) The AAA, the arbitrator and the parties may also use overnight delivery or electronic facsimile transmission (fax), to give the notices required by these rules. Where all parties and the arbitrator agree, notices may be transmitted by electronic mail (E-mail), or other methods of communication.

(c) Unless otherwise instructed by the AAA or by the arbitrator, any documents submitted by any party to the AAA or to the arbitrator shall simultaneously be provided to the other party or parties to the arbitration.

R-40. Majority Decision

When the panel consists of more than one arbitrator, unless required by law or by the arbitration agreement, a majority of the arbitrators must make all decisions.

R-41. Time of Award

The award shall be made promptly by the arbitrator and, unless otherwise agreed by the parties or specified by law, no later than 30 days from the date of closing the hearing, or, if oral hearings have been waived, from the date of the AAA's transmittal of the final statements and proofs to the arbitrator.

R-42. Form of Award

(a) Any award shall be in writing and signed by a majority of the arbitrators. It shall be executed in the manner required by law.

(b) The arbitrator need not render a reasoned award unless the parties request such an award in writing prior to appointment of the arbitrator or unless the arbitrator determines that a reasoned award is appropriate.

R-43. Scope of Award

(a) The arbitrator may grant any remedy or relief that the arbitrator deems just and equitable and within the scope of the agreement of the parties, including, but not limited to, specific performance of a contract.

(b) In addition to a final award, the arbitrator may make other decisions, including interim, interlocutory, or partial rulings, orders, and awards. In any interim, interlocutory, or partial award, the arbitrator may assess and apportion the fees, expenses, and compensation related to such award as the arbitrator determines is appropriate.

(c) In the final award, the arbitrator shall assess the fees, expenses, and compensation provided in Sections R-49, R-50, and R-51. The arbitrator may apportion such fees, expenses, and compensation among the parties in such amounts as the arbitrator determines is appropriate.

(d) The award of the arbitrator(s) may include:

(i) interest at such rate and from such date as the arbitrator(s) may deem appropriate; and

(ii) an award of attorneys' fees if all parties have requested such an award or it is authorized by law or their arbitration agreement.

R-44. Award upon Settlement

If the parties settle their dispute during the course of the arbitration and if the parties so request, the arbitrator may set forth the terms of the settlement in a "consent award." A consent award must include an allocation of arbitration costs, including administrative fees and expenses as well as arbitrator fees and expenses.

R-45. Delivery of Award to Parties

Parties shall accept as notice and delivery of the award the placing of the award or a true copy thereof in the mail addressed to the parties or their representatives at the last known addresses, personal or electronic service of the award, or the filing of the award in any other manner that is permitted by law.

R-46. Modification of Award

Within 20 days after the transmittal of an award, any party, upon notice to the other parties, may request the arbitrator, through the AAA, to correct any clerical, typographical, or computational errors in the award. The arbitrator is not empowered to redetermine the merits of any claim already decided. The other parties shall be given 10 days to respond to the request. The arbitrator shall dispose of the request within 20 days after transmittal by the AAA to the arbitrator of the request and any response thereto.

R-47. Release of Documents for Judicial Proceedings

The AAA shall, upon the written request of a party, furnish to the party, at the party's expense, certified copies of any papers in the AAA's possession that may be required in judicial proceedings relating to the arbitration.

R-48. Applications to Court and Exclusion of Liability

(a) No judicial proceeding by a party relating to the subject matter of the arbitration shall be deemed a waiver of the party's right to arbitrate.

(b) Neither the AAA nor any arbitrator in a proceeding under these rules is a necessary or proper party in judicial proceedings relating to the arbitration.

(c) Parties to an arbitration under these rules shall be deemed to have consented that judgment upon the arbitration award may be entered in any federal or state court having jurisdiction thereof.

(d) Parties to an arbitration under these rules shall be deemed to have consented that neither the AAA nor any arbitrator shall be liable to any party in any action for damages or injunctive relief for any act or omission in connection with any arbitration under these rules.

R-49. Administrative Fees

As a not-for-profit organization, the AAA shall prescribe an initial filing fee and a case service fee to compensate it for the cost of providing administrative services. The fees in effect when the fee or charge is incurred shall be applicable. The filing fee shall be advanced by the party or parties making a claim or counterclaim, subject to final apportionment by the arbitrator in the award. The AAA may, in the event of extreme hardship on the part of any party, defer or reduce the administrative fees.

R-50. Expenses

The expenses of witnesses for either side shall be paid by the party producing such witnesses. All other expenses of the arbitration, including required travel and other expenses of the arbitrator, AAA representatives, and any witness and the cost of any proof produced at the direct request of the arbitrator, shall be borne equally by the parties, unless they agree otherwise or unless the arbitrator in the award assesses such expenses or any part thereof against any specified party or parties.

R-51. Neutral Arbitrator's Compensation

(a) Arbitrators shall be compensated at a rate consistent with the arbitrator's stated rate of compensation.

(b) If there is disagreement concerning the terms of compensation, an appropriate rate shall be established with the arbitrator by the AAA and confirmed to the parties.

(c) Any arrangement for the compensation of a neutral arbitrator shall be made through the AAA and not directly between the parties and the arbitrator.

R-52. Deposits

The AAA may require the parties to deposit in advance of any hearings such sums of money as it deems necessary to cover the expense of the arbitration, including the arbitrator's fee, if any, and shall render an accounting to the parties and return any unexpended balance at the conclusion of the case.

R-53. Interpretation and Application of Rules

The arbitrator shall interpret and apply these rules insofar as they relate to the arbitrator's powers and duties. When there is more than one arbitrator and a difference arises among them concerning the meaning or application of these rules, it shall be decided by a majority vote. If that is not possible, either an arbitrator or a party may refer the question to the AAA for final decision. All other rules shall be interpreted and applied by the AAA.

R-54. Suspension for Nonpayment

If arbitrator compensation or administrative charges have not been paid in full, the AAA may so inform the parties in order that one of them may advance the required payment. If such payments are not made, the arbitrator may order the suspension or termination of the proceedings. If no arbitrator has yet been appointed, the AAA may suspend the proceedings.

EXPEDITED PROCEDURES

E-1. Limitation on Extensions

Except in extraordinary circumstances, the AAA or the arbitrator may grant a party no more than one seven-day extension of time to respond to the demand for arbitration or counterclaim as provided in Section R-4.

E-2. Changes of Claim or Counterclaim

A claim or counterclaim may be increased in amount, or a new or different claim or counterclaim added, upon the agreement of the other party, or the consent of the arbitrator. After the arbitrator is appointed, however, no new or different claim or counterclaim may be submitted except with the arbitrator's consent. If an increased claim or counterclaim exceeds $75,000, the case will be administered under the regular procedures unless all parties and the arbitrator agree that the case may continue to be processed under the Expedited Procedures.

E-3. Serving of Notices

In addition to notice provided by Section R-39(b), the parties shall also accept notice by telephone. Telephonic notices by the AAA shall subsequently be confirmed in writing to the parties. Should there be a failure to confirm in writing any such oral notice, the proceeding shall nevertheless be valid if notice has, in fact, been given by telephone.

E-4. Appointment and Qualifications of Arbitrator

(a) The AAA shall simultaneously submit to each party an identical list of five proposed arbitrators drawn from its National Roster from which one arbitrator shall be appointed.

(b) The parties are encouraged to agree to an arbitrator from this list and to advise the AAA of their agreement. If the parties are unable to agree upon an arbitrator, each party may strike two names from the list and return it to the AAA within seven days from the date of the AAA's mailing to the parties. If for any reason the appointment of an arbitrator cannot be made from the list, the AAA may make the appointment from other members of the panel without the submission of additional lists.

(c) The parties will be given notice by the AAA of the appointment of the arbitrator, who shall be subject to disqualification for the reasons specified in Section R-17. The parties shall notify the AAA within seven days of any objection to the arbitrator appointed. Any such objection shall be for cause and shall be confirmed in writing to the AAA with a copy to the other party or parties.

E-5. Exchange of Exhibits

At least two business days prior to the hearing, the parties shall exchange copies of all exhibits they intend to submit at the hearing. The arbitrator shall resolve disputes concerning the exchange of exhibits.

E-6. Proceedings on Documents

Where no party's claim exceeds $10,000, exclusive of interest and arbitration costs, and other cases in which the parties agree, the dispute shall be resolved by submission of documents, unless any party requests an oral hearing, or the arbitrator determines that an oral hearing is necessary. The arbitrator shall establish a fair and equitable procedure for the submission of documents.

E-7. Date, Time, and Place of Hearing

In cases in which a hearing is to be held, the arbitrator shall set the date, time, and place of the hearing, to be scheduled to take place within 30 days of confirmation of the arbitrator's appointment. The AAA will notify the parties in advance of the hearing date.

E-8. The Hearing

(a) Generally, the hearing shall not exceed one day. Each party shall have equal opportunity to submit its proofs and complete its case. The arbitrator shall determine the order of the hearing, and may require further submission of documents within two days after the hearing. For good cause shown, the arbitrator may schedule additional hearings within seven business days after the initial day of hearings.

(b) Generally, there will be no stenographic record. Any party desiring a stenographic record may arrange for one pursuant to the provisions of Section R-26.

E-9. Time of Award

Unless otherwise agreed by the parties, the award shall be rendered not later than 14 days from the date of the closing of the hearing or, if oral hearings have been waived, from the date of the AAA's transmittal of the final statements and proofs to the arbitrator.

E-10. Arbitrator's Compensation

Arbitrators will receive compensation at a rate to be suggested by the AAA regional office.

PROCEDURES FOR LARGE, COMPLEX COMMERCIAL DISPUTES

L-1. Administrative Conference

Prior to the dissemination of a list of potential arbitrators, the AAA shall, unless the parties agree otherwise, conduct an administrative conference with the parties and/or their attorneys or other representatives by conference call. The conference will take place within 14 days after the commencement of the arbitration. In the event the parties are unable to agree on a mutually acceptable time for the conference, the AAA may contact the parties individually to discuss the issues contemplated herein. Such administrative conference shall be conducted for the following purposes and for such additional purposes as the parties or the AAA may deem appropriate:

(a) to obtain additional information about the nature and magnitude of the dispute and the anticipated length of hearing and scheduling;

(b) to discuss the views of the parties about the technical and other qualifications of the arbitrators;

(c) to obtain conflicts statements from the parties; and

(d) to consider, with the parties, whether mediation or other non-adjudicative methods of dispute resolution might be appropriate.

L-2. Arbitrators

(a) Large, Complex Commercial Cases shall be heard and determined by either one or three arbitrators, as may be agreed upon by the parties. If the parties are unable to agree upon the number of arbitrators and a claim or counterclaim involves at least $1,000,000, then three arbitrator(s) shall hear and determine the case. If the parties are unable to agree on the number of arbitrators and each claim and counterclaim is less than $1,000,000, then one arbitrator shall hear and determine the case.

(b) The AAA shall appoint arbitrator(s) as agreed by the parties. If they are unable to agree on a method of appointment, the AAA shall appoint arbitrators from the Large, Complex Commercial Case Panel, in the manner provided in the Regular Commercial Arbitration Rules. Absent agreement of the parties, the arbitrator(s) shall not have served as the mediator in the mediation phase of the instant proceeding.

L-3. Preliminary Hearing

As promptly as practicable after the selection of the arbitrator(s), a preliminary hearing shall be held among the parties and/or their attorneys or other representatives and the arbitrator(s). Unless the parties agree otherwise, the preliminary hearing will be conducted by telephone conference call rather than in person. At the preliminary hearing the matters to be considered shall include, without limitation:

(a) service of a detailed statement of claims, damages and defenses, a statement of the issues asserted by each party and positions with respect thereto, and any legal authorities the parties may wish to bring to the attention of the arbitrator(s);

(b) stipulations to uncontested facts;

(c) the extent to which discovery shall be conducted;

(d) exchange and premarking of those documents which each party believes may be offered at the hearing;

(e) the identification and availability of witnesses, including experts, and such matters with respect to witnesses including their biographies and expected testimony as may be appropriate;

(f) whether, and the extent to which, any sworn statements and/or depositions may be introduced;

(g) the extent to which hearings will proceed on consecutive days;

(h) whether a stenographic or other official record of the proceedings shall be maintained;

(i) the possibility of utilizing mediation or other non-adjudicative methods of dispute resolution; and

(j) the procedure for the issuance of subpoenas.

By agreement of the parties and/or order of the arbitrator(s), the prehearing activities and the hearing procedures that will govern the arbitration will be memorialized in a Scheduling and Procedure Order.

L-4. Management of Proceedings

(a) Arbitrator(s) shall take such steps as they may deem necessary or desirable to avoid delay and to achieve a just, speedy and cost-effective resolution of Large, Complex Commercial Cases.

(b) Parties shall cooperate in the exchange of documents, exhibits and information within such party's control if the arbitrator(s) consider such production to be consistent with the goal of achieving a just, speedy and cost-effective resolution of a Large, Complex Commercial Case.

(c) The parties may conduct such discovery as may be agreed to by all the parties provided, however, that the arbitrator(s) may place such limitations on the conduct of such discovery as the arbitrator(s) shall deem appropriate. If the parties cannot agree on production of documents and other information, the arbitrator(s), consistent with the expedited nature of arbitration, may establish the extent of the discovery.

(d) At the discretion of the arbitrator(s), upon good cause shown and consistent with the expedited nature of arbitration, the arbitrator(s) may order depositions of, or the propounding of interrogatories to, such persons who may possess information determined by the arbitrator(s) to be necessary to determination of the matter.

(e) The parties shall exchange copies of all exhibits they intend to submit at the hearing 10 business days prior to the hearing unless the arbitrator(s) determine otherwise.

(f) The exchange of information pursuant to this rule, as agreed by the parties and/or directed by the arbitrator(s), shall be included within the Scheduling and Procedure Order.

(g) The arbitrator is authorized to resolve any disputes concerning the exchange of information.

(h) Generally hearings will be scheduled on consecutive days or in blocks of consecutive days in order to maximize efficiency and minimize costs.

OPTIONAL RULES FOR EMERGENCY MEASURES OF PROTECTION

O-1. Applicability

Where parties by special agreement or in their arbitration clause have adopted these rules for emergency measures of protection, a party in need of emergency relief prior to the constitution of the panel shall notify the AAA and all other parties in writing of the nature of the relief sought and the reasons why such relief is required on an emergency basis. The application shall also set forth the reasons why the party is entitled to such relief. Such notice may be given by facsimile transmission, or other reliable means, but must include a statement certifying that all other parties have been notified or an explanation of the steps taken in good faith to notify other parties.

O-2. Appointment of Emergency Arbitrator

Within one business day of receipt of notice as provided in Section O-1, the AAA shall appoint a single emergency arbitrator from a special AAA panel of emergency arbitrators designated to rule on emergency applications. The emergency arbitrator shall immediately disclose any circumstance likely, on the basis of the facts disclosed in the application, to affect such arbitrator's impartiality or independence. Any challenge to the appointment of the emergency arbitrator must be made within one business day of the communication by the AAA to the parties of the appointment of the emergency arbitrator and the circumstances disclosed.

O-3. Schedule

The emergency arbitrator shall as soon as possible, but in any event within two business days of appointment, establish a schedule for consideration of the application for emergency relief. Such schedule shall provide a reasonable opportunity to all parties to be heard, but may provide for proceeding by telephone conference or on written submissions as alternatives to a formal hearing.

O-4. Interim Award

If after consideration the emergency arbitrator is satisfied that the party seeking the emergency relief has shown that immediate and irreparable loss or damage will result in the absence of emergency relief, and that such party is entitled to such relief, the emergency arbitrator may enter an interim award granting the relief and stating the reasons therefore.

O-5. Constitution of the Panel

Any application to modify an interim award of emergency relief must be based on changed circumstances and may be made to the emergency arbitrator until the panel is constituted; thereafter such a request shall be addressed to the panel. The emergency arbitrator shall have no further power to act after the panel is constituted unless the parties agree that the emergency arbitrator is named as a member of the panel.

O-6. Security

Any interim award of emergency relief may be conditioned on provision by the party seeking such relief of appropriate security.

O-7. Special Master

A request for interim measures addressed by a party to a judicial authority shall not be deemed incompatible with the agreement to arbitrate or a waiver of the right to arbitrate. If the AAA is directed by a judicial authority to nominate a special master to consider and report on an application for emergency relief, the

AAA shall proceed as provided in Section O-1 of this article and the references to the emergency arbitrator shall be read to mean the special master, except that the special master shall issue a report rather than an interim award.

O-8. Costs

The costs associated with applications for emergency relief shall initially be apportioned by the emergency arbitrator or special master, subject to the power of the panel to determine finally the apportionment of such costs.

APPENDIX G

Revised January 2005

JAMS Comprehensive Arbitration Rules & Procedures

Comprehensive Arbitration Rules & Procedures

Table of Contents

Rule 1. Scope of Rules 2
Rule 2. Party-Agreed Procedures 2
Rule 3. Amendment of Rules 2
Rule 4. Conflict with Law 2
Rule 5. Commencing an Arbitration 2
Rule 6. Preliminary and Administrative Matters 3
Rule 7. Number of Arbitrators and Appointment of Chairperson 3
Rule 8. Service 3
Rule 9. Notice of Claims 4
Rule 10. Changes of Claims 4
Rule 11. Interpretation of Rules and Jurisdictional Challenges 4
Rule 12. Representation 5
Rule 13. Withdrawal from Arbitration 5
Rule 14. *Ex Parte* Communications 5
Rule 15. Arbitrator Selection and Replacement 5
Rule 16. Preliminary Conference 6
Rule 17. Exchange of Information 6
Rule 18. Summary Disposition of a Claim or Issue 7
Rule 19. Scheduling and Location of Hearing 7
Rule 20. Pre-Hearing Submissions 7
Rule 21. Securing Witnesses and Documents
         for the Arbitration Hearing 8
Rule 22. The Arbitration Hearing 8
Rule 23. Waiver of Hearing 9
Rule 24. The Award 9
Rule 25. Enforcement of the Award 10
Rule 26. Confidentiality and Privacy 10
Rule 27. Waiver 10
Rule 28. Settlement and Consent Award 10
Rule 29. Sanctions 11
Rule 30. Disqualification of the Arbitrator as a Witness
         or Party and Exclusion of Liability 11
Rule 31. Fees 11
Rule 32. Bracketed (or High-Low) Arbitration Option 11
Rule 33. Final Offer (or Baseball) Arbitration Option 12
Rule 34. Optional Arbitration Appeal Procedure 12

Rule 1. Scope of Rules

(a) The JAMS Comprehensive Arbitration Rules and Procedures ("Rules") govern binding Arbitrations of disputes or claims that are administered by JAMS and in which the Parties agree to use these Rules or, in the absence of such agreement, any disputed claim or counterclaim that exceeds $250,000, not including interest or attorneys' fees, unless other Rules are prescribed.

(b) The Parties shall be deemed to have made these Rules a part of their Arbitration agreement whenever they have provided for Arbitration by JAMS under its Comprehensive Rules or for Arbitration by JAMS without specifying any particular JAMS Rules and the disputes or claims meet the criteria of the first paragraph of this Rule.

(c) The authority and duties of JAMS are prescribed in the agreement of the Parties and in these Rules, and may be carried out through such of JAMS representatives as it may direct.

(d) JAMS may, in its discretion, assign the administration of an Arbitration to any of its offices.

(e) The term "Party" as used in these Rules includes Parties to the Arbitration and their counsel or representatives.

Rule 2. Party-Agreed Procedures

The Parties may agree on any procedures not specified herein or in lieu of these Rules that are consistent with the applicable law and JAMS policies (including, without limitation, Rules 15(i), 30 and 31). The Parties shall promptly notify JAMS of any such Party-agreed procedures and shall confirm such procedures in writing. The Party-agreed procedures shall be enforceable as if contained in these Rules.

Rule 3. Amendment of Rules

JAMS may amend these Rules without notice. The Rules in effect on the date of the commencement of an Arbitration (as defined in Rule 5) shall apply to that Arbitration, unless the Parties have specified another version of the Rules.

Rule 4. Conflict with Law

If any of these Rules, or a modification of these Rules agreed on by the Parties, is determined to be in conflict with a provision of applicable law, the provision of law will govern, and no other Rule will be affected.

Rule 5. Commencing an Arbitration

(a) The Arbitration is deemed commenced when JAMS confirms in a Commencement Letter one of the following:

(i) The submission to JAMS of a post-dispute Arbitration agreement fully executed by all Parties and that specifies JAMS administration or use of any JAMS Rules; or

(ii) The submission to JAMS of a pre-dispute written contractual provision requiring the Parties to arbitrate the dispute or claim and which specifies JAMS administration or use of any JAMS Rules or which the Parties agree shall be administered by JAMS; or

(iii) The oral agreement of all Parties to participate in an Arbitration administered by JAMS or conducted pursuant to any JAMS Rules, confirmed in writing by the Parties; or

(iv) A court order compelling Arbitration at JAMS.

(b) The Commencement Letter shall confirm that one of the above requirements for commencement has been met and that JAMS has received any payment required under the applicable fee schedule. The date of commencement of the Arbitration is the date of the Commencement Letter.

(c) If a Party who has signed a pre-dispute written contractual provision specifying these Rules or JAMS administration fails to agree to participate in the Arbitration process, JAMS shall confirm in writing that Party's failure to respond or participate and, pursuant to Rule

22, the Arbitrator shall schedule, and provide appropriate notice of a Hearing or other opportunity for the Party demanding the Arbitration to demonstrate its entitlement to relief.

(d) The definition of "commencement" in these Rules is not intended to be applicable to any legal requirement, such as the statute of limitations or a contractual limitations period, unless actually so specified by that requirement.

Rule 6. Preliminary and Administrative Matters

(a) JAMS may convene, or the Parties may request, administrative conferences to discuss any procedural matter relating to the administration of the Arbitration.

(b) At the request of a Party and in the absence of Party agreement, JAMS may make a determination regarding the location of the Hearing, subject to Arbitrator review. In determining the location of the Hearing such factors as the subject matter of the dispute, the convenience of the Parties and witnesses and the relative resources of the Parties shall be considered.

(c) If, at any time, any Party has failed to pay fees or expenses in full, JAMS may order the suspension or termination of the proceedings. JAMS may so inform the Parties in order that one of them may advance the required payment. An administrative suspension shall toll any other time limits contained in these Rules, applicable statutes or the Parties' agreement.

(d) JAMS does not maintain a duplicate file of documents filed in the Arbitration. If the Parties wish to have any documents returned to them, they must advise JAMS in writing within 30 days of the conclusion of the Arbitration. If special arrangements are required regarding file maintenance or document retention, they must be agreed to in writing and JAMS reserves the right to impose an additional fee for such special arrangements.

(e) If more than one arbitration is filed at JAMS, and if JAMS or the Arbitrator determines there are common issues of fact or law,

JAMS or the Arbitrator may consolidate the Arbitrations.

Rule 7. Number of Arbitrators and Appointment of Chairperson

(a) The Arbitration shall be conducted by one neutral Arbitrator unless all Parties agree otherwise. In these Rules, the term "Arbitrator" shall mean, as the context requires, the Arbitrator or the panel of Arbitrators in a tripartite Arbitration.

(b) In cases involving more than one Arbitrator the Parties shall agree on, or in the absence of agreement JAMS shall designate, the Chairperson of the Arbitration Panel. If the Parties and the Arbitrator agree, the Chairperson may, acting alone, decide discovery and procedural matters.

(c) Where the Parties have agreed that each Party is to name one Arbitrator, the Arbitrators so named shall be neutral and independent of the appointing Party unless the Parties have agreed that they shall be non-neutral.

Rule 8. Service

(a) Service under these Rules is effected by providing one copy of the document with original signatures to each Party and two copies in the case of a sole Arbitrator and four copies in the case of a tripartite panel to JAMS. Service may be made by hand-delivery, overnight delivery service or U.S. mail. Service by any of these means is considered effective upon the date of deposit of the document. Service by facsimile transmission is considered effective upon transmission, but only if followed within one week of delivery by service of an appropriate number of copies and originals by one of the other service methods.

(b) In computing any period of time prescribed or allowed by these Rules for a Party to do some act within a prescribed period after the service of a notice or other paper on the Party and the notice or paper is served on the Party only by U.S. Mail, three (3) calendar days shall be added to the prescribed period.

Rule 9. Notice of Claims

(a) If a matter has been submitted for Arbitration after litigation has been commenced in court regarding the same claim or dispute, the pleadings in the court case, including the complaint and answer (with affirmative defenses and counterclaims), may be filed with JAMS within fourteen (14) calendar days of the date of commencement, and if so filed, will be considered part of the record of the Arbitration. It will be assumed that the existence of such pleadings constitutes appropriate notice to the Parties of such claims, remedies sought, counterclaims and affirmative defenses. If necessary, such notice may be supplemented pursuant to Rule 9(b).

(b) If a matter has been submitted to JAMS prior to or in lieu of the filing of a case in court or prior to the filing of an answer, the Parties shall give each other notice of their respective claims, remedies sought, counterclaims and affirmative defenses (including jurisdictional challenges). Such notice may be served upon the other Parties and filed with JAMS, in the form of a demand for Arbitration, response or answer to demand for Arbitration, counterclaim or answer or response to counterclaim. Any pleading shall include a short statement of its factual basis.

(c) Notice of claims, remedies sought, counterclaims and affirmative defenses may be served simultaneously, in which case they should be filed with JAMS within fourteen (14) calendar days of the date of commencement of the Arbitration, or by such other date as the Parties may agree. The responding Parties may, however, in their sole discretion, wait to receive the notice of claim before serving any response, including counterclaims or affirmative defenses. In this case, the response, including counterclaims and affirmative defenses, should be served on the other Parties and filed with JAMS within fourteen (14) calendar days of service of the notice of claim. If the notice of claim has been served on the responding Parties prior to the date of commencement, the response, including counterclaims and affirmative defenses, shall be served within fourteen (14) calendar days from the date of commencement.

(d) Any Party that is a recipient of a counterclaim may reply to such counterclaim, including asserting jurisdictional challenges. In such case, the reply must be served on the other Parties and filed with JAMS within fourteen (14) calendar days of having received the notice of counterclaim. No claim, remedy, counterclaim or affirmative defense will be considered by the Arbitrator in the absence of prior notice to the other Parties, unless all Parties agree that such consideration is appropriate notwithstanding the lack of prior notice.

Rule 10. Changes of Claims

After the filing of a claim and before the Arbitrator is appointed, any Party may make a new or different claim. Such claim shall be made in writing, filed with JAMS and served on the other Parties. Any response to the new claim shall be made within fourteen (14) calendar days after service of such claim. After the Arbitrator is appointed, no new or different claim may be submitted except with the Arbitrator's approval. A Party may request a Hearing on this issue. Each Party has the right to respond to any new claim in accordance with Rule 9(c).

Rule 11. Interpretation of Rules and Jurisdictional Challenges

(a) Once appointed, the Arbitrator shall resolve disputes about the interpretation and applicability of these Rules and conduct of the Arbitration Hearing. The resolution of the issue by the Arbitrator shall be final.

(b) Whenever in these Rules a matter is to be determined by "JAMS" (such as in Rules 6, 11(d), 15(d), (f) or (g), 24(i) or 31(e)), such determination shall be made in accordance with JAMS administrative procedures.

(c) Jurisdictional and arbitrability disputes, including disputes over the existence, validity, interpretation or scope of the agreement under which Arbitration is sought, and who are proper Parties to the Arbitration, shall be submitted to and ruled on by the Arbitrator. The Arbitrator has the authority to determine jurisdiction and arbitrability issues as a preliminary matter.

(d) Disputes concerning the appointment of the Arbitrator and the venue of the Arbitration, if that determination is relevant to the selection of the Arbitrator, shall be resolved by JAMS.

(e)   The Arbitrator may upon a showing of good cause or sua sponte, when necessary to facilitate the Arbitration, extend any deadlines established in these Rules, provided that the time for rendering the Award may only be altered in accordance with Rules 22(i) or 24.

Rule 12. Representation
The Parties may be represented by counsel or any other person of the Party's choice. Each Party shall give prompt written notice to the Case Manager and the other Parties of the name, address and telephone and fax numbers of its representative. The representative of a Party may act on the Party's behalf in complying with these Rules.

Rule 13. Withdrawal from Arbitration
(a)   No Party may terminate or withdraw from an Arbitration after the issuance of the Commencement Letter (see Rule 5) except by written agreement of all Parties to the Arbitration.

(b)   A Party that asserts a claim or counterclaim may unilaterally withdraw that claim or counterclaim without prejudice by serving written notice on the other Parties and on the Arbitrator. However, the opposing Parties may, within fourteen (14) calendar days of service of notice of the withdrawal of the claim or counterclaim, request that the Arbitrator order that the withdrawal be with prejudice.

Rule 14. *Ex Parte* Communications
No Party may have any *ex parte* communication with a neutral Arbitrator regarding any issue related to the Arbitration. Any necessary *ex parte* communication with JAMS, whether before, during or after the Arbitration Hearing, shall be conducted through JAMS. The Parties may agree to permit *ex parte* communication between a Party and a non-neutral Arbitrator.

Rule 15. Arbitrator Selection and Replacement
(a)   Unless the Arbitrator has been previously selected by agreement of the Parties, JAMS may attempt to facilitate agreement among the Parties regarding selection of the Arbitrator.

(b)   If the Parties do not agree on an Arbitrator, JAMS shall send the Parties a list of at least five (5) Arbitrator candidates in the case of a sole Arbitrator and ten (10) Arbitrator candidates in the case of a tripartite panel. JAMS shall also provide each Party with a brief description of the background and experience of each Arbitrator candidate.

(c)   Within seven (7) calendar days of service upon the Parties of the list of names, each Party may strike two (2) names in the case of a sole Arbitrator and three (3) names in the case of a tripartite panel, and shall rank the remaining Arbitrator candidates in order of preference. The remaining Arbitrator candidate with the highest composite ranking shall be appointed the Arbitrator. JAMS may grant a reasonable extension of the time to strike and rank the Arbitrator candidates to any Party without the consent of the other Parties.

(d)   If this process does not yield an Arbitrator or a complete panel, JAMS shall designate the sole Arbitrator or as many members of the tripartite panel as are necessary to complete the panel.

(e)   If a Party fails to respond to the list of Arbitrator candidates within seven (7) calendar days of service by the Parties of the list, JAMS shall deem that Party to have accepted all of the Arbitrator candidates.

(f)   Entities whose interests are not adverse with respect to the issues in dispute shall be treated as a single Party for purposes of the Arbitrator selection process. JAMS shall determine whether the interests between entities are adverse for purposes of Arbitrator selection, considering such factors as whether the entities are represented by the same attorney and whether the entities are presenting joint or separate positions at the Arbitration.

(g)   If, for any reason, the Arbitrator who is selected is unable to fulfill the Arbitrator's duties, a successor Arbitrator shall be chosen in accordance with this Rule. If a member of a panel of Arbitrators becomes unable to fulfill his or her duties after the beginning of a Hearing but before the issuance of an Award, a new Arbitrator will be chosen in accordance with this Rule unless, in the case of a tripartite panel, the Parties agree to proceed with the remaining two Arbitrators. JAMS will make the final determination as to whether an Arbitrator is unable to fulfill his or her duties, and that decision shall be final.

(h) Any disclosures regarding the selected Arbitrator shall be made as required by law or within ten (10) calendar days from the date of appointment. The obligation of the Arbitrator to make all required disclosures continues throughout the Arbitration process.

(i) At any time during the Arbitration process, a Party may challenge the continued service of an Arbitrator for cause. The challenge must be based upon information that was not available to the Parties at the time the Arbitrator was selected. A challenge for cause must be in writing and exchanged with opposing Parties who may respond within seven (7) days of service of the challenge. JAMS shall make the final determination on such challenge. Such determination shall take into account the materiality of the facts and any prejudice to the parties. That decision will be final.

Rule 16. Preliminary Conference

At the request of any Party or at the direction of the Arbitrator, a Preliminary Conference shall be conducted with the Parties or their counsel or representatives. The Preliminary Conference may address any or all of the following subjects:

(a) The exchange of information in accordance with Rule 17 or otherwise;

(b) The schedule for discovery as permitted by the Rules, as agreed by the Parties or as required or authorized by applicable law;

(c) The pleadings of the Parties and any agreement to clarify or narrow the issues or structure the Arbitration Hearing;

(d) The scheduling of the Hearing and any prehearing exchanges of information, exhibits, motions or briefs;

(e) The attendance of witnesses as contemplated by Rule 21;

(f) The scheduling of any dispositive motion pursuant to Rule 18;

(g) The premarking of exhibits; preparation of joint exhibit lists and the resolution of the admissibility of exhibits;

(h) The form of the Award; and

(i) Such other matters as may be suggested by the Parties or the Arbitrator.

The Preliminary Conference may be conducted telephonically and may be resumed from time to time as warranted.

Rule 17. Exchange of Information

(a) The Parties shall cooperate in good faith in the voluntary, prompt and informal exchange of all non-privileged documents and other information relevant to the dispute or claim immediately after commencement of the Arbitration.

(b) The Parties shall complete an initial exchange of all relevant, non-privileged documents, including, without limitation, copies of all documents in their possession or control on which they rely in support of their positions, names of individuals whom they may call as witnesses at the Arbitration Hearing, and names of all experts who may be called to testify at the Arbitration Hearing, together with each expert's report that may be introduced at the Arbitration Hearing, within twenty-one (21) calendar days after all pleadings or notice of claims have been received. The Arbitrator may modify these obligations at the Preliminary Conference.

(c) Each Party may take one deposition of an opposing Party or of one individual under the control of the opposing Party. The Parties shall attempt to agree on the time, location and duration of the deposition, and if the Parties do not agree these issues shall be determined by the Arbitrator. The necessity of additional depositions shall be determined by the Arbitrator based upon the reasonable need for the requested information, the availability of other discovery options and the burdensomeness of the request on the opposing Parties and the witness.

(d) As they become aware of new documents or information, including experts who may be called upon to testify, all Parties continue to be obligated to provide relevant, non-privileged documents, to supplement their identification of witnesses and experts and to honor any informal agreements or understandings between the Parties regarding documents or information to be exchanged. Documents that have not been previously exchanged, or witnesses and experts not previously identified, may not be considered by the Arbitrator at the Hearing, unless agreed by the Parties or upon a showing of good cause.

(e) The Parties shall promptly notify JAMS when an unresolved dispute exists regarding discovery issues. JAMS shall arrange a conference with the Arbitrator, either by telephone or in person, and the Arbitrator shall decide the dispute. With the written consent of all Parties, and in accordance with an agreed written procedure, the Arbitrator may appoint a special master to assist in resolving a discovery dispute.

Rule 18. Summary Disposition of a Claim or Issue

(a) The Arbitrator shall decide a Motion for Summary Disposition of a particular claim or issue, either by agreement of all interested Parties or at the request of one Party, provided other interested Parties have reasonable notice to respond to the request.

(b) JAMS shall facilitate the Parties' agreement on a briefing schedule and record for the Motion. If no agreement is reached, the Arbitrator shall set the briefing and Hearing schedule and contents of the record.

Rule 19. Scheduling and Location of Hearing

(a) The Arbitrator, after consulting with the Parties that have appeared, shall determine the date, time and location of the Hearing. The Arbitrator and the Parties shall attempt to schedule consecutive Hearing days if more than one day is necessary.

(b) If a Party has failed to answer a claim or has otherwise failed to participate in the arbitration process, the Arbitrator may set the Hearing without consulting with that Party. The non-participating Party shall be served with a Notice of Hearing at least thirty (30) calendar days prior to the scheduled date unless the law of the relevant jurisdiction allows for or the Parties have agreed to shorter notice.

Rule 20. Pre-Hearing Submissions

(a) Subject to any schedule adopted in the Preliminary Conference (Rule 16), at least fourteen (14) calendar days before the Arbitration Hearing, the Parties shall exchange a list of the witnesses they intend to call, including any experts, a short description of the anticipated testimony of each such witness, an estimate of the length of the witness's direct testimony, and a list of exhibits. In addition, at least fourteen (14) calendar days before the Arbitration Hearing, the Parties shall identify all exhibits intended to be used at the Hearing and exchange copies of such exhibits to the extent that any such exhibit has not been previously exchanged. The Parties should pre-mark exhibits and shall attempt themselves to resolve any disputes regarding the admissibility of exhibits prior to the Hearing. The list of witnesses, with the description and estimate of the length of their testimony and the copies of all exhibits that the Parties intend to use at the Hearing, in pre-marked form, should also be provided to JAMS for transmission to the Arbitrator, whether or not the Parties have stipulated to the admissibility of all such exhibits.

(b) The Arbitrator may require that each Party submit concise written statements of position, including summaries of the facts and evidence a Party intends to present, discussion of the applicable law and the basis for the requested Award or denial of relief sought. The statements, which may be in the form of a letter, shall be filed with JAMS and served upon the other Parties, at least seven (7) calendar days before the Hearing date. Rebuttal statements or other pre-Hearing written submissions may be permitted or required at the discretion of the Arbitrator.

7

Revised 2005

Rule 21. Securing Witnesses and Documents for the Arbitration Hearing

At the written request of another Party, all other Parties shall produce for the Arbitration Hearing all specified witnesses in their employ or under their control without need of subpoena. The Arbitrator may issue subpoenas for the attendance of witnesses or the production of documents. Pre-issued subpoenas may be used in jurisdictions which permit them. In the event a Party or a subpoenaed person objects to the production of a witness or other evidence, the Party may file an objection with the Arbitrator, who will promptly rule on the objection, weighing both the burden on the producing Party and the need of the proponent for the witness or other evidence.

Rule 22. The Arbitration Hearing

(a)   The Arbitrator will ordinarily conduct the Arbitration Hearing in the manner set forth in these Rules. The Arbitrator may vary these procedures if it is determined reasonable and appropriate to do so.

(b)   The Arbitrator shall determine the order of proof, which will generally be similar to that of a court trial.

(c)   The Arbitrator shall require witnesses to testify under oath if requested by any Party, or otherwise in the discretion of the Arbitrator.

(d)   Strict conformity to the rules of evidence is not required, except that the Arbitrator shall apply applicable law relating to privileges and work product. The Arbitrator shall consider evidence that he or she finds relevant and material to the dispute, giving the evidence such weight as is appropriate. The Arbitrator may be guided in that determination by principles contained in the Federal Rules of Evidence or any other applicable rules of evidence. The Arbitrator may limit testimony to exclude evidence that would be immaterial or unduly repetitive, provided that all Parties are afforded the opportunity to present material and relevant evidence.

(e)   The Arbitrator shall receive and consider relevant deposition testimony recorded by transcript or videotape, provided that the other Parties have had the opportunity to attend and cross-examine. The Arbitrator may in his or her discretion consider witness affidavits or other recorded testimony even if the other Parties have not had the opportunity to cross-examine, but will give that evidence only such weight as the Arbitrator deems appropriate.

(f)   The Parties will not offer as evidence, and the Arbitrator shall neither admit into the record nor consider, prior settlement offers by the Parties or statements or recommendations made by a mediator or other person in connection with efforts to resolve the dispute being arbitrated, except to the extent that applicable law permits the admission of such evidence.

(g)   The Hearing or any portion thereof may be conducted telephonically with the agreement of the Parties or in the discretion of the Arbitrator.

(h)   When the Arbitrator determines that all relevant and material evidence and arguments have been presented, the Arbitrator shall declare the Hearing closed. The Arbitrator may defer the closing of the Hearing until a date agreed upon by the Arbitrator and the Parties, to permit the Parties to submit post-Hearing briefs, which may be in the form of a letter, and/or to make closing arguments. If post-Hearing briefs are to be submitted, or closing arguments are to be made, the Hearing shall be deemed closed upon receipt by the Arbitrator of such briefs or at the conclusion of such closing arguments.

(i)   At any time before the Award is rendered, the Arbitrator may, on his or her own initiative or on application of a Party for good cause shown, re-open the Hearing. If the Hearing is re-opened and the re-opening prevents the rendering of the Award within the time limits specified by these Rules, the time limits will be extended for an appropriate period of time.

(j)   The Arbitrator may proceed with the Hearing in the absence of a Party who, after receiving notice of the Hearing pursuant to Rule 19, fails to attend. The Arbitrator may not render an Award solely on the basis of the default or absence of the Party, but shall require any Party seeking relief to submit such evidence as the Arbitrator may require for the rendering of an Award. If the Arbitrator reasonably believes that a Party will not attend the Hearing, the Arbitrator may schedule the Hearing as a telephonic Hearing and may receive the evidence necessary to render an Award by affidavit. The notice of Hearing shall specify if it will be in person or telephonic.

(k) (i) Any Party may arrange for a stenographic or other record to be made of the Hearing and shall inform the other Parties in advance of the Hearing. The requesting Party shall bear the cost of such stenographic record. If all other Parties agree to share the cost of the stenographic record, it shall be made available to the Arbitrator and may be used in the proceeding.

(ii) If there is no agreement to share the cost of the stenographic record, it may not be provided to the Arbitrator and may not be used in the proceeding unless the Party arranging for the stenographic record either agrees to provide access to the stenographic record at no charge or on terms that are acceptable to the Parties and the reporting service.

(iii) If the Parties agree to an Optional Arbitration Appeal Procedure (see Rule 34), they shall ensure that a stenographic or other record is made of the Hearing and shall share the cost of that record.

(iv) The Parties may agree that the cost of the stenographic record shall or shall not be allocated by the Arbitrator in the Award.

Rule 23. Waiver of Hearing
The Parties may agree to waive the oral Hearing and submit the dispute to the Arbitrator for an Award based on written submissions and other evidence as the Parties may agree.

Rule 24. The Award
(a) Absent good cause for an extension, and except as provided in Rule 22(i) or 31(d), the Arbitrator shall render the Award within thirty (30) calendar days after the date of the closing of the Hearing (as defined in Rule 22(h)) or, if a Hearing has been waived, within thirty (30) calendar days after the receipt by the Arbitrator of all materials specified by the Parties. The Arbitrator shall provide the Award to JAMS for issuance in accordance with this rule.

(b) Where a panel of Arbitrators has heard the dispute, the decision and Award of a majority of the panel shall constitute the Arbitration Award and shall be binding on the Parties.

(c) Unless the Parties specify a different standard, in determining the Award the Arbitrator shall be guided by principles of law and equity as applied to the facts found at the Arbitration Hearing. The Arbitrator may grant any remedy or relief that is just and equitable and within the scope of the Parties' agreement, including but not limited to specific performance of a contract.

(d) In addition to the final Award, the Arbitrator may make other decisions, including interim or partial rulings, orders and Awards.

(e) Interim Measures. The Arbitrator may take whatever interim measures are deemed necessary, including injunctive relief and measures for the protection or conservation of property and disposition of disposable goods. Such interim measures may take the form of an interim Award, and the Arbitrator may require security for the costs of such measures. Any recourse by a Party to a court for interim or provisional relief shall not be deemed incompatible with the agreement to arbitrate or a waiver of the right to arbitrate.

(f) In any Award, order or ruling, the Arbitrator may also assess Arbitration fees, Arbitrator compensation and expenses if provided by agreement of the Parties, allowed by applicable law or pursuant to Rule 31(c), in favor of any Party.

(g) The Award will consist of a written statement signed by the Arbitrator regarding the disposition of each claim and the relief, if any, as to each claim. Unless all Parties agree otherwise, the Award shall also contain a concise written statement of the reasons for the Award.

(h) After the Award has been rendered, and provided the Parties have complied with Rule 31, the Award shall be issued by serving copies on the Parties. Service may be made by U.S. Mail. It need not be sent certified or registered.

(i) Within seven (7) calendar days after issuance of the Award, any Party may serve upon the other Parties and on JAMS a request that the Arbitrator correct any computational, typographical or other similar error in an Award (including the reallocation of fees pursuant to Rule 31(c)), or the Arbitrator may sua sponte propose to correct such errors in an Award. A Party opposing such correction shall have seven (7) calendar days in which to file any objection. The Arbitrator may make any necessary and appropriate correction to the Award within fourteen (14) calendar days of receiving a request or seven (7) calendar days after the Arbitrator's proposal to do so. The corrected Award shall be served upon the Parties in the same manner as the Award.

(j) The Award is considered final, for purposes of either an Optional Arbitration Appeal Procedure pursuant to Rule 34 or a judicial proceeding to enforce, modify or vacate the Award pursuant to Rule 25, fourteen (14) calendar days after service is deemed effective if no request for a correction is made, or as of the effective date of service of a corrected Award.

Rule 25. Enforcement of the Award

Proceedings to enforce, confirm, modify or vacate an Award will be controlled by and conducted in conformity with the Federal Arbitration Act, 9 U.S.C. Sec 1 et seq. or applicable state law.

Rule 26. Confidentiality and Privacy

(a) JAMS and the Arbitrator shall maintain the confidential nature of the Arbitration proceeding and the Award, including the Hearing, except as necessary in connection with a judicial challenge to or enforcement of an Award, or unless otherwise required by law or judicial decision.

(b) The Arbitrator may issue orders to protect the confidentiality of proprietary information, trade secrets or other sensitive information.

(c) Subject to the discretion of the Arbitrator or agreement of the Parties, any person having a direct interest in the Arbitration may attend the Arbitration Hearing. The Arbitrator may exclude any non-Party from any part of a Hearing.

Rule 27. Waiver

(a) If a Party becomes aware of a violation of or failure to comply with these Rules and fails promptly to object in writing, the objection will be deemed waived, unless the Arbitrator determines that waiver will cause substantial injustice or hardship.

(b) If any Party becomes aware of information that could be the basis of a challenge for cause to the continued service of the Arbitrator, such challenge must be made promptly, in writing, to the Arbitrator or JAMS. Failure to do so shall constitute a waiver of any objection to continued service by the Arbitrator.

Rule 28. Settlement and Consent Award

(a) The Parties may agree, at any stage of the Arbitration process, to submit the case to JAMS for mediation. The JAMS mediator assigned to the case may not be the Arbitrator or a member of the Appeal Panel, unless the Parties so agree pursuant to Rule 28(b).

(b) The Parties may agree to seek the assistance of the Arbitrator in reaching settlement. By their written agreement to submit the matter to the Arbitrator for settlement assistance, the Parties will be deemed to have agreed that the assistance of the Arbitrator in such settlement efforts will not disqualify the Arbitrator from continuing to serve as Arbitrator if settlement is not reached; nor shall such assistance be argued to a reviewing court as the basis for vacating or modifying an Award.

(c) If, at any stage of the Arbitration process, all Parties agree upon a settlement of the issues in dispute and request the Arbitrator to embody the agreement in a Consent Award, the Arbitrator shall comply with such request unless the Arbitrator believes the terms of the agreement are illegal or undermine the integrity of the Arbitration process. If the Arbitrator is concerned about the possible consequences of the proposed Consent Award, he or she shall inform the Parties of that concern and may request additional specific information from the Parties regarding the proposed Consent Award. The Arbitrator may refuse to enter the proposed Consent Award and may withdraw from the case.

Rule 29. Sanctions

The Arbitrator may order appropriate sanctions for failure of a Party to comply with its obligations under any of these Rules. These sanctions may include, but are not limited to, assessment of costs, exclusion of certain evidence, or in extreme cases ruling on an issue submitted to Arbitration adversely to the Party who has failed to comply.

Rule 30. Disqualification of the Arbitrator as a Witness or Party and Exclusion of Liability

(a) The Parties may not call the Arbitrator, the Case Manager or any other JAMS employee or agent as a witness or as an expert in any pending or subsequent litigation or other proceeding involving the Parties and relating to the dispute that is the subject of the Arbitration. The Arbitrator, Case Manager and other JAMS employees and agents are also incompetent to testify as witnesses or experts in any such proceeding.

(b) The Parties shall defend and/or pay the cost (including any attorneys' fees) of defending the Arbitrator, Case Manager and/or JAMS from any subpoenas from outside Parties arising from the Arbitration.

(c) The Parties agree that neither the Arbitrator, Case Manager nor JAMS is a necessary Party in any litigation or other proceeding relating to the Arbitration or the subject matter of the Arbitration, and neither the Arbitrator, Case Manager nor JAMS, including its employees or agents, shall be liable to any Party for any act or omission in connection with any Arbitration conducted under these Rules, including but not limited to any disqualification of or recusal by the Arbitrator.

Rule 31. Fees

(a) Each Party shall pay its pro-rata share of JAMS fees and expenses as set forth in the JAMS fee schedule in effect at the time of the commencement of the Arbitration, unless the Parties agree on a different allocation of fees and expenses. JAMS agreement to render services is jointly with the Party and the attorney or other representative of the Party in the Arbitration. The non-payment of fees may result in an administrative suspension of the case in accordance with Rule 6(c).

(b) JAMS requires that the Parties deposit the fees and expenses for the Arbitration prior to the Hearing and may preclude a Party that has failed to deposit its pro-rata or agreed-upon share of the fees and expenses from offering evidence of any affirmative claim at the Hearing. JAMS may waive the deposit requirement upon a showing of good cause.

(c) The Parties are jointly and severally liable for the payment of the fees and expenses of JAMS. In the event that one Party has paid more than its share of the fees, the Arbitrator may award against any other Party any costs or fees that such Party owes with respect to the Arbitration.

(d) Entities whose interests are not adverse with respect to the issues in dispute shall be treated as a single Party for purposes of JAMS assessment of fees. JAMS shall determine whether the interests between entities are adverse for purpose of fees, considering such factors as whether the entities are represented by the same attorney and whether the entities are presenting joint or separate positions at the Arbitration.

Rule 32. Bracketed (or High-Low) Arbitration Option

(a) At any time before the issuance of the Arbitration Award, the Parties may agree, in writing, on minimum and maximum amounts of damages that may be awarded on each claim or on all claims in the aggregate. The Parties shall promptly notify JAMS and provide to JAMS a copy of their written agreement setting forth the agreed-upon maximum and minimum amounts.

(b)   JAMS shall not inform the Arbitrator of the agreement to proceed with this option or of the agreed-upon minimum and maximum levels without the consent of the Parties.

(c)   The Arbitrator shall render the Award in accordance with Rule 24.

(d)   In the event that the Award of the Arbitrator is in between the agreed-upon minimum and maximum amounts, the Award shall become final as is. In the event that the Award is below the agreed-upon minimum amount, the final Award issued shall be corrected to reflect the agreed-upon minimum amount. In the event that the Award is above the agreed-upon maximum amount, the final Award issued shall be corrected to reflect the agreed-upon maximum amount.

Rule 33. Final Offer (or Baseball) Arbitration Option

(a)   Upon agreement of the Parties to use the option set forth in this Rule, at least seven (7) calendar days before the Arbitration Hearing, the Parties shall exchange and provide to JAMS written proposals for the amount of money damages they would offer or demand, as applicable, and that they believe to be appropriate based on the standard set forth in Rule 24 (c). JAMS shall promptly provide a copy of the Parties' proposals to the Arbitrator, unless the Parties agree that they should not be provided to the Arbitrator. At any time prior to the close of the Arbitration Hearing, the Parties may exchange revised written proposals or demands, which shall supersede all prior proposals. The revised written proposals shall be provided to JAMS, which shall promptly provide them to the Arbitrator, unless the Parties agree otherwise.

(b)   If the Arbitrator has been informed of the written proposals, in rendering the Award the Arbitrator shall choose between the Parties' last proposals, selecting the proposal that the Arbitrator finds most reasonable and appropriate in light of the standard set forth in Rule 24(c). This provision modifies Rule 24(g) in that no written statement of reasons shall accompany the Award.

(c)   If the Arbitrator has not been informed of the written proposals, the Arbitrator shall render the Award as if pursuant to Rule 24, except that the Award shall thereafter be corrected to conform to the closest of the last proposals, and the closest of the last proposals will become the Award.

(d)   Other than as provided herein, the provisions of Rule 24 shall be applicable.

Rule 34. Optional Arbitration Appeal Procedure

At any time before the Award becomes final pursuant to Rule 24, the Parties may agree to the JAMS Optional Arbitration Appeal Procedure. All Parties must agree in writing for such procedure to be effective. Once a Party has agreed to the Optional Arbitration Appeal Procedure, it cannot unilaterally withdraw from it, unless it withdraws, pursuant to Rule 13, from the Arbitration.

APPENDIX H

AMERICAN ARBITRATION ASSOCIATION (AAA) International Arbitration Rules

As Amended and Effective July 1, 2003. Reproduced with the permission of the American Arbitration Association

Article 1

1. Where parties have agreed in writing to arbitrate disputes under these International Arbitration Rules or have provided for arbitration of an international dispute by the International Centre for Dispute Resolution or the American Arbitration Association without designating particular rules, the arbitration shall take place in accordance with these rules, as in effect at the date of commencement of the arbitration, subject to whatever modifications the parties may adopt in writing.

2. These rules govern the arbitration, except that, where any such rule is in conflict with any provision of the law applicable to the arbitration from which the parties cannot derogate, that provision shall prevail.

3. These rules specify the duties and responsibilities of the administrator, the International Centre for Dispute Resolution, a division of the American Arbitration Association. The administrator may provide services through its Centre, located in New York, or through the facilities of arbitral institutions with which it has agreements of cooperation.

R-1. Commencing the Arbitration—Notice of Arbitration and Statement of Claim

Article 2

1. The party initiating arbitration ("claimant") shall give written notice of arbitration to the administrator and at the same time to the party against whom a claim is being made ("respondent").

2. Arbitral proceedings shall be deemed to commence on the date on which the administrator receives the notice of arbitration.

3. The notice of arbitration shall contain a statement of claim including the following:

(a) a demand that the dispute be referred to arbitration;

(b) the names, addresses and telephone numbers of the parties;

(c) a reference to the arbitration clause or agreement that is invoked;

(d) a reference to any contract out of or in relation to which the dispute arises;

(e) a description of the claim and an indication of the facts supporting it;

(f) the relief or remedy sought and the amount claimed; and

(g) may include proposals as to the means of designating and the number of arbitrators, the place of arbitration and the language(s) of the arbitration.

4. Upon receipt of the notice of arbitration, the administrator shall communicate with all parties with respect to the arbitration and shall acknowledge the commencement of the arbitration.

Statement of Defense and Counterclaim

Article 3

1. Within 30 days after the commencement of the arbitration, a respondent shall submit a written statement of defense, responding to the issues raised in the notice of arbitration, to the claimant and any other parties, and to the administrator.

2. At the time a respondent submits its statement of defense, a respondent may make counterclaims or assert setoffs as to any claim covered by the agreement to arbitrate, as to which the claimant shall within 30 days submit a written statement of defense to the respondent and any other parties and to the administrator.

3. A respondent shall respond to the administrator, the claimant and other parties within 30 days after the commencement of the arbitration as to any proposals the claimant may have made as to the number of arbitrators, the place of the arbitration or the language(s) of the arbitration, except to the extent that the parties have previously agreed as to these matters.

4. The arbitral tribunal, or the administrator if the arbitral tribunal has not yet been formed, may extend any of the time limits established in this article if it considers such an extension justified.

Amendments to Claims

Article 4

During the arbitral proceedings, any party may amend or supplement its claim, counterclaim or defense, unless the tribunal considers it inappropriate to allow such amendment or supplement because of the party's delay in making it, prejudice to the other parties or any other circumstances. A party may not amend or supplement a claim or counterclaim if the amendment or supplement would fall outside the scope of the agreement to arbitrate.

R-2. The Tribunal —Number of Arbitrators

Article 5

If the parties have not agreed on the number of arbitrators, one arbitrator shall be appointed unless the administrator determines in its discretion that three arbitrators are appropriate because of the large size, complexity or other circumstances of the case.

Appointment of Arbitrators

Article 6

1. The parties may mutually agree upon any procedure for appointing arbitrators and shall inform the administrator as to such procedure.

2. The parties may mutually designate arbitrators, with or without the assistance of the administrator. When such designations are made, the parties shall notify the administrator so that notice of the appointment can be communicated to the arbitrators, together with a copy of these rules.

3. If within 45 days after the commencement of the arbitration, all of the parties have not mutually agreed on a procedure for appointing the arbitrator(s) or have not mutually agreed on the designation of the arbitrator(s), the administrator shall, at the written request of any party, appoint the arbitrator(s) and designate the presiding arbitrator. If all of the parties have mutually agreed upon a procedure for appointing the arbitrator(s), but all appointments have not been made within the time limits provided in that procedure, the administrator shall, at the written request of any party, perform all functions provided for in that procedure that remain to be performed.

4. In making such appointments, the administrator, after inviting consultation with the parties, shall endeavor to select suitable arbitrators. At the request of any party or on its own initiative, the administrator may appoint nationals of a country other than that of any of the parties.

5. Unless the parties have agreed otherwise no later than 45 days after the commencement of the arbitration, if the notice of arbitration names two or more claimants or two or more respondents, the administrator shall appoint all the arbitrators.

Impartiality and Independence of Arbitrators

Article 7

1. Arbitrators acting under these rules shall be impartial and independent. Prior to accepting appointment, a prospective arbitrator shall disclose to the administrator any circumstance likely to give rise to justifiable doubts as to the arbitrator's impartiality or independence. If, at any stage during the arbitration,

new circumstances arise that may give rise to such doubts, an arbitrator shall promptly disclose such circumstances to the parties and to the administrator. Upon receipt of such information from an arbitrator or a party, the administrator shall communicate it to the other parties and to the tribunal.

2. No party or anyone acting on its behalf shall have any ex parte communication relating to the case with any arbitrator, or with any candidate for appointment as party-appointed arbitrator except to advise the candidate of the general nature of the controversy and of the anticipated proceedings and to discuss the candidate's qualifications, availability or independence in relation to the parties, or to discuss the suitability of candidates for selection as a third arbitrator where the parties or party designated arbitrators are to participate in that selection. No party or anyone acting on its behalf shall have any ex parte communication relating to the case with any candidate for presiding arbitrator.

Challenge of Arbitrators
Article 8

1. A party may challenge any arbitrator whenever circumstances exist that give rise to justifiable doubts as to the arbitrator's impartiality or independence. A party wishing to challenge an arbitrator shall send notice of the challenge to the administrator within 15 days after being notified of the appointment of the arbitrator or within 15 days after the circumstances giving rise to the challenge become known to that party.

2. The challenge shall state in writing the reasons for the challenge.

3. Upon receipt of such a challenge, the administrator shall notify the other parties of the challenge. When an arbitrator has been challenged by one party, the other party or parties may agree to the acceptance of the challenge and, if there is agreement, the arbitrator shall withdraw. The challenged arbitrator may also withdraw from office in the absence of such agreement. In neither case does withdrawal imply acceptance of the validity of the grounds for the challenge.

Article 9

If the other party or parties do not agree to the challenge or the challenged arbitrator does not withdraw, the administrator in its sole discretion shall make the decision on the challenge.

Replacement of an Arbitrator
Article 10

If an arbitrator withdraws after a challenge, or the administrator sustains the challenge, or the administrator determines that there are sufficient reasons to accept the resignation of an arbitrator, or an arbitrator dies, a substitute arbitrator shall be appointed pursuant to the provisions of Article 6, unless the parties otherwise agree.

Article 11

1. If an arbitrator on a three-person tribunal fails to participate in the arbitration for reasons other than those identified in Article 10, the two other arbitrators shall have the power in their sole discretion to continue the arbitration and to make any decision, ruling or award, notwithstanding the failure of the third arbitrator to participate. In determining whether to continue the arbitration or to render any decision, ruling or award without the participation of an arbitrator, the two other arbitrators shall take into account the stage of the arbitration, the reason, if any, expressed by the third arbitrator for such nonparticipation, and such other matters as they consider appropriate in the circumstances of the case. In the event that the two other arbitrators determine not to continue the arbitration without the participation of the third arbitrator, the administrator on proof satisfactory to it shall declare the office vacant, and a substitute arbitrator shall be appointed pursuant to the provisions of Article 6, unless the parties otherwise agree.

2. If a substitute arbitrator is appointed under either Article 10 or Article 11, the tribunal shall determine at its sole discretion whether all or part of any prior hearings shall be repeated.

R-3. General Conditions
Representation

Article 12

Any party may be represented in the arbitration. The names, addresses and telephone numbers of representatives shall be communicated in writing to the other parties and to the administrator. Once the tribunal has been established, the parties or their representatives may communicate in writing directly with the tribunal.

Place of Arbitration

Article 13

1. If the parties disagree as to the place of arbitration, the administrator may initially determine the place of arbitration, subject to the power of the tribunal to determine finally the place of arbitration within 60 days after its constitution. All such determinations shall be made having regard for the contentions of the parties and the circumstances of the arbitration.

2. The tribunal may hold conferences or hear witnesses or inspect property or documents at any place it deems appropriate. The parties shall be given sufficient written notice to enable them to be present at any such proceedings.

Language

Article 14

If the parties have not agreed otherwise, the language(s) of the arbitration shall be that of the documents containing the arbitration agreement, subject to the power of the tribunal to determine otherwise based upon the contentions of the parties and the circumstances of the arbitration. The tribunal may order that any documents delivered in another language shall be accompanied by a translation into the language(s) of the arbitration.

Pleas as to Jurisdiction

Article 15

1. The tribunal shall have the power to rule on its own jurisdiction, including any objections with respect to the existence, scope or validity of the arbitration agreement.

2. The tribunal shall have the power to determine the existence or validity of a contract of which an arbitration clause forms a part. Such an arbitration clause shall be treated as an agreement independent of the other terms of the contract. A decision by the tribunal that the contract is null and void shall not for that reason alone render invalid the arbitration clause.

3. A party must object to the jurisdiction of the tribunal or to the arbitrability of a claim or counterclaim no later than the filing of the statement of defense, as provided in Article 3, to the claim or counterclaim that gives rise to the objection. The tribunal may rule on such objections as a preliminary matter or as part of the final award.

Conduct of the Arbitration

Article 16

1. Subject to these rules, the tribunal may conduct the arbitration in whatever manner it considers appropriate, provided that the parties are treated with equality and that each party has the right to be heard and is given a fair opportunity to present its case.

2. The tribunal, exercising its discretion, shall conduct the proceedings with a view to expediting the resolution of the dispute. It may conduct a preparatory conference with the parties for the purpose of organizing, scheduling and agreeing to procedures to expedite the subsequent proceedings.

3. The tribunal may in its discretion direct the order of proof, bifurcate proceedings, exclude cumulative or irrelevant testimony or other evidence, and direct the parties to focus their presentations on issues the decision of which could dispose of all or part of the case.

4. Documents or information supplied to the tribunal by one party shall at the same time be communicated by that party to the other party or parties.

Further Written Statements

Article 17

1. The tribunal may decide whether the parties shall present any written statements in addition to statements of claims and counterclaims and statements of defense, and it shall fix the periods of time for submitting any such statements.

2. The periods of time fixed by the tribunal for the communication of such written statements should not exceed 45 days. However, the tribunal may extend such time limits if it considers such an extension justified.

Notices

Article 18

1. Unless otherwise agreed by the parties or ordered by the tribunal, all notices, statements and written communications may be served on a party by air mail, air courier, facsimile transmission, telex, telegram or other written forms of electronic communication addressed to the party or its representative at its last known address or by personal service.

2. For the purpose of calculating a period of time under these rules, such period shall begin to run on the day following the day when a notice, statement or written communication is received. If the last day of such period is an official holiday at the place received, the period is extended until the first business day which follows. Official holidays occurring during the running of the period of time are included in calculating the period.

Evidence

Article 19

1. Each party shall have the burden of proving the facts relied on to support its claim or defense.

2. The tribunal may order a party to deliver to the tribunal and to the other parties a summary of the documents and other evidence which that party intends to present in support of its claim, counterclaim or defense.

3. At any time during the proceedings, the tribunal may order parties to produce other documents, exhibits or other evidence it deems necessary or appropriate.

Hearings

Article 20

1. The tribunal shall give the parties at least 30 days advance notice of the date, time and place of the initial oral hearing. The tribunal shall give reasonable notice of subsequent hearings.

2. At least 15 days before the hearings, each party shall give the tribunal and the other parties the names and addresses of any witnesses it intends to present, the subject of their testimony and the languages in which such witnesses will give their testimony.

3. At the request of the tribunal or pursuant to mutual agreement of the parties, the administrator shall make arrangements for the interpretation of oral testimony or for a record of the hearing.

4. Hearings are private unless the parties agree otherwise or the law provides to the contrary. The tribunal may require any witness or witnesses to retire during the testimony of other witnesses. The tribunal may determine the manner in which witnesses are examined.

5. Evidence of witnesses may also be presented in the form of written statements signed by them.

6. The tribunal shall determine the admissibility, relevance, materiality and weight of the evidence offered by any party. The tribunal shall take into account applicable principles of legal privilege, such as those involving the confidentiality of communications between a lawyer and client.

Interim Measures of Protection

Article 21

1. At the request of any party, the tribunal may take whatever interim measures it deems necessary, including injunctive relief and measures for the protection or conservation of property.

2. Such interim measures may take the form of an interim award, and the tribunal may require security for the costs of such measures.

3. A request for interim measures addressed by a party to a judicial authority shall not be deemed incompatible with the agreement to arbitrate or a waiver of the right to arbitrate.

4. The tribunal may in its discretion apportion costs associated with applications for interim relief in any interim award or in the final award.

Experts

Article 22

1. The tribunal may appoint one or more independent experts to report to it, in writing, on specific issues designated by the tribunal and communicated to the parties.

2. The parties shall provide such an expert with any relevant information or produce for inspection any relevant documents or goods that the expert may require. Any dispute between a party and the expert as to the relevance of the requested information or goods shall be referred to the tribunal for decision.

3. Upon receipt of an expert's report, the tribunal shall send a copy of the report to all parties and shall give the parties an opportunity to express, in writing, their opinion on the report. A party may examine any document on which the expert has relied in such a report.

4. At the request of any party, the tribunal shall give the parties an opportunity to question the expert at a hearing. At this hearing, parties may present expert witnesses to testify on the points at issue.

Default

Article 23

1. If a party fails to file a statement of defense within the time established by the tribunal without showing sufficient cause for such failure, as determined by the tribunal, the tribunal may proceed with the arbitration.

2. If a party, duly notified under these rules, fails to appear at a hearing without showing sufficient cause for such failure, as determined by the tribunal, the tribunal may proceed with the arbitration.

3. If a party, duly invited to produce evidence or take any other steps in the proceedings, fails to do so within the time established by the tribunal without showing sufficient cause for such failure, as determined by the tribunal, the tribunal may make the award on the evidence before it.

Closure of Hearing

Article 24

1. After asking the parties if they have any further testimony or evidentiary submissions and upon receiving negative replies or if satisfied that the record is complete, the tribunal may declare the hearings closed.

2. The tribunal in its discretion, on its own motion or upon application of a party, may reopen the hearings at any time before the award is made.

Waiver of Rules

Article 25

A party who knows that any provision of the rules or requirement under the rules has not been complied with, but proceeds with the arbitration without promptly stating an objection in writing thereto, shall be deemed to have waived the right to object.

Awards, Decisions, and Rulings

Article 26

1. When there is more than one arbitrator, any award, decision or ruling of the arbitral tribunal shall be made by a majority of the arbitrators. If any arbitrator fails to sign the award, it shall be accompanied by a statement of the reason for the absence of such signature.

2. When the parties or the tribunal so authorize, the presiding arbitrator may make decisions or rulings on questions of procedure, subject to revision by the tribunal.

Form and Effect of the Award

Article 27

1. Awards shall be made in writing, promptly by the tribunal, and shall be final and binding on the parties. The parties undertake to carry out any such award without delay.

2. The tribunal shall state the reasons upon which the award is based, unless the parties have agreed that no reasons need be given.

3. The award shall contain the date and the place where the award was made, which shall be the place designated pursuant to Article 13.

4. An award may be made public only with the consent of all parties or as required by law.

5. Copies of the award shall be communicated to the parties by the administrator.

6. If the arbitration law of the country where the award is made requires the award to be filed or registered, the tribunal shall comply with such requirement.

7. In addition to making a final award, the tribunal may make interim, interlocutory or partial orders and awards.

8. Unless otherwise agreed by the parties, the administrator may publish or otherwise make publicly available selected awards, decisions and rulings that have been edited to conceal the names of the parties and other identifying details or that have been made publicly available in the course of enforcement or otherwise.

Applicable Laws and Remedies

Article 28

1. The tribunal shall apply the substantive law(s) or rules of law designated by the parties as applicable to the dispute. Failing such a designation by the parties, the tribunal shall apply such law(s) or rules of law as it determines to be appropriate.

2. In arbitrations involving the application of contracts, the tribunal shall decide in accordance with the terms of the contract and shall take into account usages of the trade applicable to the contract.

3. The tribunal shall not decide as amiable compositeur or ex aequo et bono unless the parties have expressly authorized it to do so.

4. A monetary award shall be in the currency or currencies of the contract unless the tribunal considers another currency more appropriate, and the tribunal may award such pre-award and post-award interest, simple or compound, as it considers appropriate, taking into consideration the contract and applicable law.

5. Unless the parties agree otherwise, the parties expressly waive and forego any right to punitive, exemplary or similar damages unless a statute requires that compensatory damages be increased in a specified manner. This provision shall not apply to any award of arbitration costs to a party to compensate for dilatory or bad faith conduct in the arbitration.

Settlement or Other Reasons for Termination

Article 29

1. If the parties settle the dispute before an award is made, the tribunal shall terminate the arbitration and, if requested by all parties, may record the settlement in the form of an award on agreed terms. The tribunal is not obliged to give reasons for such an award.

2. If the continuation of the proceedings becomes unnecessary or impossible for any other reason, the tribunal shall inform the parties of its intention to terminate the proceedings. The tribunal shall thereafter issue an order terminating the arbitration, unless a party raises justifiable grounds for objection.

Interpretation or Correction of the Award

Article 30

1. Within 30 days after the receipt of an award, any party, with notice to the other parties, may request the tribunal to interpret the award or correct any clerical, typographical or computation errors or make an additional award as to claims presented but omitted from the award.

2. If the tribunal considers such a request justified, after considering the contentions of the parties, it shall comply with such a request within 30 days after the request.

Costs

Article 31

The tribunal shall fix the costs of arbitration in its award. The tribunal may apportion such costs among the parties if it determines that such apportionment is reasonable, taking into account the circumstances of the case.

Such costs may include:

(a) the fees and expenses of the arbitrators;

(b) the costs of assistance required by the tribunal, including its experts;

(c) the fees and expenses of the administrator;

(d) the reasonable costs for legal representation of a successful party; and

(e) any such costs incurred in connection with an application for interim or emergency relief pursuant to Article 21.

Compensation of Arbitrators

Article 32

Arbitrators shall be compensated based upon their amount of service, taking into account their stated rate of compensation and the size and complexity of the case. The administrator shall arrange an appropriate daily or hourly rate, based on such considerations, with the parties and with each of the arbitrators as soon as practicable after the commencement of the arbitration. If the parties fail to agree on the terms of compensation, the administrator shall establish an appropriate rate and communicate it in writing to the parties.

Deposit of Costs

Article 33

1. When a party files claims, the administrator may request the filing party to deposit appropriate amounts as an advance for the costs referred to in Article 31, paragraphs (a), (b) and (c).

2. During the course of the arbitral proceedings, the tribunal may request supplementary deposits from the parties.

3. If the deposits requested are not paid in full within 30 days after the receipt of the request, the administrator shall so inform the parties, in order that one or the other of them may make the required payment. If such payments are not made, the tribunal may order the suspension or termination of the proceedings.

4. After the award has been made, the administrator shall render an accounting to the parties of the deposits received and return any unexpended balance to the parties.

Confidentiality

Article 34

Confidential information disclosed during the proceedings by the parties or by witnesses shall not be divulged by an arbitrator or by the administrator. Except as provided in Article 27, unless otherwise agreed by the parties, or required by applicable law, the members of the tribunal and the administrator shall keep confidential all matters relating to the arbitration or the award.

Exclusion of Liability

Article 35

The members of the tribunal and the administrator shall not be liable to any party for any act or omission in connection with any arbitration conducted under these rule s, except that they may be liable for the consequences of conscious and deliberate wrongdoing.

Interpretation of Rules

Article 36

The tribunal shall interpret and apply these rules insofar as they relate to its powers and duties. The administrator shall interpret and apply all other rules.

APPENDIX I

1958 New York Convention on the Recognition and Enforcement of Foreign Arbitral Awards

Reproduced with permission of THE 1958 NEW YORK CONVENTION on the recognition and enforcement of foreign arbitral awards

The Convention on the Recognition and Enforcement of Foreign Arbitral Awards was signed at the United Nations Conference on International Commercial Arbitration held in New York in June 1958.

The complete text of the Convention is given below for information. Attention is however particularly drawn to Articles I to VII, which contain the essential substance of the Convention. The remaining articles are primarily concerned with procedural matters.

Article 1

1. This Convention shall apply to the recognition and enforcement of arbitral awards made in the territory of a State other than the State where the recognition and enforcement of such awards are sought, and arising out of differences between persons, whether physical or legal. It shall also apply to arbitral awards not considered as domestic awards in the State where their recognition and enforcement are sought.

2. The term "arbitral awards" shall include not only awards made by arbitrators appointed for each case but also those made by permanent arbitral bodies to which the parties have submitted.

3. When signing, ratifying or acceding to this Convention, or notifying extension under Article X hereof, any State may on the basis of reciprocity declare that it will apply the Convention to the recognition and enforcement of awards made only in the territory of another Contracting State. It may also declare that it will apply the Convention only to differences arising out of legal relationships, whether contractual or not, which are considered as commercial under the national law of the State making such declaration.

Article II

1. Each Contracting State shall recognize an agreement in writing under which the parties undertake to submit to arbitration all or any differences which have arisen or which may arise between them in respect of a defined legal relationship, whether contractual or not, concerning a subject matter capable of settlement of arbitration.

2. The term "agreement in writing" shall include an arbitral clause in a contract or an arbitration agreement, signed by the parties or contained in an exchange of letters or telegrams.

3. The court of a Contracting State, when seized of an action in a matter in respect of which the parties have made an agreement within the meaning of this article, shall, at the request of one of the parties, refer the parties to arbitration, unless it finds that the said agreement is null and void, inoperative or incapable of being performed.

Article III

Each Contracting State shall recognize arbitral awards as binding and enforce them in accordance with the rules of procedure of the territory where the award is relied upon, under the conditions laid down in the following articles. There shall not be imposed substantially more onerous conditions or higher fees or charges on the recognition or enforcement of arbitral awards to which this Convention applies than are imposed on the recognition or enforcement of domestic arbitral awards.

Article IV

1. To obtain the recognition and enforcement mentioned in the preceding article, the party applying for recognition and enforcement shall, at the time of the application, supply:

(a) the duly authenticated original award or a duly certified copy thereof;

(b) the original agreement referred to in Article II or a duly certified copy thereof.

2. If the said award or agreement is not made in an official language of the country in which the award is relied upon, the party applying for recognition and enforcement of the award shall produce a translation of these documents into such language. The translation shall be certified by an official or sworn translator or by a diplomatic or consular agent.

Article V

1. Recognition and enforcement of the award may be refused, at the request of the party against whom it is invoked, only if that party furnishes to the competent authority where the recognition and enforcement is sought, proof that:

(a) the parties to the agreement referred to in Article II were, under the law applicable to them, under some incapacity, or the said agreement is not valid under the law to which the parties have subjected it or, failing any indication thereon, under the law of the country where the award was made; or

(b) the party against whom the award is invoked was not given proper notice of the appointment of the arbitrator or of the arbitration proceedings or was otherwise unable to present his case; or

(c) the award deals with a difference not contemplated by or not falling within the terms of the submission to arbitration, or it contains decisions on matters beyond the scope of the submission to arbitration, provided that, if the decision on matters submitted to arbitration can be separated from those not so submitted, that part of the award which contains decisions on matters submitted to arbitration may be recognized and enforced: or

(d) the composition of the arbitral authority or the arbitral procedure was not in accordance with the agreement of the parties, or, failing such agreement, was not in accordance with the law of the country where the arbitration took place; or

(e) the award has not yet become binding on the parties, or has been set aside or suspended by a competent authority of the country in which, or under the law of which, that award was made.

2. Recognition and enforcement of an arbitral award may also be refused if the competent authority in the country where recognition and enforcement is sought finds that:

(a) the subject matter of the difference is not capable of settlement by arbitration under the law of that country; or

(b) the recognition or enforcement of the award would be contrary to the public policy of that country.

Article VI

If an application for the setting aside or suspension of the award has been made to be a competent authority referred to in Article V paragraph (1) [e], the authority before which the award is sought to be relied upon may, if it considers it proper, adjourn the decision on the enforcement of the award and may also, on the application of the party claiming enforcement of the award, order the other party to give suitable security.

Article VII

1. The provisions of the present Convention shall not affect the validity of multilateral or bilateral agreements concerning the recognition and enforcement of arbitral awards entered into by the Contracting States nor deprive any interested party of any right he may have to avail himself of an arbitral award in the manner and to the extent allowed by the law or the treaties of the country where such award is sought to be relied upon.

2. The Geneva Protocol on Arbitration Clauses of 1923 and the Geneva Convention on the Execution of Foreign Arbitral Awards of 1927 shall cease to have effect between the Contracting States on their becoming bound and to the extent that they become bound, by this Convention.

Article VIII

1. This Convention shall be open until 31 December 1958 for signature on behalf of any Member of the United Nations and also on behalf of any other State which is or hereafter becomes a member of any specialized agency of the United Nations, or which is or hereafter becomes a party to the Statute of the International Court of Justice, or any other State to which an invitation has been addressed by the General Assembly of the United Nations.

2. This Convention shall be ratified and the instrument of ratification shall be deposited with the Secretary General of the United Nations.

Article IX

1. This Convention shall be open for accession to all States referred to in Article VIII.

2. Accession shall be effected by the deposit of an instrument of accession with the Secretary General of the United Nations.

Article X

1. Any State may, at the time of signature, ratification or accession, declare that this Convention shall extend to all or any of their territories for the international relations of which it is responsible. Such a declaration shall take effect when the Convention enters into force for the State concerned.

2. At any time thereafter any such extension shall be made by notification addressed to the Secretary General of the United Nations and shall take effect as from the ninetieth day after the day of receipt by the Secretary General of the United Nations of this notification, or as from the date of entry into force of the Convention for the State concerned, whichever is the later.

3. With respect to those territories to which this Convention is not extended at the time of signature, ratification or accession, each State concerned shall consider the possibility of taking the necessary steps in order to extend the application of this Convention to such territories, subject, where necessary for constitutional reasons, to the consent of the Governments of such territories.

Article XI

1. In the case of a federal or non-unitary State, the following provisions shall apply:

a)   With respect to those articles of this Convention that come within the legislative jurisdiction of the federal authority, the obligations of the federal Government shall to this extent be the same as those of Contracting States which are not federal States;

b)   With respect to those articles of this Convention that come within the legislative jurisdiction of constituent states or provinces which are not, under the constitutional system of the federation, bound to take legislative action, the federal Government shall bring such articles with a favourable recommendation to the notice of the appropriate authorities of constituent states or provinces at the earliest possible moment;

c)   A federal State party to this Convention shall, at the request of any other Contracting State transmitted through the Secretary General of the United Nations, supply a statement of the law and practice of the federation and its constituent units in regard to any particular provision of this Convention, showing the extent to which effect has been given to that provision by legislative or other action.

Article XII

1. This Convention shall come into force on the ninetieth day following the date of deposit of the third instrument of ratification or accession.

2. For each State ratifying or acceding to this Convention after the deposit of the third instrument of ratification or accession, this Convention shall enter into force on the ninetieth day after deposit by such State of its instrument of ratification or accession.

Article XIII

1. Any Contracting State may denounce this Convention by a written notification to the Secretary General of the United Nations. Denunciation shall take effect one year after the date of receipt of the notification by the Secretary General.

2. Any State which has made a declaration or notification under Article X may, at any time thereafter, by notification to the Secretary General of the United Nations, declare that this Convention shall cease to extend to the territory concerned one year after the date of the receipt of the notification by the Secretary General.

3. This Convention shall continue to be applicable to arbitral awards in respect of which recognition or enforcement proceedings have been instituted before the denunciation takes effect.

Article XIV

A Contracting State shall not be entitled to avail itself at the present Convention against other Contracting States except to the extent that it is itself bound to apply the Convention.

Article XV

The Secretary General of the United Nations shall notify the States contemplated in article VIII of the following:

> a)   Signatures and ratifications in accordance with article VIII;
>
> b)   Accessions in accordance with article IX;
>
> c)   Declarations and notifications under articles I, X and XI;
>
> d)   The date upon which this Convention enters into force in accordance with article XII;
>
> e)   Denunciations and notifications in accordance with article XIII.

Article XVI

1. This Convention, of which the Chinese, English, French, Russian and Spanish texts shall be equally authentic, shall be deposited in the archives of the United Nations.

2. The Secretary General of the United Nations shall transmit a certified copy of this Convention to the States contemplated in article VIII.

APPENDIX J

American Arbitration Association
Supplementary Procedures for Online Arbitration

**Reprinted with the permission of the American Arbitration Association
(Effective July 1, 2001)**

1.   Introduction

The purpose of the Supplementary Procedures for Online Arbitration is to permit, where the parties have agreed to arbitration under these Supplementary Procedures, arbitral proceedings to be conducted and resolved exclusively via the Internet. The Supplementary Procedures provide for all party submissions to be made online, and for the arbitrator, upon review of such submissions, to render an award and to communicate it to the parties via the Internet. These Supplementary Procedures further authorize the parties and the arbitrator in certain circumstances to use methods of communication other than the Internet.

Definitions

a. **Administrative Site** refers to the Internet site www.adr.org. At the Administrative Site, parties may initiate arbitration under the Supplementary Procedures and pay filing fees and other administrative costs. The Administrative Site also provides schedules of applicable fees and costs, technical guidelines regarding the format of submissions, as well as other important information and resources.

b. **Arbitrator** refers to a sole arbitrator or a three person panel appointed according to the Supplementary Procedures.

c. **Case Site** refers to the Internet site established to maintain the case files and submissions. All of the parties' written submissions shall be posted on the Case Site, and no one other than the AAA, the parties, and the Arbitrator shall have access to the Case Site.

d. **Hearing,** whether used in the singular or plural, refers to any meeting or meetings of the parties before the Arbitrator, whether conducted in-person or by telephone, video-conference, or other means.

e. **Internet and online** are used interchangeably to refer to the world-wide electronic online medium.

f. **Portal Terms** shall refer to the terms and conditions of use of the Case Site and Administrative Site, as may be amended from time to time by the AAA.

g. **Submit** refers to (i) the electronic transmittal of pleadings, exhibits, communications, or other documents to the Case Site, or (ii) such other method of transmitting pleadings, exhibits, communications, or other documents as may be authorized by the Arbitrator under Section 12(a). Submissions refers to all such pleadings, exhibits, communications, or other documents, however transmitted.

h. **Writing** refers not only to the customary definition of "writing" but also to an "electronic record" as the term is defined the Uniform Electronic Transactions Act (U.L.A.), § 2.

Procedures

1.   Agreement to Arbitrate under these Supplementary Procedures

a. The parties shall be deemed to have made these Supplementary Procedures a part of their arbitration agreement whenever they have provided for arbitration by the American Arbitration Association (the "AAA") under its Supplementary Procedures for online Arbitration. These Supplementary Procedures may also be used, by agreement of the parties and Arbitrator, in arbitrations initiated under other sets of rules. The Supplementary Procedures and any amendment to them shall apply in the form in effect at the time of commencement of the arbitration. The parties, by agreement in writing, may vary the procedures set forth in these Supplementary Procedures.

b. The Supplementary Procedures are supplemental to the AAA's Commercial Dispute Resolution Procedures, or any other set of applicable AAA rules, which shall remain applicable except where modified by the Supplementary Procedures.

c. The AAA may decide that an arbitration shall not be conducted under the Supplementary Procedures where a party lacks the capacity to participate in the arbitration in accordance with these Procedures, or where the AAA otherwise finds, in its discretion, that an arbitration should not be conducted under these Procedures. In the event that the AAA makes such a determination, the arbitration shall be conducted in accordance with the Commercial Dispute Resolution Procedures or other applicable AAA rules.

d. By agreeing to the Supplementary Procedures, the parties also agree to the Portal Terms in effect at the time of commencement of the arbitration.

e. When the parties agree to arbitrate under the Supplementary Procedures, they thereby authorize the AAA to administer the arbitration.

2.   Serving of Notices and Calculation of Time Periods

a. Except as otherwise agreed by the parties and approved by the Arbitrator, all submissions provided for under the Supplementary Procedures shall be deemed to have been made when received at the Case Site. The date and time of receipt shall be that stated in the confirmatory e-mail sent from the Case Site to the party making the submission.

b. For the purposes of calculating a period of time under the Supplementary Procedures, such period shall begin to run from the date of receipt at the Case Cite.

3.   The Claim in Arbitration

a. The Claimant shall initiate the arbitration by submitting to the Administrative Site a claim in arbitration (the "Claim"), which shall include: the parties' arbitration agreement; any agreement between the parties regarding the number, identity, qualifications, and/or the manner of selection of the Arbitrator; basic documents insofar as reasonably susceptible to electronic transmittal; and a statement of the nature of the dispute, the legal arguments which support the Claim, the amount involved, if any, and the remedy sought.

b. In addition to the foregoing, the Claim shall provide the following information:

> 1) the e-mail address at which the Claimant will receive e-mail communications from the Case Site;
>
> 2) the last known valid e-mail address of the Respondent; and
>
> 3) the names, postal addresses, and telephone and facsimile numbers of the parties.

c. The Claimant shall pay the appropriate filing fee within five days of submitting the Claim to the Administrative Site. Such fee may be paid electronically or by any other method prescribed by the AAA.

4.   Notification of Complaint

a. Upon receipt of the appropriate filing fee from the Claimant, the AAA shall review the Claim to ascertain whether it complies with Section 3. Once the AAA has satisfied itself of the foregoing, the AAA shall, within five business days, establish a Case Site upon which the Claim shall immediately be made available. The AAA shall notify the parties by e-mail of the Internet address for the Case Site. The arbitration shall be deemed commenced on the date upon which the Case Site was established, as reflected in the confirmatory e-mails sent by the AAA to the parties.

b. If the AAA finds that notification to the Respondent via e-mail is not possible, the AAA may decide that the Supplementary Procedures should not apply.

c. If the AAA determines that the Claim is administratively deficient, the AAA shall not create a Case Site and shall promptly notify the Claimant of the deficiencies identified.

5.   Response to Claim

Within thirty calendar days following the establishment of the Case Site, the Respondent shall submit to the Case Site a response, which shall include:

> 1) the response to the Claim, together with the facts, documents, and legal arguments supporting such response;
>
> 2) any objection to the jurisdiction of the Arbitrator, to the number, identity, qualifications, and/or manner of selection of the Arbitrator, or to the applicability of the Supplementary Procedures;
>
> 3) the e-mail address at which the Respondent will receive e-mail communications from the Case Site; and
>
> 4) if the Respondent has a counterclaim, a submission satisfying the requirements for a Claim set out in Section 3.

6.   Response to Counterclaim

Where the Respondent has submitted a counterclaim, the Claimant shall submit to the Case Site a response within thirty calendar days from the date upon which the Respondent's counterclaim was submitted to the Case Site. The response shall include the information sufficient to meet the requirements of a response to a Claim set out in Section 5.

7.   Extensions of Time

The AAA or the Arbitrator may, for good cause shown, extend the period of time for the Respondent to submit its response to the Claim or for the Claimant to submit its response to any counterclaim. Any such request made to the Arbitrator shall be submitted to the Case Site. Any such request made to the AAA shall be both submitted to the Case Site and sent by e-mail to the AAA as provided in Section 12(b).

8.   Language of the Arbitration

Unless otherwise agreed by the parties, the language of the arbitration shall be that of the document(s) containing the arbitration agreement, subject to the power of the Arbitrator to determine otherwise.

9.   Hearings

a. Unless either party requests and the Arbitrator agrees to a Hearing, the Arbitrator will make the award based on the submissions. In the absence of a request for a Hearing, the Arbitrator will render the award within thirty days of the closing of the proceeding.

b. At a Hearing, witness testimony may be received, cross-examination of witnesses may be conducted, and additional documentary evidence may be received as approved by the Arbitrator.

10.   Place of Award

The parties may agree in writing upon the place of the award, and the Arbitrator shall designate this as the place of the award in the award. In the absence of such an agreement between the parties, the Arbitrator shall decide and shall designate the place of the award in the award.

11.   Communication of the Award to the Parties

The Arbitrator shall submit the award to the Case Site. The award shall be deemed to have been made when submitted, which date shall be stated in the confirmatory e-mail sent from the Case Site to the parties notifying them that the award has been submitted. The Case Site shall remain available to the parties for thirty days from the date upon which the award was submitted.

12.   Additional Methods of Communication

a. The Arbitrator may authorize a method of communicating with the Arbitrator other than the above-described use of the Case Site.

b. The AAA shall provide to the parties and to the Arbitrator an e-mail address for those communications between the parties and the AAA or between the Arbitrator and the AAA which are not to be made available to all parties and the Arbitrator through submission to the Case Site (e.g., administrative queries).

APPENDIX K

The Code of Ethics for Arbitrators in Commercial Disputes —2004 Revision

@American Arbitration Association
@American Bar Association

The Code of Ethics for Arbitrators in Commercial Disputes was originally prepared in 1977 by a joint committee consisting of a special committee of the American Arbitration Association and a special committee of the American Bar Association. The Code was revised in 2003 by an ABA Task Force and special committee of the AAA. Both the original 1977 Code and the 2003 Revision have been approved and recommended by both organizations.

Preamble

The use of arbitration to resolve a wide variety of disputes has grown extensively and forms a significant part of the system of justice on which our society relies for a fair determination of legal rights. Persons who act as arbitrators therefore undertake serious responsibilities to the public, as well as to the parties. Those responsibilities include important ethical obligations.

Few cases of unethical behavior by commercial arbitrators have arisen. Nevertheless, this Code sets forth generally accepted standards of ethical conduct for the guidance of arbitrators and parties in commercial disputes, in the hope of contributing to the maintenance of high standards and continued confidence in the process of arbitration.

This Code provides ethical guidelines for many types of arbitration but does not apply to labor arbitration, which is generally conducted under the Code of Professional Responsibility for Arbitrators of Labor-Management Disputes.

There are many different types of commercial arbitration. Some proceedings are conducted under arbitration rules established by various organizations and trade associations, while others are conducted without such rules. Although most proceedings are arbitrated pursuant to voluntary agreement of the parties, certain types of disputes are submitted to arbitration by reason of particular laws. This Code is intended to apply to all such proceedings in which disputes or claims are submitted for decision to one or more arbitrators appointed in a manner provided by an agreement of the parties, by applicable arbitration rules, or by law. In all such cases, the persons who have the power to decide should observe fundamental standards of ethical conduct. In this Code, all such persons are

399

called "arbitrators," although in some types of proceeding they might be called "umpires," "referees," "neutrals," or have some other title.

Arbitrators, like judges, have the power to decide cases. However, unlike full-time judges, arbitrators are usually engaged in other occupations before, during, and after the time that they serve as arbitrators. Often, arbitrators are purposely chosen from the same trade or industry as the parties in order to bring special knowledge to the task of deciding. This Code recognizes these fundamental differences between arbitrators and judges.

In those instances where this Code has been approved and recommended by organizations that provide, coordinate, or administer services of arbitrators, it provides ethical standards for the members of their respective panels of arbitrators. However, this Code does not form a part of the arbitration rules of any such organization unless its rules so provide.

Note on Neutrality

In some types of commercial arbitration, the parties or the administering institution provide for three or more arbitrators. In some such proceedings, it is the practice for each party, acting alone, to appoint one arbitrator (a "party-appointed arbitrator") and for one additional arbitrator to be designated by the party-appointed arbitrators, or by the parties, or by an independent institution or individual. The sponsors of this Code believe that it is preferable for all arbitrators—including any party-appointed arbitrators —to be neutral, that is, independent and impartial, and to comply with the same ethical standards. This expectation generally is essential in arbitrations where the parties, the nature of the dispute, or the enforcement of any resulting award may have international aspects. However, parties in certain domestic arbitrations in the United States may prefer that party-appointed arbitrators be non-neutral and governed by special ethical considerations. These special ethical considerations appear in Canon X of this Code.

This Code establishes a presumption of neutrality for all arbitrators, including party-appointed arbitrators, which applies unless the parties' agreement, the arbitration rules agreed to by the parties or applicable laws provide otherwise. This Code requires all party-appointed arbitrators, whether neutral or not, to make pre-appointment disclosures of any facts which might affect their neutrality, independence, or impartiality. This Code also requires all party-appointed arbitrators to ascertain and disclose as soon as practicable whether the parties intended for them to serve as neutral or not. If any doubt or uncertainty exists, the party-appointed arbitrators should serve as neutrals unless and until such doubt or uncertainty is resolved in accordance with Canon IX. This Code expects all arbitrators, including those serving under Canon X, to preserve the integrity and fairness of the process.

Note on Construction

Various aspects of the conduct of arbitrators, including some matters covered by this Code, may also be governed by agreements of the parties, arbitration rules to which the parties have agreed, applicable law, or other applicable ethics rules, all of which should be consulted by the arbitrators. This Code does not take the place of or supersede such laws, agreements, or arbitration rules to which the parties have agreed and should be read in conjunction with other rules of ethics. It does not establish new or additional grounds for judicial review of arbitration awards.

All provisions of this Code should therefore be read as subject to contrary provisions of applicable law and arbitration rules. They should also be read as subject to contrary agreements of the parties. Nevertheless, this Code imposes no obligation on any arbitrator to act in a manner inconsistent with the arbitrator's fundamental duty to preserve the integrity and fairness of the arbitral process.

Canons I through VIII of this Code apply to all arbitrators. Canon IX applies to all party-appointed arbitrators, except that certain party-appointed arbitrators are exempted by Canon X from compliance with certain provisions of Canons I-IX related to impartiality and independence, as specified in Canon X.

CANON I.   AN ARBITRATOR SHOULD UPHOLD THE INTEGRITY AND FAIRNESS OF THE ARBITRATION PROCESS.

A.   An arbitrator has a responsibility not only to the parties but also to the process of arbitration itself, and must observe high standards of conduct so that the integrity and fairness of the process will be preserved. Accordingly, an arbitrator should recognize a responsibility to the public, to the parties whose rights will be decided, and to all other participants in the proceeding. This responsibility may include pro bono service as an arbitrator where appropriate.

B.   One should accept appointment as an arbitrator only if fully satisfied:

(1)   that he or she can serve impartially;

(2)   that he or she can serve independently from the parties, potential witnesses, and the other arbitrators;

(3)   that he or she is competent to serve; and

(4)   that he or she can be available to commence the arbitration in accordance with the requirements of the proceeding and thereafter to devote the time and attention to its completion that the parties are reasonably entitled to expect.

C. After accepting appointment and while serving as an arbitrator, a person should avoid entering into any business, professional, or personal relationship, or acquiring any financial or personal interest, which is likely to affect impartiality or which might reasonably create the appearance of partiality. For a reasonable period of time after the decision of a case, persons who have served as arbitrators should avoid entering into any such relationship, or acquiring any such interest, in circumstances which might reasonably create the appearance that they had been influenced in the arbitration by the anticipation or expectation of the relationship or interest. Existence of any of the matters or circumstances described in this paragraph C does not render it unethical for one to serve as an arbitrator where the parties have consented to the arbitrator's appointment or continued services following full disclosure of the relevant facts in accordance with Canon II.

D. Arbitrators should conduct themselves in a way that is fair to all parties and should not be swayed by outside pressure, public clamor, and fear of criticism or self-interest. They should avoid conduct and statements that give the appearance of partiality toward or against any party.

E. An arbitrator's authority is derived from the agreement of the parties. An arbitrator should neither exceed that authority nor do less than is required to exercise that authority completely. Where the agreement of the parties sets forth procedures to be followed in conducting the arbitration or refers to rules to be followed, it is the obligation of the arbitrator to comply with such procedures or rules. An arbitrator has no ethical obligation to comply with any agreement, procedures or rules that are unlawful or that, in the arbitrator's judgment, would be inconsistent with this Code.

F. An arbitrator should conduct the arbitration process so as to advance the fair and efficient resolution of the matters submitted for decision. An arbitrator should make all reasonable efforts to prevent delaying tactics, harassment of parties or other participants, or other abuse or disruption of the arbitration process.

G. The ethical obligations of an arbitrator begin upon acceptance of the appointment and continue throughout all stages of the proceeding. In addition, as set forth in this Code, certain ethical obligations begin as soon as a person is requested to serve as an arbitrator and certain ethical obligations continue after the decision in the proceeding has been given to the parties.

H. Once an arbitrator has accepted an appointment, the arbitrator should not withdraw or abandon the appointment unless compelled to do so by unanticipated circumstances that would render it impossible or impracticable to continue. When an arbitrator is to be compensated for his or her services, the arbitrator may withdraw if the parties fail or refuse to provide for payment of the compensation as agreed.

I.   An arbitrator who withdraws prior to the completion of the arbitration, whether upon the arbitrator's initiative or upon the request of one or more of the parties, should take reasonable steps to protect the interests of the parties in the arbitration, including return of evidentiary materials and protection of confidentiality.

Comment to Canon I

A prospective arbitrator is not necessarily partial or prejudiced by having acquired knowledge of the parties, the applicable law or the customs and practices of the business involved. Arbitrators may also have special experience or expertise in the areas of business, commerce, or technology which are involved in the arbitration. Arbitrators do not contravene this Canon if, by virtue of such experience or expertise, they have views on certain general issues likely to arise in the arbitration, but an arbitrator may not have prejudged any of the specific factual or legal determinations to be addressed during the arbitration.

During an arbitration, the arbitrator may engage in discourse with the parties or their counsel, draw out arguments or contentions, comment on the law or evidence, make interim rulings, and otherwise control or direct the arbitration. These activities are integral parts of an arbitration. Paragraph D of Canon I is not intended to preclude or limit either full discussion of the issues during the course of the arbitration or the arbitrator's management of the proceeding.

CANON II.   AN ARBITRATOR SHOULD DISCLOSE ANY INTEREST OR RELATIONSHIP LIKELY TO AFFECT IMPARTIALITY OR WHICH MIGHT CREATE AN APPEARANCE OF PARTIALITY.

A.   Persons who are requested to serve as arbitrators should, before accepting, disclose:

(1)   Any known direct or indirect financial or personal interest in the outcome of the arbitration;

(2)   Any known existing or past financial, business, professional or personal relationships which might reasonably affect impartiality or lack of independence in the eyes of any of the parties. For example, prospective arbitrators should disclose any such relationships which they personally have with any party or its lawyer, with any co-arbitrator, or with any individual whom they have been told will be a witness. They should also disclose any such relationships involving their families or household members or their current employers, partners, or professional or business associates that can be ascertained by reasonable efforts;

(3) The nature and extent of any prior knowledge they may have of the dispute; and

(4) Any other matters, relationships, or interests which they are obligated to disclose by the agreement of the parties, the rules or practices of an institution, or applicable law regulating arbitrator disclosure.

B. Persons who are requested to accept appointment as arbitrators should make a reasonable effort to inform themselves of any interests or relationships described in paragraph A.

C. The obligation to disclose interests or relationships described in paragraph A is a continuing duty which requires a person who accepts appointment as an arbitrator to disclose, as soon as practicable, at any stage of the arbitration, any such interests or relationships which may arise, or which are recalled or discovered.

D. Any doubt as to whether or not disclosure is to be made should be resolved in favor of disclosure.

E. Disclosure should be made to all parties unless other procedures for disclosure are provided in the agreement of the parties, applicable rules or practices of an institution, or by law. Where more than one arbitrator has been appointed, each should inform the others of all matters disclosed.

F. When parties, with knowledge of a person's interests and relationships, nevertheless desire that person to serve as an arbitrator, that person may properly serve.

G. If an arbitrator is requested by all parties to withdraw, the arbitrator must do so. If an arbitrator is requested to withdraw by less than all of the parties because of alleged partiality, the arbitrator should withdraw unless either of the following circumstances exists:

(1) An agreement of the parties, or arbitration rules agreed to by the parties, or applicable law establishes procedures for determining challenges to arbitrators, in which case those procedures should be followed; or

(2) In the absence of applicable procedures, if the arbitrator, after carefully considering the matter, determines that the reason for the challenge is not substantial, and that he or she can nevertheless act and decide the case impartially and fairly.

H. If compliance by a prospective arbitrator with any provision of this Code would require disclosure of confidential or privileged information, the prospective arbitrator should either:

(1) Secure the consent to the disclosure from the person who furnished the information or the holder of the privilege; or

(2) Withdraw.

CANON III. AN ARBITRATOR SHOULD AVOID IMPROPRIETY OR THE APPEARANCE OF IMPROPRIETY IN COMMUNICATING WITH PARTIES.

A. If an agreement of the parties or applicable arbitration rules establishes the manner or content of communications between the arbitrator and the parties, the arbitrator should follow those procedures notwithstanding any contrary provision of paragraphs B and C.

B. An arbitrator or prospective arbitrator should not discuss a proceeding with any party in the absence of any other party, except in any of the following circumstances:

(1) When the appointment of a prospective arbitrator is being considered, the prospective arbitrator:

(a) may ask about the identities of the parties, counsel, or witnesses and the general nature of the case; and

(b) may respond to inquiries from a party or its counsel designed to determine his or her suitability and availability for the appointment. In any such dialogue, the prospective arbitrator may receive information from a party or its counsel disclosing the general nature of the dispute but should not permit them to discuss the merits of the case.

(2) In an arbitration in which the two party-appointed arbitrators are expected to appoint the third arbitrator, each party-appointed arbitrator may consult with the party who appointed the arbitrator concerning the choice of the third arbitrator;

(3) In an arbitration involving party-appointed arbitrators, each party-appointed arbitrator may consult with the party who appointed the arbitrator concerning arrangements for any compensation to be paid to the party-appointed arbitrator. Submission of routine written requests for payment of compensation and expenses in accordance with such arrangements and written communications pertaining solely to such requests need not be sent to the other party;

(4) In an arbitration involving party-appointed arbitrators, each party-appointed arbitrator may consult with the party who appointed the arbitrator concerning the status of the arbitrator (i.e., neutral or non-neutral), as contemplated by paragraph C of Canon IX;

(5)   Discussions may be had with a party concerning such logistical matters as setting the time and place of hearings or making
other arrangements for the conduct of the proceedings. However, the arbitrator should promptly inform each other party
of the discussion and should not make any final determination
concerning the matter discussed before giving each absent party
an opportunity to express the party's views; or

(6)   If a party fails to be present at a hearing after having been
given due notice, or if all parties expressly consent, the arbitrator may discuss the case with any party who is present.

Unless otherwise provided in this Canon, in applicable arbitration rules or
in an agreement of the parties, whenever an arbitrator communicates in writing
with one party, the arbitrator should at the same time send a copy of the communication to every other party, and whenever the arbitrator receives any written
communication concerning the case from one party which has not already been
sent to every other party, the arbitrator should send or cause it to be sent to the
other parties.

CANON IV.   AN ARBITRATOR SHOULD CONDUCT THE PROCEEDINGS FAIRLY AND DILIGENTLY.

A.   An arbitrator should conduct the proceedings in an even-handed manner. The arbitrator should be patient and courteous to the parties, their representatives, and the witnesses and should encourage similar conduct by all participants.

B.   The arbitrator should afford to all parties the right to be heard and due
notice of the time and place of any hearing. The arbitrator should allow each
party a fair opportunity to present its evidence and arguments.

C.   The arbitrator should not deny any party the opportunity to be represented by counsel or by any other person chosen by the party.

D.   If a party fails to appear after due notice, the arbitrator should proceed
with the arbitration when authorized to do so, but only after receiving assurance
that appropriate notice has been given to the absent party.

E.   When the arbitrator determines that more information than has been
presented by the parties is required to decide the case, it is not improper for the
arbitrator to ask questions, call witnesses, and request documents or other evidence, including expert testimony.

F.   Although it is not improper for an arbitrator to suggest to the parties that
they discuss the possibility of settlement or the use of mediation, or other dispute

resolution processes, an arbitrator should not exert pressure on any party to settle or to utilize other dispute resolution processes. An arbitrator should not be present or otherwise participate in settlement discussions or act as a mediator unless requested to do so by all parties.

G. Co-arbitrators should afford each other full opportunity to participate in all aspects of the proceedings.

Comment to paragraph G

Paragraph G of Canon IV is not intended to preclude one arbitrator from acting in limited circumstances (e.g., ruling on discovery issues) where authorized by the agreement of the parties, applicable rules or law, nor does it preclude a majority of the arbitrators from proceeding with any aspect of the arbitration if an arbitrator is unable or unwilling to participate and such action is authorized by the agreement of the parties or applicable rules or law.

CANON V.   AN ARBITRATOR SHOULD MAKE DECISIONS IN A JUST, INDEPENDENT AND DELIBERATE MANNER.

A. The arbitrator should, after careful deliberation, decide all issues submitted for determination. An arbitrator should decide no other issues.

B. An arbitrator should decide all matters justly, exercising independent judgment, and should not permit outside pressure to affect the decision.

C. An arbitrator should not delegate the duty to decide to any other person.

D. In the event that all parties agree upon a settlement of issues in dispute and request the arbitrator to embody that agreement in an award, the arbitrator may do so, but is not required to do so unless satisfied with the propriety of the terms of settlement. Whenever an arbitrator embodies a settlement by the parties in an award, the arbitrator should state in the award that it is based on an agreement of the parties.

CANON VI.   AN ARBITRATOR SHOULD BE FAITHFUL TO THE RELATIONSHIP OF TRUST AND CONFIDENTIALITY INHERENT IN THAT OFFICE.

A. An arbitrator is in a relationship of trust to the parties and should not, at any time, use confidential information acquired during the arbitration proceeding to gain personal advantage or advantage for others, or to affect adversely the interest of another.

B. The arbitrator should keep confidential all matters relating to the arbitration proceedings and decision. An arbitrator may obtain help from an associate, a research assistant or other persons in connection with reaching his or her decision if the arbitrator informs the parties of the use of such assistance and such persons agree to be bound by the provisions of this Canon.

C. It is not proper at any time for an arbitrator to inform anyone of any decision in advance of the time it is given to all parties. In a proceeding in which there is more than one arbitrator, it is not proper at any time for an arbitrator to inform anyone about the substance of the deliberations of the arbitrators. After an arbitration award has been made, it is not proper for an arbitrator to assist in proceedings to enforce or challenge the award.

D. Unless the parties so request, an arbitrator should not appoint himself or herself to a separate office related to the subject matter of the dispute, such as receiver or trustee, nor should a panel of arbitrators appoint one of their number to such an office.

CANON VII. AN ARBITRATOR SHOULD ADHERE TO STANDARDS OF INTEGRITY AND FAIRNESS WHEN MAKING ARRANGE- MENTS FOR COMPENSATION AND REIMBURSEMENT OF EXPENSES.

A. Arbitrators who are to be compensated for their services or reimbursed for their expenses shall adhere to standards of integrity and fairness in making arrangements for such payments.

B. Certain practices relating to payments are generally recognized as tending to preserve the integrity and fairness of the arbitration process. These practices include:

(1) Before the arbitrator finally accepts appointment, the basis of payment, including any cancellation fee, compensation in the event of withdrawal and compensation for study and preparation time, and all other charges, should be established. Except for arrangements for the compensation of party-appointed arbitrators, all parties should be informed in writing of the terms established.

(2) In proceedings conducted under the rules or administration of an institution that is available to assist in making arrangements for payments, communication related to compensation should be made through the institution. In proceedings where no institution has been engaged by the parties to administer the arbitration, any communication with arbitrators (other than party appointed arbitrators) concerning payments should be in the presence of all parties; and

(3) Arbitrators should not, absent extraordinary circumstances, request increases in the basis of their compensation during the course of a proceeding.

CANON VIII. **AN ARBITRATOR MAY ENGAGE IN ADVERTISING OR PROMOTION OF ARBITRAL SERVICES WHICH IS TRUTHFUL AND ACCURATE.**

A. Advertising or promotion of an individual's willingness or availability to serve as an arbitrator must be accurate and unlikely to mislead. Any statements about the quality of the arbitrator's work or the success of the arbitrator's practice must be truthful.

B. Advertising and promotion must not imply any willingness to accept an appointment otherwise than in accordance with this Code.

Comment to Canon VIII

This Canon does not preclude an arbitrator from printing, publishing, or disseminating advertisements conforming to these standards in any electronic or print medium, from making personal presentations to prospective users of arbitral services conforming to such standards or from responding to inquiries concerning the arbitrator's availability, qualifications, experience, or fee arrangements.

CANON IX. **ARBITRATORS APPOINTED BY ONE PARTY HAVE A DUTY TO DETERMINE AND DISCLOSE THEIR STATUS AND TO COMPLY WITH THIS CODE, EXCEPT AS EXEMPTED BY CANON X.**

A. In some types of arbitration in which there are three arbitrators, it is customary for each party, acting alone, to appoint one arbitrator. The third arbitrator is then appointed by agreement either of the parties or of the two arbitrators, or failing such agreement, by an independent institution or individual. In tripartite arbitrations to which this Code applies, all three arbitrators are presumed to be neutral and are expected to observe the same standards as the third arbitrator.

B. Notwithstanding this presumption, there are certain types of tripartite arbitration in which it is expected by all parties that the two arbitrators appointed by the parties may be predisposed toward the party appointing them. Those arbitrators, referred to in this Code as "Canon X arbitrators," are not to be held to the standards of neutrality and independence applicable to other arbitrators. Canon X describes the special ethical obligations of party-appointed arbitrators who are not expected to meet the standard of neutrality.

C. A party-appointed arbitrator has an obligation to ascertain, as early as possible but not later than the first meeting of the arbitrators and parties, whether the parties have agreed that the party-appointed arbitrators will serve as neutrals or whether they shall be subject to Canon X, and to provide a timely report of their conclusions to the parties and other arbitrators:

(1) Party-appointed arbitrators should review the agreement of the parties, the applicable rules and any applicable law bearing upon arbitrator neutrality. In reviewing the agreement of the parties, party-appointed arbitrators should consult any relevant express terms of the written or oral arbitration agreement. It may also be appropriate for them to inquire into agreements that have not been expressly set forth, but which may be implied from an established course of dealings of the parties or well-recognized custom and usage in their trade or profession;

(2) Where party-appointed arbitrators conclude that the parties intended for the party-appointed arbitrators not to serve as neutrals, they should so inform the parties and the other arbitrators. The arbitrators may then act as provided in Canon X unless or until a different determination of their status is made by the parties, any administering institution or the arbitral panel; and

(3) Until party-appointed arbitrators conclude that the party-appointed arbitrators were not intended by the parties to serve as neutrals, or if the party-appointed arbitrators are unable to form a reasonable belief of their status from the foregoing sources and no decision in this regard has yet been made by the parties, any administering institution, or the arbitral panel, they should observe all of the obligations of neutral arbitrators set forth in this Code.

D. Party-appointed arbitrators not governed by Canon X shall observe all of the obligations of Canons I through VIII unless otherwise required by agreement of the parties, any applicable rules, or applicable law.

CANON X. EXEMPTIONS FOR ARBITRATORS APPOINTED BY ONE PARTY WHO ARE NOT SUBJECT TO RULES OF NEUTRALITY.

Canon X arbitrators are expected to observe all of the ethical obligations prescribed by this Code except those from which they are specifically excused by Canon X.

A. *Obligations under Canon I*

Canon X arbitrators should observe all of the obligations of Canon I subject only to the following provisions:

(1) Canon X arbitrators may be predisposed toward the party who appointed them but in all other respects are obligated to act in good faith and with integrity and fairness. For example, Canon X arbitrators should not engage in delaying tactics or harassment of

any party or witness and should not knowingly make untrue or misleading statements to the other arbitrators; and

(2) The provisions of subparagraphs B(1), B(2), and paragraphs C and D of Canon I, insofar as they relate to partiality, relationships, and interests are not applicable to Canon X arbitrators.

B. *Obligations under Canon II*

(1) Canon X arbitrators should disclose to all parties, and to the other arbitrators, all interests and relationships which Canon II requires be disclosed. Disclosure as required by Canon II is for the benefit not only of the party who appointed the arbitrator, but also for the benefit of the other parties and arbitrators so that they may know of any partiality which may exist or appear to exist; and

(2) Canon X arbitrators are not obliged to withdraw under paragraph G of Canon II if requested to do so only by the party who did not appoint them.

C. *Obligations under Canon III*

Canon X arbitrators should observe all of the obligations of Canon III subject only to the following provisions:

(1) Like neutral party-appointed arbitrators, Canon X arbitrators may consult with the party who appointed them to the extent permitted in paragraph B of Canon III;

(2) Canon X arbitrators shall, at the earliest practicable time, disclose to the other arbitrators and to the parties whether or not they intend to communicate with their appointing parties. If they have disclosed the intention to engage in such communications, they may thereafter communicate with their appointing parties concerning any other aspect of the case, except as provided in paragraph (3).

(3) If such communication occurred prior to the time they were appointed as arbitrators, or prior to the first hearing or other meeting of the parties with the arbitrators, the Canon X arbitrator should, at or before the first hearing or meeting of the arbitrators with the parties, disclose the fact that such communication has taken place. In complying with the provisions of this subparagraph, it is sufficient that there be disclosure of the fact that such communication has occurred without disclosing the content of the communication. A single timely disclosure of the Canon X arbitrator's intention to participate in such communications in the future is sufficient;

(4) Canon X arbitrators may not at any time during the arbitration:

    (a)   disclose any deliberations by the arbitrators on any matter or issue submitted to them for decision;

    (b)   communicate with the parties that appointed them concerning any matter or issue taken under consideration by the panel after the record is closed or such matter or issue has been submitted for decision; or

    (c)   disclose any final decision or interim decision in advance of the time that it is disclosed to all parties.

(4) Unless otherwise agreed by the arbitrators and the parties, a Canon X arbitrator may not communicate orally with the neutral arbitrator concerning any matter or issue arising or expected to arise in the arbitration in the absence of the other Canon X arbitrator. If a Canon X arbitrator communicates in writing with the neutral arbitrator, he or she shall simultaneously provide a copy of the written communication to the other Canon X arbitrator;

(5) When Canon X arbitrators communicate orally with the parties that appointed them concerning any matter on which communication is permitted under this Code, they are not obligated to disclose the contents of such oral communications to any other party or arbitrator; and

(6) When Canon X arbitrators communicate in writing with the party who appointed them concerning any matter on which communication is permitted under this Code, they are not required to send copies of any such written communication to any other party or arbitrator.

D. *Obligations under Canon IV*

Canon X arbitrators should observe all of the obligations of Canon IV.

E. *Obligations under Canon V*

Canon X arbitrators should observe all of the obligations of Canon V, except that they may be predisposed toward deciding in favor of the party who appointed them.

F. *Obligations under Canon VI*

Canon X arbitrators should observe all of the obligations of Canon VI.

G. *Obligations Under Canon VII*

Canon X arbitrators should observe all of the obligations of Canon VII.

H. *Obligations Under Canon VIII*

Canon X arbitrators should observe all of the obligations of Canon VIII.

I. *Obligations Under Canon IX*

The provisions of paragraph D of Canon IX are inapplicable to Canon X arbitrators, except insofar as the obligations are also set forth in this Canon.

APPENDIX L

Selected ABA Model Rules of Professional Conduct—
© The American Bar Association

Preamble and Scope: A Lawyer's Responsibilities

[1]   A lawyer, as a member of the legal profession, is a representative of clients, an officer of the legal system and a public citizen having special responsibility for the quality of justice.

[2]   As a representative of clients, a lawyer performs various functions. As advisor, a lawyer provides a client with an informed understanding of the client's legal rights and obligations and explains their practical implications. As advocate, a lawyer zealously asserts the client's position under the rules of the adversary system. As negotiator, a lawyer seeks a result advantageous to the client but consistent with requirements of honest dealings with others. As an evaluator, a lawyer acts by examining a client's legal affairs and reporting about them to the client or to others.

[3]   In addition to these representational functions, a lawyer may serve as a third-party neutral, a nonrepresentational role helping the parties to resolve a dispute or other matter. Some of these Rules apply directly to lawyers who are or have served as third-party neutrals. See, e.g., Rules 1.12 and 2.4. In addition, there are Rules that apply to lawyers who are not active in the practice of law or to practicing lawyers even when they are acting in a nonprofessional capacity. For example, a lawyer who commits fraud in the conduct of a business is subject to discipline for engaging in conduct involving dishonesty, fraud, deceit or misrepresentation. See Rule 8.4.

[4]   In all professional functions a lawyer should be competent, prompt and diligent. A lawyer should maintain communication with a client concerning the representation. A lawyer should keep in confidence information relating to representation of a client except so far as disclosure is required or permitted by the Rules of Professional Conduct or other law.

[5]   A lawyer's conduct should conform to the requirements of the law, both in professional service to clients and in the lawyer's business and personal affairs. A lawyer should use the law's procedures only for legitimate purposes and not to harass or intimidate others. A lawyer should demonstrate respect for the legal system and for those who serve it, including judges, other lawyers and public officials. While it is a lawyer's duty, when necessary, to challenge the rectitude of official action, it is also a lawyer's duty to uphold legal process.

[6]   As a public citizen, a lawyer should seek improvement of the law, access to the legal system, the administration of justice and the quality of service rendered by the legal profession. As a member of a learned profession, a lawyer should cultivate knowledge of the law beyond its

use for clients, employ that knowledge in reform of the law and work to strengthen legal education. In addition, a lawyer should further the public's understanding of and confidence in the rule of law and the justice system because legal institutions in a constitutional democracy depend on popular participation and support to maintain their authority. A lawyer should be mindful of deficiencies in the administration of justice and of the fact that the poor, and sometimes persons who are not poor, cannot afford adequate legal assistance. Therefore, all lawyers should devote professional time and resources and use civic influence to ensure equal access to our system of justice for all those who because of economic or social barriers cannot afford or secure adequate legal counsel. A lawyer should aid the legal profession in pursuing these objectives and should help the bar regulate itself in the public interest.

[7]   Many of a lawyer's professional responsibilities are prescribed in the Rules of Professional Conduct, as well as substantive and procedural law. However, a lawyer is also guided by personal conscience and the approbation of professional peers. A lawyer should strive to attain the highest level of skill, to improve the law and the legal profession and to exemplify the legal profession's ideals of public service.

[8]   A lawyer's responsibilities as a representative of clients, an officer of the legal system and a public citizen are usually harmonious. Thus, when an opposing party is well represented, a lawyer can be a zealous advocate on behalf of a client and at the same time assume that justice is being done. So also, a lawyer can be sure that preserving client confidences ordinarily serves the public interest because people are more likely to seek legal advice, and thereby heed their legal obligations, when they know their communications will be private.

[9]   In the nature of law practice, however, conflicting responsibilities are encountered. Virtually all difficult ethical problems arise from conflict between a lawyer's responsibilities to clients, to the legal system and to the lawyer's own interest in remaining an ethical person while earning a satisfactory living. The Rules of Professional Conduct often prescribe terms for resolving such conflicts. Within the framework of these Rules, however, many difficult issues of professional discretion can arise. Such issues must be resolved through the exercise of sensitive professional and moral judgment guided by the basic principles underlying the Rules. These principles include the lawyer's obligation zealously to protect and pursue a client's legitimate interests, within the bounds of the law, while maintaining a professional, courteous and civil attitude toward all persons involved in the legal system.

[10]   The legal profession is largely self-governing. Although other professions also have been granted powers of self-government, the legal profession is unique in this respect because of the close relationship between the profession and the processes of government and law enforcement. This connection manifested in the fact that ultimate authority over the legal profession is vested largely in the courts.

[11]   To the extent that lawyers meet the obligations of their professional calling, the occasion for government regulation is obviated. Self-regulation also helps maintain the legal profession's independence from government domination. An independent legal profession is an important force in preserving government under law, for abuse of legal authority is more readily challenged by a profession whose members are not dependent on government for the right to practice.

[12]   The legal profession's relative autonomy carries with it special responsibilities of self-government. The profession has a responsibility to assure that its regulations are conceived in the public interest and not in furtherance of parochial or self-interested concerns of the bar. Every lawyer is responsible for observance of the Rules of Professional Conduct. A lawyer should also aid in securing their observance by other lawyers. Neglect of these responsibilities compromises the independence of the profession and the public interest which it serves.

[13]   Lawyers play a vital role in the preservation of society. The fulfillment of this role requires an understanding by lawyers of their relationship to our legal system. The Rules of Professional Conduct, when properly applied, serve to define that relationship.

SCOPE

[14]   The Rules of Professional Conduct are rules of reason. They should be interpreted with reference to the purposes of legal representation and of the law itself. Some of the Rules are imperatives, cast in the terms "shall" or "shall not." These define proper conduct for purposes of professional discipline. Others, generally cast in the term "may," are permissive and define areas under the Rules in which the lawyer has discretion to exercise professional judgment. No disciplinary action should be taken when the lawyer chooses not to act or acts within the bounds of such discretion. Other Rules define the nature of relationships between the lawyer and others. The Rules are thus partly obligatory and disciplinary and partly constitutive and descriptive in that they define a lawyer's professional role. Many of the Comments use the term "should." Comments do not add obligations to the Rules but provide guidance for practicing in compliance with the Rules.

[15]   The Rules presuppose a larger legal context shaping the lawyer's role. That context includes court rules and statutes relating to matters of licensure, laws defining specific obligations of lawyers and substantive and procedural law in general. The Comments are sometimes used to alert lawyers to their responsibilities under such other law.

[16]   Compliance with the Rules, as with all law in an open society, depends primarily upon understanding and voluntary compliance, secondarily upon reinforcement by peer and public opinion and finally, when necessary, upon enforcement through disciplinary proceedings. The Rules do not, however, exhaust the moral and ethical considerations that should inform a lawyer, for no worthwhile human activity can be completely defined by legal rules. The Rules simply provide a framework for the ethical practice of law.

[17]   Furthermore, for purposes of determining the lawyer's authority and responsibility, principles of substantive law external to these Rules determine whether a client-lawyer relationship exists. Most of the duties flowing from the client-lawyer relationship attach only after the client has requested the lawyer to render legal services and the lawyer has agreed to do so. But there are some duties, such as that of confidentiality under Rule 1.6, that attach when the lawyer agrees to consider whether a client-lawyer relationship shall be established. See Rule 1.18. Whether a client-lawyer relationship exists for any specific purpose can depend on the circumstances and may be a question of fact.

[18]   Under various legal provisions, including constitutional, statutory and common law, the responsibilities of government lawyers may include authority concerning legal matters that ordinarily reposes in the client in private client-lawyer relationships. For example, a lawyer for a government agency may have authority on behalf of the government to decide upon settlement or whether to appeal from an adverse judgment. Such authority in various respects is generally vested in the attorney general and the state's attorney in state government, and their federal counterparts, and the same may be true of other government law officers. Also, lawyers under the supervision of these officers may be authorized to represent several government agencies in intergovernmental legal controversies in circumstances where a private lawyer could not represent multiple private clients. These Rules do not abrogate any such authority.

[19]   Failure to comply with an obligation or prohibition imposed by a Rule is a basis for invoking the disciplinary process. The Rules presuppose that disciplinary assessment of a lawyer's conduct will be made on the basis of the facts and circumstances as they existed at the time of the conduct in question and in recognition of the fact that a lawyer often has to act upon uncertain or incomplete evidence of the situation. Moreover, the Rules presuppose that whether or not discipline should be imposed for a violation, and the severity of a sanction, depend on all the circumstances, such as the willfulness and seriousness of the violation, extenuating factors and whether there have been previous violations.

[20]   Violation of a Rule should not itself give rise to a cause of action against a lawyer nor should it create any presumption in such a case that a legal duty has been breached. In addition, violation of a Rule does not necessarily warrant any other nondisciplinary remedy, such as disqualification of a lawyer in pending litigation. The Rules are designed to provide guidance to lawyers and to provide a structure for regulating conduct through disciplinary agencies. They are not designed to be a basis for civil liability. Furthermore, the purpose of the Rules can be subverted when they are invoked by opposing parties as procedural weapons. The fact that a Rule is a just basis for a lawyer's self-assessment, or for sanctioning a lawyer under the administration of a disciplinary authority, does not imply that an antagonist in a collateral proceeding or transaction has standing to seek enforcement of the Rule. Nevertheless, since the Rules do establish standards of conduct by lawyers, a lawyer's violation of a Rule may be evidence of breach of the applicable standard of conduct.

[21]   The Comment accompanying each Rule explains and illustrates the meaning and purpose of the Rule. The Preamble and this note on Scope provide general orientation. The Comments are intended as guides to interpretation, but the text of each Rule is authoritative.

RULE 1.1   COMPETENCE

A lawyer shall provide competent representation to a client. Competent representation requires the legal knowledge, skill, thoroughness and preparation reasonably necessary for the representation.

RULE 1.2   SCOPE OF REPRESENTATION AND ALLOCATION OF AUTHORITY BETWEEN CLIENT AND LAWYER

(a)   Subject to paragraphs (c) and (d), a lawyer shall abide by a client's decisions concerning the objectives of representation and, as required by Rule 1.4, shall consult with the client as to the means by which they are to be pursued. A lawyer may take such action on behalf of the client as is impliedly authorized to carry out the representation. A lawyer shall abide by a client's decision whether to settle a matter. In a criminal case, the lawyer shall abide by the client's decision, after consultation with the lawyer, as to a plea to be entered, whether to waive jury trial and whether the client will testify.

(b)   A lawyer's representation of a client, including representation by appointment, does not constitute an endorsement of the client's political, economic, social or moral views or activities.

(c)   A lawyer may limit the scope of the representation if the limitation is reasonable under the circumstances and the client gives informed consent.

(d)   A lawyer shall not counsel a client to engage, or assist a client, in conduct that the lawyer knows is criminal or fraudulent, but a lawyer may discuss the legal consequences of any proposed course of conduct with a client and may counsel or assist a client to make a good faith effort to determine the validity, scope, meaning or application of the law.

RULE 1.3   DILIGENCE

A lawyer shall act with reasonable diligence and promptness in representing a client.

RULE 1.4   COMMUNICATION

(a)   A lawyer shall:

(1) promptly inform the client of any decision or circumstance with respect to which the client's informed consent, as defined in Rule 1.0(e), is required by these Rules;

(2) reasonably consult with the client about the means by which the client's objectives are to be accomplished;

(3) keep the client reasonably informed about the status of the matter;

(4) promptly comply with reasonable requests for information; and

(5) consult with the client about any relevant limitation on the lawyer's conduct when the lawyer knows that the client expects assistance not permitted by the Rules of Professional Conduct or other law.

(b) A lawyer shall explain a matter to the extent reasonably necessary to permit the client to make informed decisions regarding the representation.

RULE 1.6 RULE OF CONFIDENTIALITY

(a) A lawyer shall not reveal information relating to the representation of a client unless the client gives informed consent, the disclosure is impliedly authorized in order to carry out the representation or the disclosure is permitted by paragraph (b).

(b) A lawyer may reveal information relating to the representation of a client to the extent the lawyer reasonably believes necessary:

(1) to prevent reasonably certain death or substantial bodily harm;

(2) to prevent the client from committing a crime or fraud that is reasonably certain to result in substantial injury to the financial interests or property of another and in furtherance of which the client has used or is using the lawyer's services;

(3) to prevent, mitigate or rectify substantial injury to the financial interests or property of another that is reasonably certain to result or has resulted from the client's commission of a crime of fraud in furtherance of which the client has used the lawyer's services;

(4) to secure legal advice about the lawyer's compliance with these Rules:

(5) to establish a claim or defense on behalf of the lawyer in a controversy between the lawyer and the client, to establish a defense to a criminal charge or civil claim against the lawyer based upon conduct in which the client was involved, or to respond to allegations in any proceeding concerning the lawyer's representation of the client; or

(6) to comply with other law or a court order.

RULE 1.7 CONFLICT OF INTEREST: CURRENT CLIENTS

(a) Except as provided in paragraph (b), a lawyer shall not represent a client if the representation involves a concurrent conflict of interest. A concurrent conflict of interest exists if:

(1) the representation of one client will be directly adverse to another client; or

(2) there is a significant risk that the representation of one or more clients will be materially limited by the lawyer's responsibilities to another client, a former client or a third person or by a personal interest of the lawyer.

(b)   Notwithstanding the existence of a concurrent conflict of interest under paragraph (a), a lawyer may represent a client if:

(1) the lawyer reasonably believes that the lawyer will be able to provide competent and diligent representation to each affected client;

(2) the representation is not prohibited by law;

(3) the representation does not involve the assertion of a claim by one client against another client represented by the lawyer in the same litigation or other proceeding before a tribunal; and

(4) each affected client gives informed consent, confirmed in writing.

RULE 1.9 DUTIES TO FORMER CLIENTS

(a)   A lawyer who has formerly represented a client in a matter shall not thereafter represent another person in the same or a substantially related matter in which that person's interests are materially adverse to the interests of the former client unless the former client gives informed consent, confirmed in writing.

(b)   A lawyer shall not knowingly represent a person in the same or a substantially related matter in which a firm with which the lawyer formerly was associated had previously represented a client

(1) whose interests are materially adverse to that person; and

(2) about whom the lawyer had acquired information protected by Rules 1.6 and 1.9(c) that is material to the matter; unless the former client gives informed consent, confirmed in writing.

(c)   A lawyer who has formerly represented a client in a matter or whose present or former firm has formerly represented a client in a matter shall not thereafter:

(1) use information relating to the representation to the disadvantage of the former client except as these Rules would permit or require with respect to a client, or when the information has become generally known; or

(2) reveal information relating to the representation except as these Rules would permit or require with respect to a client.

RULE 1.12 FORMER JUDGE, ARBITRATOR, MEDIATOR OR OTHER THIRD-PARTY NEUTRAL

(a)   Except as stated in paragraph (d), a lawyer shall not represent anyone in connection with a matter in which the lawyer participated personally and substantially as a judge or other adjudicative officer or law clerk to such a person or as an arbitrator, mediator or other third-party neutral, unless all parties to the proceeding give informed consent, confirmed in writing.

(b)   A lawyer shall not negotiate for employment with any person who is involved as a party or as lawyer for a party in a matter in which the lawyer is participating personally and substantially as a judge or other adjudicative officer or as an arbitrator, mediator or other third-party neutral. A lawyer serving as a law clerk to a judge or other adjudicative officer may negotiate for employment with a party or lawyer involved in a matter in which the clerk is participating personally and substantially, but only after the lawyer has notified the judge or other adjudicative officer.

(c)   If a lawyer is disqualified by paragraph (a), no lawyer in a firm with which that lawyer is associated may knowingly undertake or continue representation in the matter unless:

        (1) the disqualified lawyer is timely screened from any participation in the matter and is apportioned no part of the fee therefrom; and

        (2) written notice is promptly given to the parties and any appropriate tribunal to enable them to ascertain compliance with the provisions of this rule.

(d)   An arbitrator selected as a partisan of a party in a multimember arbitration panel is not prohibited from subsequently representing that party.

RULE 1.13   ORGANIZATION AS CLIENT

(a)   A lawyer employed or retained by an organization represents the organization acting through its duly authorized constituents.

(b)   If a lawyer for an organization knows that an officer, employee or other person associated with the organization is engaged in action, intends to act or refuses to act in a matter related to the representation that is a violation of a legal obligation to the organization, or a violation of law that reasonably might be imputed to the organization, and that is likely to result in substantial injury to the organization, then the lawyer shall proceed as is reasonably necessary in the best interest of the organization. Unless the lawyer reasonably believes that it is not necessary in the best interest of the organization to do so, the lawyer shall refer the matter to higher authority in the organization, including, if warranted by the circumstances to the highest authority that can act on behalf of the organization as determined by applicable law.

(c)   Except as provided in paragraph (d), if

        (1) despite the lawyer's efforts in accordance with paragraph (b)

the highest authority that can act on behalf of the organization insists upon or fails to address in a timely and appropriate manner an action, or a refusal to act, that is clearly a violation of law, and

(2) the lawyer reasonably believes that the violation is reasonably certain to result in substantial injury to the organization, then the lawyer may reveal information relating to the representation whether or not Rule 1.6 permits such disclosure, but only if and to the extent the lawyer reasonably believes necessary to prevent substantial injury to the organization.

(d)　　Paragraph (c) shall not apply with respect to information relating to a lawyer's representation of an organization to investigate an alleged violation of law, or to defend the organization or an officer, employee or other constituent associated with the organization against a claim arising out of an alleged violation of law.

(e)　　A lawyer who reasonably believes that he or she has been discharged because of the lawyer's actions taken pursuant to paragraphs (b) or (c), or who withdraws under circumstances that require or permit the lawyer to take action under either of those paragraphs, shall proceed as the lawyer reasonably believes necessary to assure that the organization's highest authority is informed of the lawyer's discharge or withdrawal.

RULE 2.4　LAWYER SERVING AS THIRD-PARTY NEUTRAL

(a)　　A lawyer serves as a third-party neutral when the lawyer assists two or more persons who are not clients of the lawyer to reach a resolution of a dispute or other matter that has arisen between them. Service as a third-party neutral may include service as an arbitrator, a mediator or in such other capacity as will enable the lawyer to assist the parties to resolve the matter.

(b)　　A lawyer serving as a third-party neutral shall inform unrepresented parties that the lawyer is not representing them. When the lawyer knows or reasonably should know that a party does not understand the lawyer's role in the matter, the lawyer shall explain the difference between the lawyer's role as a third-party neutral and a lawyer's role as one who represents a client.

RULE 3.3　CANDOR TOWARD THE TRIBUNAL

(a)　　A lawyer shall not knowingly:

(1) make a false statement of fact or law to a tribunal or fail to correct a false statement of material fact or law previously made to the tribunal by the lawyer;

(2) fail to disclose to the tribunal legal authority in the controlling jurisdiction known to the lawyer to be directly adverse to the position of the client and not disclosed by opposing counsel; or

(3) offer evidence that the lawyer knows to be false. If a lawyer, the lawyer's client, or a witness called by the lawyer, has offered material

evidence and the lawyer comes to know of its falsity, the lawyer shall take reasonable remedial measures, including, if necessary, disclosure to the tribunal. A lawyer may refuse to offer evidence, other than the testimony of a defendant in a criminal matter, that the lawyer reasonably believes is false.

(b)   A lawyer who represents a client in an adjudicative proceeding and who knows that a person intends to engage, is engaging or has engaged in criminal or fraudulent conduct related to the proceeding shall take reasonable remedial measures, including, if necessary, disclosure to the tribunal.

(c)   The duties stated in paragraphs (a) and (b) continue to the conclusion of the proceeding, and apply even if compliance requires disclosure of information otherwise protected by Rule 1.6.

(d)   In an ex parte proceeding, a lawyer shall inform the tribunal of all material facts known to the lawyer that will enable the tribunal to make an informed decision, whether or not the facts are adverse.

RULE 3.4   FAIRNESS TO OPPOSING PARTY AND COUNSEL

A lawyer shall not:

(a)   unlawfully obstruct another party' s access to evidence or unlawfully alter, destroy or conceal a document or other material having potential evidentiary value. A lawyer shall not counsel or assist another person to do any such act;

(b)   falsify evidence, counsel or assist a witness to testify falsely, or offer an inducement to a witness that is prohibited by law;

(c)   knowingly disobey an obligation under the rules of a tribunal except for an open refusal based on an assertion that no valid obligation exists;

(d)   in pretrial procedure, make a frivolous discovery request or fail to make reasonably diligent effort to comply with a legally proper discovery request by an opposing party;

(e)   in trial, allude to any matter that the lawyer does not reasonably believe is relevant or that will not be supported by admissible evidence, assert personal knowledge of facts in issue except when testifying as a witness, or state a personal opinion as to the justness of a cause, the credibility of a witness, the culpability of a civil litigant or the guilt or innocence of an accused; or

(f)   request a person other than a client to refrain from voluntarily giving relevant information to another party unless:

(1) the person is a relative or an employee or other agent of a client; and

(2) the lawyer reasonably believes that the person's interests will not be adversely affected by refraining from giving such information.

RULE 3.5 IMPARTIALITY AND DECORUM OF THE TRIBUNAL

A lawyer shall not:

(a)   seek to influence a judge, juror, prospective juror or other official by means prohibited by law;

(b)   communicate ex parte with such a person during the proceeding unless authorized to do so by law or court order;

(c)   communicate with a juror or prospective juror after discharge of the jury if:

(1) the communication is prohibited by law or court order;

(2) the juror has made known to the lawyer a desire not to communicate; or

(3) the communication involves misrepresentation, coercion, duress or harassment; or

(d)   engage in conduct intended to disrupt a tribunal.

RULE 4.1 TRUTHFULNESS IN STATEMENTS TO OTHERS

In the course of representing a client a lawyer shall not knowingly:

(a) make a false statement of material fact or law to a third person; or

(b) fail to disclose a material fact to a third person when disclosure is necessary to avoid assisting a criminal or fraudulent act by a client, unless disclosure is prohibited by Rule 1.6.

RULE 4.3 DEALING WITH UNREPRESENTED PERSON

In dealing on behalf of a client with a person who is not represented by counsel, a lawyer shall not state or imply that the lawyer is disinterested. When the lawyer knows or reasonably should know that the unrepresented person misunderstands the lawyer's role in the matter, the lawyer shall make reasonable efforts to correct the misunderstanding. The lawyer shall not give legal advice to an unrepresented person, other than the advice to secure counsel, if the lawyer knows or reasonably should know that the interests of such a person are or have a reasonable possibility of being in conflict with the interests of the client.

RULE 4.4 RESPECT FOR RIGHTS OF THIRD PERSONS

(a)   In representing a client, a lawyer shall not use means that have no substantial purpose other than to embarrass, delay, or burden a third person, or use methods of obtaining evidence that violate the legal rights of such a person.

(b)   A lawyer who receives a document relating to the representation of the lawyer's client and knows or reasonably should know that the document was inadvertently sent shall promptly notify the sender.

APPENDIX M

American Bar Association Litigation Section—
© The American Bar Association

Civility Guidelines

The material contained in this section is adapted from Manuel San Juan, "ABA Litigation Section's Civility Guidelines," February 2001 *The Federal Lawyer* 51.

In 1998, the American Bar Association's Litigation Section issued a set of Guidelines for Litigation Conduct to address what it viewed as a decline in professionalism and civility among lawyers. Modeled on the Standards of Professional Conduct adopted by the United States Court of Appeals for the Seventh Circuit, the ABA Section of Litigation's Guidelines are purely aspirational and are not used as a basis for liability or discipline. You should draw these Guidelines to the attention of other arbitration advocates, as necessary, when inappropriate or unprofessional behavior of lawyers tends to threaten the intended purpose, the integrity, or the character of the arbitration process. Guidelines that appear to directly pertain to the arbitration process include:

Lawyer's duties to other counsel

1. We will practice our profession with a continuing awareness that our role is to zealously advance the legitimate interests of our clients. In our dealings with others, we will not reflect the ill feelings of our clients. We will treat all other counsel, parties, and witnesses in a civil and courteous manner, not only in court, but also in all other written and oral communications. We will refrain from acting upon or manifesting bias or prejudice based upon race, sex, religion, national origin, disability, age, sexual orientation, or socioeconomic status toward any participant in the legal process.

2. We will not, even when called upon by a client to do so, abuse or indulge in offensive conduct directed to other counsel, parties, or witnesses. We will abstain from disparaging personal remarks or acrimony toward other counsel, parties, or witnesses. We will treat adverse witnesses and parties with fair consideration.

3. We will not encourage or knowingly authorize any person under our control to engage in conduct that would be improper if we engaged in such conduct.

4. We will not, absent good cause attribute bad motives or improper conduct to other counsel.

. . .

6. We will in good faith adhere to all express promises and to agreements with other counsel, whether oral or in writing, and to all agreements implied by the circumstances or local customs.

. . .

9. In civil actions, we will stipulate to relevant matters if they are undisputed and if no good faith advocacy basis exists for not stipulating.

. . .

10. We will not use any form of discovery or discovery scheduling as a means of harassment.

11. Whenever circumstances allow, we will make good faith efforts to resolve by agreement objections before presenting them to the [tribunal].

12. We will not time the filing or service of motions or pleadings in any way that unfairly limits another party's opportunity to respond.

13. We will not request an extension of time solely for the purpose of unjustified delay or to obtain unfair advantage.

14. We will consult other counsel regarding scheduling matters in a good faith effort to avoid scheduling conflicts.

15. We will endeavor to accommodate previously scheduled dates for hearings, depositions, meeting, conferences, vacations, seminars, or other functions that produce good faith calendar conflicts on the part of other counsel.

16. We will promptly notify other counsel, and . . . other persons, when . . . meetings, or conferences are to be canceled or postponed.

17. We will agree to reasonable requests for extensions of time and for waiver of procedural formalities, provided our clients' legitimate rights will not be materially or adversely affected.

18. We will not cause any default or dismissal to be entered without first notifying opposing counsel when we know his or her identity, unless the rules provide otherwise.

19. We will take depositions only when actually needed. We will not take depositions for the purposes of harassment or other improper purpose.

20. We will not engage in any conduct during a deposition that would not be appropriate in the presence of an [arbitrator].

21. We will not obstruct questioning during a deposition or object to deposition questions unless permitted under applicable law.

22. During depositions, we will ask only those questions we reasonably believe are necessary, and appropriate, for the prosecution or defense of an action.

23. We will carefully craft document production requests so they are limited to those documents we reasonably believe are necessary, and appropriate, for the prosecution or defense of an action. We will not design production requests to place an undue burden or expense on a party, or for any other improper purpose.

24. We will respond to document requests reasonably and not strain to interpret requests in an artificially restrictive manner to avoid disclosure of relevant and non-privileged documents. We will not produce documents in a manner designed to hide or obscure the existence of particular documents, or to accomplish Any other improper purpose.

25. We will carefully craft interrogatories so they are limited to those matters we reasonably believe are necessary, and appropriate, for the prosecution or defense of an action, and we will not design them to place an undue burden or expense on a party, or for any other improper purpose.

26. We will respond to interrogatories reasonably and will not strain to interpret them in an artificially restrictive manner to avoid disclosure of relevant and non-privileged information, or for any other improper purpose.

27. We will base our discovery objections on a good faith belief in their merit and will not object solely for the purpose of withholding or delaying the disclosure of relevant information, or for any other improper purpose.

28. When a draft order is to be prepared by counsel to reflect an [arbitrator's] ruling, we will draft an order that accurately and completely reflects the [arbitrator's] ruling. We will promptly prepare and submit a proposed order to other counsel and attempt to reconcile any differences before the draft order is present to the [arbitrator].

29. We will not ascribe a position to another counsel that counsel has not taken.

30. Unless permitted or invited by the [arbitrator], we will not send copies of correspondence between counsel to the [arbitrator].

31. Nothing contained in these Guidelines is intended or shall be construed to inhibit vigorous advocacy, including vigorous cross-examination.

Lawyers' Duties to the [arbitrator(s)]

1. We will speak and write civilly and respectfully in all communications with the [arbitrator(s)].

2. We will be punctual and prepared for all . . . appearances so that all hearings, conferences, and trials may commence on time; if delayed, we will notify the [arbitrator(s)], if possible.

3. We will be considerate of the time constraints and pressures on the [arbitrator(s)] … inherent in their effort to administer justice.

4. We will not engage in any conduct that brings disorder or disruption to the [hearing]. We will advise our clients and witnesses appearing in [the hearing] of the proper conduct expected and required there and, to the best of our ability, prevent our clients and witnesses from creating disorder or disruption.

5. We will not knowingly misrepresent, mischaracterize, misquote, or miscite facts or authorities in any oral or written communication to the [arbitrator(s)].

6. We will not write letters to the [arbitrator(s)] In connection with a pending action, unless invited or permitted by the [arbitrator(s].

7. Before dates for hearings . . . are set, or if that is not feasible, immediately after such date has been set, we will attempt to verify the availability of necessary participants and witnesses so we can promptly notify the court of any likely problems.

APPENDIX N

Uniform Arbitration Act—

(Reprinted with permission, Copyright NCCUL.)

(Last Revisions Completed Year 2000)

Drafted by the

NATIONAL CONFERENCE OF COMMISSIONERS
ON UNIFORM STATE LAWS

and by it

APPROVED AND RECOMMENDED FOR ENACTMENT
IN ALL THE STATES

at its

ANNUAL CONFERENCE

ANNUAL CONFERENCE

MEETING IN ITS ONE-HUNDRED-AND-NINTH YEAR

ST. AUGUSTINE, FLORIDA

JULY 28–AUGUST 4, 2000

WITHOUT COMMENTS

UNIFORM ARBITRATION ACT

The Committee that acted for the National Conference of Commissioners on Uniform State Laws in preparing the Revised Uniform Arbitration Act is as follows:

FRANCIS J. PAVETTI, 83 Huntington Street, New London, CT 06320,
Chair

FRANCISCO L. ACEVEDO, P.O. Box 190998, 16th Floor, Banco Popular Center, Hato Rey, PR 00919

RICHARD T. CASSIDY, 100 Main Street, P.O. Box 1124, Burlington, VT 05402

M. MICHAEL CRAMER, 216 N. Adams Street, Rockville, MD 20850

BARRY C. HAWKINS, One Landmark Square, 17th Floor, Stamford, CT 06901

TIMOTHY J. HEINSZ, University of Missouri-Columbia, School of Law, 203 Hulston Hall, Columbia, MO 65211,
National Conference Reporter

ROGER C. HENDERSON, University of Arizona, James E. Rogers College of Law, Mountain and Speedway Streets, Tucson, AZ 85721,
Committee on Style *Liaison*

JEREMIAH MARSH, Suite 4300, Three First National Plaza, Chicago, IL 60602

RODNEY W. SATTERWHITE, P.O. Box 1540, Midland, TX 79702

JAMES A. WYNN, JR., Court of Appeals, One W. Morgan Street, P.O. Box 888, Raleigh, NC 27602

JOAN ZELDON, Superior Court, 500 Indiana Avenue, N.W., Room 1640, Washington, DC 20001

EX OFFICIO

JOHN L. McCLAUGHERTY, P.O. Box 553, Charleston, WV 25322,
President

STANLEY M. FISHER, 1100 Huntington Building, 925 Euclid Avenue, Cleveland, OH 44115-1475,
Division Chair

AMERICAN BAR ASSOCIATION ADVISORS

RICHARD CHERNICK, 3055 Wilshire Boulevard, 7th Floor, Los Angeles, CA 90010-1108,
*Co-Adviso*r

JAMES L. KNOLL, 1500 S.W. Taylor Street, Portland, OR 97205,
Tort and Insurance Practice Section Advisor

JOHN K. NOTZ, JR., 3300 Quaker Tower, 321 N. Clark Street, Chicago, IL 60610-4795,
Senior Lawyers Division Advisor

YARKO SOCHYNSKY, 350 The Embarcadero, 6th Floor, San Francisco, CA 94105-1250,
Real Property, Probate and Trust Law Section Advisor

RONALD M. STURTZ, 27 Badger Drive, Livingston, NJ 07039,
Co-Advisor

MAX ZIMNY, Floor 3, 1710 Broadway, New York, NY 10019-5254,
Labor and Employment Law Section Advisor

EXECUTIVE DIRECTOR

FRED H. MILLER, University of Oklahoma, College of Law, 300 Timberdell Road, Norman, OK 73019,
Executive Director

WILLIAM J. PIERCE, 1505 Roxbury Road, Ann Arbor, MI 48104,
Executive Director Emeritus

Copies of this Act may be obtained from:

NATIONAL CONFERENCE OF COMMISSIONERS
ON UNIFORM STATE LAWS
211 E. Ontario Street, Suite 1300
Chicago, Illinois 60611
312/915-0195 • www.nccusl.org

UNIFORM ARBITRATION ACT
TABLE OF CONTENTS [summary]

SECTION 1.   DEFINITIONS
SECTION 2.   NOTICE
SECTION 3.   WHEN [ACT] APPLIES
SECTION 4.   EFFECT OF AGREEMENT TO ARBITRATE;
             NONWAIVABLE PROVISIONS
SECTION 5.   [APPLICATION] FOR JUDICIAL RELIEF
SECTION 6.   VALIDITY OF AGREEMENT TO ARBITRATE
SECTION 7.   [MOTION] TO COMPEL OR STAY ARBITRATION
SECTION 8.   PROVISIONAL REMEDIES
SECTION 9.   INITIATION OF ARBITRATION
SECTION 10. CONSOLIDATION OF SEPARATE ARBITRATION
             PROCEEDINGS
SECTION 11. APPOINTMENT OF ARBITRATOR; SERVICE AS A
             NEUTRAL ARBITRATOR
SECTION 12. DISCLOSURE BY ARBITRATOR
SECTION 13. ACTION BY MAJORITY
SECTION 14. IMMUNITY OF ARBITRATOR; COMPETENCY TO TESTIFY;
             ATTORNEY'S FEES AND COSTS
SECTION 15. ARBITRATION PROCESS
SECTION 16. REPRESENTATION BY LAWYER
SECTION 17. WITNESSES; SUBPOENAS; DEPOSITIONS; DISCOVERY
SECTION 18. JUDICIAL ENFORCEMENT OF PREAWARD RULING
             BY ARBITRATOR
SECTION 19. AWARD
SECTION 20. CHANGE OF AWARD BY ARBITRATOR
SECTION 21. REMEDIES; FEES AND EXPENSES OF ARBITRATION
             PROCEEDING
SECTION 22. CONFIRMATION OF AWARD
SECTION 23. VACATING AWARD
SECTION 24. MODIFICATION OR CORRECTION OF AWARD
SECTION 25. JUDGMENT ON AWARD; ATTORNEY'S FEES
             AND LITIGATION EXPENSES
SECTION 26. JURISDICTION
SECTION 27. VENUE
SECTION 28. APPEALS
SECTION 29. UNIFORMITY OF APPLICATION AND CONSTRUCTION
SECTION 30. RELATIONSHIP TO ELECTRONIC SIGNATURES
             IN GLOBAL AND NATIONAL COMMERCE ACT
SECTION 31. EFFECTIVE DATE
SECTION 32. REPEAL
SECTION 33. SAVINGS CLAUSE

UNIFORM ARBITRATION ACT

Prefatory Note

The Uniform Arbitration Act (UAA), promulgated in 1955, has been one of the most successful Acts of the National Conference of Commissioners on Uniform State Laws. Forty-nine jurisdictions have arbitration statutes; 35 of these have adopted the UAA and 14 have adopted substantially similar legislation. A primary purpose of the 1955 Act was to insure the enforceability of agreements to arbitrate in the face of oftentimes hostile state law. That goal has been accomplished. Today arbitration is a primary mechanism favored by courts and parties to resolve disputes in many areas of the law. This growth in arbitration caused the Conference to appoint a Drafting Committee to consider revising the Act in light of the increasing use of arbitration, the greater complexity of many disputes resolved by arbitration, and the developments of the law in this area.

The UAA did not address many issues which arise in modern arbitration cases. The statute provided no guidance as to (1) who decides the arbitrability of a dispute and by what criteria; (2) whether a court or arbitrators may issue provisional remedies; (3) how a party can initiate an arbitration proceeding; (4) whether arbitration proceedings may be consolidated; (5) whether arbitrators are required to disclose facts reasonably likely to affect impartiality; (6) what extent arbitrators or an arbitration organization are immune from civil actions; (7) whether arbitrators or representatives of arbitration organizations may be required to testify in another proceeding; (8) whether arbitrators have the discretion to order discovery, issue protective orders, decide motions for summary dispositions, hold prehearing conferences and otherwise manage the arbitration process; (9) when a court may enforce a preaward ruling by an arbitrator; (10) what remedies an arbitrator may award, especially in regard to attorney's fees, punitive damages or other exemplary relief; (11) when a court can award attorney's fees and costs to arbitrators and arbitration organizations; (12) when a court can award attorney's fees and costs to a prevailing party in an appeal of an arbitrator's award; and (13) which sections of the UAA would not be waivable, an important matter to insure fundamental fairness to the parties will be preserved, particularly in those instances where one party may have significantly less bargaining power than another; and (14) the use of electronic information and other modern means of technology in the arbitration process. The Revised Uniform Arbitration Act (RUAA) examines all of these issues and provides state legislatures with a more up-to-date statute to resolve disputes through arbitration.

There are a number of principles that the Drafting Committee agreed upon at the outset of its consideration of a revision to the UAA. First, arbitration is a consensual process in which autonomy of the parties who enter into arbitration agreements should be given primary consideration, so long as their agreements conform to notions of fundamental fairness. This approach provides parties with the opportunity in most instances to shape the arbitration process to their own particular needs. In most instances the RUAA provides a default mechanism if the parties do not have a specific agreement on a particular issue. Second, the underlying reason many parties choose arbitration is the relative speed, lower cost, and greater efficiency of the process. The law should take these factors, where applicable, into account. For example, section 10 allows consolidation of issues involving multiple parties. Such a provision can be of special importance in adhesion situations where there are numerous persons with essentially the same claims against a party to the arbitration agreement. Finally, in most cases parties intend the decisions of arbitrators to be final with minimal court involvement unless there is clear unfairness or a denial of justice. This contractual nature of arbitration means that the provision to vacate awards in section 23 is limited. This is so even where an arbitrator may award attorney's fees, punitive damages or other exemplary relief under section 21. Section 14 insulates arbitrators from unwarranted litigation to insure their independence by providing them with immunity.

Other new provisions are intended to reflect developments in arbitration law and to insure that the process is a fair one. Section 12 requires arbitrators to make important disclosures to the parties. Section 8 allows courts to grant provisional remedies in certain circumstances to protect the integrity of the arbitration process. Section 17 includes limited rights to discovery while recognizing the importance of expeditious arbitration proceedings.

In light of a number of decisions by the United States Supreme Court concerning the Federal Arbitration Act (FAA), any revision of the UAA must take into account the doctrine of preemption. The rule of preemption, whereby FAA standards and the emphatically pro-arbitration perspective of the FAA control, applies in both the federal courts and the state courts. To date, the preemption-related opinions of the Supreme Court have centered in large part on the two key issues that arise at the front end of the arbitration process—enforcement of the agreement to arbitrate and issues of substantive arbitrability. Prima Paint Corp. v. Flood & Conklin Mfg. Co., 388 U.S. 35 (1967); Moses H. Cone Mem'l Hosp. v. Mercury Constr. Corp., 460 U.S. 1 (1983); Southland Corp. v. Keating, 465 U.S. 2 (1984); Perry v. Thomas, 482 U.S. 483 (1987); Allied-Bruce Terminix Cos. v. Dobson, 513 U.S. 265 (1995); Doctor's Assocs. v. Cassarotto, 517 U.S. 681 (1996). That body of case law establishes that state law of any ilk, including adaptations of the RUAA, mooting or limiting contractual agreements to arbitrate must yield to the pro-arbitration public policy voiced in sections 2, 3, and 4 of the FAA.

The other issues to which the FAA speaks definitively lie at the back end of the arbitration process. The standards and procedure for vacatur, confirmation and modification of arbitration awards are the subject of sections 9, 10, 11, and 12 of the FAA. In contrast to the "front end" issues of enforceability and substantive arbitrability, there is no definitive Supreme Court case law speaking to the preemptive effect, if any, of the FAA with regard to these "back end" issues. This dimension of FAA preemption of state arbitration law is further complicated by the strong majority view among the United States Circuit Courts of Appeals that the section 10(a) standards are not the exclusive grounds for vacatur.

Nevertheless, the Supreme Court's unequivocal stand to date as to the preemptive effect of the FAA provides strong reason to believe that a similar result will obtain with regard to section 10(a) grounds for vacatur. If it does, and if the Supreme Court eventually determines that the section 10(a) standards are the sole grounds for vacatur of commercial arbitration awards, FAA preemption of conflicting state law with regard to the "back end" issues of vacatur (and confirmation and modification) would be certain. If the Court takes the opposite tack and holds that the section 10(a) grounds are not the exclusive criteria for vacatur, the preemptive effect of section 10(a) would most likely be limited to the rule that state arbitration acts cannot eliminate, limit or modify any of the four grounds of party and arbitrator misconduct set out in section 10(a). Any definitive federal "common law," pertaining to the nonstatutory grounds for vacatur other than those set out in section 10(a), articulated by the Supreme Court or established as a clear majority rule by the United States Courts of Appeals, likely would preempt contrary state law. A holding by the Supreme Court that the Section 10(a) grounds are not exclusive would also free the States to codify other grounds for vacatur beyond those set out in section 10(a). These various, currently nonstatutory grounds for vacatur are discussed at length in the section C to the Comment to section 23.

An important caveat to the general rule of FAA preemption is found in Volt Information Sciences, Inc. v. Stanford University, 489 U.S. 468 (1989) and Mastrobuono v. Shearson Lehman Hutton, Inc., 514 U.S. 52 (1995). The focus in these cases is on the effect of FAA preemption on choice-of-law provisions routinely included in commercial contracts. Volt and Mastrobuono establish that a clearly expressed contractual agreement by the parties to an arbitration contract to conduct their arbitration under state law rules effectively trumps the preemptive effect of the FAA. If the parties elect to govern their contractual arbitration mechanism by the law of a particular State and thereby limit the issues that they will arbitrate or the procedures under which the arbitration will be conducted, their bargain will be honored—as long as the state law principles invoked by the choice-of-law provision do not conflict with the FAA's prime directive that agreements to arbitrate be enforced. See, e.g., ASW Allstate Painting & Constr. Co. v. Lexington Ins. Co., 188 F.3d 307 (5th Cir. 1999); Russ Berrie & Co. v. Gantt,

988 S.W.2d 713 (Tex. Ct. App. 1999). It is in these situations that the RUAA will have most impact. Section 4(a) of the RUAA also explicitly provides that the parties to an arbitration agreement may waive or vary the terms of the Act to the extent otherwise permitted by law. Thus, when parties choose to contractually specify the procedures to be followed under their arbitration agreement, the RUAA contemplates that the contractually-established procedures will control over contrary state law, except with regard to issues designated as "nonwaivable" in section 4(b) and (c) of the RUAA.

The contractual election to proceed under state law instead of the FAA will be honored presuming that the state law is not antithetical to the pro-arbitration public policy of the FAA. Southland and Terminix leave no doubt that anti-arbitration state law provisions will be struck down because preempted by the federal arbitration statute.

Besides arbitration contracts where the parties choose to be governed by state law, there are other areas of arbitration law where the FAA does not preempt state law, in the absence of definitive federal law set out in the FAA or determined by the federal courts. First, the Supreme Court has made clear its belief that ascertaining when a particular contractual agreement to arbitrate is enforceable is a matter to be decided under the general contract law principles of each State. The sole limitation on state law in that regard is the Court's assertion that the enforceability of arbitration agreements must be determined by the same standards as are used for all other contracts. Terminix, 513 U.S. at 281 (1995) (quoting Volt, 489 U.S. at 474 (1989)) and quoted in Cassarotto, 517 U.S. 681, 685 (1996); and Cassarotto, 517 U.S. at 688 (quoting Scherk v. Alberto-Culver Co., 417 U.S. 506, 511 (1974)). Arbitration agreements may not be invalidated under state laws applicable only to arbitration provisions. Id. The FAA will preempt state law that does not place arbitration agreements on an "equal footing" with other contracts.

During the course of its deliberations the Drafting Committee considered at length another issue with strong preemption undertones—the question of whether the RUAA should explicitly sanction contractual provisions for "opt-in" review of challenged arbitration awards beyond that presently contemplated by the FAA and current state arbitration acts. "Opt-in" provisions of two types are in limited use today. The first variant permits a party who is dissatisfied with the arbitral result to petition directly to a designated state court and stipulates that the court may vacate challenged awards, typically for errors of law or fact. The second type of "opt-in" contractual provision establishes an appellate arbitral mechanism to which challenged arbitration awards can be submitted for review, again most typically for errors of law or fact.

As explained in detail in section B of the Comment to section 23, there were a number of reasons that resulted in the decision not to include statutory sanction of the "opt-in" device for expanded judicial review in the RUAA: (1) the current uncertainty as to the legality of a state statutory sanction of the "opt-in" device, (2) the "disconnect" between the Act's purpose of fostering the use of arbitration as a final and binding alternative to traditional litigation in a court of law, and (3) the inclusion of a statutory provision that would permit the parties to contractually render arbitration decidedly non-final and non-binding. Simply stated, the potential gain to be realized by codifying a right to opt-into expanded judicial review that has not yet been definitively confirmed to exist does not outweigh the potential threat that adoption of an opt-in statutory provision would create for the integrity and viability of the RUAA as a template for state arbitration acts.

Unlike the "opt-in" judicial review mechanism, there are few, if any, legal concerns raised by statutory sanction of "opt-in" provisions for appellate arbitral review. Nevertheless, as explained in the Section B of the Comments to section 23, because the current, contract-based view of arbitration establishes that the parties are free to design the inner workings of their arbitration procedures in any manner they see fit, the Drafting Committee determined that codification of that right in the RUAA would add nothing of substance to the existing law of arbitration.

The decision not to statutorily sanction either form of the "opt-in" device in the RUAA leaves the issue of the legal propriety of this means for securing review of awards to the developing case law under the FAA and state arbitration statutes. Parties remain free, within the constraints imposed by the existing and developing law, to agree to contractual provisions for arbitral or judicial review of challenged awards.

It is likely that matters not addressed in the FAA are also open to regulation by the States. State law provisions regulating purely procedural dimensions of the arbitration process (e.g., discovery [RUAA Section 17], consolidation of claims [RUAA Section 10], and arbitrator immunity [RUAA Section 14]) likely will not be subject to preemption. Less certain is the effect of FAA preemption with regard to substantive issues like the authority of arbitrators to award punitive damages (RUAA Section 21) and the standards for arbitrator disclosure of potential conflicts of interest (RUAA Section 12) that have a significant impact on the integrity and/or the adequacy of the arbitration process. These "borderline" issues are not purely procedural in nature but unlike the "front end" and "back end" issues they do not go to the essence of the agreement to arbitrate or effectuation of the arbitral result. Although there is no concrete guidance in the case law, preemption of state law dealing with such matters seems unlikely as long as it cannot be characterized as anti-arbitration or as intended to limit the enforceability or viability of agreements to arbitrate.

The subject of international arbitration is not specifically addressed in the RUAA. Twelve States have passed arbitration statutes directed to international arbitration. Seven States have based their statutes on the Model Arbitration Law proposed in 1985 by the United Nations Commission on International Trade Law (UNCITRAL). Other States have approached international arbitration in a variety of ways, such as adopting parts of the UNCITRAL Model Law together with provisions taken directly from the 1958 United Nations Convention on Recognition and Enforcement of Foreign Arbitral Awards (commonly referred to as the New York Convention) or by devising their own international arbitration provisions.

Any provisions of these state international arbitration statutes that are inconsistent with the New York Convention, to which the United States adhered in 1970 (terms of the New York Convention can be found at 9 U.S.C. § 201), or with the federal legislation in chapter 2 of Title 9 of the United States Code are preempted. Chapter 2 creates federal-question jurisdiction in the federal district courts for any case "falling under the [New York] Convention" and permits removal of any such case from a state court to the federal court "at any time prior to trial." 9 U.S.C. §§ 203, 205. The statute covers any commercial agreement to arbitrate and the resultant arbitration award unless the matter involves only American citizens and has no reasonable relationship to any foreign country and the courts have broadly applied the statute. Therefore, it is unlikely that state arbitration law will have major application to an international case. There are two instances where state arbitration law might apply in the international context: (1) where the parties designate a specific state arbitration law to govern the international arbitration and (2) where all parties to an arbitration proceeding involving an international transaction decide to proceed on a matter in state court and do not exercise their rights of removal under chapter 2 of Title 9 and the relevant provision of state arbitration law is not preempted by federal arbitration law or the New York Convention. In these relatively rare cases, the state courts will refer to the RUAA unless the State has enacted a special international arbitration law.

Because few international cases are likely to be dealt with in state courts and because of the diversity of state law already enacted for international cases, the Drafting Committee decided not to address international arbitration as a specific subject in the revision of the UAA; however, the Committee utilized provisions of the UNCITRAL Model Law, the New York Convention, and the 1996 English Arbitration Act as sources of statutory language for the RUAA.

The members of the Drafting Committee to revise the Uniform Arbitration Act wish to acknowledge our deep indebtedness and appreciation to Professor Stephen Hayford and Professor Thomas Stipanowich who devoted extensive amounts of time by providing invaluable advice throughout the entire drafting process.

UNIFORM ARBITRATION ACT

SECTION 1. DEFINITIONS. In this [Act]:

(1) "Arbitration organization" means an association, agency, board, commission, or other entity that is neutral and initiates, sponsors, or administers an arbitration proceeding or is involved in the appointment of an arbitrator.

(2) "Arbitrator" means an individual appointed to render an award, alone or with others, in a controversy that is subject to an agreement to arbitrate.

(3) "Court" means [a court of competent jurisdiction in this State].

(4) "Knowledge" means actual knowledge.

(5) "Person" means an individual, corporation, business trust, estate, trust, partnership, limited liability company, association, joint venture, government; governmental subdivision, agency, or instrumentality; public corporation; or any other legal or commercial entity.

(6) "Record" means information that is inscribed on a tangible medium or that is stored in an electronic or other medium and is retrievable in perceivable

SECTION 2. NOTICE.

(a) Except as otherwise provided in this [Act], a person gives notice to another person by taking action that is reasonably necessary to inform the other person in ordinary course, whether or not the other person acquires knowledge of the notice.

(b) A person has notice if the person has knowledge of the notice or has received notice.

(c) A person receives notice when it comes to the person's attention or the notice is delivered at the person's place of residence or place of business, or at another location held out by the person as a place of delivery of such communications.

SECTION 3. WHEN [ACT] APPLIES.

(a) This [Act] governs an agreement to arbitrate made on or after [the effective date of this [Act]].

(b) This [Act] governs an agreement to arbitrate made before [the effective date of this [Act]] if all the parties to the agreement or to the arbitration proceeding so agree in a record.

(c) On or after [a delayed date], this [Act] governs an agreement to arbitrate whenever made.

SECTION 4. EFFECT OF AGREEMENT TO ARBITRATE NON WAIVABLE PROVISIONS.

(a) Except as otherwise provided in subsections (b) and (c), a party to an agreement to arbitrate or to an arbitration proceeding may waive or, the parties may vary the effect of, the requirements of this [Act] to the extent permitted by law.

(b) Before a controversy arises that is subject to an agreement to arbitrate, a party to the agreement may not:

> (1) waive or agree to vary the effect of the requirements of Section 5(a), 6(a), 8, 17(a), 17(b), 26, or 28;
>
> (2) agree to unreasonably restrict the right under Section 9 to notice of the initiation of an arbitration proceeding;
>
> (3) agree to unreasonably restrict the right under Section 12 to disclosure of any facts by a neutral arbitrator; or
>
> (4) waive the right under Section 16 of a party to an agreement to arbitrate to be represented by a lawyer at any proceeding or hearing under this [Act], but an employer and a labor organization may waive the right to representation by a lawyer in a labor arbitration.

(c) A party to an agreement to arbitrate or arbitration proceeding may not waive, or the parties may not vary the effect of, the requirements of this section or

SECTION 5. [APPLICATION] FOR JUDICIAL RELIEF.

(a) Except as otherwise provided in Section 28, an [application] for judicial relief under this [Act] must be made by [motion] to the court and heard in the manner provided by law or rule of court for making and hearing [motions].

(b) Unless a civil action involving the agreement to arbitrate is pending, notice of an initial [motion] to the court under this [Act] must be served in the manner provided by law for the service of a summons in a civil action. Otherwise, notice of the motion must be given in the manner provided by law or rule of court for serving [motions] in pending cases.

SECTION 6. VALIDITY OF AGREEMENT TO ARBITRATE.

(a) An agreement contained in a record to submit to arbitration any existing or subsequent controversy arising between the parties to the agreement is valid, enforceable, and irrevocable except upon a ground that exists at law or in equity for the revocation of a contract.

(b) The court shall decide whether an agreement to arbitrate exists or a controversy is subject to an agreement to arbitrate.

(c) An arbitrator shall decide whether a condition precedent to arbitrability has been fulfilled and whether a contract containing a valid agreement to arbitrate is enforceable.

(d) If a party to a judicial proceeding challenges the existence of, or claims that a controversy is not subject to, an agreement to arbitrate, the arbitration proceeding may continue pending final resolution of the issue by the court, unless

SECTION 7. [MOTION] TO COMPEL OR STAY ARBITRATION.

(a) On [motion] of a person showing an agreement to arbitrate and alleging another person's refusal to arbitrate pursuant to the agreement:

> (1) if the refusing party does not appear or does not oppose the [motion], the court shall order the parties to arbitrate; and

> (2) if the refusing party opposes the [motion], the court shall proceed summarily to decide the issue and order the parties to arbitrate unless it finds that there is no enforceable agreement to arbitrate.

(b) On [motion] of a person alleging that an arbitration proceeding has been initiated or threatened but that there is no agreement to arbitrate, the court shall proceed summarily to decide the issue. If the court finds that there is an enforceable agreement to arbitrate, it shall order the parties to arbitrate.

(c) If the court finds that there is no enforceable agreement, it may not pursuant to subsection (a) or (b) order the parties to arbitrate.

(d) The court may not refuse to order arbitration because the claim subject to arbitration lacks merit or grounds for the claim have not been established.

(e) If a proceeding involving a claim referable to arbitration under an alleged agreement to arbitrate is pending in court, a [motion] under this section must be made in that court. Otherwise a [motion] under this section may be made in any court as provided in Section 27.

(f) If a party makes a [motion] to the court to order arbitration, the court on just terms shall stay any judicial proceeding that involves a claim alleged to be subject to the arbitration until the court renders a final decision under this section.

(g) If the court orders arbitration, the court on just terms shall stay any judicial proceeding that involves a claim subject to the arbitration. If a claim subject to the arbitration is severable, the court may limit the stay to that claim.

SECTION 8. PROVISIONAL REMEDIES.

(a) Before an arbitrator is appointed and is authorized and able to act, the court, upon [motion] of a party to an arbitration proceeding and for good cause shown, may enter an order for provisional remedies to protect the effectiveness of the arbitration proceeding to the same extent and under the same conditions as if the controversy were the subject of a civil action.

(b) After an arbitrator is appointed and is authorized and able to act:

(1) the arbitrator may issue such orders for provisional remedies, including interim awards, as the arbitrator finds necessary to protect the effectiveness of the arbitration proceeding and to promote the fair and expeditious resolution of the controversy, to the same extent and under the same conditions as if the controversy were the subject of a civil action and

(2) a party to an arbitration proceeding may move the court for a provisional remedy only if the matter is urgent and the arbitrator is not able to act timely or the arbitrator cannot provide an adequate remedy.

(c) A party does not waive a right of arbitration by making a [motion] under subsection (a) or (b).

SECTION 9.   INITIATION OF ARBITRATION.

(a) A person initiates an arbitration proceeding by giving notice in a record to the other parties to the agreement to arbitrate in the agreed manner between the parties or, in the absence of agreement, by certified or registered mail, return receipt requested and obtained, or by service as authorized for the commencement of a civil action. The notice must describe the nature of the controversy and the remedy sought.

(b) Unless a person objects for lack or insufficiency of notice under Section 15(c) not later than the beginning of the arbitration hearing, the person by appearing at the hearing waives any objection to lack of or insufficiency of notice.

SECTION 10. CONSOLIDATION OF SEPARATE ARBITRATION PROCEEDINGS.

(a) Except as otherwise provided in subsection (c), upon [motion] of a party to an agreement to arbitrate or to an arbitration proceeding, the court may order consolidation of separate arbitration proceedings as to all or some of the claims if:

(1) there are separate agreements to arbitrate or separate arbitration proceedings between the same persons or one of them is a party to a separate agreement to arbitrate or a separate arbitration proceeding with a third person;

(2) the claims subject to the agreements to arbitrate arise in substantial part from the same transaction or series of related transactions;

(3) the existence of a common issue of law or fact creates the possibility of conflicting decisions in the separate arbitration proceedings; and

(4) prejudice resulting from a failure to consolidate is not outweighed by the risk of undue delay or prejudice to the rights of or hardship to parties opposing consolidation.

(b) The court may order consolidation of separate arbitration proceedings as to some claims and allow other claims to be resolved in separate arbitration proceedings.

(c) The court may not order consolidation of the claims of a party to an agreement to arbitrate if the agreement prohibits consolidation.

SECTION 11. APPOINTMENT OF ARBITRATOR; SERVICE AS A NEUTRAL ARBITRATOR.

(a) If the parties to an agreement to arbitrate agree on a method for appointing an arbitrator, that method must be followed, unless the method fails. If the parties have not agreed on a method, the agreed method fails, or an arbitrator appointed fails or is unable to act and a successor has not been appointed, the court, on [motion] of a party to the arbitration proceeding, shall appoint the arbitrator. An arbitrator so appointed has all the powers of an arbitrator designated in the agreement to arbitrate or appointed pursuant to the agreed method.

(b) An individual who has a known, direct, and material interest in the outcome of the arbitration proceeding or a known, existing, and substantial relationship with a party may not serve as an arbitrator required by an agreement to be

SECTION 12. DISCLOSURE BY ARBITRATOR.

(a) Before accepting appointment, an individual who is requested to serve as an arbitrator, after making a reasonable inquiry, shall disclose to all parties to the agreement to arbitrate and arbitration proceeding and to any other arbitrators any known facts that a reasonable person would consider likely to affect the impartiality of the arbitrator in the arbitration proceeding, including:

(1) a financial or personal interest in the outcome of the arbitration proceeding; and

(2) an existing or past relationship with any of the parties to the agreement to arbitrate or the arbitration proceeding, their counsel or representatives, a witness, or another arbitrators.

(b) An arbitrator has a continuing obligation to disclose to all parties to the agreement to arbitrate and arbitration proceeding and to any other arbitrators any facts that the arbitrator learns after accepting appointment which a reasonable person would consider likely to affect the impartiality of the arbitrator.

(c) If an arbitrator discloses a fact required by subsection (a) or (b) to be disclosed and a party timely objects to the appointment or continued service of the arbitrator based upon the fact disclosed, the objection may be a ground under Section 23(a)(2) for vacating an award made by the arbitrator.

(d) If the arbitrator did not disclose a fact as required by subsection (a) or (b), upon timely objection by a party, the court under Section 23(a)(2) may vacate an award.

(e) An arbitrator appointed as a neutral arbitrator who does not disclose a known, direct, and material interest in the outcome of the arbitration proceeding or a known, existing, and substantial relationship with a party is presumed to act with evident partiality under Section 23(a)(2).

(f) If the parties to an arbitration proceeding agree to the procedures of an arbitration organization or any other procedures for challenges to arbitrators before an award is made, substantial compliance with those procedures is a condition precedent to a [motion] to vacate an award on that ground under Section 23(a)(2).

SECTION 13. ACTION BY MAJORITY.

If there is more than one arbitrator, the powers of an arbitrator must be exercised by a majority of the arbitrators, but all of them shall conduct the hearing under Section 15(c).

SECTION 14. IMMUNITY OF ARBITRATOR; COMPETENCY TO TESTIFY; ATTORNEY'S FEES AND COSTS.

(a) An arbitrator or an arbitration organization acting in that capacity is immune from civil liability to the same extent as a judge of a court of this State acting in a judicial capacity.

(b) The immunity afforded by this section supplements any immunity under other law.

(c) The failure of an arbitrator to make a disclosure required by Section 12 does not cause any loss of immunity under this section.

(d) In a judicial, administrative, or similar proceeding, an arbitrator or representative of an arbitration organization is not competent to testify, and may not be required to produce records as to any statement, conduct, decision, or ruling occurring during the arbitration proceeding, to the same extent as a judge of a court of this State acting in a judicial capacity. This subsection does not apply:

(1) to the extent necessary to determine the claim of an arbitrator, arbitration organization, or representative of the arbitration organization against a party to the arbitration proceeding; or

(2) to a hearing on a [motion] to vacate an award under Section 23(a)(1) or (2) if the [movant] establishes prima facie that a ground for vacating the award exists.

(e) If a person commences a civil action against an arbitrator, arbitration organization, or representative of an arbitration organization arising from the services of the arbitrator, organization, or representative or if a person seeks to compel an arbitrator or a representative of an arbitration organization to testify or produce records in violation of subsection (d), and the court decides that the arbitrator, arbitration organization, or representative of an arbitration organization is immune from civil liability or that the arbitrator or representative of the organization is not competent to testify, the court shall award to the arbitrator, organization, or representative reasonable attorney's fees and other reasonable

SECTION 15. ARBITRATION PROCESS.

(a) An arbitrator may conduct an arbitration in such manner as the arbitrator considers appropriate for a fair and expeditious disposition of the proceeding. The authority conferred upon the arbitrator includes the power to hold conferences with the parties to the arbitration proceeding before the hearing and, among other matters, determine the admissibility, relevance, materiality and weight of any evidence.

(b) An arbitrator may decide a request for summary disposition of a claim or particular issue:

(1) if all interested parties agree; or
(2) upon request of one party to the arbitration proceeding if that party gives notice to all other parties to the proceeding, and the other parties have a reasonable opportunity to respond.

(c) If an arbitrator orders a hearing, the arbitrator shall set a time and place and give notice of the hearing not less than five days before the hearing begins. Unless a party to the arbitration proceeding makes an objection to lack or insufficiency of notice not later than the beginning of the hearing, the party's appearance at the hearing waives the objection. Upon request of a party to the arbitration proceeding and for good cause shown, or upon the arbitrator's own initiative, the arbitrator may adjourn the hearing from time to time as necessary but may not postpone the hearing to a time later than that fixed by the agreement to arbitrate for making the award unless the parties to the arbitration proceeding consent to a later date. The arbitrator may hear and decide the controversy upon the evidence produced although a party who was duly notified of the arbitration proceeding did not appear. The court, on request, may direct the arbitrator to conduct the hearing promptly and render a timely decision.

(d) At a hearing under subsection (c), a party to the arbitration proceeding has a right to be heard, to present evidence material to the controversy, and to cross-examine witnesses appearing at the hearing.

(e) If an arbitrator ceases or is unable to act during the arbitration proceeding, a replacement arbitrator must be appointed in accordance with Section 11 to continue the proceeding and to resolve the controversy.

SECTION 16. REPRESENTATION BY LAWYER.

A party to an arbitration proceeding may be represented by a lawyer.

SECTION 17. WITNESSES; SUBPOENAS; DEPOSITIONS; DISCOVERY.

(a) An arbitrator may issue a subpoena for the attendance of a witness and for the production of records and other evidence at any hearing and may administer oaths. A subpoena must be served in the manner for service of subpoenas in a civil action and, upon [motion] to the court by a party to the arbitration proceeding or the arbitrator, enforced in the manner for enforcement of subpoenas in a civil action.

(b) In order to make the proceedings fair, expeditious, and cost effective, upon request of a party to or a witness in an arbitration proceeding, an arbitrator may permit a deposition of any witness to be taken for use as evidence at the hearing, including a witness who cannot be subpoenaed for or is unable to attend a hearing. The arbitrator shall determine the conditions under which the deposition is taken.

(c) An arbitrator may permit such discovery as the arbitrator decides is appropriate in the circumstances, taking into account the needs of the parties to the arbitration proceeding and other affected persons and the desirability of making the proceeding fair, expeditious, and cost effective.

(d) If an arbitrator permits discovery under subsection (c), the arbitrator may order a party to the arbitration proceeding to comply with the arbitrator's discovery-related orders, issue subpoenas for the attendance of a witness and for the production of records and other evidence at a discovery proceeding, and take action against a noncomplying party to the extent a court could if the controversy were the subject of a civil action in this State.

(e) An arbitrator may issue a protective order to prevent the disclosure of privileged information, confidential information, trade secrets, and other information protected from disclosure to the extent a court could if the controversy were the subject of a civil action in this State.

(f) All laws compelling a person under subpoena to testify and all fees for attending a judicial proceeding, a deposition, or a discovery proceeding as a witness apply to an arbitration proceeding as if the controversy were the subject of a civil action in this State.

(g) The court may enforce a subpoena or discovery-related order for the attendance of a witness within this State and for the production of records and other evidence issued by an arbitrator in connection with an arbitration proceeding in another State upon conditions determined by the court so as to make the arbitration proceeding fair, expeditious, and cost effective. A subpoena or discovery-related order issued by an arbitrator in another State must be served in the manner provided by law for service of subpoenas in a civil action in this State and, upon [motion] to the court by a party to the arbitration proceeding or the arbitrator, enforced in the manner provided by law for enforcement of subpoenas in a civil action in this State.

SECTION 18. JUDICIAL ENFORCEMENT OF PREAWARD RULING BY ARBITRATOR.

If an arbitrator makes a preaward ruling in favor of a party to the arbitration proceeding, the party may request the arbitrator to incorporate the ruling into an award under Section 19. A prevailing party may make a [motion] to the court for an expedited order to confirm the award under Section 22, in which case the court shall summarily decide the [motion]. The court shall issue an order to confirm the award unless the court vacates, modifies, or corrects the award under Section 23 or 24.

SECTION 19. AWARD.

(a) An arbitrator shall make a record of an award. The record must be signed or otherwise authenticated by any arbitrator who concurs with the award. The arbitrator or the arbitration organization shall give notice of the award, including a copy of the award, to each party to the arbitration proceeding.

(b) An award must be made within the time specified by the agreement to arbitrate or, if not specified therein, within the time ordered by the court. The court may extend or the parties to the arbitration proceeding may agree in a record to extend the time. The court or the parties may do so within or after the time specified or ordered. A party waives any objection that an award was not timely made unless the party gives notice of the objection to the arbitrator before receiving notice of the award.

SECTION 20. CHANGE OF AWARD BY ARBITRATOR.

(a) On [motion] to an arbitrator by a party to an arbitration proceeding, the arbitrator may modify or correct an award:

(1) upon a ground stated in Section 24(a)(1) or (3);
(2) because the arbitrator has not made a final and definite award upon a claim submitted by the parties to the arbitration proceeding; or

(3) to clarify the award.

(b) A [motion] under subsection (a) must be made and notice given to all parties within 20 days after the movant receives notice of the award.

(c) A party to the arbitration proceeding must give notice of any objection to the [motion] within 10 days after receipt of the notice.

(d) If a [motion] to the court is pending under Section 22, 23, or 24, the court may submit the claim to the arbitrator to consider whether to modify or correct the award:

(1) upon a ground stated in Section 24(a)(1) or (3);
(2) because the arbitrator has not made a final and definite award upon a claim submitted by the parties to the arbitration proceeding; or
(3) to clarify the award.

(e) An award modified or corrected pursuant to this section is subject to Sections 19(a), 22, 23, and 24.

SECTION 21. REMEDIES; FEES AND EXPENSES OF ARBITRATION PROCEEDING.

(a) An arbitrator may award punitive damages or other exemplary relief if such an award is authorized by law in a civil action involving the same claim and the evidence produced at the hearing justifies the award under the legal standards otherwise applicable to the claim.

(b) An arbitrator may award reasonable attorney's fees and other reasonable expenses of arbitration if such an award is authorized by law in a civil action involving the same claim or by the agreement of the parties to the arbitration proceeding.

(c) As to all remedies other than those authorized by subsections (a) and (b), an arbitrator may order such remedies as the arbitrator considers just and appropriate under the circumstances of the arbitration proceeding. The fact that such a remedy could not or would not be granted by the court is not a ground for refusing to confirm an award under Section 22 or for vacating an award under Section 23.

(d) An arbitrator's expenses and fees, together with other expenses, must be paid as provided in the award.

(e) If an arbitrator awards punitive damages or other exemplary relief under subsection (a), the arbitrator shall specify in the award the basis in fact justifying and the basis in law authorizing the award and state separately the amount of the punitive damages or other exemplary relief.

SECTION 22. CONFIRMATION OF AWARD..

After a party to an arbitration proceeding receives notice of an award, the party may make a [motion] to the court for an order confirming the award at which time the court shall issue a confirming order unless the award is modified or corrected pursuant to Section 20 or 24 or is vacated pursuant to Section 23.

SECTION 23. VACATING AWARD.

(a) Upon [motion] to the court by a party to an arbitration proceeding, the court shall vacate an award made in the arbitration proceeding if:

(1) the award was procured by corruption, fraud, or other undue means;

(2) there was:

(A) evident partiality by an arbitrator appointed as a neutral arbitrator;

(B) corruption by an arbitrator; or

(C) misconduct by an arbitrator prejudicing the rights of a party to the arbitration proceeding;

(3) an arbitrator refused to postpone the hearing upon showing of sufficient cause for postponement, refused to consider evidence material to the controversy, or otherwise conducted the hearing contrary to Section 15, so as to prejudice substantially the rights of a party to the arbitration proceeding;

(4) an arbitrator exceeded the arbitrator's powers;

(5) there was no agreement to arbitrate, unless the person participated in the arbitration proceeding without raising the objection under Section 15(c) not later than the beginning of the arbitration hearing; or

(6) the arbitration was conducted without proper notice of the initiation of an arbitration as required in Section 9 so as to prejudice substantially the rights of a party to the arbitration proceeding.

(b) A [motion] under this section must be filed within 90 days after the [movant] receives notice of the award pursuant to Section 19 or within 90 days after the [movant] receives notice of a modified or corrected award pursuant to Section 20, unless the [movant] alleges that the award was procured by corruption, fraud, or other undue means, in which case the [motion] must be made within 90 days after the ground is known or by the exercise of reasonable care would have been known by the [movant].

(c) If the court vacates an award on a ground other than that set forth in subsection (a)(5), it may order a rehearing. If the award is vacated on a ground stated in subsection (a)(1) or (2), the rehearing must be before a new arbitrator. If the award is vacated on a ground stated in subsection (a)(3), (4), or (6), the rehearing may be before the arbitrator who made the award or the arbitrator's successor. The arbitrator must render the decision in the rehearing within the same time as that provided in Section 19(b) for an award.

(d) If the court denies a [motion] to vacate an award, it shall confirm the award unless a [motion] to modify or correct the award is pending.

Comment

A. **Comment on Section 23(a)(2), (5), (6), and (c)**

SECTION 24. MODIFICATION OR CORRECTION OF AWARD.

(a) Upon [motion] made within 90 days after the [movant] receives notice of the award pursuant to Section 19 or within 90 days after the [movant] receives notice of a modified or corrected award pursuant to Section 20, the court shall modify or correct the award if:

(1) there was an evident mathematical miscalculation or an evident mistake in the description of a person, thing, or property referred to in the award;

(2) the arbitrator has made an award on a claim not submitted to the arbitrator and the award may be corrected without affecting the merits of the decision upon the claims submitted; or

(3) the award is imperfect in a matter of form not affecting the merits of the decision on the claims submitted.

(b) If a [motion] made under subsection (a) is granted, the court shall modify or correct and confirm the award as modified or corrected. Otherwise, unless a motion to vacate is pending, the court shall confirm the award.

(c) A [motion] to modify or correct an award pursuant to this section may be joined with a [motion] to vacate the award.

SECTION 25. JUDGMENT ON AWARD; ATTORNEY'S FEES AND LITIGATION EXPENSES.

(a) Upon granting an order confirming, vacating without directing a rehearing, modifying, or correcting an award, the court shall enter a judgment in conformity therewith. The judgment may be recorded, docketed, and enforced as any other judgment in a civil action.

(b) A court may allow reasonable costs of the [motion] and subsequent judicial proceedings.

(c) On [application] of a prevailing party to a contested judicial proceeding under Section 22, 23, or 24, the court may add reasonable attorney's fees and other reasonable expenses of litigation incurred in a judicial proceeding after the award is made to a judgment confirming, vacating without directing a rehearing, modifying, or correcting an award.

SECTION 26. JURISDICTION.

(a) A court of this State having jurisdiction over the controversy and the parties may enforce an agreement to arbitrate.

(b) An agreement to arbitrate providing for arbitration in this State confers exclusive jurisdiction on the court to enter judgment on an award under this [Act].

SECTION 27. VENUE.

A [motion] pursuant to Section 5 must be made in the court of the [county] in which the agreement to arbitrate specifies the arbitration hearing is to be held or, if the hearing has been held, in the court of the [county] in which it was held. Otherwise, the [motion] may be made in the court of any [county] in which an adverse party resides or has a place of business or, if no adverse party has a residence or place of business in this State, in the court of any [county] in this State. All subsequent [motions] must be made in the court hearing the initial [motion] unless the court otherwise directs.

SECTION 28. APPEALS.

(a) An appeal may be taken from:

(1) an order denying a [motion] to compel arbitration;

(2) an order granting a [motion] to stay arbitration;

(3) an order confirming or denying confirmation of an award;

(4) an order modifying or correcting an award;

(5) an order vacating an award without directing a rehearing; or

(6) a final judgment entered pursuant to this [Act].

(b) An appeal under this section must be taken as from an order or a judgment in a civil action.

SECTION 29. UNIFORMITY OF APPLICATION AND CONSTRUCTION.

In applying and construing this uniform act, consideration must be given to the need to promote uniformity of the law with respect to its subject matter among States that enact it.

SECTION 30. RELATIONSHIP TO ELECTRONIC SIGNATURES IN GLOBAL AND NATIONAL COMMERCE ACT.

The provisions of this Act governing the legal effect, validity, and enforceability of electronic records or electronic signatures, and of contracts performed with the use of such records or signatures conform to the requirements of Section 102 of the Electronic Signatures in Global and National Commerce Act.

SECTION 31. EFFECTIVE DATE.

This [Act] takes effect on [effective date].

SECTION 32. REPEAL.

Effective on [delayed date should be the same as that in Section 3(c)], the [Uniform Arbitration Act] is repealed.

> 2. This repeal section is based on Section 1205 of the Revised Uniform Partnership Act and Section 1209 of the 1996 Amendments constituting the Uniform Limited Liability Partnership Act. Both of these statutes have transition provisions similar to Section 3 of the RUAA.

SECTION 33. SAVINGS CLAUSE.

This [Act] does not affect an action or proceeding commenced or right accrued before this [Act] takes effect. Subject to Section 3 of this [Act], an arbitration agreement made before the effective date of this [Act] is governed by the [Uniform Arbitration Act].

APPENDIX O

The Federal Arbitration Act
Reprinted with permission. Copyrighted material of the National Conference of Commisioners on Uniform State Laws (NCCUSL 2004).

CHAPTER 1. GENERAL PROVISIONS

Section 1. "Maritime transactions" and "commerce" defined; exceptions to operation of title

"Maritime transaction", as herein defined, means charter parties, bills of lading of water carriers, agreements relating to wharfage, supplies furnished vessels or repairs to vessels, collisions, or any other matters in foreign commerce which, if the subject of controversy, would be embraced within admiralty jurisdiction; "commerce", as herein defined, means commerce among the several States or with foreign nations, or in any Territory of the United States or in the District of Columbia, or between any such Territory and another, or between any such Territory and any State or foreign nation, or between the District of Columbia and any State or Territory or foreign nation, but nothing herein contained shall apply to contracts of employment of seamen, railroad employees, or any other class of workers engaged in foreign or interstate commerce.

Section 2. Validity, irrevocability, and enforcement of agreements to arbitrate

A written provision in any maritime transaction or a contract evidencing a transaction involving commerce to settle by arbitration a controversy thereafter arising out of such contract or transaction, or the refusal to perform the whole or any part thereof, or an agreement in writing to submit to arbitration an existing controversy arising out of such a contract, transaction, or refusal, shall be valid, irrevocable, and enforceable, save upon such grounds as exist at law or in equity for the revocation of any contract.

Section 3. Stay of proceedings where issue therein referable to arbitration

If any suit or proceeding be brought in any of the courts of the United States upon any issue referable to arbitration under an agreement in writing for such arbitration, the court in which such suit is pending, upon being satisfied that the issue involved in such suit or proceeding is referable to arbitration under such an agreement, shall on application of one of the parties stay the trial of the action until such arbitration has been had in accordance with the terms of the agreement, providing the applicant for the stay is not in default in proceeding with such arbitration.

Section 4. Failure to arbitrate under agreement; petition to United States court having jurisdiction for order to compel arbitration; notice and service thereof; hearing and determination.

A party aggrieved by the alleged failure, neglect, or refusal of another to arbitrate under a written agreement for arbitration may petition any United States district court which, save for such agreement, would have jurisdiction under Title 28, in a civil action or in admiralty of the subject matter of a suit arising out of the controversy between the parties, for an order directing that such arbitration proceed in the manner provided for in such agreement. Five days' notice in writing of such application shall be served upon the party in default. Service thereof shall be made in the manner provided by the Federal Rules of Civil Procedure. The court shall hear the parties, and upon being satisfied that the making of the agreement for arbitration or the failure to comply therewith is not in issue, the court shall make an order directing the parties to proceed to arbitration in accordance with the terms of the agreement. The hearing and proceedings, under such agreement, shall be within the district in which the petition for an order directing such arbitration is filed. If the making of the arbitration agreement or the failure, neglect, or refusal to perform the same be in issue, the court shall proceed summarily to the trial thereof. If no jury trial be demanded by the party alleged to be in default, or if the matter in dispute is within admiralty jurisdiction, the court shall hear and determine such issue. Where such an issue is raised, the party alleged to be in default may, except in cases of admiralty, on or before the return day of the notice of application, demand a jury trial of such issue, and upon such demand the court shall make an order referring the issue or issues to a jury in the manner provided by the Federal Rules of Civil Procedure, or may specially call a jury for that purpose. If the jury find that no agreement in writing for arbitration was made or that there is no default in proceeding thereunder, the proceeding shall be dismissed. If the jury find that an agreement for arbitration was made in writing and that there is a default in proceeding thereunder, the court shall make an order summarily directing the parties to proceed with the arbitration in accordance with the terms thereof.

Section 5. Appointment of arbitrators or umpire

If in the agreement provision be made for a method of naming or appointing an arbitrator or arbitrators or an umpire, such method shall be followed; but if no method be provided therein, or if a method be provided and any party thereto shall fail to avail himself of such method, or if for any other reason there shall be a lapse in the naming of an arbitrator or arbitrators or umpire, or in filling a vacancy, then upon the application of either party to the controversy the court shall designate and appoint an arbitrator or arbitrators or umpire, as the case may require, who shall act under the said agreement with the same force and effect as if he or they had been specifically named therein; and unless otherwise provided in the agreement the arbitration shall be by a single arbitrator.

Section 6. Application heard as motion

Any application to the court hereunder shall be made and heard in the manner provided by law for the making and hearing of motions, except as otherwise herein expressly provided.

Section 7. Witnesses before arbitrators; fees; compelling attendance

The arbitrators selected either as prescribed in this title or otherwise, or a majority of them, may summon in writing any person to attend before them or any of them as a witness and in a proper case to bring with him or them any book, record, document, or paper which may be deemed material as evidence in the case. The fees for such attendance shall be the same as the fees of witnesses before masters of the United States courts. Said summons shall issue in the name of the arbitrator or arbitrators, or a majority of them, and shall be signed by the arbitrators, or a majority of them, and shall be directed to the said person and shall be served in the same manner as subpoenas to appear and testify before the court; if any person or persons so summoned to testify shall refuse or neglect to obey said summons, upon petition the United States district court for the district in which such arbitrators, or a majority of them, are sitting may compel the attendance of such person or persons before said arbitrator or arbitrators, or punish said person or persons for contempt in the same manner provided by law for securing the attendance of witnesses or their punishment for neglect or refusal to attend in the courts of the United States.

Section 8. Proceedings begun by libel in admiralty and seizure of vessel or property

If the basis of jurisdiction be a cause of action otherwise justiciable in admiralty, then, notwithstanding anything herein to the contrary, the party claiming to be aggrieved may begin his proceeding hereunder by seizure of the vessel or other property of the other party according to the usual course of admiralty proceedings, and the court shall then have jurisdiction to direct the parties to proceed with the arbitration and shall retain jurisdiction to enter its decree upon the award.

Section 9. Award of arbitrators; confirmation; jurisdiction; procedure

If the parties in their agreement have agreed that a judgment of the court shall be entered upon the award made pursuant to the arbitration, and shall specify the court, then at any time within one year after the award is made any party to the arbitration may apply to the court so specified for an order confirming the award, and thereupon the court must grant such an order unless the award is vacated, modified, or corrected as prescribed in sections 10 and 11 of this title. If no court is specified in the agreement of the parties, then such application may be made to the United States court in and for the district within which such award was made. Notice of the application shall be served upon the adverse party, and thereupon the court shall have jurisdiction of such party as though he had appeared generally in the proceeding. If the adverse party is a resident of the district within which the award was made, such service shall be made upon the adverse party or his attorney as prescribed by law for service of notice of motion in an action in the same court. If the adverse party shall be a nonresident, then the notice of the application shall be served by the marshal of any district within which the adverse party may be found in like manner as other process of the court.

Section 10. Same; vacation; grounds; rehearing

(a) In any of the following cases the United States court in and for the district wherein the award was made may make an order vacating the award upon the application of any party to the arbitration

(1) Where the award was procured by corruption, fraud, or undue means.

(2) Where there was evident partiality or corruption in the arbitrators, or either of them.

(3) Where the arbitrators were guilty of misconduct in refusing to postpone the hearing, upon sufficient cause shown, or in refusing to hear evidence pertinent and material to the controversy; or of any other misbehavior by which the rights of any party have been prejudiced.

(4) Where the arbitrators exceeded their powers, or so imperfectly executed them that a mutual, final, and definite award upon the subject matter submitted was not made.

(5) Where an award is vacated and the time within which the agreement required the award to be made has not expired the court may, in its discretion, direct a rehearing b the arbitrators.

(b) The United States district court for the district wherein an award was made that was issued pursuant to section 590 of title 5 may make an order vacating the award upon the application of a person, other than a party to the arbitration, who is adversely affected or aggrieved by the award, if the use of arbitration or the award is clearly inconsistent with the factors set forth in section 582 of Title 5.

Section 11. Same; modification or correction; grounds; order

In either of the following cases the United States court in and for the district wherein the award was made may make an order modifying or correcting the award upon the application of any party to the arbitration

(a) Where there was an evident material miscalculation of figures or an evident material mistake in the description of any person, thing, or property referred to in the award.

(b) Where the arbitrators have awarded upon a matter not submitted to them, unless it is a matter not affecting the merits of the decision upon the matter submitted.

(c) Where the award is imperfect in matter of form not affecting the merits of the controversy.

The order may modify and correct the award, so as to effect the intent thereof and promote justice between the parties.

Section 12. Notice of motions to vacate or modify; service; stay of proceedings

Notice of a motion to vacate, modify, or correct an award must be served upon the adverse party or his attorney within three months after the award is filed or delivered. If the adverse party is a resident of the district within which the award was made, such service shall be made upon the adverse party or his attorney as prescribed by law for service of notice of motion in an action in the same court. If the adverse party shall be a nonresident then the notice of the application shall be served by the marshal of any district within which the adverse party may be found in like manner as other process of the court. For the purposes of the motion any judge who might make an order to stay the proceedings in an action brought in the same court may make an order, to be served with the notice of motion, staying the proceedings of the adverse party to enforce the award.

Section 13. Papers filed with order on motions; judgment; docketing; force and effect; enforcement

The party moving for an order confirming, modifying, or correcting an award shall, at the time such order is filed with the clerk for the entry of judgment thereon, also file the following papers with the clerk:

(a) The agreement; the selection or appointment, if any, of an additional arbitrator or umpire; and each written extension of the time, if any, within which to make the award.

(b) The award.

(c) Each notice, affidavit, or other paper used upon an application to confirm, modify, or correct the award, and a copy of each order of the court upon such an application.

The judgment shall be docketed as if it was rendered in an action.

The judgment so entered shall have the same force and effect, in all respects, as, and be subject to all the provisions of law relating to, a judgment in an action; and it may be enforced as if it had been rendered in an action in the court in which it is entered.

Section 14. Contracts not affected
This title shall not apply to contracts made prior to January 1, 1926.

Section 15. Inapplicability of the Act of State doctrine
Enforcement of arbitral agreements, confirmation of arbitral awards, and execution upon judgments based on orders confirming such awards shall not be refused on the basis of the Act of State doctrine.

Section 16. Appeals
(a) An appeal may be taken from

(1) an order

(A) refusing a stay of any action under section 3 of this title,

(B) denying a petition under section 4 of this title to order arbitration to proceed,

(C) denying an application under section 206 of this title to compel arbitration,

(D) confirming or denying confirmation of an award or partial award, or

(E) modifying, correcting, or vacating an award;

(2) an interlocutory order granting, continuing, or modifying an injunction against an arbitration that is subject to this title; or

(3) a final decision with respect to an arbitration that is subject to this title.

(b) Except as otherwise provided in section 1292 (b) of title 28, an appeal may not be taken from an interlocutory order

(1) granting a stay of any action under section 3 of this title;

(2) directing arbitration to proceed under section 4 of this title;

(3) compelling arbitration under section 206 of this title; or

(4) refusing to enjoin an arbitration that is subject to this title.

THE FEDERAL ARBITRATION ACT

Section 201. Enforcement of Convention

The Convention on the Recognition and Enforcement of Foreign Arbitral Awards of June 10, 1958, shall be enforced in United States courts in accordance with this chapter.

Section 202. Agreement or award falling under the Convention

An arbitration agreement or arbitral award arising out of a legal relationship, whether contractual or not, which is considered as commercial, including a transaction, contract, or agreement described in section 2 of this title, falls under the Convention. An agreement or award arising out of such a relationship which is entirely between citizens of the United States shall be deemed not to fall under the Convention unless that relationship involves property located abroad, envisages performance or enforcement abroad, or has some other reasonable relation with one or more foreign states. For the purpose of this section a corporation is a citizen of the United States if it is incorporated or has its principal place of business in the United States.

Section 203. Jurisdiction; amount in controversy

An action or proceeding falling under the Convention shall be deemed to arise under the laws and treaties of the United States. The district courts of the United States (including the courts enumerated in section 460 of Title 28) shall have original jurisdiction over such an action or proceeding, regardless of the amount in controversy.

Section 204. Venue

An action or proceeding over which the district courts have jurisdiction pursuant to section 203 of this title may be brought in any such court in which save for the arbitration agreement an action or proceeding with respect to the controversy between the parties could be brought, or in such court for the district and division which embraces the place designated in the agreement as the place of arbitration if such place is within the United States.

Section 205. Removal of cases from State courts

Where the subject matter of an action or proceeding pending in a State court relates to an arbitration agreement or award falling under the Convention, the defendant or the defendants may, at any time before the trial thereof, remove such action or proceeding to the district court of the United States for the district and division embracing the place where the action or proceeding is pending. The procedure for removal of causes otherwise provided by law shall apply, except that the ground for removal provided in this section need not appear on the face of the complaint but may be shown in the petition for removal. For the purposes of Chapter 1 of this title any action or proceeding removed under this section shall be deemed to have been brought in the district court to which it is removed.

Section 206. Order to compel arbitration; appointment of arbitrators

A court having jurisdiction under this chapter may direct that arbitration be held in accordance with the agreement at any place therein provided for, whether that place is within or without the United States. Such court may also appoint arbitrators in accordance with the provisions of the agreement.

Section 207. Award of arbitrators; confirmation; jurisdiction; proceeding

Chapter 1 applies to actions and proceedings brought under this chapter to the extent that chapter is not in conflict with this chapter or the Convention as ratified by the United States.

Section 208. Chapter 1; residual application

Chapter 1 applies to actions and proceedings brought under this chapter to the extent that chapter is not in conflict with this chapter or the Convention as ratified by the United States.

CHAPTER 3. INTER-AMERICAN CONVENTION ON INTERNA-TIONAL COMMERCIAL ARBITRATION

Section 301. Enforcement of Convention

The Inter-American Convention on International Commercial Arbitration of January 30, 1975, shall be enforced in United States courts in accordance with this chapter.

Section 302. Incorporation by reference

Sections 202, 203, 204, 205, and 207 of this title shall apply to this chapter as if specifically set forth herein, except that for the purposes of this chapter "the Convention" shall mean the Inter-American Convention.

Section 303. Order to compel arbitration; appointment of arbitrators; locale

(a) A court having jurisdiction under this chapter may direct that arbitration be held in accordance with the agreement at any place therein provided for, whether that place is within or without the United States. The court may also appoint arbitrators in accordance with the provisions of the agreement.

(b) In the event the agreement does not make provision for the place of arbitration or the appointment of arbitrators, the court shall direct that the arbitration shall be held and the arbitrators be appointed in accordance with Article 3 of the Inter-American Convention.

Section 304. Recognition and enforcement of foreign arbitral decisions and awards; reciprocity

Arbitral decisions or awards made in the territory of a foreign State shall, on the basis of reciprocity, be recognized and enforced under this chapter only if that State has ratified or acceded to the Inter-American Convention.

Section 305. Relationship between the Inter-American Convention and the Convention on the Recognition and Enforcement of Foreign Arbitral Awards of June 10, 1958

When the requirements for application of both the Inter-American Convention and the Convention on the Recognition and Enforcement of Foreign Arbitral Awards of June 10, 1958, are met, determination as to which Convention applies shall, unless otherwise expressly agreed, be made as follows:

(1) If a majority of the parties to the arbitration agreement are citizens of a State or States that have ratified or acceded to the Inter-American Convention and are member States of the Organization of American States, the Inter-American Convention shall apply.

(2) In all other cases the Convention on the Recognition and Enforcement of Foreign Arbitral Awards of June 10, 1958, shall apply.

Section 306. Applicable rules of Inter-American Commercial Arbitration Commission

(a)For the purposes of this chapter the rules of procedure of the Inter-American Commercial Arbitration Commission referred to in Article 3 of the Inter-American Convention shall, subject to subsection (b) of this section, be those rules as promulgated by the Commission on July 1, 1988.

(b) In the event the rules of procedure of the Inter-American Commercial Arbitration Commission are modified or amended in accordance with the procedures for amendment of the rules of that Commission, the Secretary of State, by regulation in accordance with section 553 of Title 5, consistent with the aims and purposes of this Convention, may prescribe that such modifications or amendments shall be effective for purposes of this chapter.

Section 307. Chapter 1; residual application

Chapter 1 applies to actions and proceedings brought under this chapter to the extent chapter 1 is not in conflict with this chapter or the Inter-American Convention as ratified by the United States.

APPENDIX P

Organizations Offering ADR Services

ORGANIZATION	LOCATION AND CONTACT INFORMATION	TYPES OF DIS-PUTES
EASTERN UNITED STATES		
American Arbitration Association	www.adr.org New York, N.Y. (212) 484-4000 Boston, Mass. (617) 451-6600 Atlanta, Ga. (404) 325-0101 Miami, Fla. (305) 358-7777	General civil
Arbitration Forums Inc.	www.arb.file.org Tampa, Fla. (813) 931-4004	Insurance claims
Clean Sites	Alexandria, Va. (703) 683-8522	Environmental
JAMS, Inc.	www.jamsadr.com Boston, Mass. (617) 228-0200 New York, N.Y. (212) 751-2700 Washington, D.C. (202) 942-9180 Atlanta, Ga. (213) 620-1133	General civil
International Centre for Settlement of investment Disputes (Public International Organization)	www.worldbank.org Washington, D.C. (202) 477-1234	International investment
Resolution Resources Inc.	www.clrp.com Atlanta, Ga. (404) 215-9800	General civil
World Wildlife Fund	www.worldwildlife.org Washington, D.C. (202) 293-4800	Environmental, natural resources

ORGANIZATION	LOCATION AND CONTACT INFORMATION	TYPES OF DISPUTES
CENTRAL UNITED STATES		
ADR Systems of America, LLC	www.adrsystems.com e-mail: adrsystems@aol.com Chicago, Illinois (312) 960-2260	General civil
American Arbitration	www.adr.org Chicago, Ill (312) 616-6560 Denver, Colorado (303) 831-0823 Cincinnati, Ohio (513) 241-8434 Minneapolis, Minnesota (612) 332-6545 St. Louis, Missouri (314) 621-7175	General civil
Center for Resolution of Disputes	www.cfrdemediation.com Cincinnati, Ohio (513) 721-4466	Private and public disputes
Chicago International Dispute Resolution Association (CIDRA)	www.cidra.org Chicago, Illinois (312) 409-1373	International
Global solutions	e-mail: globalbohn.msn.com Inverness, Illinois (847) 358-8856	Commercial and International

JAMS, Inc.	Chicago, Illinois (312) 739-0200 www.jams.com Indianapolis, Indiana (317) 231-6320 www.vbradr.com Denver, Colorado (303) 534-1254 www.jamsadr.com Dallas, Texas (214) 744-5267 www.jamsadr.com Houston, Texas (713) 651-1400 www.jamsadr.com	General civil
Judicial Dispute Resolution, Inc.	e-mail: jdrinc@jdrinc.com Chicago, Illinois (312) 917-2888	General civil
Mediation Research and Education Project, Inc.	www.mrep.org Chicago, Ill (810) 356-0870	Coal industry, manufacturing, communications, education

ORGANIZATION	LOCATION AND CONTACT INFORMATION	TYPES OF DISPUTES
WESTERN UNITED STATES		
American Arbitration Association	www.adr.org San Francisco, California (415) 981-3901 Los Angeles, California (213) 383-6516 Seattle, Washington (206) 622-6435	General civil
CDR Associates	www.mediate.org Boulder, Colo. (303) 442-7367	Commercial, government
JAMS, Inc.	www.jamsadr.org San Francisco, California (415) 982-5267 Los Angeles, California (213) 620-1133 Portland, Oregon (800) 626-5267 Tacoma, Washington (206) 627-3059 Seattle, Washington (206) 622-5267	General civil
Judicial Arbiter Group, Inc.	www.jaginc.com Colorado Springs, Colorado (719) 473-8282 Denver, Colorado (303) 572-1919	General civil
United States Arbitration and Mediation, Inc.;	www.usamwa.com Seattle, Washington (206) 467-0794	Commercial, tort

ORGANIZATION	CONTACT INFORMATION	PRINCIPLE SERVICES
NONPROFIT ORGANIZATIONS THAT STUDY AND PROMOTE ADR		
ABA Section of Dispute Resolution 740 15th Street, N.W. Washington, DC 20005	www.abanet.org/dispute e-mail: dispute@abanet.org (202) 662-1680	ADR services to ABA members and general public
Association for Conflict Resolution 1015 18th St. N.W. Washington, DC 20036	www.acresolution.org info@acresolution.org (202) 464-9700	
CPR Institute for Dispute Resolution 366 Madison Avenue New York, NY 10017	www.cpradr.org (212) 949-6490	Promotes ADR through corporate policy statements
American Arbitration Association 1633 Broadway New York, NY 10020	www.adr.org e-mail: usadrpub@arb.com (212) 484-4000	ADR publications, training, meetings, and seminars.
Center for Analysis of Alternative dispute Resolution Systems 11 E. Adams St. Suite 500 Chicago, IL 60603	www.caadrs.org e-mail: caadrs@caadrs.org (312) 922-6475, ext. 924	Conducts studies of the effectiveness of court-sponsored ADR programs
Center for Conflict Resolution 11 E. Adams St. Suite 500 Chicago, IL 60603	www.caads.org (312) 922-6464	ADR training and mediation center

469